A Dance
along the Precipice

A Dance along the Precipice

The Political and Economic Dimensions of the International Debt Problem

Edited by

William N. Eskridge, Jr.
University of Virginia
School of Law

Lexington Books
D.C. Heath and Company/Lexington, Massachusetts/Toronto

Library of Congress Cataloging in Publication Data

Main entry under title:

A Dance along the precipice.

Papers presented at the Eighth Sokol Colloquium, held at the University of Virginia, March 1984.
Includes Index.
1. Debts, External—Developing countries—Congresses. 2. Debt relief—Developing countries—Congresses. I. Eskridge, William N. II. Sokol Colloquium (8th : 1984 : University of Virginia)
HJ8899.D36   1985   336.3′ 435′ 091724   85-5789
ISBN 0-669-10899-5 (alk. paper)

Published simultaneously in Canada
Printed in the United States of America on acid-free paper
International Standard Book Number: 0-669-10899-5
Library of Congress Catalog Card Number: 85-5789

To Tugar

Contents

Figures

Tables

Preface and Acknowledgments

The Sokol Colloquia on Private International Law were established at the University of Virginia School of Law in 1976 through a grant from the Gustave Sokol Fund. The colloquia are designed to promote the study of comparative and international law by having distinguished scholars, practitioners, and government officials meet and address vital issues of concern to the international community. The papers of each of the seven previous colloquia have been published to make them available to a wider audience.

The present book represents the scholarly result of the Eighth Sokol Colloquium, held in March 1984 at the University of Virginia. The subject was the international debt problem. The three topics examined at the colloquium and in this book are the origins of the international debt problem, including political and economic origins; the dynamics of the process of debt restructuring, by which the private and official lenders, the borrowing countries, and government regulators have coped with the crises resulting from short-term country illiquidity; and the prospects for the future, as well as proposals for new directions in dealing with the problem.

The success of each colloquium is due to the intellectual efforts and skills of the participants and to other persons involved in the project. Danielle N. Cormier was the chief planner and coordinator of the colloquium, and the many compliments received about the high level of organization and efficiency were owed to her. The officers and members of the John Bassett Moore Society of International Law ably assisted Mrs. Cormier and provided invaluable aid in publicizing and planning the colloquium. My research associates Stephanie Humbert, Richard Kaminski, and Abby Tabb (soon-to-be Esquires) helped to edit the papers, check the citations (as well as uncover many of them), and proofread text and footnotes of this volume. Darlene Williams organized the volume for me and made certain that materials were produced with splendid timeliness. George Nash suggested the title to me several years ago.

Special thanks are due to Richard B. Lillich, the director of the Sokol Fund for seven fruitful years, and to Ronald Sokol, Esquire, and the Gustave Sokol Fund for their initiative and generosity that have made books such as the present one possible.

Introduction

W hen a typical American family purchases a home, it borrows most of the money from a financial institution, with the home as security for the mortgage loan. Since 1979 many families have obtained adjustable-rate mortgages, in which the interest rate and (usually) the monthly payment fluctuate periodically in connection with an index of the money market. Real estate brokers, homebuilders, and lenders themselves have come up with all sorts of gimmicks to persuade homebuyers to take out these adjustable mortgages. "Teaser rates" well below those for fixed-rate mortgages may attract many homebuyers to adjustable mortgages. Homebuyers have often been shocked to learn later that the teaser rate does not remain in place very long and that volatility of the interest rate exposes them to large swings in monthly payments. When rates went up in 1979–81 and 1983–84, homebuyers suffered from payment shock, and many defaulted on their mortgage loans, thus losing their homes. Notwithstanding some congressional concern and alarming default rates in 1984, federal banking regulators have done little more than sympathize with the hapless homebuyers.

From 1973 to 1982 Mexico, Brazil, and Argentina did much the same thing that homebuyers did from 1977 to 1984: they borrowed a lot of money at adjustable interest rates. And, again like many homebuyers, they faced virtual insolvency in the early 1980s, when interest rates rose to historically high levels and the economy reeled from a worldwide recession. The problem of Mexico, Brazil, and Argentina, and the problem of several dozen other developing countries, generated a crisis, however. The same federal agencies that have been happy to let the market "protect" helpless homebuyers were galvanized into action when Mexico announced in August 1982 that it could not make its regular debt payments; the regulators have maintained an active interest in the international debt problem since then and occasionally have intervened directly. Counsel for the banks and for the borrowers have elegantly articulated the dimensions of the crisis to the public, and the media have created a cottage industry of news about the debt crisis, assigning some of their brainiest reporters and analysts to keep track of every development.

Why has so much more attention been lavished on the sovereign debt problem than on the home mortgage problem? The sums of money at stake— several hundred billion dollars in each case—are not so different. The impact on people's lives cannot be the reason. Many families have already been pinched by teaser-rate adjustable mortgages, and many will face financial disaster if interest rates go up steeply in either 1985 or 1986. The economic and legal policy issues implicated in the sovereign debt problem strike me as no more interesting than those relating to the home mortgage problem (and I have written on both). The failures of the financial market mechanisms in each case are fascinating and challenging.

Perhaps one reason for the enormous attention to the sovereign debt problem is that it is a political drama on a grand scale. The dramatis personae are big self-governing entities whose interaction commands our attention. The borrowers (or, in some cases, the guarantors of loans) are themselves sovereign countries and their agencies and instrumentalities. The borrowers that receive the most attention (Mexico, Brazil, Argentina) are the three largest countries in Latin America, and their geopolitical importance to the United States is obvious. The lenders, the big banks, are semisovereign entities. They not only control enormous sums of money, but their continued financial health is perceived to be critical for the economic stability of the United States and the world economic community. The political importance of the borrowers and lenders has drawn in the United States and the governments of other members of the Organisation for Economic Co-operation and Development (OECD). The role of the United States has, for the most part, been welcomed by the other participants. The borrowers see the United States as a source of temporary, "bridge" loans and a potent lobbying force, and the banks view the United States as a lender of last resort that will bail them out if the crisis cannot be resolved. A fourth group of participants are multilateral financial institutions, especially the International Monetary Fund (IMF) and the Bank for International Settlements (BIS). Creatures of the post–World War II cooperation in various arenas of international finance, these institutions are sources of money to prevent default and, more important, are said to be honest brokers among the various interests. The IMF now conditions most of its loans to the troubled sovereign borrowers upon their agreement to take hard economic austerity measures *and* upon the banks' agreement to lend new money or to reschedule maturing indebtedness or both.

The participants in the international debt drama are sovereign, and their concerns and incentives are in large part political. A central theme that emerges in this book is that the international debt problem is a political problem as well as an economic one. Indeed, the political and economic dimensions of the crisis tend to merge. At stake is power, not just power over the use of large sums of money, but also power in the transnational finance market, geopolitical power, distributional power affecting the lives of millions of people. The consequences of the interaction of the Latin American borrowers, the commercial bank lenders, the United States and other OECD Western governments, and the IMF are far-reaching and unpredictable.

The theme of the interconnection of economics and politics in the debt crisis is apparent in each of the three parts of this book. The first part explores the political and economic origins of the problem from the perspectives of an eminent economist with the Federal Reserve Bank of New York, an international banker, and a law professor. In the second part, counsel for the leading U.S. lender, counsel for several borrowing countries, and a business school scholar of international finance explore the dynamics of debt restructuring and the strategies of some of the key participants in the process. The final part places the dynamics of debt restructuring in a broader context and suggests directions for reform and further effort. Contributors include a renowned political scientist specializing in Latin American political systems, a law professor, and counsel for regional banks and a borrowing country.

Origins

Apart from its academic interest, there are two very good reasons for examining the origins of the international debt problem. One reason is that an historical understanding of the origins of the problem contributes to greater understanding of its seriousness and the prospects, and directions, for its resolution.

Much of the popular literature and some of the more sophisticated treatments of the origins of the debt problem place almost exclusive emphasis on the economic external shocks. This explanation posits that the debt crisis was, as the World Bank argued in 1984, the result of an unexpected mixture of circumstances—oil price increases induced by the Organization of Petroleum Exporting Countries (OPEC) in 1973 and 1978–79 and, after 1978, prolonged recession in industrial countries, an unusually strong dollar, and high real interest rates (the nominal interest rate minus the rate of inflation). That is, the international financial system and its sovereign borrowers were simply unlucky. The upward surge in oil prices led Latin American and other developing countries to take on vast new loans after 1973, which became difficult for the debtors to service (to make yearly payments of principal and interest) after 1978, when the worldwide recession cut into their export earnings and rising real interest rates increased the interest charges. The external shocks explanation is a reassuring one for Western financial and political systems, because the global economic recovery and the decline of OPEC ought to rescue the system from the crisis. Once the external shocks disappear or are ameliorated, the crisis will dissipate.

This explanation seems simplistic and incomplete. Many countries, such as South Korea and Taiwan, subject to the same or greater external shocks as other developing countries have been able to accumulate a large external debt without problems; other countries, such as Mexico and Venezuela, on balance benefited from the external shocks but now have problems paying for their large external indebtedness. As a result of these and other anomalies, more sophisticated explanations for the crisis are emerging. The first three chapters of this book contribute to this more sophisticated approach, which stresses that the problem of how to handle external shocks became a crisis when both borrowers and lenders made substantial mistakes of policy between 1973 and 1982.

Roger Kubarych, senior vice-president and deputy director of research of the Federal Reserve Bank of New York, cogently argues in chapter 1 that there were six reasons why less developed countries (LDCs) borrowing money in the 1970s were vulnerable to the severe external shocks of 1979–82. Five of the mistakes were made by the LDCs themselves. (1) They were too optimistic about their continued prospects for growth in the uncertain world economy of the 1970s and did not adequately consider the possibility of recession when they borrowed so much money in the 1970s. (2) LDCs financed their development needs in the 1970s mostly through bank loans at floating interest rates; they failed to follow a more balanced plan of obtaining more of their capital needs through official loans at more fixed rates and foreign direct investment. (3) LDCs followed misguided domestic economic policies and (4) tolerated uncontrolled budget deficits in their public sectors. (5) Finally, these countries suffered from internal fraud and corruption and massive capital flight, which drained them of their capital before it was put to productive use. Mr. Kubarych attributes one mistake to governments of industrialized countries, which actively encouraged unprecedented level of LDC lending by private banks in the 1970s.

Louis Schirano, vice-president of one of the great money center banks in the United States, confesses in chapter 2 that the banks made mistakes as well. Faced with huge deposits of OPEC profits in the 1970s and a shortage of loan opportunities, the banks made loans to the LDCs that were paying the price for OPEC's oil. Because international banking is highly competitive and close-knit, argues Mr. Schirano, the trickle of sovereign lending that had taken place in the 1960s became a "fever of international lending" in the 1970s. No one paid very close attention to the historical risks of LDC lending or to the soon alarming levels of loans to individual countries. Propelled by a herd instinct and short-term profitability of sovereign lending, the banks made an almost unlimited volume of loans until late in 1982, when the herd of bankers recoiled from the volume of loans, and international loans to the main borrowing countries all but collapsed.

The "shocks-and-mistakes" explanation set forth in chapters 1 and 2 is a very attractive one today, because it is realistic and sophisticated, without sacrificing all of the optimism of the original external shocks explanation. If the external shocks dissipate *and* the LDCs and the bankers learn from their mistakes, then the crisis will be resolved, and perhaps future crises averted. In chapter 3, I explore this approach and suggest a longer range historical approach that complements the shocks and mistakes explanation by positing structural reasons for the mistakes. Drawing from models and sources of Latin American sociopolitical dynamics, I argue that an ideology of growth development in Latin American LDCs impelled them to seek significantly larger amounts of foreign capital after 1966 to sustain the rapid growth considered necessary to justify government legitimacy and to avert economic sacrifices by any of the powerful corporatist segments whose support was necessary to the government's survival. The banks lent enormous sums of money for structural reasons related to previous manias and panics: sovereign loans offered good short-term profits, and bankers underestimated or ignored country risk. The decline of the Bretton Woods system of international financial rules and the pro-loan attitude of Western governments left international lending virtually unregulated and exposed to crashes and panics to which it had historically been subject. As Messrs. Kubarych and Schirano point out, neither borrowers nor lenders were behaving according to classical economic rationality. My further point is that in political or historical terms their behavior made a lot of sense, and that the overlending and some kind of crisis were inevitable.

A second reason for studying the origins of the international debt problem is indicated by the last part of chapter 3: the problem is an excellent opportunity to test the validity of various development models and to understand better the dynamics of national economic systems and their relation to other systems. Modernization theory views development as an endogenous process of industrialization and economic growth and emphasizes the role of capital accumulation in achieving growth. The debt problem and its origins have exposed traditional theory to criticism insofar as they suggest that infusions of capital have not necessarily led to sustained economic growth and have instead tightened ties of dependency of borrowing countries which threaten those countries' economic viability.

Dependency theory may explain the debt crisis better. Under this approach to development, the industrialized "core" states of the world create structures that tie growth in "peripheral" (underdeveloped) countries to growth in the core countries. The result is that most or all of the benefits of growth redound to the benefit of people in core countries. The debt crisis can be viewed as an example of the difficulty peripheral countries encounter from their dependency ties—and the unfairness of the dependency relationship.

Even though the responsibility for the problem seems to rest with the governing elites of the borrowing countries, the banks, and Western governments, most of the costs of the solution are being borne by the people of the borrowing countries, the costs being high unemployment, lower standards of living, foreclosed growth opportunities. The debt crisis may be exacerbating political and economic inequality in the world and within certain developing countries. Dependency theory is a persuasive context for understanding the deeper problems, of which the debt crisis is only a symptom. A third theory, the world systems approach, is a more useful way to describe the international debt problem. Although opportunities for true development are scarce, they exist, if the developing country can exercise the political discipline to make present sacrifices in times of economic opportunity. Latin American countries at present do not have the social or political capacity to emerge from their dependent status in the world system, and they will face continuing problems in the future.

In the context of development theory, there are two ways in which the origins of the international debt crisis are political as well as economic. First, the crisis is an illustration of some of the economic contradictions and political unfairness inherent in traditional development theory and practice. The theory, that capital infusions will lead to growth, is an ideological device that obscures the process by which people of the world are subordinated to the interests of elites. The term "development" itself may be something of a misnomer, for the possibilities for material advancement within the capitalist world system are limited and in many instances are accomplished only through the sacrifice of other values. Moreover, the international debt problem is a reminder of the vulnerability of Latin American countries to political and economic decisions made in industrial countries. Western bankers and regulators call the shots, and Latin America feels the impact.

Dynamics

The political dimensions of the international debt problem are equally, if not more, apparent in the dynamics by which the borrowers, lenders, and others have sought to deal with it. The trigger for the crisis came on August 12, 1982, when the Mexican minister of finance and public credit informed the United States that Mexico did not have the hard currency to meet its scheduled principal and interest payments. Although the U.S. government and the bankers were quite taken aback by this announcement, their prompt response was the "Mexican rescue," as Joseph Kraft has so aptly named it. In the first stage of the rescue, "official" lenders provided Mexico with money or prospects for money so that the country would not default on its loans and could continue to import basic goods and services. The support package stitched together in August 1982 included almost $8 billion in advance payments on future oil shipments by the United States; new credit extended (or promised) by the United States, the BIS, and the IMF; and a U.S. commitment to guarantee loans for food and other basic imports.

These official measures, or the prospect for them, were only temporary. There was a consensus that Mexico's problem was a deeper one: under current market conditions, the country could not repay the short-term debt falling due in 1982 and did not even have the cash flow to meet principal and interest payments. Thus Mexico asked its private creditors to restructure its external debt. An advisory group of banks was formed to serve as a communications link in connection with Mexico's proposal, that is, to serve as the negotiating representative of the hundreds of banks with loans to Mexico.

Extensions of maturing loans by the banks as a group gave the main participants—Mexico, the banks, the United States, the IMF—time to restructure the country's debt. The first step was a deal between Mexico and the IMF, in which the former agreed to undertake a stabilization program designed to improve the country's balance of trade so as to generate enough hard currency to resume scheduled debt payments. The stabilization program consisted of deep cuts in government spending and overall reduction in the public sector's deficit; a ceiling on net external borrowing; exchange rate and interest rate measures to assure the competitiveness of Mexican exports in world markets, to promote domestic savings, and to prevent capital flight; and severe reductions in imports and annual growth. The program was Mexico's quid pro quo. In return for new loans and extended maturities, Mexico would undertake policies designed to improve its prospects for making scheduled payments in the future.

The second step was a deal between the IMF and the commercial banks. The IMF's managing director announced in December 1982 that he was prepared to recommend an IMF loan if the IMF were assured of the banks' own commitment to lend Mexico $5 billion in new money and to reschedule much of the country's debt. The bank advisory committee, Federal Reserve officials, and representatives of the Office of Comptroller General lobbied more than 500 banks to participate as a group in the new loans and the rescheduling of old loans. When the advisory committee reported that almost all of the $5 billion had been committed, the IMF approved a three-year extended IMF arrangement for $3.9 billion.

The third step was a series of deals between Mexico and the U.S. commercial banks to restructure the Mexican indebtedness. This involved two sets of contractual agreements. The first were new money credit agreements, finalized in March 1983. More than 500 banks participated in the agreements. The second agreements rescheduled the public Mexican debt to commercial banks which would have fallen due between August 22, 1982 and December 31, 1984.

The Mexican rescue suggests a pattern of action followed for other countries (including Brazil, Argentina, Peru, Venezuela, and other developing countries in Latin America and elsewhere) after August 1982. Once the country confessed inability to make scheduled debt payments, Western governments (through their central banks or otherwise) or multilateral financial institutions would arrange temporary loans and the private banks would agree to maturity extensions for debt falling due pending resolution of the problem. Next, the country would adopt a stabilization program, typically after agreement with the IMF. The IMF and the banks would extend new credit to the country, and the banks would then reschedule loans that had matured or were about to mature.

Alfred Mudge, partner in a Wall Street law firm, has represented Citibank in connection with debt restructuring negotiations with Mexico in 1982–83 and in 1984 and is familiar with the restructuring arrangement for other countries. He describes, in chapter 4, the process by which the banks organize themselves and the incentives and strategies they follow in this process. He observes that the individual bank creditors have differing economic incentives and differing roles in the restructure process. The job of counsel is to draft an agreement that represents a consensus of debtors, general bank creditors, agent banks, bank advisory groups, and servicing banks.

One striking feature of Mr. Mudge's account is that it depicts a classic legal problem—the borrower cannot keep up with scheduled payments on its debt—to which there are not workable legal solutions. Contrast Mexico's problem in August 1982 with that of the homebuyer who has an adjustable-rate mortgage. Neither is in a position to make scheduled payments, and each is in default. Default on one payment permits the lender to "accelerate" payment of the entire debt. The commercial bank is liable to do just that to the homebuyer, but is quite unlikely to do that to Mexico. Mr. Mudge suggests one reason why: the bank is part of a syndicate of many banks, and the individual bank cannot easily accelerate unless it has the consent of other banks. There is another, more fundamental, reason. In the case of the homebuyer, the bank may take possession of the home in the event of default, since in a home mortgage, the house is collateral for the loan. There is little or nothing to take possession of when the debtor in default is Mexico. The bank acts at some risk if it believes it can waltz down to Mexico City and initiate proceedings to attach government buildings. While Mexico has a number of assets in the United States, under applicable U.S. law most of Mexico's assets in this country are protected by its sovereign immunity. Being a country makes a difference.

Because there is not necessarily any reliable legal mechanism to enforce the loan instrument's terms against Mexico or other delinquent debtors, the resolution has been a negotiated one. The various actors work together to prevent a default and then negotiate a way for the country's indebtedness and its economy to be reconstituted so that future payments might be made. All the participants have incentives for this negotiation process to work. The banks might themselves be rendered insolvent by the default of one of the biggest borrowers or several smaller ones; the debtor countries want continued access to world financial markets to finance trade and to obtain development capital; and the Western governments and multilateral financial institutions want to preserve financial stability. Thus described, this sounds like a pretty reasonable, principled, apolitical process. It is not. It is complex and highly politicized and may be quite unfair, as chapters 5 and 6 demonstrate.

James Hurlock is Alfred Mudge's *doppelgänger*. Where the latter is a leading counsel for banks, the former is a key partner at the leading law firm for the borrowing countries. Their views of the restructuring process are very different. Where Mr. Mudge depicts a diversity of bank interests that complicate the process of negotiated restructurings, Mr. Hurlock depicts the banks as a monolithic group often insensitive to the special needs of Third World sovereign borrowers. Thus the banks as a group insist that the borrowing country pay all interest arrearages, including penalties and interest on interest, before the banks will agree to lend new money and to reschedule soon-to-mature indebtedness. Even when the banks agreed to lend new money in 1983–84, it was often just enough to permit the country to pay the banks the interest and penalty payments owed in those years.

Mr. Hurlock also charges that the banks approach the debt negotiations with only short-term goals in mind. Their focus is on maintaining current income flows and preventing the write-off of their sovereign loans; they want to err on the side of too few concessions to the borrowing countries and do not mind restructuring the same country's debt more than once if the first plan does not work. After all, the banks receive various fees "up front" (and the servicing and agent banks receive extra fees for their duties) every time the process occurs. As a result of the short-term approach, the process has worked unevenly. Mexico's restructuring was successful, and in 1984 the banks were willing to reschedule a larger portion of the debt over a longer repayment term. Brazil's restructuring was less successful, and there were so many problems in 1983 that a new restructuring (including $6.5 billion in new money) was necessary in early 1984. Argentina's restructuring was less successful than that of Brazil. The initial restructuring required a longer period of negotiation, and it was largely unsuccessful because of its short-term character and because of Argentina's inability to comply with the IMF stabilization program. In 1984 Argentina and its creditors struggled to reach agreement; a tentative agreement was reached at the end of the year. But it is still short term, and there may be a third round of restructuring in 1985 or 1986 for Argentina.

Mr. Hurlock's complaints are based upon his perception that the debt renegotiations are politically stacked in favor of the banks, who call the shots (not always very wisely). Although both sides have incentives to work out the debt problem, the borrowing country may have more at stake. Its exclusion from international financial circles could, it fears, trigger severe economic consequences for its people and possible political instability. While the banks are aware that default by one of the three largest borrowers (Mexico, Brazil, Argentina) might render many of them insolvent, they may with good reason believe that the U.S. government would intervene to prevent that, as it did in the case of Continental Illinois. Moreover, Mr. Hurlock argues, the banks have important allies—the central banks of the main industrial states, the IMF, BIS, the World Bank, and so on. All of these have one important common interest, that is to force austerity programs onto the borrowing country that will produce a quick turnaround in the country's current account balance. A quick turnaround is convenient for the international financial system to which all of these participants are politically dedicated, but the price in human and political terms for the borrowing country is both severe and excessive. Additionally, the austerity measures typically require virtual elimination of capital goods imports by the borrowing countries. As a result, the countries not only forgo present growth needed to support a growing population, but also may forgo future growth levels that a more moderate adjustment program might achieve.

Mr. Hurlock's analysis focuses on the politics of the interactions of commercial banks and sovereign borrowers, and he argues that the banks come out ahead. Philip Wellons, associate professor of business administration at the Harvard Business School, focuses on interbank politics and bank–government politics in chapter 6. His conclusions are, essentially, that the big money center banks come out ahead. They are able to draw governments into the process to diminish their risks and losses and to coerce regional banks (though in a rather ambiguous and mild way) to cooperate in solving a crisis the big banks generated. Professor Wellons posits that the big international banks of the Group of Five (the United States, the United Kingdom, Japan, West Germany, France) take political action at three different levels—in their home countries, in the borrowing countries, and internationally—to pursue their strategic goals.

In order to prevent default or a payment moratorium by a borrowing country to which they have lent a lot of money, the big banks must not only reschedule much of the debt, but also ensure the flow of new loans, preferably not exclusively by them. Politics is the way the big banks achieve these goals in the process of debt restructuring, argues Professor Wellons. Through interbank politics, the big banks seek new money commitments from "outliers," the banks whose relative exposure is often not large enough to justify their making fresh loans simply to minimize the possibility of default. If the outliers fail to contribute to commitments of new money, there might be a chain reaction of refusals that would sabotage the process and leave the big banks with the sole lending responsibility and the possibility of big losses. Typically, therefore, the big banks enlist the aid of their home governments and bank regulators to persuade the outliers to cooperate. The IMF and the central banks of other countries also lobby the outliers in favor of an agreement to restructure, as does the government of the borrowing country. This political process was particularly important in "persuading" the regional banks to participate in the 1982–83 Mexican restructuring and the 1984–85 Argentine restructuring.

A second type of politics during the restructuring process, according to Professor Wellons, is bail-out politics: one or more official lenders provide new money to the Third World borrower. At the international level, BIS often provides bridge loans, and the IMF typically forwards new money in connection with the borrower's agreement to a stabilization program. The IMF, of course, has devised its own political gambit: it will not commit any money to a borrowing country until and unless the banks agree to lend a certain amount of new money and to reschedule maturing indebtedness. At the home level, the big banks have been very successful in having public funds augment their own funds. As Professor Wellons points out, the willingness of the United States to contribute these large sums varies directly with the perceived importance of the borrowing country to U.S. foreign affairs and trade relations. Thus the 1982–83 Mexican restructuring received more official assistance than the 1982–83 Brazilian restructuring, which in turn received more official assistance than the 1983 Argentine restructuring. At the borrowers' level, interestingly, some of the debtor countries help with bridge loans. For example, several Latin American countries provided money for an Argentine bridge loan in 1984.

The strategic goals of the big international banks are not limited to cutting their losses during the restructuring process. They would also like to improve their competitive position vis-à-vis the regional banks and one another after the restructuring is complete. Thus the big banks have typically dominated the advisory committees. These banks hope that having taken the lead in restructuring they will have first choice of loans once the borrowing country is restored to creditworthiness. Citibank has taken a leading role in the advisory committees for Mexico, Brazil, Argentina, and Peru, which may give it a competitive advantage over its competitors in future lending. The big banks as a group hope to get a more profitable share of the Latin American credit market from the regional banks because of their assertedly more constructive role in the restructuring process and the personal relationships that have surely been established.

The dynamics of the process of solving the debt crisis are intrinsically political, and the variety of political participants and incentives makes the whole process very complex and sometimes unpredictable. Resort to political channels is necessary, however, because the legal mechanisms for resolving the problem are primitive and unworkable. In order to prevent most of the lenders from opting out of the process and to push the borrowing country to make hard decisions, political pressures have proved useful. But this political process is subject to charges of unfairness. If, as Mr. Hurlock claims, the bargaining position of the debtor country is seldom more than weak and the banks, the IMF, and Western governments impose ever-increasing demands for austerity and sacrifice on the debtor country, the process may be exacerbating the gap between the haves and the have nots in the world. If, as may be inferred from Professor Wellons's argument, the big banks are able to shift some of their costs and losses to smaller banks and the public sector, there may be a misallocation of resources and insufficient incentives for the big banks to follow more prudent lending policies in the future.

Prospects and Proposals

There are two broad categories of pundits of the international debt crisis, the optimists and the pessimists. A good many of the pundits in 1983 were pessimists, because most of the largest debtor countries were tumbling into crisis and because the economic indicators were less than encouraging. One pundit who was an optimist was William Cline of the Institute for International Economics. He produced a series of econometric projections for the leading debtor countries in 1983 and predicted that, with a 3 percent growth in industrial countries, most of the debtors would return to creditworthy status within several years. In general Mr. Cline's projections have been prescient, and he was able to make a triumphant presentation to the Foreign Relations Committee of the U.S. House of Representatives in August 1984 in support of his thesis that an increase in world trade will resolve the problem, and there can be an expeditious return to voluntary lending. Indeed developments between August 1984 and January 1985 ought to augment this optimism, since interest rates have declined and United States growth in 1984 was a surprising 7 percent.

Others are more guarded. They remember that in 1978 the experts were on the whole quite satisfied that the level of Third World external debt was not too high. For example, as Mr. Kubarych says in chapter 1, the ability of the banks and the borrowers to work out useful restructurings and the growth in industrial countries in 1984 and the projections for 1985 justify some optimism. But he cautions that the debtor countries are still highly vulnerable because of high real interest rates, capital flight, and other problems.

Andrew Quale, partner in a law firm representing commercial banks in both creditor and debtor countries, who has served as an advisor to the ministries of finance of two debtor countries and is adjunct professor of law at the University of Virginia, is less optimistic, at least in the near term. In chapter 7, he warns that the participants affected by the international debt problem are in for a roller coaster ride for a number of years. He sees the debt problem as part of a global disequilibrium of high interest rates, an over-valued dollar, and excessive indebtedness. Professor Quale does not share William Cline's optimism that growth of the OECD countries will immediately translate into a quick solution of the debt crisis, because such growth will have uneven benefits for developing countries. Increases in U.S. imports in 1983 went almost entirely to Canada, Japan, South Korea, and Taiwan. It remains to be seen whether the increased trade projected for Latin America for 1985 will be as significant as Mr. Cline's models project. Perhaps the most justifiable optimism exists for Mexico and Brazil, observes Professor Quale, but other debtor countries (such as Chile and Peru) did not profit very much from the economic upturn in 1984. Additionally, the austerity programs imposed upon these countries by the debt crisis may impair their ability to take advantage of new export opportunities in the industrialized countries. Much, and probably most, of the import reduction was achieved by forgoing capital goods needed to maintain and expand productive capacity. Exporters in the debtor countries may have difficulty competing with exporters in industrialized countries and in South Korea and Taiwan who have been able to preserve or improve their capital investment during the crisis.

There may also be political dynamics that should dampen any premature optimism about the international debt crisis. Riordan Roett, authority on Latin American political systems and director of the School of Advanced International Studies at the Johns Hopkins University, argues that an exclusively economic approach to resolving the debt crisis is not sufficient. He demonstrates in chapter 9 that there are two important political consequences of the foreign debt crisis of Latin America. First, the external indebtedness and the series of IMF-sponsored austerity programs imperil the decided but fragile trend toward redemocratization in Latin America. Unlike the Anglo-American experience, democracy in Latin America since 1930 has tended to alternate with military dictatorships. Between 1964 and 1973, for example, many Latin American countries reverted to authoritarian governments, and in most instances the new military dictators remained in power for a long time. The military governments implemented expensive national security and growth plans that contributed to the debt explosion of the 1970s, only to see their policies discredited after 1978. Between 1979 and January 1985 nine Latin American countries have enjoyed a transition from dictatorship to democracy. But this trend toward redemocratization is fragile because the new governments have been immediately tested by the dilemma of massive indebtedness: they must pay the debts accumulated by the preceding, military governments, but in doing so their own political viability may be threatened. The declines in real wages, the unemployment, the cuts in public benefits and subsidies, and the declines in consumption that typify IMF stabilization programs may have precisely the opposite, destabilizing effects politically.

Given this threat to Latin American redemocratization, Dr. Roett shows that the debt problem has a second political consequence: it involves the national security and diplomatic interests of the United States. As the world's premier democracy, the United States has long pursued a policy of encouraging democracies in the world, and especially in our own hemisphere. The United States has correctly perceived that the greater accountability and rationality of democratic governments renders them forces for peace in the hemisphere. The adventurism of Argentina in the Malvinas/Falklands War was only too typical of military governments in the region. Finally, the United States' own diplomatic position might be severely undermined by a heavy-handed approach by U.S. banks and the U.S-dominated IMF. Coming on the heels of the United States' botched handling of the war between Argentina and the United Kingdom, the debt crisis could harden the rift between this country and its hemisphere neighbors.

Professor Quale and Dr. Roett propose a series of constructive measures that should be taken to ameliorate the risks of the debt problem. They recognize the political barriers to implementing most of their proposals but argue persuasively that the political as well as economic urgency and importance of the international debt crisis command political response by the United States.

Global Growth and Lower Interest Rates. Pessimists agree with optimists that growth in the OECD countries will be beneficial to the debtor countries but warn of two policies that might undermine some of the potential benefits of such growth. One is the pull toward protectionism, which almost every knowledgeable commentator believes should be resisted. A second, and potentially more troubling, policy is the tolerance of high real interest rates in the United States. Although on a downward swing as of January 1985, real interest rates are still at historically high levels, and a major cause is the stubbornly enormous federal deficits generated in large part by changes in the federal tax laws enacted in 1981. No one with any sense disagrees with that diagnosis, yet no one in any position of power seems willing to admit the obvious and raise taxes. A political impasse between the president and Congress may help keep interest rates far above the rate of inflation in 1985–86. This impasse must be broken.

Professor Quale argues that, in the event that the impasse persists, attention must be focused on reducing the rates of interest charged by the banks. The political problem here is that to achieve any meaningful relief for the debtor countries, the banks would have to reduce their rates by 3 percent to 5 percent, which they certainly will not do on their own. Nor is there any chance that the U.S. government will require the banks to make this sacrifice, because the big banks have a powerful influence on the policy of the federal banking regulators, who depend on the banks for information and cooperation. Professor Quale suggests a thoughtful and creative solution: reduce interest rates below market, capitalize the difference between payments at the market level and payments at the low-interest level, and issue new notes evidencing that capitalized interest. He argues that the accountants and the regulators ought to allow the banks to do this without requiring a write-down in such loans, although the banks voluntarily should increase their loan loss reserves to reflect part of the capitalized interest. This proposal deserves serious consideration. It would not require unreasonable sacrifices by the banks but would permit the debtor countries to try to solve their problems without having to adopt adjustment programs as severe as the programs and restructurings of 1983.

Continuation of New Loans and Extension of Debt Maturity. A related proposal urged in both chapter 7 and chapter 9 is that the U.S. banks and their regulators take a leadership role in moving international debt management into a new phase. The first phase was ad hoc; the banks and the borrowers and the OECD governments "muddled through" by providing new loans and rescheduling maturing indebtedness due in the coming year or two, thus staving off default but not providing the borrowing countries much breathing time. Dr. Roett and Professor Quale strongly favor continued new loans by private banks and, more important, long-term rescheduling. That is, a more substantial portion of the country's loans (those maturing over four to six years rather than one to two years) would be rescheduled over a longer period of time (ten to twenty-five years). The advantage of the long-term approach is that the borrowing country is relieved of the economic uncertainty associated with year-to-year rescheduling and has more breathing room to return its economy to growth. The Mexican 1984 restructuring followed this philosophy, and Brazil will likely negotiate a similar deal in 1985.

The political problem with this proposal is that the banks are only willing to do it for the success stories, the countries that need it the least, and for perfectly understandable political reasons. The banks fear that unless the specter of debt renegotiation hangs over the political system of an Argentina, efforts to comply with IMF stabilization goals will be halfhearted. Even if one bank were willing to gamble on a long-term approach for Argentina, it is unlikely that the banks as a group would go along. And without their cooperation, nothing can be done. (Indeed, only a concerted political campaign was able to sell the more conservative 1984 restructuring to Argentina's private creditors.) The IMF and the United States and the other OECD governments should apply greater pressure in favor of this long-term approach, perhaps offering incentives to banks that cooperate.

Increased Commitment to Official Lending. One way to get more money to the borrowing countries on "concessionary" terms (lower interest rates, longer maturities) would be to increase the level of official lending. Cynthia

Lichtenstein of the Boston College Law School in chapter 8 traces the process by which the United States in 1983 increased its IMF quota by almost 50 percent. From the perspective of U.S. policy, a larger role for the IMF and other multilateral financial institutions would be useful, because they could take some of the pressure off of the banks, would give the countries better terms, and would accompany these services with stabilization agreements. Professor Lichtenstein's study of the 1983 legislation, however, makes one doubtful that the political process will move any further in this direction.

The IMF funding law was only proposed by the Reagan Administration after the debt crisis dramatically broke in 1982, and one suspects that any additional initiative (especially in a year of more nickel-and-dime budget cuts) will not be forthcoming unless the crisis generates a renewed sense of dramatic urgency. Also, the law encountered serious opposition in Congress. Legislators, especially in the U.S. House of Representatives, complained that the money was needed for domestic programs and was a bail-out for the banks. Moreover, chapter 8 shows that Congress exacted a quid pro quo from the executive branch. In return for Congress's funding the increased commitment to the IMF, the federal bank regulators were required to tighten their regulation of lending to sovereign entities. The real danger, Professor Lichtenstein observes, is that Congress will deprive the regulators of the flexibility they need to encourage banks to make new loans and to reschedule sovereign debt. The regulators in this case have, with considerable deftness, implemented the congressional rules without impairing their flexibility. But the implicit danger is that the next legislation in the area will shackle them more explicitly.

Dr. Roett supports increased official lending and adds a further proposal: developmental foreign aid to the neediest Latin American debtors. Patterned on the administration's Caribbean Basin Initiative, the proposal would assure special export incentives, low-interest loans or grants for development purposes, and direct investment encouragement as a "Mini-Marshall Plan" for Latin America. This proposal is strikingly sensible, for it would ameliorate the internal shocks resulting from draconian IMF stabilization programs and would contribute to better relations between the United States and Latin America. On the other hand political pressures render the prospect of aid and export incentives unlikely in the near future. The political challenge is to persuade U.S. policymakers in the executive and legislative branches of government that these policies are urgently needed to protect the economic, political, and diplomatic interests of the United States.

Developing Country Policies to Discourage Capital Flight and Encourage Domestic and Foreign Investment. Because the origins of the international debt crisis lie in the policies of the debtor countries as well as those of the system of international finance, Professor Quale recommends policies to lower the rate of inflation in the debtor countries so that it is lower than the rate of interest paid on savings and to control the flow of foreign exchange more effectively. He also urges these countries to encourage direct foreign investment by multinational corporations, so that they will not have to rely so heavily on bank loans to finance their development. These, too, are sensible recommendations along the lines of classical economic theory. One problem is that high inflation in countries like Brazil has structural causes that impede a quick solution. Even with IMF austerity programs, the inflation rates in Brazil and Argentina were 100 percent or more in 1984. It is in fact not clear what policies these countries could adopt that would solve that nagging problem. And even if the policy choices were clear, it is far from evident that the nonrobust political systems of those countries would be able to implement them, especially if (as seems likely) one or more of the powerful corporatist interests had to make sacrifices.

In that event Professor Quale's suggestion that Latin America rely on direct foreign investment rather than bank loans is appealing. The advantage of foreign investment is that the country does not have to pay interest. Such investment, moreover, is supposed to introduce modern technology that will increase the host country's productive capacity. There may be nationalist political opposition to more foreign investment, however. More important, direct foreign investment itself often creates debt. As set forth in more detail in chapter 3, subsidiaries of multinational enterprises in Latin American countries may cause cash to flow out of the countries rather than into them, because (1) much of their investment capital is raised in the local capital markets; (2) the companies' export earnings are offset by their capital imports and their repatriation of profits; and (3) the companies' oligopolistic position in the local market generates supernormal profits, which are largely repatriated. In this way direct foreign investment may further deplete the hard currency positions of these countries. Of course some of those means of depletion can be regulated by requiring local part ownership, local supply of raw materials and components, and limitations on profit repatriation—and Latin American countries have enacted such regulations. The regulations can be evaded through transfer pricing and the like, but, more important, those are the regulations that discourage direct foreign investment. The dilemma for the Latin American country seeking to follow Professor Quale's advice is this: unregulated direct foreign investment may have adverse cash flow consequences for the host country, but regulations to control this problem tend to discourage such investment.

The four sets of proposals advocated by Professor Quale and Dr. Roett—global growth and lower interest rates, more new lending and substantial extension of debt maturity, increased commitment by OECD governments to official lending, and more prudent domestic policies by the Latin American borrowers—are ones for which political action will be needed at many different levels. The United States will have to take even more of a leadership role than it has heretofore. The question is whether it will. The answer to that question depends on how urgent the United States believes the crisis to be, and whether it poses direct threats to U.S. interests. Professor Quale and Dr. Roett persuasively argue that the crisis is urgent and that it does pose severe dangers and risks for the economic and national security of the United States.

Stated more broadly, the international debt problem poses substantial risks for all of the political participants. The participants are engaged in a dance along the precipice. On every side yawn chasms of disaster, representing dangers to the system of international financial flows, world political stability and cooperation, and the ability of the people of the world to go about the business of improving their economic prospects. One false step along the precipice may send several, if not all, of the dancers careening into one of these pits. A sure-footed approach to the risks of the terrain will assure the dancers that the disaster below never occurs.

Part I
Origins

1
The Financial Vulnerability of the LDCs: Six Factors

Roger M. Kubarych

T he international debt crisis poses a severe test of the world's financial fabric. For 1983 alone, according to World Bank estimates, twenty-seven countries rescheduled over $67 billion in debt to commercial banks and governments.[1] The magnitude of this debt is unprecedented, constituting more than all previous reschedulings combined. The severity of these debt servicing problems is intricately related to international economic developments of the past few years. In particular, the recent world recession was the worst in some time; furthermore, interest rates rose to unusually high levels as the industrial countries pursued anti-inflationary policies.

Why were the less developed countries (LDCs) so vulnerable? This chapter focuses on six features that played a large part in spawning the debt servicing crises these countries face now. It also examines current approaches to repayment problems and identifies the constraints on alternative solutions. The overall outlook may be labeled tenuous optimism; there are many favorable signs but there is considerable uncertainty about their strength.

Reasons for LDC Vulnerability

At least six different factors spawned the crisis in debt servicing: false expectations by LDCs, their unsatisfactory financial planning, industrialized countries' encouragement of bank lending to LDCs, LDCs' policy mistakes, their large government budget deficits, and capital flight from LDCs.

Optimistic LDC Expectations and Economic Shocks

The first factor contributing to the international debt crisis is the mistaken assumption the LDCs made, both about the world economy and about the economic response of industrial countries in the late 1970s. Rising oil prices in 1979 impelled many debtor countries to increase their foreign borrowing to finance imports and their reserve goals. They assumed that the inflation triggered by the oil price shocks would be dealt with gradually by industrial countries, without severe impact on interest rates and trade levels. That assumption was wrong. In the United States, the Federal Reserve Board attacked inflation vigorously through its control of the supply of money. Thus, the real growth (netting out inflation) of M1, an indicator of monetary expansion and contraction, was negative during three years of restrictive monetary policies (table 1–1). These policies did ultimately help curb inflation, but they had two further consequences that contributed to the LDC debt crisis.

The strong measures industrial countries took to combat inflation contributed to a recession—with unemployment, diminished demand, falling primary commodity prices—that exacerbated the deterioration in the terms of trade for many LDCs. As demand for their exports fell, and prices tumbled, and domestic growth all but halted, their current account deficits grew substantially, from $11.3 billion in 1973 to $107.7 billion in 1981 (table 1–2). Even more important was the significant rise in real interest rates. Although nominal rates were high in the 1970s, real interest rates had remained low or negative because of the high rates of inflation (table 1–3), thus permitting easier paydown of debt by LDCs in those years. The decline in the inflation rate, combined with the rise of nominal interest rates resulting from restrictive monetary policies, produced unusually high real interest rates by 1981–83 (table 1–3). The high interest rates impelled debtor countries to borrow more heavily than ever before, in part to meet the higher interest payments—and the new money was on loan at very high rates. Total debt owed by developing countries to banks doubled between 1978 and June 1982 (table 1–4).

The unfortunate consequence of these unexpected external shocks was that LDCs incurred more debt than they would have otherwise, and were less

Table 1–1
Money Growth, Inflation, and Interest Rates in Major Industrial Countries

	1976	1977	1978	1979	1980	1981	1982	1983
Nominal[a] MI growth	10.2%	8.8%	10.9%	9.6%	6.6%	6.0%	6.7%	9.5%
Real M1 growth	1.0	3.3	3.6	−0.4	−3.8	−1.2	3.0	3.7
Consumer prices	8.3	8.5	7.2	9.1	11.9	9.9	7.5	5.0
Real[b] interest rates								
Short-term	0.0	−0.7	−0.2	1.4	2.4	4.3	4.0	4.3
Long-term	1.4	1.0	0.9	1.2	1.9	4.2	5.4	6.0

Sources: Real money growth and interest rates: IMF, *World Economic Outlook* (1984), pp. 115, table 1.7; 120–21, tables 2.2, 2.6.
Nominal M1 growth and consumer prices: IMF, *International Financial Statistics* (August 1984) and 1983 Yearbook, *passim* ("change in money" tables; "change in consumer prices" tables).
[a]M1 is the currency outside banks and private sector demand deposits.
[b]Excess nominal rate over GNP deflator.

Table 1–2
Nonoil Developing Countries: Current Account Financing, 1973–1982
(billions of U.S. dollars)

	1973	1974	1975	1976	1977	1978	1979	1980	1981	1982
Current account deficit[a]	$11.3	$37.0	$46.3	$32.6	$28.9	$41.3	$61.0	$89.0	$107.7	$86.8
Use of reserves	-10.4	-2.7	1.6	-13.0	-12.5	-17.4	-12.6	-4.5	-2.1	7.1
Non-debt-creating flows, net	10.3	14.6	11.8	12.6	14.4	17.9	23.9	24.1	28.0	25.1
Direct investment flows, net	4.2	5.3	5.3	5.0	5.4	7.3	8.9	10.1	13.9	11.4
Net external borrowing[b]	11.4	25.1	32.9	33.0	27.0	40.8	49.7	69.3	81.8	54.6
Long-term borrowing, net[c]	11.9	18.1	27.1	28.0	24.6	37.2	36.5	47.2	62.7	41.0
From official sources	4.9	6.8	11.7	10.5	11.4	13.8	13.3	17.6	23.0	19.5
From private sources	6.8	11.3	15.4	17.5	13.2	23.4	23.2	29.6	39.7	21.5

Source: IMF, *Annual Report* (1983), p. 33.
[a]Net total of balances on goods, services, and private transfers, as defined in the IMF's *Balance of Payments Statistics* (with sign reversed).
[b]Includes any net use of nonreserve claims on nonresidents, errors and omissions in reported balance-of-payments statements for individual countries, and minor deficiencies in coverage.
[c]On a balance-of-payments basis.

Table 1–3

U.S. Interest Rates: Nominal and Real, 1976–1983

	1976	1977	1978	1979	1980	1981	1982	1983
Long-term								
Nominal	7.6%	7.4%	8.4%	9.4%	11.5%	13.9%	13.0%	11.0%
Real	2.3	1.5	0.9	0.7	2.1	4.2	6.6	6.7
Short-term								
Nominal	5.0	5.3	7.2	10.1	11.4	14.0	10.6	8.6
Real	−0.2	−0.5	−0.2	1.3	2.1	4.3	4.3	4.3

Source: IMF, *World Economic Outlook* (1984), pp. 120–21, tables 2.6, 2.7.

financially able to repay it. The ability of a country to service its foreign debt depends on how much hard currency (typically, dollars) it obtains from export sales and foreign direct investment. As their trade positions worsened, debtor LDCs were forced to borrow new funds from their creditors, in order to meet interest payments on old debt, while simultaneously incurring new debts.

Imperfect LDC Financial Planning

A second factor contributing to LDC vulnerability stems from their imperfect financial planning. Specifically, this entailed too much debt incurred on floating interest rates, insufficient currency diversification, excessive contracting with commercial banks, and inadequate direct foreign investment in debtor countries.

By the end of 1983 the nonoil LDCs had accumulated an external debt of over $660 billion in a variety of forms (see table 1–5). Official lending (by the IMF, the World Bank, and others) at concessional interest rates reflected only a small portion of that amount. And even less took the form of private fixed-rate financing in the bond market. Instead, most private debt, whether long term or short term in maturity, was negotiated at floating interest rates. Debt contracted on floating rather than fixed rates constituted 70 percent of the total debt outstanding in 1983, compared to 60 percent in 1973. One implication of this is that debtor countries became increasingly vulnerable to the increases in interest rates that occurred after 1978 (tables 1–1 and 1–3).

To compound this problem, too much of the debt, particularly in Latin America, was contracted in U.S. dollars rather than over a range of international currencies. By failing to use diversification strategies, debtor countries exposed themselves to tremendous risk and bore heavy costs when the U.S. dollar became exceptionally strong. Had the nonoil LDCs diversified their new and maturing bank debt between 1979 and 1982, the combined savings

Table 1–4
Bank Claims on Nonoil Developing Countries
(billions of U.S. dollars)

Year	Claims on All Countries				Claims on Argentina, Brazil, and Mexico			
	U.S. Banks	*Non-U.S. Banks*	*Total*	*U.S. Share of Total*	*U.S. Banks*	*Non-U.S. Banks*	*Total*	*U.S. Share of Total*
1975	$34.3	$ 28.5	$ 62.7	54.5%	$18.7	$12.8	$ 31.5	59.4%
1976	43.1	37.8	80.9	53.3	24.7	17.8	42.5	58.1
1977	46.9	47.4	94.3	49.7	25.8	24.4	50.2	51.3
1978	52.2	79.1	131.3	39.8	26.8	36.4	63.2	42.4
1979	61.8	109.2	171.0	36.1	29.9	53.1	83.0	36.0
1980	75.4	134.8	210.2	35.9	37.0	71.1	108.1	34.2
1981	92.8	160.7	253.5	36.6	46.7	87.8	134.5	34.7
1982a	98.6	169.7	268.3	36.7	52.4	92.6	145.0	36.1

Source: Statement by Paul A. Volcker, chairman, Board of Governors of the Federal Reserve System, before the Committee on Banking, Finance and Urban Affairs, House of Representatives, February 2, 1983, table II.
aAs of June.

Table 1–5
Total External Debt of the Nonoil LDCs
(billions of U.S. dollars)

Debt	1973	1978	1982	1983
Total: nonoil LDCs	$130	$334	$633	$669
Short-term	18	52	125	102
Long-term	112	283	508	569
From official sources	51	116	189	212
From private sources	61	166	319	355
Nonoil LDC debt, by area				
Africa (excluding South Africa)		37	62	66
Asia		78	153	165
Europe		47	72	75
Middle East		27	46	51
Western hemisphere		132	283	294
Total: major borrowers[a]		312	576	607
Short-term		60	140	120
Long-term		252	436	487
From official sources		88	128	142
From private sources		163	308	344

Source: IMF, *World Economic Outlook* (1984), p. 205, table 35.

[a]Brazil, Mexico, Argentina, Korea, Indonesia, Venezuela, Israel, India, Chile, Egypt, Yugoslavia, Turkey, Algeria, Philippines, South Africa, Portugal, Nigeria, Thailand, Malaysia, Peru, Pakistan, Morocco, Romania, Colombia, and Hungary (in order of amount of debt at the end of 1982).

from lower interest costs and exchange rate gains could have amounted to over $30 billion.[2]

Yet another aspect of poor financial planning is that too much debt was contracted with banks, as opposed to other lenders such as institutions and individual bond purchasers (table 1–6). In large part this was due to transnational banks' increased willingness to lend to LDCs in the early 1970s. The demand for credit from traditional clients was declining just as large deposits from oil-exporting countries were flowing into the large private international banks. Besides the pressure on banks to recycle petrodollars, the countries themselves found it easier to deal with private sources of money than with the official ones, since the former typically attached no conditions on the use of disbursed funds and responded to loan requests more quickly. One consequence of such extensive private debt is that the LDC debt problem was transformed into a banking system problem, with all the attendant management difficulties.

Finally, the LDCs seem not to have considered the optimal allocation of debt financing between debt and equity investments. Visions of national ownership and control of industries prevailed instead. They thus eliminated

Table 1–6
External Financing by Nonoil LDCs
(billions of U.S. dollars)

	1978	1979	1980	1981	1982	1983
Financial requirements	$58	$74	$95	$114	$78	$62
Current account deficit	42	62	88	109	82	56
Increase in reserves	16	12	7	5	-4	6
Sources of financing	58	74	95	114	78	62
Officials flows[a]	26	31	40	47	50	44
Official transfers	8	12	13	14	13	13
Private flows	40	46	70	84	47	28
Net borrowing from banks[b]	22	23	28	29	16	40
Net direct investment	7	9	9	13	11	8
Residual[c]	-8	-3	-15	-17	-19	-10

Source: IMF, *World Economic Outlook* (1984), p. 197, table 28.
[a]Including use of IMF credit.
[b]Long-term borrowing only. 1983 borrowing mostly reflects a change from short-term or long-term borrowing.
[c]Unrecorded capital flight.

or reduced opportunities for foreign direct investment at the very time when increasing direct equity investment would have been more prudent.

Industrial Countries' Encouragement of Loans to LDCs

The third factor producing greater vulnerability was that banks from the major industrial countries were directly and indirectly encouraged by their own governments to lend to the debtor countries. Governments were prepared to endorse the recycling of OPEC's oil earnings through the world's commercial banking system, but not to deal directly with the consequences of the major shift in wealth to the OPEC countries. Undoubtedly, bankers in most industrial countries believed, with a certain measure of justification, that their governments effectively stood behind loans to LDCs.

But note that, proportionately, the major increase in lending during the 1979–81 period, when the lending grew most rapidly, was not by American banks. In fact, U.S. bank lending was relatively low in those years, while that of other industrial countries was very rapid. Lending by the United States to the most troubled debtors of Latin America, for example, now accounts for only about 35 percent to 40 percent of the total, whereas it accounted for more than half of the claims before 1978 (table 1–4). That is, the international debt crisis is not solely a U.S. problem; it is a world problem whose solutions require cooperative efforts.

Table 1-7
Exchange Rate Changes for Selected Debtor Countries

	1978	1979	1980	1981	1982	1983
Argentina						
Nominal exchange rate	−95.10%	−65.0%	−39.4%	−139.1%	−489.1%	−306.2%
Real effective exchange rate	n.a.	41.0	31.2	−7.8	−44.1	−15.6
Brazil						
Nominal rate	−27.8	−49.1	−95.6	−76.7	−92.8	−221.4
Real effective exchange rate	n.a.	−9.6	−9.7	23.3	5.6	−18.6
Mexico						
Nominal rate	−0.9	−0.2	−0.6	−6.8	−124.3	−118.4
Real effective exchange rate	n.a.	5.8	11.7	12.9	−27.4	−13.0

Source: IMF, *International Financial Statistics*, various issues, and calculations based on IMF data.

LDC Policy Mistakes

Policy mistakes constitute the fourth factor for LDC vulnerability to the debt crisis. I am defining a "policy mistake" as a course of action taken by a government that leads to its own undermining, to unintended or counterproductive side effects, or to distortions in markets. For the LDCs such misguided undertakings ranged from maintaining overvalued exchange rates to tolerating accelerating inflation.

Overvalued exchange rates, which do not reasonably reflect the true value of foreign exchange to the debtor countries, leave gaping mismatches between price levels at home and abroad. But, for reasons of political expediency or national pride, many LDCs overvalued their currency in the 1970s. An overvalued currency has the unfortunate effect of pricing a country's exporters out of world markets. Imports become relatively inexpensive for LDC buyers, and LDC exports become correspondingly expensive abroad. The end result is a worsened trade balance for LDCs. Eventually, though, currency overvaluation requires remedial action, and in fact virtually all of the major debtor countries have had to undergo major currency depreciations to help restore external balance (table 1–7).

Another questionable policy lay in the realm of subsidies, which LDC governments granted in excessive numbers to a variety of special interest groups. Such subsidies increase budget deficits, which must be financed either through creation of money or through private borrowing. Money financing exacerbates the inflation already plaguing many debtor countries.

A third policy error is reflected in the fact that almost all of the heavily indebted countries had negative real interest rates for extended periods of time. Negative real interest rates lead to inflation by stimulating too much investment, spending, and borrowing as well as too little savings. Nearly every one of the countries with debt servicing problems had negative real interest rates for several years *before* the debt crisis (table 1–8).

Finally, the most common policy fault of countries vulnerable to debt servicing problems was accepting substantial inflation. The LDCs that are servicing their debts on time right now—Korea, Malaysia, Indonesia, Thailand, and Taiwan, for example—are LDCs without severe inflation (table 1–9). The countries having problems are those that have had massive and, too often, accelerating inflation (table 1–9).

LDC Budget Deficits

The fifth factor contributing to LDC vulnerability derives from their uncontrolled budget deficits. The United States itself is running huge budget deficits. But in the United States, individuals and companies in the domestic private sector are and have been willing to finance the deficits. By contrast,

Table 1–8
Interest Rates and Consumer Price Changes for Selected Debtor Countries

	1978	1979	1980	1981	1982	1983
Argentina						
Interest rate[a]	86.6%	72.6%	72.0%	86.8%	103.4%	176.4%
Inflation rate[b]	170.0	139.7	87.6	131.3	209.7	433.7
Real interest rate	– 83.4	– 67.7	– 15.6	– 44.5	– 106.3	– 257.3
Brazil						
Interest rate	58.3	55.6	54.0	110.0	21.0	23.0
Inflation rate	38.1	76.0	86.3	100.6	101.8	177.9
Real interest rate	20.2	– 20.4	– 32.3	9.4	– 80.8	– 154.9
Mexico						
Interest rate	12.0	16.8	26.2	31.8	52.5	54.7
Inflation rate	16.2	20.0	29.8	28.7	98.9	80.8
Real interest rate	– 4.2	– 3.2	– 3.6	3.1	– 46.4	– 26.1

Sources: Interest rate levels: Morgan Guaranty Trust, *World Financial Markets* (December 1981) and (August 1984).
Inflation levels: IMF, *International Financial Statistics,* various issues.
[a]Commercial bank deposit rates (December rates).
[b]Consumer price index (end of year over end of year).

few developing countries can induce adequate private financing. As a result, LDCs have been financing much of their deficits from abroad. This makes budgetary programming vulnerable to shifts in credit availability and tempts governments to rely on inflationary financing. Not surprisingly, LDCs with large government deficits, such as Brazil and Mexico and Argentina (table 1–10), also suffer from high rates of inflation (table 1–9).

Table 1–9
Wholesale Price Growth Rates for Selected Countries

	1979	1980	1981	1982	1983
South Korea	18.8%	38.9%	20.4%	4.7%	0.2%
Malaysia[a]	3.6	6.7	9.7	5.8	n.a.
Indonesia	48.7	26.7	11.1	n.a.	n.a.
Thailand	11.2	20.1	9.5	0.9	2.1
Taiwan[b]	13.8	21.6	7.6	– 0.7	n.a.
Argentina	149.3	75.4	109.6	256.2	360.8
Brazil	55.9	106.5	108.2	92.0	168.3
Mexico	18.3	24.5	24.4	56.1	107.4

Source: IMF, *International Financial Statistics* (August 1984).
[a]Wholesale price index not available; consumer price index used instead.
[b]Not an IMF member. Data from country source.

Table 1–10
Government Deficits as Percentage of Gross Domestic Product,
Consolidated Public Sector

	1978	1980	1981	1982
Brazil	1.4%[a]	2.3%[a]	6.5%[b]	6.1%[b]
Argentina	7.2	8.6	14.3	14.2
Mexico	7.1	7.5	14.9	16.5
Peru	1.7	6.4	8.2	6.6
Venezuela	−1.1	−1.2	−2.0	6.0

Sources: Central bank bulletins, various countries and issues.

Note: Negative numbers indicate a budget surplus.

[a]Excluding public sector enterprises and indexation of interest on public debt.

[b]Including public sector enterprises but excluding indexed interest on public debt, which equaled 80 percent of GDP in 1982.

Capital Flight from LDCs

The sixth factor encompasses problems such as internal fraud or corruption and massive capital flight. The magnitudes involved here are staggering. Recent analysis suggests that perhaps 40 percent (or $40–50 billion) of all bank lending into Latin America from 1979 to the end of 1981 ended up as capital outflows from those countries. The consequences are obvious. Much of the money on loan to these countries has not been invested productively. Had it contributed to productivity, the countries would now be better able to generate the exports (and foreign exchange) needed to service their debts. In several Latin American countries and in one or two countries in Asia and Africa, corruption and capital flight, more than other factors, are largely responsible for their inability to service their debts.

Resolving this kind of problem is difficult. The hope is that capital flight will reverse when economic recovery is attained. The preconditions for such a recovery include keeping exchange rates in line, keeping real interest rates positive, and subjecting government decision making to budgetary restraint. But although these are necessary conditions for restoring financial stability, they may not be sufficient to stem the tide of outflows and encourage capital inflows.

Taken together, the six factors outlined intensified the fundamental economic problems LDCs faced after 1979: world recession and high interest rates. Had these conditions been avoided, the same economic and financial conditions would have entailed far less severe consequences.

Prospects for the Future

The current rescheduling arrangements, imperfect as they may be, have been implemented with a great deal of effort and have held matters together for about two years now. The formula used is fairly set: banks do not lend any new money unless there is an economic adjustment program in place between the borrowing country and the IMF. The official sector (the governments and central banks of the industrial countries) will assist where needed but also require an agreement between the IMF and the debtor country. And since the IMF itself factors in anticipated bank lending in designing its programs, the creditors' decisions are linked.[3]

Almost all the countries with the most serious debt servicing problems have reached agreements with the IMF and are now pursuing their adjustment programs under its supervision—with varying degrees of success. But the possibility that a country will fail to follow through with its IMF program presents the prospect of an unfortunate discontinuity in the process.

For this and other reasons, an increasing number of people feel a sense of frustration and dissatisfaction about the restructuring approach. They yearn for a more systematic method of problem solving than what appears to be case-by-case crisis management. This wish is not easy to fulfill. Devising a comprehensive method requires first coming to terms with the six factors just described. Furthermore, the very success achieved so far in certain countries may dull the sense of urgency for imaginative action.

And, even more important, several powerful constraints limit the possibilities for new financing agreements. First of all, little money from the official sector is likely to be made available to substitute for new lending banks provided in these reschedulings. There is no political pressure in the United States for providing money through Congress, and other countries tend to follow the lead of the United States.

Nor are multinational corporations likely to see incentives for increasing their direct investments in LDCs until the situation stabilizes. Currently problems for corporations include delayed or blocked profit remittances, troublesome relationships with their subsidiaries (where they must put in new money without being able to receive interest), and price controls limiting the profits they can earn in an inflationary environment. Since governments in the debtor countries have not changed their policies convincingly enough to encourage foreign direct investment, multinationals cannot be expected to provide large amounts of new money in the near future.

Finally, the very process of rescheduling generates attrition, both of regional banks in the United States and of some fairly sizable banks in Europe. Some banks have not only withdrawn from lending to the private sector but are also hesitant to join in new loans to the public sector. It may become increasingly difficult to maintain full participation in the rescheduling efforts.

In short, it appears now that the LDCs will only gain access to new funds through restructuring agreements devised in cooperation with the IMF. This means that the LDCs must conform to the IMF's often stringent requirements and face all the associated social and political repercussions.

But according to several expert analysts, LDC commitment to the IMF programs should yield positive results by 1986–87. Growth rates in these countries should return to rates considered average in the 1970s. Debt service ratios will resemble those prevalent in the late 1970s, when banks were voluntarily making loans to the LDCs.[4] Of course, such analyses are inevitably speculative. To many people, it seems difficult to imagine everything working out smoothly in this scenario.

How good are the possibilities for a turnaround? The United States has had an outstanding year of growth. Europe may soon see more vigorous recovery. Yet many expect that such growth, combined with low inflation, will not last, primarily because of the large budget deficits in the United States and the protracted demands for credit that they will engender. Thus, although the economic setting now favors the LDCs, it is unlikely to remain as consistently favorable in the future. We have reason for optimism, but an optimism tempered by the knowledge that the debt crisis is not over, and that LDCs remain politically and economically vulnerable.

Notes

1. The World Bank, *World Debt Tables* (Washington, D.C.: World Bank, 1984).
2. See appendix A, "Currency Diversification and LDC Debt," by Andrew Mohl and Dorothy Sobol.
3. See chapter 4 and chapter 5 of this book.
4. Ronald Leven and David Roberts, "Latin America's Prospects for Recovery," *Federal Reserve Bank New York Quarterly Review* (Autumn 1983).

2
A Banker's View

Louis G. Schirano

One day early in 1984 I found myself in a very comfortable law firm conference room with a number of other bankers and lawyers, in a meeting of the Mexico Advisory Committee. It was the middle of the afternoon, and I found my mind drifting a little during one of those somewhat less than vigorous discussions on the definition of something consequential like the term "business day." I happened to glance up at the wall, and staring down at us was a marvelous photograph of Winston Churchill. One of the great things about Churchill is that his words are so applicable to situations in which we find ourselves today. Contemplating the photograph, I thought of Churchill's "Battle of Britain" speech, and I began to smile. The other bankers asked me what I found so amusing about this very serious, deadening discussion. I pointed to Churchill's photograph, and said: "I think he's looking down at us and saying, 'Never in the course of human history has so much been owed by so few to so many'."[1]

This is hardly a hyperbolic description of the crisis in which the leading international commercial banks have found themselves in the 1980s. Several hundred billion dollars are on loan to less developed countries that are hard pressed to make their regular interest payments on their external debt. While the prospect of default by a major debtor country such as Mexico or Brazil is now considered unlikely, the banks and their officers are still concerned about the overall level of indebtedness and the ability of other Third World countries to service it, even if the world economy continues to rebound from the recession of 1981–82. Because of this concern and the historical distance we now have from the triggering events of August 1982, when Mexico, one of the most creditworthy of the less developed countries we thought, admitted inability to maintain its interest payments, many of us in the financial industry have been considering the causes of the crisis.

In a sense the international debt crisis is an irony. Curiously, although banks are supposed to be in the risk business (for example, I run a division called "Risk Management"), they really don't like to take risks. Bankers lend money, with the typical assumption that they will get it all back. So when the possibility arises that a bank will actually lose a lot of money that has been lent out and will not be able to foreclose on anything, the reaction is generally one of shock, dismay and, most important, a search for someone to blame. Who is to blame? In assessing today's situation, a banker cannot blame himself, because that would be stupid. What institution would continue to employ the banker who, admittedly, made hundreds of millions of dollars of what are in retrospect unwise loans? Nor can he blame his boss, because that would be really stupid. Unless the banker has absolutely no moral scruples, he cannot blame the people who work for him, because they probably need the job more than he does. But if the bank executive wants to save face (and possibly his job), he has to explain the mistakes somehow.

One easy solution would be to blame Walter Wriston. After all, Walter Wriston, the powerful head of Citicorp in the 1970s, told us that foreign sovereign loans were safe (look at the record), make us all rich, and they made Citibank (Citicorp's main enterprise) the largest bank in the United States. He also hired Irving Friedman, who made a lasting impression on international finance and commerce when he said: "Countries don't go broke!" Now, if prominent, indeed brilliant, economists and bankers like Irving Friedman and Walter Wriston can say something like that, obviously there's no risk in international lending. And so, certain in the knowledge that we had found banking's promised land (or continents as the case may be), we developed an international loan market for sovereign credit that totaled $115 billion by 1981.[2] And then the bubble burst.

Who went wrong? As the international banking community struggles to manage the crisis, its members are reexamining its causes. One thesis of this chapter is that the causes and cures (or obstacles to cures) are interrelated. Coping with the crisis requires understanding its origins. A second thesis is that three features of international bank lending are critical to understanding the causes of the problem, and obstacles to an easy solution: profitability, capital transfers, and interest rates. All of these factors are extremely important to the development of the debt crisis, and all are extremely important to solving it.

Profits and International Lending

As I said, bankers are not risk takers. By nature, a commercial bank will try to find loan opportunities that have the least amount of risk in whatever environment it finds itself. It is an old joke among bankers that they will lend you money only if you do not need it. No bank, not Citibank or Bankers Trust or anyone else, will lend money to Brazil at any kind of interest rate if there are enough opportunities to lend money on Park Avenue, simply because the proximity of Park Avenue makes any loan less risky. But if there are no opportunities to lend money on Park Avenue and banks have funds on hand, banks will lend money elsewhere, because banks cannot make profits (and indeed they incur losses) just by sitting on their money.

The leading international banks found themselves in an anomalous position in the early 1970s. They had, since the mid-1960s, been expanding their international operations and had been making some loans to foreign states to finance balance-of-payments deficits. Banks had not done much of this in the period after World War II, but it was a natural extension of many other lending activities traditionally performed by banks.[3] Two developments in 1973–75 made it inevitable that banks would lend more money to developing countries. The first was the price increase for oil by the Organization of Petroleum Exporting Countries (OPEC), which created a big demand on the part of developing countries for loans and a tremendous supply of new bank deposits by the oil-rich members of OPEC. The second development was the recession in the United States and other countries. During the recession, corporate and other traditional bank customers were not borrowing nearly enough to soak up all the new OPEC deposits. With huge deposits accumulating and insufficient borrowing by traditional (and preferred) clients, the banks found it only natural to recycle petrodollars through loans to developing countries. Everyone believed this was a wonderfully useful and symmetric arrangement, and among the biggest boosters of all were the federal officials who regulate the banks (the Board of Governors of the Federal Reserve System, the comptroller general, the Federal Deposit Insurance Corporation). Their enthusiasm paled in comparison, however, to that of Treasury officials in every Western nation, who, faced with the seeming impossibility of concerted and appropriate action, opted to do nothing and to allow the world's commercial banks to set right their failure.

A second contributing factor is the fact that banks are very competitive. If Citibank is lending money to Uruguay, then chances are that Bankers Trust is also lending money to Uruguay. And bankers are not only highly competitive, but (frankly) they are not always very bright. Banks travel in packs: when one bank moves in one direction, all the other big and little banks follow along. Why do they do it? Well, there's safety in numbers, and in many cases it is to support the legitimate needs of their domestic clients—if General Motors opens operations in Brazil, its lenders will support it. In other cases it is to support the growth of the banks. Take a look at Citicorp, for example: during the high point of its international lending, when domestic earnings were depressed, fully 40 percent of net earnings came from its activities in Brazil. Now, that is an extraordinarily large amount of money. And other banks are perfectly well aware of Citicorp's success, so they imitate it by doing the same thing—lending millions of dollars overseas. To keep up with one another, the leading banks all engaged in a great deal of foreign sovereign lending.

One might infer from the fervor of international lending in the 1970s that it was making banks terribly profitable. On the whole, that inference would be wrong. The highest profit ratio of any "money center" bank was that of

Morgan Guaranty, and even their return was considerably less than 1 percent on their earning assets. The fact is that banks as a whole are not very profitable institutions. They are not very profitable in their domestic lending operations because the competition is so stringent, and they are positively unprofitable in their commercial banking operations.[4] Since 1976 (or perhaps 1978), banks have all but decided they cannot remain profitable by lending money alone—and certainly not in this country. There are three reasons for this: (1) there are 20,000 banks competing with one another; (2) there are myriad ways people can borrow money or get money without going through commercial banks; and (3) there has been the explosive growth of non-U.S. banks in U.S. markets, and these banks, because of different capital structures that domestic banks cannot duplicate, are able to compete effectively and take away many of the markets previously available to U.S. banks. Indeed, some would hold that the legislative approach to banking in the United States favors foreign banks.

If profits cannot be made by lending money, what does a bank do? It gets out of banking—by wholesaling operations or by developing a vast market share, purchasing other businesses (or banks), getting into different lines of work, and computerizing—all of which cost a whole lot of money to do. How does a bank get that kind of capital? In the last ten years, the largest component of the increase in bank capital has been retained earnings. Thus the profitability from the lending operations of the large international banks had to be maintained in order to assist those banks in diversifying into businesses and to get out of a basic business that was becoming very unprofitable. Everything was going fine until Mexico told us that it could not service its debt.

The Crisis and Muddling Through

In 1981 and 1982 there were signs that things were not quite right. Then came August 12, 1982, when the Mexican minister of finance met with his country's creditors in the Federal Reserve Bank of New York (about three o'clock in the afternoon) and said: "We can't pay anymore." To say that the financial community was taken aback is to seriously understate the reaction. But at first the response was to view the event as a passing phenomenon— Mexico was merely experiencing a cash flow problem, and there was no serious, systemic debt problem. Indeed, at a meeting of the American Bankers Association in New York in December 1982, I heard the most amusing quote I think I have ever heard from a banker: "The only problem with international banking today is the perceived inability on the part of some countries to service debt." In part, the government of the United States aided in this view, for following the meeting with Minister Silva Herzog, the most extraordinary support package ever put together for one sovereign by another was assembled in record time by the United States.[5]

Unfortunately, eight days after that notable addition to banking lore, Brazil's banking situation fell apart. The two largest sovereign debtors, countries with enormous development potential and rich resources, were at the same moment unable to service their debt. At that point the banks got scared— very scared, because they began to realize that these were not just ad hoc problems. But they were still not sure. Soon after that, at a meeting of the Mexico Advisory Committee, a senior member of that committee said: "You know, I've become convinced in my own mind that there is not a market solution to Mexico's problems." Nine people fell off their chairs—three of them because they knew it all along and were surprised it had taken others so long to figure it out, and six more because they could not believe what they had just been told. The crisis was now real and bankers reacted in their normal way. They traveled in packs. They formed steering committees or advisory committees and they called their lawyers.

The result was rooms full of people, and they would be asked: How are we going to deal with this? And the answer was, "Let's get a consensus." Wall Street lawyers told the bankers: "You reach your consensus, and we lawyers will tell you whether and how it can work legally." Were the banks serious about solving the problem? In one sense they were, but in the main, the bankers were not trying to work out a plan for the long-term solvency of Brazil and Mexico. The banks wanted only to prevent default and keep interest payments current. They worked very hard, through their advisory committees, to do this. They were assisted by their attorneys, their governments, and the International Monetary Fund (IMF). Their goals were short term, not long term. The banks wanted to solve today's crisis, not tomorrow's: in short, to muddle through. The stated purpose in all of these exercises was to create an environment in which Mexico and Brazil (and any one else for that matter) could return to this "voluntary market." The stated purpose was real, and important; the unstated purpose was to keep the interest current and that was an even more important short-term goal. Why? Because the profitability of international banking is absolutely vital.

Banks rarely look for long-term solutions, generally leaving that job to the IMF. Why do bankers tend to take such a short-range view, especially now that we've seen that the IMF is not infallible?[6] One reason is that the Fund has the personnel and expertise to devise programs that will restore the country's ability to repay debt. Although the large international banks do their own country risk analyses now, they do not have the staff or the expertise to perform complex macroeconomic and political analysis. Furthermore, there is a reluctance among most banks to get involved in the "political arena." They see themselves as private institutions and believe that the governments of international financial institutions should handle delicate political matters. I submit that, in fact, international banks have been operating in the political arena for some time now, and ought to recognize that fact. As a consequence, I submit that banks can no longer ignore the long-term prospects of borrowing countries; muddling through individual situations on an ad hoc basis is no longer sufficient policy.

Obstacles to a Longer-Term Solution

I am not sure where we go from here. Obviously, from the banks' point of view, profitability has to be maintained. But if the banks take the extreme position that all interest has to be current and sustained at full market rates, there will be a polarization. On the one side, people say this short-term strategy of muddling through may not work; the banks must make sacrifices.[7] On the other side the banks are saying there should be more governmental involvement, rather than sacrifices of profitability by the banks.[8] Frankly, I think both positions are correct. At some point these two lines of thought will have to intersect. Two of the issues to be addressed are how developing countries will obtain the capital they need, and what level of interest rates will be charged.

The problem loans under discussion are to developing countries. By definition, such a country needs capital inflows from other countries. Yet since 1982 there has been a net outflow of capital from every country in Latin America. Indeed, the only country in the western hemisphere that has had a net capital inflow is the United States. It is obvious that in order for the developing countries to escape their problems, there must be net inflows of capital. Some have criticized the banks for not making more money available. The banks' position has been that they cannot solve this problem, especially for countries that have sizable levels of capital flight. The trend in the negotiations during 1984 seems to be that the banks are willing to lend new money and to extend maturities to the developing countries, if the Western governments or international financial institutions such as the IMF also contribute capital. I believe this direction is a constructive one. If the developing country, pursuant to an IMF program or otherwise, is able to reduce the level of capital flight and improve its ability to service external indebtedness, the banks should continue to make loans.

Let us understand one thing, however. The debt crisis has its origins in many causes, the single most important being capital flight. In certain countries, this has reached outrageous proportions and is misnamed; it is no longer flight, but theft, in vast amounts directly by public servants or with their assistance. Bankers can do just so much. Unless the conditions that foster this disgrace are ended and the practice stamped out, progress will not occur.

Another point is important to keep in mind. Bankers at this stage are beginning to recognize the concept that I call the "level of sustainable debt." That is, bankers are looking at the individual countries, such as Brazil, and are beginning to ask: "Is $98 billion a level of debt that Brazil can realistically sustain?" I do not know the answer for Brazil, but I do think there is a number there, and bankers and the country itself have to find it. The level of the debt for each country will not remain at current (or even higher) levels and simply be rolled over. Some of these countries have accumulated too much debt, and they will have to scale back over time.

The second important question is the level of interest rates. A 1 percent increase in the interest rate means $900 million in extra debt servicing for Brazil; $800 million in extra debt servicing for Mexico. Thus if banks reduced the interest rate charged on loans to Mexico by ¾ percent, that would produce a savings to Mexico of $600 million per year (in fact, the rate was reduced to produce savings of about $350 million). Increases in the prime rate early in 1984 wiped out any savings that Mexico had achieved, while a drop in the prime rate later in 1984 restored many of those gains. One has to keep the general level of interest rates in mind while discussing the international debt problem. The bank view, a proper one, is that the level of interest rates is an "exogenous" factor, one over which neither the banks nor the borrowers have any control. The United States' own monetary and fiscal policies to a great extent determine the rates banks can offer and stay profitable. If interest rates do go up, it will be extremely difficult, even with the best minds available, to do anything about international debt. Critics have demanded that banks renegotiate loans at concessionary (below normal market) interest rates. While banks have resisted this demand, they have compromised a great deal on this issue. The 1984 renegotiation of Mexican loans imposed a near concessionary rate of interest as a reward for Mexico's progress in meeting the stabilization objectives of its IMF program.

One final complexity should be noted: this is not just a problem of the United States. The debt owed to the U.S. banks is probably only 35 to 40 percent of the total. The rest is owed to European and Japanese banks, which operate under an entirely different system of regulations from those in the United States. Non-U.S. banks perhaps have different philosophies as to what a bank is or what a bank can be. Commercial banks in the United States are run very much like American industrial corporations. They are supposed to make profits, and they are supposed to make more profits each year. Indeed, it is not unusual to see a chairman of the board get up and say: "Our five-year profit projection is X, Y, and Z." Most banks outside the United States do not necessarily think that way. Their philosophy is that banks make money, but banks may not make as much money next year as they make this year, and they may even make considerably less. They do not have the pressures on them that American banks have to increase profitability. Therefore, they are quite willing, in some cases, to get rid of problems simply by writing them off. Now what happens if a West German bank says it does not want to worry about Mexico anymore? (In fact, some banks have been writing off their Mexican loans by about 15 percent a year.) The different responses of banks from different countries may create further problems in future negotiations.

I should like to end on a personal note. There has been a great effort to make things "look" better. A colleague of mine, in thinking about some of these efforts, wrote me a note, in which he said: "Sometimes I wonder, that when the Great Trumpet sounds up yonder, and when I am asked what I did with my life, will I have to respond that I spent most of my life at 280 Park Avenue playing three card monte and trying to convince everyone that if you change the definition the problem disappears. Or will I ever be able to say I traded mostly on what William Faulkner termed 'the Old American truths of the heart, the old universal truths—love and honor, pity, compassion, and sacrifice'."[9] Some days, I'd rather not be asked.

Notes

1. Churchill's original speech, delivered August 20, 1940, may be found in Great Britain, Parliamentary Debates, House of Commons, 5th Series CCLXIV, p. 1166.

2. Obviously, I do not mean any of the remarks about Walter Wriston personally. He just typifies an attitude that almost all of us shared in the 1970s.

3. International lending generally got its start financing international trade (and this continues to be a major part of a bank's international operations). But it is a small step to take from financing trade (or "transactions with the smell of salt water," as one of my colleagues terms them) to near trade transactions, then to nontrade transactions, and finally to balance-of-payments transactions. Normally, the latter is the last thing in which banks will want to engage, but when done, it is justified that on the basis of what was carried on years before, the bank has sufficient knowledge of the economic conditions to minimize the dangers of the loans. See generally Philip Wellons, *World Money and Credit: The Crisis and Its Causes* (Cambridge, Mass.: Harvard University Press, 1983), p. 23ff.

4. Services like checking and the like are probably more expensive for the bank to perform than the fees banks get for performing them.

5. The Federal Reserve Board of Governors takes the basic position that the U.S. government will not bail out the banks or otherwise become involved. That may be so, but two weeks later that same minister of finance walked out of New York with a $5 billion package of loans and guarantees arranged primarily by our government—$900 million from the Federal Reserve in swap loans, $2 billion from the U.S. Treasury in the form of early payments for Mexican oil, and $1.8 billion or so from the Bank for International Settlements. So much for nongovernmental involvement. It is true, as the federal officials say, that Mexico is a "special case" because of the border it shares with the United States and its importance as a supplier of oil. I suspect, however, that before we are finished a few more special situations will be discovered.

6. In the opinion of many of us in the industry, the IMF stabilization program for Mexico in 1982–83 was a success. But the programs for Peru, Brazil (phase I), Argentina, Yugoslavia, and Chile (January 1983) were not.

7. See, for example, Riordan Roett, chapter 9 of this book.

8. See, for example, Philip Wellons, chapter 6 of this book.

9. William Faulkner, acceptance speech at the award ceremonies for the Nobel Prize for Literature, 1950.

3
Santa Claus and Sigmund Freud: Structural Contexts of the International Debt Problem

William N. Eskridge, Jr.

Never have so many countries owed so much money to so many banks, with so little prospect of repayment. For more than two years the international financial system has staggered under the burden of a debt crisis, in which a group of nonoil developing countries (NODCs)[1] and their lenders have struggled to prevent default on a level of external debt which is by most measures excessive. The most dramatic debt figures are those for the major Latin American borrowers. In January 1985, Brazil's estimated external debt was almost $100 billion, and that of Mexico and Argentina at least $96 billion and $45 billion, respectively.[2] The nine largest banks in the United States have over 110 percent of their capital exposed in loans to these three debtor states, and over 200 percent exposed to NODCs as a whole.[3] Many of the outstanding bank loans required some form of renegotiation in 1983 and 1984. Although prospects for the debtor states to continue to service their debts have brightened considerably due to the worldwide economic recovery, sober analysts nonetheless warn that the crisis has deeper implications and may remain a concern for several years.[4]

With so much at stake, there has been considerable discussion on the causes and origins of the crisis, especially for the Latin American countries that are the focus of this chapter. The literature is dominated by econometrics. Most of these economic studies emphasize the external shocks (higher oil prices, rising real interest rates, worldwide recession) experienced by NODCs between 1973 and 1982 (especially 1979–82). More recent studies suggest that the external shocks alone did not cause the debt crisis. Rather, they were triggers of a problem which became a crisis because of mistakes made by NODC borrowers and the international financial system. This "shocks-and-mistakes" explanation is realistic and analytically sophisticated. The first section of this chapter draws upon these studies to recreate the short-term historical context

A longer version of this chapter was published as an article in *Virginia Journal of International Law* 25 (1985):281.

for the debt crisis. A shocks-and-mistakes approach is useful in understanding that the debt problem is a consequence of a complex array of interconnected trends and events.

On the other hand the ten-year time frame of the shocks-and-mistakes explanation renders it ahistorical and unsystematic. The explanation tends to ignore longer range trends and structures that made the actions now considered "mistakes" quite reasonable or inevitable when they were taken. Drawing from models of international finance, Latin American sociopolitical dynamics, and bank regulation, the second section of this chapter argues that the rapid accumulation of too much international sovereign debt was the result of a variety of "structural" problems. The ideology of growth development in Latin American NODCs impelled them to seek foreign capital so that their development plans would not be disrupted by the external shocks. Accommodative political structures prevented these countries from facing hard economic realities so long as they were able to borrow money. And, for awhile, the flow of funds seemed limitless. The availability of petrodollar deposits and the bankers' systematic underappreciation of sovereign risk contributed to a bank mania of NODC loans. The decline of the Bretton Woods system of international financial cooperation and the virtual dearth of Western bank regulation of foreign sovereign lending left the field critically exposed to crashes and panics to which it had historically been subject. When the banks suddenly realized the problems with the NODC loans, there was a contagious collapse of confidence which precipitated the crisis. Total panic or a crash has only been averted by "involuntary lending" and a continuing series of debt restructurings.

Under this "structuralist" explanation, there are neither fools nor villains. The mistakes made by the various participants were either hard to avoid or impelled by historical trends beyond the comprehension of any but the most cassandric observer. While more descriptively complete than the shocks-and-mistakes explanation, this structuralist approach might itself be too confining a context for understanding the international debt problem. The third section of this chapter analyzes the problem as part of, or a symptom of, a larger crisis of development and development theory. Traditional theory, based upon a Western modernization paradigm, views development as an endogenous national process of industrialization and economic growth and emphasizes the role of capital accumulation in achieving growth. The debt crisis has underlined weaknesses in the traditional theory: infusions of capital have not necessarily led to sustained economic growth and have, instead, tightened ties of dependency of borrowing countries which threaten those countries' economic viability.

A second theory of development, the dependency paradigm, explains the debt crisis more coherently. The industrialized "core" states of the world create international economic structures that ensure the dependency of the states of the "periphery," so that they can be exploited by states of the core.

Growth of peripheral states is tied to growth of core states. The benefits of growth and the costs of crises are unevenly distributed, in favor of the core states. The debt crisis is an example of the dependency relationship: Latin American countries have become addicted to Western capital infusions, which benefit Western transnational banks and corporations more than the countries. When unusual economic circumstances upset the flow of capital, the Latin American countries, and their people, have borne most of the costs. The normative framework of dependency theory is a valuable perspective on the debt crisis, although as a theory of historical dynamics it is limited by its failure to recognize the ways in which at least some peripheral states have benefited from foreign capital and in which core states are equally vulnerable, because of their unstable system of international finance.

A third paradigm, based on world systems theory, may be a more accurate way to view the debt crisis historically. Although the core capitalist countries continue to lead and dominate the world system, countries in the periphery can seize opportunities to advance in the world system, at least to become part of the "semiperiphery" of partially industrialized states and regional sociopolitical powers. The world economic situation has been in flux since 1968, when the United States' hegemony began to erode due to its political humiliation in Vietnam and the economic dysfunctions of inflation, erratic interest rates, and unmanageable trade deficits. The decline of the main core state has been both a test and an opportunity for the "newly industrializing countries" (NICs). It is an opportunity for the NICs to ascend, primarily by reliance on their state-centered approach to capitalism. It is also a test to determine whether individual NICs have the economic discipline and internal political strength to weather the crisis. A few countries (South Korea, Taiwan) have passed this test (for now), in part by sacrificing other values. Most countries, as the debt problem attests, remain mired in the periphery or semiperiphery.

The international debt problem is a crisis only within the context of the modernization paradigm. Indeed, it exposes that model of development to ridicule. Under other paradigms of development, the debt problem is merely the symptom of broader problems. "Late developing" countries face severe obstacles to their economic plans and are highly vulnerable to economic and political decisions of industrial countries. The debt dilemma demonstrates the difficulty of Latin American development within the world system. Indeed, it raises anew the fairness questions of unequal opportunity and distribution of risks and rewards under the existing world system.

External Shocks-and-Mistakes Context of the International Debt Problem

Working in large part from data gathered by the International Monetary Fund (IMF) and the World Bank, sophisticated analyses published by authors

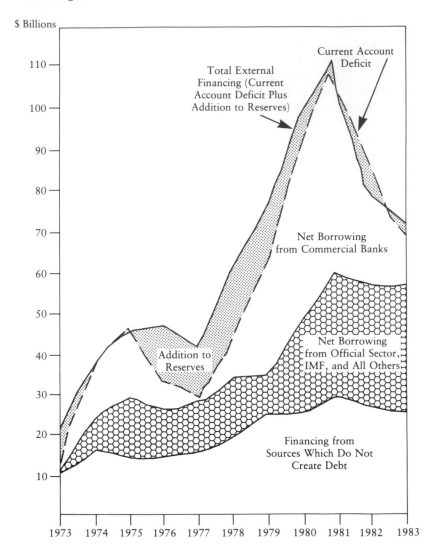

Sources: Citibank; International Monetary Fund, *World Economic Outlook*.

Figure 3–1. Nonoil Developing Country Sources of External Finance

working under the auspices of the Brookings Institution, the Institute for International Economics, the Organisation for Economic Co-operation and Development (OECD), and the Federal Reserve Banks have stressed the role of both exogenous (external shocks) and endogenous (policy mistakes) factors leading to the debt crisis in 1982. Specifically, the NODCs, especially those in Latin America, responded to the 1973 and 1979 oil price shocks by borrowing more money than they should have; the banks were eager to lend more money than they should have; the regulators raised no objections to the excessive lending, even after it became apparent that the loans represented a clear threat to the banks' solvency. Finally, the other shocks of 1979–82—recession and declining prices for NODC products, rising interest rates, and a strong dollar—made the servicing burdens intolerable for the debtor countries which in turn failed to adjust to the drastically changed conditions. When the banks finally realized that problems existed, the whole house of cards caved in.

Too Much Sovereign Borrowing in Response to the Oil Price Shocks, 1973–82

The sharp rise in the price of oil in 1973–74 and again in 1978–79 was an important exogenous cause of the debt crisis. William Cline of the Institute for International Economics calculates that the value of NODC oil imports increased from 6 percent of their total merchandise imports in 1973 to about 20 percent in 1980–83; between 1974 and 1982 NODCs paid $260 billion (real dollars, adjusted for inflation) extra because of the price shocks.[5] This precipitous and largely adverse shift in the terms of trade left the NODCs with potentially enormous current account deficits.

At least three responses were possible to these actual or projected increases in current account deficits. The NODCs could have (1) sought to reduce the trade imbalance by discouraging imports and increasing exports to make up for the increased sums needed to pay for oil; (2) attracted the capital needed to finance the payments deficits, either by an enhanced domestic savings effort or by more direct foreign investment; or (3) borrowed the money from foreign official and private lenders.[6] Typically, countries employed a combination of these mechanisms. For example, some of the Asian developing countries, such as Singapore and Taiwan, combined export expansion, an enhanced public savings effort, and direct foreign investment to cover their increased oil payments. Very few countries were able to perform this economic feat, however, and these countries tended to be "upper income developing countries." A second group of countries, including Kenya and other African states, adjusted through import substitution and enhanced public savings, but at the price of slower export growth than in the 1960s. Unlike the first group, these countries also had to resort to a substantial amount of external borrowing to cover the remainder of the oil import deficit. Most of these countries were "lower- or middle-income developing countries."[7] Finally, many countries relied heavily on external financing to cover the deficits. These countries tended to be fast-developing, upper income developing countries in Latin America.

In sum, for NODCs as a whole (and especially for the third group of countries), increased domestic savings, export growth, and import substitution did not cover the higher oil prices. The consequences are represented graphically in figure 3–1: the NODCs generally ran substantial current account deficits after 1973. And the deficits increased in size, from an overall NODC deficit of $11 billion in 1973 to $108 billion in 1981, until 1982, when the deficit fell back to $87 billion (appendix B, table B–1 sets forth these and other detailed figures). Direct foreign investment remained modest. Rather than using foreign exchange reserves to cover those deficits (indeed, they generally added to those reserves in the 1970s), most NODCs paid for the deficits by borrowing money. As a result, the external debt of NODCs quintupled between 1973 and 1982, increasing at an average annual rate of 19 percent (appendix B, table B–2); 70 percent to 80 percent of this debt was owed by the public sector.[8] Even after accounting for inflation, the debt more than doubled, increasing at an average annual rate of 8.7 percent (appendix B, table B–2).

External debt for NODCs as a whole rose from 22 percent of their gross domestic product (GDP) in 1973 to 36 percent in 1982; the ratio of debt to exports rose from 115 percent in 1973 to 144 percent in 1982 (appendix B, table B–2). Even more dramatic were the trends for the main Latin American borrowers. Brazil's external debt increased by a factor of 6.4 between 1973 and 1982, Mexico's by a factor of 9.5, Argentina's by a factor of 5.9 (appendix B, table B–3)—all well ahead of the general fivefold increase for NODCs as a whole. Similarly, the ratio of debt to exports rose sharply for these three largest borrowers in the period 1973–82: from 106.2 to 365.3 for Brazil, from 154.6 to 248.6 for Mexico, and from 140.8 to 353.5 for Argentina (appendix B, table B–3).

This level of debt was, for many countries, more than was prudent under the circumstances and reflected mistaken judgments by both the borrowing countries and the lending banks. Latin American NODCs, for their part, believed their payment balances were temporary and that difficult policy adjustments restricting growth and domestic consumption could be avoided or postponed by foreign borrowing.[9] Foreign borrowing appealed to the governments as a substitute for currency depreciation and import restrictions, especially in light of the brisk inflation of the 1970s, which made the real rates of interest (nominal interest rate minus rate of inflation) paid by these countries minimal and in some years actually negative.[10] For these reasons Latin American NODCs borrowed heavily in the 1970s, and their short-term growth continued. The long-term prospects worsened, though: the elites continued their high level of import consumption, state enterprises and projects had insufficient incentives to economize, and the current account deficit increased each year. According to a recent Brookings Institution study by Thomas Enders and Richard Mattione, foreign financing in the 1970s enabled the Latin American countries to pay for current account deficits that rose from 2.2 percent of the GDP in 1971–73 to 3.8 percent in 1976–79 and 5.0 percent in 1980. In the same period (1970–80), the average real exchange rate of Latin American currencies increased by 31 percent, and public sector deficits increased to between 5 percent and 8 percent of the GDP for the largest countries.[11] As a result of these trends and of the continuing high price of oil, payment imbalances were not temporary. The excessive borrowing, it turned out, had been a miscalculation.

The borrowing countries could not have obtained these huge loans from their traditional sources—the IMF, the World Bank, and Western governments—because of their limited funds and more stringent guidelines and restrictions.[12] The sovereign borrowers therefore obtained most of their new loans from private banks. The banks were just as eager to make the large volume of loans as the countries were to take the money. Bankers viewed international lending as a profitable activity, and a number of financial cheerleaders, notably Walter Wriston of Citicorp, vociferously espoused the view that international lending was the wave of the future.[13] One reason to make these sovereign loans was the pool of petrodollars deposited by members of the Organization of Petroleum Exporting Countries (OPEC) in the banks and the shortage of profitable loan opportunities to absorb the petrodollars.[14] In order to maintain earnings on their large reserves of petrodollars, banks were happy to lend money to developing countries.[15] Indeed, one recent account of the debt problem describes the leading international bankers as so many "traveling salesmen" or "hucksters" who used a hard sell to persuade countries to borrow enormous sums of money, which was provided by far-flung syndicates of banks, each contributing millions of dollars based on little more than telexes describing the deals.[16]

Whatever the general validity of such an indictment of bankers' ethics, they (and the bank regulators) made two very big mistakes. One was that they underestimated the possibility that countries would overborrow and then default on their loans, or at least not be able to pay current principal and interest. Bankers told one another repeatedly that "countries don't go broke,"[17] but to the extent that failure to make interest and principal payments is the same thing, this was not right. The second mistake was excessive concentration by the largest banks in loans to similarly situated sovereigns, an elementary failure to diversify their portfolio of risks. In 1979 the nine leading U.S. banks had on loan to the three main debtor countries (Brazil, Mexico, Argentina) more than 100 percent of their paid-in capital, and by 1984 the figure for several of the banks exceeded 150 percent.[18] Had any one of those countries defaulted, the banks' shareholders would have lost much of their investment, and several banks might have become insolvent themselves. Yet the bank regulators—the Comptroller of the Currency, the Federal Deposit Insurance Corporation, and the Federal Reserve Board in the United States—did almost nothing about either error until 1979, when they instituted a largely ineffectual system of country lending guidelines (not mandatory rules).[19] Only in 1983, under the threat of stringent congressional legislation, did the regulators propose binding rules to prevent banks from making too many ill-advised international loans.[20]

Debtor Countries' Vulnerability to Higher Interest Rates and Worldwide Recession, 1979–82

The level of debt for NODCs as a whole, and particularly for the leading debtor countries in Latin America, posed problems both for the debtor countries and for the international financial system because it represented a postponement of hard economic choices. Nonetheless, between 1976 and 1979, the debt situation appeared under control. Exports of the leading debtor countries seemed more than enough to service the growing external indebtedness.[21] The world of international debt changed dramatically after 1978, however. The second OPEC oil price shock not only placed new pressure on NODC current account balances but also triggered severe deflationary policies, higher interest rates, and diminished demand for imports in the Western industrial countries (chiefly the United States). Although, astonishingly, bankers were still falling over one another to make NODC sovereign loans, the combination of higher oil prices, lower demand for developing country goods, and higher interest rates after 1979 severely impaired the ability of many of the sovereign debtors to service their debts.

The NODC borrowers were particularly vulnerable to the post-1978 crisis because of the terms of their private bank loans. Sovereign loans from official sources (IMF, World Bank, Western governments) in the 1950s and 1960s came with constraining conditions but concessionary terms, such as below market fixed interest rates and an easy repayment schedule over a long term. The nonconcessionary nature of the large volume of bank loans in the 1970s presented very substantial future risks for the heavily indebted countries. First, the private loans tended to carry floating interest rates: the rates were periodically adjusted to be one to two points above the London Inter Bank Offered Rate (LIBOR). Roger Kubarych of the Federal Reserve Bank of New York estimates that international sovereign debt contracted at floating interest rates constituted 70 percent of the total in 1983.[22] And the floating-rate debt was concentrated in a few countries: Brazil, Mexico, Argentina, South Korea, and Chile owed 87 percent of the total floating-interest debt in 1983.[23] These countries, as a result, were highly vulnerable to swings in the interest rate.

Second, most of the external debt was contracted in U.S. dollars, rather than in a diversified range of hard currencies, thus exposing the debtor countries to the risk that the dollar would prove unusually strong.[24] Third, much of the external debt was short term. From 1972 to 1974 the maturities of NODC sovereign debt were typically in the range of ten to twelve years, but after 1974 the average maturities fell back to five to seven years.[25] Again, the major borrowers led the way: in 1983 about 20 percent of their external debt was short term, compared with less than 10 percent for other countries (appendix B, table B-4). One disadvantage of this increase in short-term debt was that when new loans were negotiated, the borrowing country would not only have to pay the going interest rate, but also various fees (commitment fees, participation fees, and management fees where a banking syndicate was involved).[26] As a result of the risk spread assessed by banks and these various fees and commissions, the effective interest rate on these loans was sometimes as much as 4 percent above LIBOR.[27]

These risks materialized in the period 1979–82, when the Western countries, led by the United States, responded to the second round of OPEC price increases by a severe cutback in the money supply, the chief result of which was steep interest rate increases. Market rates for new or rolled over loans jumped to 13.0 percent in 1979, 15.4 percent in 1980, and 17.5 percent in 1982 (appendix B, table B-5); the average nominal rates of interest paid on all external debt (the new short-term debt at high current rates plus long-term debt at lower rates) increased from 4.5 percent in 1973–77 to 8.5 percent in 1981–82.[28] More important, because the rate of inflation fell after 1980, the real rate of interest (nominal rate minus rate of inflation) charged on new loans soared to 7.5 percent in 1981 and 11.0 percent in 1982; overall, the average real rate of interest on all NODC indebtedness increased from an aggregate − 6 percent for 1973–77 to one of + 3 percent for 1981–82, and went even higher in 1983–84. Based only upon the interest rates that might have been expected from the period 1961–80, William Cline estimates that real interest rates were 5.8 percentage points higher than expected in 1981 and 9.3 percentage points higher in 1982.[29]

A second consequence of U.S. monetary policies was appreciation in the value of the dollar—an unfavorable development for debtor countries, which had to repay loans in dollars. Thus the dollar appreciated by 11 percent in 1981 and 17 percent through November 1982. Though it lost some strength in 1983, it remained at strong levels well above those of the 1970s and overall appreciated against the Japanese yen, the West German mark, and other "hard" currencies.[30] It is estimated that the dollar in 1984 was 40 percent stronger than it was in 1980.

A third, less direct, result of new monetary policies was a worldwide recession in 1980–82. Real growth in the industrialized countries fell from 3.2 percent per year (1973–79) to 1.2 percent (1980–81) to − 0.3 percent (1982).[31] Industrialized countries, chiefly the United States, are the main export markets for most NODCs, especially those in Latin America. Consequently, export growth for NODCs, which had been 8.1 percent in 1971–80 and 9.9 percent in 1981, fell to 1.8 percent in 1982.[32] The impact of the recession was much harder for developing countries than for the industrialized ones, because commodity export prices are more sensitive to the business cycle. The IMF estimates that export prices for NODCs fell in 1982 to 90 percent of their 1980 value, while import prices remained about the same (after fluctuating upward in 1981).[33]

In short, at the very time when debtor countries desperately needed strong export sales to pay the suddenly mounting costs of servicing their high-interest debt in overvalued dollars, their export earnings were falling. The result of this dilemma, represented graphically in figure 3–2, is that total debt and debt servicing payments surpassed export growth after 1978. Between 1973

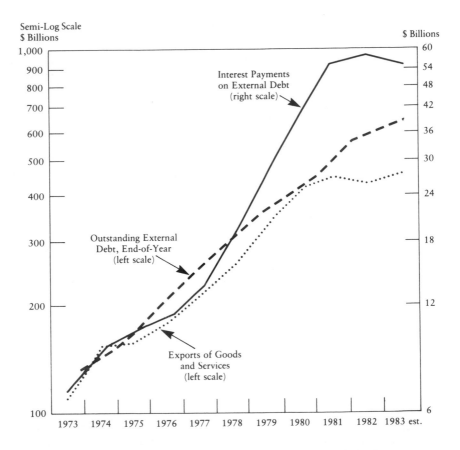

Sources: Citibank; International Monetary Fund, *World Economic Outlook.*

Figure 3–2. Nonoil Developing Country External Debt, Exports, and Interest Payments

and 1977 the ratio of debt service payments to exports of goods and services hovered around 15 percent for NODCs as a group; the figure shot up to 19 percent in 1978–79 and reached 23 percent by 1982 (appendix B, table B–2). Again, the leading Latin American borrowers were significantly worse off: the ratio of debt service to exports in 1982 was 87 percent for Brazil, 59 percent for Mexico, and 103 percent for Argentina (appendix B, table B–3). For these countries, export earnings were barely able to keep up with scheduled debt payments in 1982.

Risky planning by both borrowers and lenders left the NODCs highly vulnerable to the problems of the early 1980s, though it is fair to say that no one would have predicted such a confluence of events in 1977. Cline estimates that the NODCs as a group "lost approximately $141 billion in higher interest payments, lower export receipts, and higher import costs as the consequence of adverse macroeconomic developments" after 1978.[34] Other analysts estimate that these countries lost another $30 billion through their failure to diversify their currency repayments.[35] Not surprisingly, the impact of the external shocks differed from country to country. Enders and Mattione conclude that the cumulative negative shocks were enormous for Brazil ($48.5 billion) and substantial for Argentina ($13.4 billion), Colombia ($6.8 billion), and Chile ($4.8 billion). Because Peru, Mexico, and Venezuela were on balance oil-exporting nations in 1979–82, however, Enders and Mattione conclude that they incurred "positive shocks" (they were better off, considering the higher oil prices, higher interest rates, and recessionary world market).[36] A similar study by Bela Balassa and Desmond McCarthy disputes this conclusion for Mexico and Peru.[37] The point, however, is that while it is clear that Mexico, for example, was much less severely impacted by the various external shocks than Brazil, to take the worst case, it was nonetheless Mexico, and not Brazil, which found itself unable to service its debt in August 1982. The explanation for the debt crisis rests, it would appear, not alone with the large-scale lending of the 1970s and the unprepared for cataclysm of 1979–82. One must also look at the policy responses of the debtor countries to the last series of oil price, interest rate, and trade shocks.

Debtor Countries' Policy Errors Exacerbating the
Debt Servicing Problem, 1979–82

Although the banks were willing, even anxious, to lend them ever more money (until 1982), NODCs facing substantial adverse external shocks after 1979 should have (according to classic adjustment theory) adopted policies to attract hard currency which could be used to service the external debt. Even those countries with positive or small negative shocks needed to avoid policies that could turn a favorable situation into a disaster.[38] First, countries were well advised to avoid overvalued exchange rates, namely official rates that do not reflect the value of the currency on the free market. Overvalued exchange rates discourage exports by making them relatively more expensive and encourage imports by making them relatively less expensive. The result harms both the trade and current account balances. Overvalued exchange rates also encourage capital flight: if the NODC's currency is not really worth the official rate, the citizens will want to convert their money into a hard currency.

Second, classic adjustment policy would require that the borrowing countries reduce or eliminate special subsidies, state enterprise deficits, and trade restrictions, because they impede the operation of free markets and efficient allocation of productive efforts. Third, the vulnerable debtor countries needed to minimize public sector deficits and restrain expansion of the money supply to control inflation. Inflation, like overvalued currency, tends to harm the terms of trade by rendering exports more costly abroad and foreign imports less expensive to domestic consumers. Moreover, if domestic interest rates are lower than the rate of inflation (negative real interest rates), domestic saving decreases, and capital flight into overseas dollar accounts may occur.

Adjustment efforts differed from country to country. Countries such as Mexico, Venezuela, and Argentina, in particular, followed very poor policies, which induced or facilitated more than $40 billion in capital flight between 1979 and 1982.[39] Enders and Mattione argue that "internal causes of the [international debt] crisis were more significant than were external causes."[40] Although this thesis is not necessarily accepted wisdom, the internal factors were critical, for they contributed to bank skepticism about Latin American lending. When the banks curtailed their lending to the region in 1982,[41] the international debt crisis truly was triggered.

That Mexico, which suffered less than most other Latin American countries from the external shocks of 1979–82, was the first to confess inability to service its debts is explained in large part by the policies its government followed. Because Mexico had become a net oil exporter by 1979 and saw continued increases in the price of oil, the government followed a highly expansionistic policy, with large government deficits (over 18 percent of GDP by 1982), a severely overvalued peso (until 1982), and state enterprise losses averaging 6.2 percent of GDP (appendix B, table B–6). Although the economy was in fact 25 percent larger in 1982 than it had been in 1978, the consequences of these policies were predictably sad: inflation ran out of control (reaching 59 percent in 1982), and real interest rates were negative, leading to a massive capital flight from Mexican pesos into more stable currencies (appendix B, table B–6). More than $17 billion thereby left the country in 1981–82, contributing nearly one-fifth of the total external debt. Nonoil exports were crippled, and imports soared, as a result of the domestic inflation and the overvalued peso. The enormous government deficit had mortgaged the country, based upon the prospect of continuing oil price increases.[42]

Deteriorating oil market conditions in 1981–82 alerted Mexico to the fact that it had overextended itself. In February 1982 the government devalued the peso by 67 percent, and efforts were made to reduce the federal deficit. Price controls were tightened. Flexible interest and exchange rate policies were instituted to prevent new overvaluation of the peso. Notwithstanding these efforts, inflation continued at an alarming rate, and international loan flows dried up. Because it was relying on oil revenues and new loans that did not materialize in the volume expected for 1982, Mexico was unable to meet its scheduled debt payments in August 1982. The United States and the Bank for International Settlements extended Mexico emergency credits. In December the IMF concluded a loan of SDR 3.61 billion ($3.86 billion); in return Mexico agreed to reductions in the public sector deficit and the current account deficit and a greater effort against inflation. The commercial banks arranged $5 billion in new loans in March 1983, and much of the Mexican public debt was rescheduled in the summer of 1983.[43] A second major rescheduling of a substantial part of the Mexican debt was accomplished in the summer of 1984, in which Mexico was rewarded for progress against inflation with a longer maturity for the loans and interest rate concessions.

Argentina has not fared as well. Highly sensitive to external markets and terms of trade, Argentina nonetheless followed, almost in textbook fashion, policies designed to aggravate the substantial negative external shocks caused by oil price increases, higher interest rates, and diminished trade.[44] A severely overvalued peso (until 1982), public sector deficits which reached 14 percent of the GDP, inflation over 100 percent, and severe negative real interest rates left Argentina in a desperate condition in 1981 (appendix B, table B–6), with a $30 billion foreign debt (51 percent of it due in 12 months), massive capital flight and current account deficits, declining government revenues, and bankruptcy and illiquidity in the foundering private sector. Some efforts were made after March 1981 to ameliorate the problem—including devaluations of the peso and reductions in the current account deficit and the level of wage increases—but they proved unavailing in light of political instability and the war with Great Britain.

The Falklands–Malvinas War not only contributed to the government deficits and inflation, but undermined the confidence of Western bankers that Argentina could manage its own affairs. When foreign bank funds dried up in 1982, Argentina was forced to ask for relief. Argentina obtained from the IMF a loan of SDR 2.02 billion ($2.16 billion) in January 1983, conditioned upon an IMF adjustment program to reduce government deficits and inflation. Commercial banks extended a $1.1 billion loan at the same time, which they supplemented with more new money later in 1983.[45] Problems in meeting the IMF program goals appeared in 1983, and in 1984 Argentina fell into arrears on its servicing payments. After months of difficult renegotiations, in December 1984 Argentina reached agreement with the IMF for a further $1.66 billion loan and, tentatively, with its bank advisory group for $4.2 billion in new loans and a rescheduling of much of its debt.[46]

Most Latin American countries adjusted to the external shocks better than did Mexico and Argentina, but after the Falklands–Malvinas War and the Mexican crisis of August 1982 the banks drastically reduced their lending in the entire region. Outstanding U.S. bank loans increased only $1.2 billion in the last six months of 1982, compared with $7.3 billion with latter half of 1981.[47] This psychological chain reaction, tied to the notorious herd instinct of banks, precipitated a series of other Latin American reschedulings in 1983, the chief one being that for Brazil.

Brazil was a NODC that made an effort to adjust to the substantial external shocks it suffered, though its efforts, and its success, were only partial. While a proposed stabilization program was not implemented and the government followed an inflationary, high-growth policy through most of 1979, in late 1979 and 1980 Brazil devalued the cruzeiro by 25 percent, abolished subsidies to domestic industry, and followed restrictive monetary and fiscal policies. By 1981 these policies had brought growth to a halt and discouraged the corrosive capital flight that afflicted Mexico.[48] On the other hand the government's deficits exceeded 12 percent of the GDP in both 1981 and 1982, contributing to an inflation rate of over 100 percent per year and creating negative interest rates, which discouraged domestic savings and investment (appendix B, table B–6). In short, Brazil was able to reduce the effects of the severe external shocks, but not to eliminate them.

In part because of the Mexican crisis, Brazil after September 1982 was unable to obtain enough new loans to cover its current account deficit. Thus in early 1983 Brazil turned to the IMF, which extended SDR 4.96 billion ($5.3 billion) in return for the government's commitment to encourage export growth, reduce current account deficits, and slow inflation. At about the same time, the private banks agreed to new loan commitments of $4.4 billion and to a rescheduling of $4.7 billion due in 1983, contingent upon Brazil's following the IMF program.[49] In fact it soon became apparent that Brazil would not be able to meet those IMF conditions, and a milder program (plus $6.5 billion in new loans from commercial banks) was agreed to in the fall of 1983; in January 1985 Brazil and its private creditors have been moving toward agreement on a longer term rescheduling of much of the private indebtedness.[50]

By the middle of 1983 the external debts of Peru, Venezuela, and Chile were also being rescheduled as part of this financial chain reaction, and previous renegotiations continued in Bolivia, Costa Rica, Ecuador, and Nicaragua.[51] In the cases of Venezuela (which enjoyed a large positive shock but failed to manage it to create permanent growth opportunities) and Peru (which had no net adverse shocks until 1982 and was trying to adjust at least in part), the early restructurings were precipitated by the abrupt cut-off of new funds to the region rather than any urgent need in 1982 to reevaluate their particular external debt levels.[52] Just as decisively as they had earlier encouraged almost limitless sovereign borrowing, the banks in 1982–83 grew nervous and began a long cycle of renegotations and IMF adjustment programs as prerequisites for new money in most parts of the now less creditworthy Latin American region.

Under the emerging economic policy analysis recounted, there is no single cause for the debt crisis. Among the contributing causes were the external shocks (oil price increases, high real interest rates, deterioration in terms of trade and trade level); poor planning and risk assessment by the borrowing countries, the banks, and the people who were supposed to have been regulating the banks; poor policy responses by some of the debtor countries to the external shocks after 1979; and a herdlike crisis mentality that gripped bankers after the first few countries faltered in their debt servicing.

Political, Institutional, and Economic Structural Context of the International Debt Crisis

The shocks-and-mistakes explanation for the debt crisis set forth above is a persuasive one on its own terms, but is not a wholly satisfactory context in which to analyze the debt crisis. To begin with, it is ahistorical. The current problem is not entirely unique. Charles Kindleberger has demonstrated that "manias" of foreign lending occurred in 1808–10, 1823–25, 1856–61, 1885–90, 1910–13, and 1924–28. Those periods of manic lending were stimulated by an external economic crisis that led to a euphoric period of lending, which in turn snapped back in a series of "revulsions."[53] Latin American countries, for example, were regular borrowers and defaulters on the European bond market after 1820.[54] There is nothing new about international debt crises. But the present problem is in many respects unique. To understand the unique causes of this crisis, one must examine not just the shocks and mistakes of the last decade, but also the massive reordering of the world's politics, economics, and finance after World War II.

Another shortcoming of the short-term economic analysis of the crisis is that it begs a number of questions by implicitly attributing the crisis to fortuity (external shocks) and error (policy mistakes). As history, this sort of approach calls for elaboration. Why do large groups of sophisticated and intelligent people make such enormous mistakes? The modern historian is reluctant to believe them idiots or blunderers and, therefore, seeks explanation for systematic errors in the structures and institutions of society. To what extent were the external shocks truly fortuitous? Why have Latin American countries fallen into illiquidity, while other NODCs have not? While individual events may have an adventitious quality (the OPEC price increases), the modern historian finds patterns where the traditional historian or the ahistorical analyst would see accidents. Even if the external shocks go away, are there dangers to international lending and Latin American development of which the present crisis is a symptom?

My argument is that structural weaknesses (uncritical dedication to growth, but without the ability to make hard decisions in support of long-term growth) of Latin American governments and politics plus historical changes resulting in a substantial deregulation of international financing led to a great mania of sovereign lending after 1966, followed quite inevitably by a revulsion when external events revealed vulnerability. The revulsion did not, however, lead to a crash, because of the unique nature of international sovereign lending and a revival of international regulatory attention. But the revulsion has created a continuing problem, which private and public institutions are now struggling to resolve. Some kind of reckoning, in short, was inevitable. Although its timing and some of its dimensions have been affected by the external shocks, the debt crisis is the result of colliding structural changes in Latin American development strategies, the business of international lending, and its regulation (or lack thereof).

Latin American Politics and the Ideology of Growth

Through most of the nineteenth century, the newly independent Latin American states were socially, politically, and economically dominated by oligarchies derived from the landowning class of the colonial period. Most of the countries were authoritarian, elitist, hierarchical, corporatist—especially those countries in the gold-producing areas that Spain and Portugal had most actively colonized (Mexico, Brazil, Peru, Colombia, Bolivia). Although nominally democracies, political power rested with a corrupt bureaucracy and executive that protected the interest of the elites. Economically, the countries imported manufactured and luxury goods and exported primary commodities (coffee, bananas, minerals, meat). Between 1870 and the present, Latin America underwent at least three phases of growth, each punctuated by a crisis in that growth. Table 3–1 summarizes the characteristics of each period.[55]

Change came slowly in the first growth period (1870–1930). A modest middle class consisting of merchants, bureaucrats, and craftsmen existed in the Latin American countries in the nineteenth century. But it was conservative, dependent on the state, and undynamic because it was tied to an agrarian commodity export economy. In Argentina, Brazil, Peru, and Chile the old landed wealth and the newer commercial wealth joined forces to produce stable oligarchic democracies. Other countries, most notably Mexico and

Table 3–1
Periods of Growth Development in Latin America

	Growth Philosophy	Social Forces	Political Patterns
1870–1930	Primary commodity export	Modernization of some elites; rise of entrepreneurial middle sector; creation of a working group in cities	Either oligarchic democracy or rule by *caudillos* (military dictators)
1930–1960s	Horizontal import substitution, especially in larger states	Establishment of entrepreneurial and technocratic elites; unions; embourgeoisement of the military and the Church	Cycle of democracy and military rule
1960s–1980s	Variety of strategies: socialism, vertical and horizontal import substitution, and export expansion	Sharpening of class conflict and population pressures; increasing dilemmas of growth and justice issues	Bureaucratic, authoritarian, with trend to democracy 1979–1985

Venezuela, saw *caudillos*, military dictators, seize power for periods of time. Both types of leaders, however, introduced modern features into the economy, including an improved infrastructure and some industry.[56] Modernization was both cause and incentive for an expansion of the countries' primary commodity exports (coffee from Brazil and Colombia, bananas from Central America, meat and wool from Argentina and Uruguay, copper from Chile and Peru). Modernization also stimulated some local industry and generated new social groups, including an entrepreneurial and more dynamic urban middle class and a labor group.

The gradual social diversification of the Latin American countries had profound effects on both the politics and economic programs of those countries. Politically, the middle class upset the oligarchical, corporatist order but did not necessarily displace it. Backed up by the military, the agrarian oligarchies that had long ruled the countries were not eager to relinquish power to middle class coalitions. On the other hand the demands and needs of a larger middle class and worker population could not be ignored lightly. The typical political strategy of the ruling elites was co-option of the middle class. The oligarchy would grant the middle sectors some political participation and power in return for their support of the existing regime.

The worldwide Great Depression after 1929 was a major turning point, because it exposed the weakness of the oligarchic policies. As the prices of primary commodities plummeted in the 1930s, opportunities for growth evanesced, and existing oligarchic governments were supplanted. Although Latin American countries suffered at least a decade of little or no growth after 1930, the political, social, and economic structures on the rise in this second period of development (the 1930s through the 1960s) are critical in understanding the origins of the debt crisis of the 1980s. Politically, this second period was one of crisis and transition in Latin America—away from the stability of the discredited oligarchical rule.[57] There was a political lacuna, filled at first in some countries (Chile, Mexico, Uruguay, Venezuela) by entrepreneurial middle class democracy, and in other countries (Brazil, Argentina, Cuba, Dominican Republic, Honduras, Nicaragua, Paraguay, Guatemala) by dictators whose state-building efforts were influenced by modernization aspirations. Five corporate groups—the large landowners, the military, the Church, the entrepreneurial middle class, and the unions—were socially and politically relevant after 1930. The post-1930 structure is only an elaboration of the nineteenth-century hierarchy. These groups vied for control of power and policy, but no one group or cluster of groups was able to preserve lasting domination. As a result, the relative political stability of oligarchic rule (1870–1930) gave way to instability after 1930.

As Riordan Roett demonstrates, for most of the Latin American countries, the political model for this second period is a cyclical one, in which populist democracy alternated with authoritarian (usually military) rule.[58] Brazil is a classic example of the cyclical model.[59] Brazil's First Republic (oligarchy) lost its legitimacy when its commodity-export policy was crushed by the Great Depression, and it was overthrown in a military coup led by General Getúlio Vargas, who ruled as a dictator but was responsive to the demands of the new entrepreneurial middle class and worker groups. Vargas was himself overthrown by a military coup in 1945 but returned to office in the 1950 presidential elections. Civilian middle-class-oriented presidents governed from 1955 to 1964, but when the economy faltered in 1961–64 the military again intervened.

The unstable cycle of democracy and dictatorship also characterized the political systems of Argentina, Peru, Colombia, Venezuela, Ecuador, Uruguay, Bolivia, Honduras, El Salvador, and Panama between 1930 and the 1960s, although each country followed its own unique pattern of coping with the tensions among the five or more power groups in society.[60] For example, Juan Perón gained and maintained power in Argentina by building a coalition of unions, managers, and the military. His controversial attacks on landowning elites and authoritarian measures triggered a coup deposing him in 1955, but Argentine politics for the next thirty years revolved in large part around a cycle of quasi-populist democracy alternating with military rule. Political clashes in other major Latin American countries—Colombia, Venezuela, Peru—were sporadically violent as well as unstable. Two groups of Latin American countries did not adhere to the cyclical model. Mexico and Chile, for example, had democratic elections through the 1960s, in part because their dominant political parties were organized around and catered to the main interest groups (landowners, the middle class, the unions, and the military).[61] In Nicaragua and Paraguay, the crisis of the 1930s led to the rule of a series of reactionary dictators.[62]

The cycle of democracy and dictatorship in Latin America in this second period contributed to, or reflected, two structural weaknesses in the countries' political systems. One was the impermanency in the governments, which impaired their ability to formulate long-term policy. Neither the elected leaders nor the authoritarian ones were in power long enough to carry out systematic policy. At its extreme a political system characterized by the cyclical model conditions the population to expect a change of government when things start going wrong.[63] Even when a government may implement a policy, of course, it might be overturned when the government itself is overthrown.

A second weakness is that hard decisions, those requiring sacrifice by major groups in the country, such as redistribution of property or income, are not made. Since all groups are politically relevant, and no one group is able to hold power alone for very long, each power group agrees tacitly not to harm the interests of the other groups.[64] This system of mutual accommodation among the corporatist powers yields either no policy, harming no group, or contradictory policies, whereby a group harmed by one policy gets as compensation some other policy that is in its interest.[65] This sort of system has great difficulty coping with crises. The fragility of the government even under the best of circumstances makes it hazardous to risk alienating its supporters or intensifying its opposition, by demanding unpopular sacrifices. Thus, if the democratic government makes a hard decision, it stands to lose the next election or be overthrown by the military. If the authoritarian government makes a hard decision, it may lose its usually questionable legitimacy and fall under renewed pressure to hold free elections. Even the more stable democracies, such as Chile and Mexico, have had this second problem. Stability in Mexico after the 1917 Revolution depended upon the ability of the governing party to accommodate a variety of interest groups, culminating in many contradictory policies.[66] The long-lived democracy in Chile proved vulnerable to military overthrow in 1973 when its leader, Salvador Allende, proposed novel policies that provoked intense opposition from the military and landowning elites.[67]

Economically, Latin American governments in the second period embraced the middle class entrepreneurial policy of growth. Even when it did not actually hold power, the middle class influenced policy, in part because it offered greater competence and efficiency to the government and in part because the Depression had discredited the development philosophy of the landowning elites, which was to export primary commodities and to import manufactured goods.[68] Moreover, the middle class penetrated the military and the Church and thus infected these important power groups with their

values of economic growth and long-range planning. The ideology of productive growth heralded by the new middle class posited that (1) the purpose
of development is to become more like the wealthy economies of the industrialized countries; (2) Latin American countries will not develop by relying
on primary commodities as their chief economic activity and therefore must
diversify into manufacturing activities; and (3) to catch up with the industrialized countries the Latin American countries need a rapid and decisive
growth in gross domestic product, which also dictated an industrializing
strategy because the greatest portion of added value in a product typically
comes from manufacture, not from the primary commodity.[69] Unlike the
pre-1930 growth philosophy, the approach of the second period required active government encouragement plus massive inflows of capital for purposes
of industrial production.

With the post–World War II boom in world trade, the creation of international financial organs to encourage Third World development, and the
improvement in the terms of trade for Latin American primary commodities,
the period 1950 to 1970 saw remarkable economic growth in the leading
Latin American countries. Mexican GDP grew at an average annual rate of
6.7 percent from 1956 to 1970,[70] Brazil's real GDP grew at 7.8 percent annually from 1956 to 1962, slowed down to 3.7 percent annually from 1962
to 1967 and then speeded up to 10.15 percent from 1968 to 1973.[71] Venezuela's GDP grew by an average rate of 5.7 percent per year from 1960 to
1975; Chile, Peru, and Argentina enjoyed substantial albeit uneven growth.[72]
The dynamo generating the impressive growth rates was industry. Mexico's
industrial sector grew by 9 percent a year from 1954 to 1976; Brazil's industrial sector grew more than 10 percent per year from 1956 to 1962 and
almost 13 percent per year from 1967 to 1973, more than double the growth
rates for the agricultural sector. Obviously, the effect of such disproportionate
rates of growth was that the industrial sector became increasingly important
(also, of course, making the entrepreneurial middle class more prominent).
By one recent estimate, industry's share of Brazil's GDP increased from 26
percent to 36 percent from 1950 to 1970, while agriculture's share declined
from 25 percent to 10 percent; similar but less dramatic trends are reported
for Mexico.[73]

The primary developmental policy to foster productive growth in the
1930s to 1950s was "horizontal" import substitution, replacing imported
consumer goods with goods manufactured within the countries.[74] The policy
of import substitution was most firmly embraced by the big countries in the
region—Argentina, Brazil, and Mexico—for they had large internal markets
(large consumer populations) that could sustain substantial supplying industries. This was an easy way to grow rapidly, since resources could be allocated to sectors where they would yield great returns. Smaller countries followed this policy somewhat, but less purposively. Peru, Venezuela, and Chile,

for example, still relied on commodity exports for much of their growth in the 1960s. Because of their very small internal markets, Central American countries did not seriously initiate import substitution efforts until the 1960s, after formation of a Central American Common Market.

Import substitution was hardly a panacea, though. For the largest countries, import substitution reached a natural limit in the 1960s. Once the most profitable markets were tapped by domestic industry, marginal returns began to fall. The result was slower and more erratic growth and, all too often, political crisis and new avenues of growth explored by authoritarian governments that took control. Problems with import substitution as a mechanism for industrialization ushered in a third period of growth from the 1960s to the 1980s. Several examples reveal the diversity of responses by countries in the region.

Brazil's growth slowed after 1962, triggering a military coup in 1964.[75] The military governments from 1964 to 1985 sought, above all else, to maintain high growth rates. Their approach was to emphasize "vertical" import substitution (domestic production of capital goods) and export expansion. As a result, the growth industries during Brazil's economic miracle of 1967–73 were minerals, metal products, machinery, electrical equipment, transport equipment, rubber products, and chemicals.[76] The new export-led model of development envisioned by the Brazilian government contemplated the solidification of a modern productive sector of the economy, which would be fully integrated with international capitalism.[77]

The establishment of a long-term authoritarian government was not unique to Brazil. Military authoritarian governments replaced democratic ones in Argentina (1966 and 1976), Peru and Panama (1968), Bolivia (1969), Ecuador and Honduras (1972), and Uruguay and Chile (1973), in each instance justifying its long-term control as a means of redirecting the country's policy to improve the country's economic growth.

After modest, albeit irregular, growth in the 1960s, Chile under the Allende government (1970–73) experimented with a socialist approach to growth development, including redistribution of land and nationalization of major industries. In the short term, these policies were not successful, triggering the military coup of 1973. The military government sought to achieve high growth rates in the 1970s by opening up the economy to free trade and foreign investment, with mixed success. Peru, like Chile and Brazil, enjoyed only sluggish growth in the 1960s, and the lack of suitable economic direction was one justification for the military coup of General Velasco in 1968. His government, while authoritarian, followed policies of redistribution and nationalization akin to those of Allende's Chile rather than Pinochet's Chile.

Although the third period of Latin American growth development was a time of political and economic experimentation, the fundamental problems of society were not solved by the military governments, which like the civilian ones became captives of their growth philosophy as a means of satisfying the relevant interest groups—for awhile. In fact, nine Latin American countries returned to civilian democratic rule between 1979 and March 1985.[78]

An integral part of the middle class ideology of productive growth that has dominated policy after 1930 has been the idea that capital is critical to rapid development. Because private accumulation has not been sufficient, the capital for development has had to come from somewhere else. Latin American governments themselves have been a major source of investment capital, through subsidies to favored industries, capitalization of state-owned trading and manufacturing enterprises, and creation of an infrastructure (roads, communications, education) capable of sustaining modernizing growth. The Brazilian and Mexican governments own about half of the capitalized value of their countries' fifty largest firms. Brazil's state sector has been particularly active, dominating some of the major export industries and increasing its share of GDP from 17 percent (in 1947) to 37 percent (1973) by one estimate.[79] Argentina, Peru, and Venezuela have also stressed the role of government expenditures and state-subsidized enterprises in their development—as evidenced by the large deficits in these areas after 1979 (appendix B, table B–6). Only Chile under military rule has moved away from state financial involvement in the economy.

Latin American planners generally assumed that government capital was not sufficient; external sources were also needed. Foreign direct investment was the main source of external capital in the second growth period. For example, 49 percent of the sales volume of Brazil's top 1,000 nonfinancial firms in 1974 could be attributed to firms owned or controlled by foreign multinational corporations. Peru in 1969 saw foreign-controlled subsidiaries account for 69 percent of sales; figures for Mexico and Argentina for 1972 were 27 percent and 31 percent, respectively.[80] Overall for Spanish Latin America, U.S. investment in 1970 was 1.18 times the total domestic governmental revenues (appendix B, table B–7). Foreign control was most pronounced in industries geared mainly for exports, such as the rubber, machinery, chemicals industries. Between 1950 and 1966, direct foreign investment was the main external source of development capital in Latin America.

A third necessary source of capital for Latin American growth development was indebtedness. It was widely assumed by Western and Latin American economists that development would entail current account deficits and substantial foreign debt.[81] Especially after 1966 (the third growth period), foreign loans became the predominant form of capital transfer from abroad, in part due to increasing objections in Latin American countries to foreign ownership of the nations' resources and means of production.[82] A great deal of Brazil's economic miracle after 1967 was fueled by external debt, which quadrupled between 1968 and 1973; in 1970, the overall ratio of external debt to total exports was 150 percent.[83] In Spanish Latin America, the overall ratio of external debt to total exports increased from 41 percent in 1950 to 115 percent in 1970 (appendix B, table B–8). By the early 1970s external indebtedness had surpassed direct foreign investment as the main source of capital in most of these countries.

Given the social, political, and economic policy structures described here, it is easy to see why most Latin American political leaders after 1973 responded to oil price increases by increasing indebtedness rather than by adopting other policies. Import substitution could produce only limited reductions in the payment deficits because the most likely domestic markets were already localized, and export expansion required further capital investment in imported technology, components, and materials, and thus further debt or disfavored foreign ownership. The only viable alternative to more debt was to slow growth. And that the governments were generally not willing to do: twenty years of growth exercised an enormous gravitational force on decision making. Growth was the government's raison d'être, and its cessation might be its coup de grace. Authoritarian governments acutely aware of their shaky legitimacy and democratic governments nervous about military intervention were prepared to make distributional decisions so long as the economic pie was expanding and unions and the entrepreneurial class could gain without penalizing the landowners. But they were not willing to force redistributional decisions mandated by a shrinking pie, whereby one group would have to make sacrifices. Consequently, the governments had a powerful incentive to borrow almost any amount of money to postpone the hard choices.

Different countries responded in different ways, but they generally followed this pattern. (Appendix B, table B–3 shows the geometric increase in debt for each country.) The authoritarian governments in Brazil and Peru, for example, were dominated by middle class, technocratic growth goals and saw themselves as engines of more efficient development. Rather than curtail their growth plans and antagonize the unions and entrepreneurs, those countries increased their external indebtedness sixfold (Brazil) and fourfold (Peru). Less liberal authoritarian regimes in Chile and Argentina expanded their external indebtedness to placate the military (through arms build-ups and, in the case of Argentina, a war) as well as the middle class and other relevant groups. The Mexican democracy during the governments from 1970 to 1982 explicitly followed a policy of continuing growth *and* improving the lot of the poor. This entailed large increases in government deficits, as well as a ninefold increase in external debt (appendix B, tables B–3 and B–6). Venezuela, which like Mexico became a leading oil exporter, followed a similar policy, grounded upon the hope that oil wealth would keep the pie expanding. Colombia, alone among the large Latin American debtors, saw only modest increases. Whatever the actual form of government, these and most other Latin American countries consciously followed the path of least political resistance. Rather than force groups to make present sacrifices, the countries borrowed a lot of money.

The Decline and Fall of the Bretton Woods Accords: The
Reemergence of Uncontrolled Private International Lending

Of course, no matter how much Latin American (and other) countries might have wanted to finance enormous current account deficits through external borrowing in the 1970s, they could not have done so if the banks had not been prepared to lend unprecedented sums of money. Apart from the availability of "petrodollars" (OPEC funds on deposit) to lend, two structural phenomena explain the willingness of banks to overextend themselves. The first structural factor is the Minsky–Kindleberger theory of manias and panics, which is historically applicable to international sovereign lending.[84] After an external political or economic shock (called a "displacement"), there will be an increase in speculative activity in which certain investments are thought by some to be superprofitable in the period of uncertainty. Others join in this activity, creating a mania of speculation, fueled by a collective euphoria, an unjustified optimism about the investment opportunity. (Increased speculation does indeed make the activity highly profitable in the short term.) When the speculation bottoms out, there is a period of uncertainty and distress, followed sooner or later by a revulsion against the speculative activity and then often by a panic or crash. This cycle of mania and panic characterized international sovereign lending, especially to Latin American countries, in the nineteenth century and was repeated after 1966. The displacement was inflation caused by U.S. deficits and the OPEC price increases; the mania was euphoric private bank lending to NODCs (especially in Latin America); revulsion finally came in 1982, when everyone realized that the loans could not be repaid.

The banks, of course, had not been caught up in the cyclical mania and panic of sovereign lending since the 1920s. One critical reason for this was the Bretton Woods system of controlled international finance, the decline of which is the second structural factor leading to bankers' eagerness to make unprecedented amounts of sovereign loans. The accords reached at Bretton Woods after World War II were meant to provide a stable international monetary and trade climate, with the United States as the guarantor of international economic stability.[85] Under this system, the dollar (fully redeemable in gold) would replace gold as the ultimate standard of value, and other currencies would have fixed exchange rates against the dollar. The IMF was established to regulate currency exchange rates (and approve changes in the rates if a country were chronically in deficit) and to provide access to credit to allow countries to adjust to short-term economic difficulties. The World Bank was established to make loans to enable countries to improve their infrastructure. A corollary to Bretton Woods was that the United States provided foreign aid and loans, first to Europe in the Marshall Plan and then to underdeveloped countries, to help the world economy recover from World War II.

In most respects the Bretton Woods system provided a workable world financial environment for economic development. International trade flourished, providing technological imports and a market for exports by developing countries. Foreign direct investment flourished, providing technology, know-how, and capital for industrial development. And developing countries could obtain funds from the IMF to smooth over trade imbalances, from the World Bank to fund development and infrastructure projects, and from Western governments (especially the United States) to pay for food and other imports from industrial countries. These official international lenders, moreover, made the loans for long terms and at concessionary interest rates. The disadvantages of official loans were that the lenders often attached conditions (the IMF insisted on measures to redress poor trade balances, for example) and did not have unlimited monies to lend. But these were really advantages, because the ideology of productive growth so fervently embraced by developing countries and the weaknesses of their political systems, especially in Latin America, made them all too prone to overborrow if they were not so constrained. Indeed, from 1956 to 1979 developing countries regularly confessed inability to service their debts, and their official creditors (typically under the auspices of the Paris Club) would restructure the debt so that it could be serviced.[86]

The Bretton Woods arrangement in large part unraveled in the 1960s, and its demise set the stage for an unprecedented amount of NODC sovereign debt. The United States partially withdrew as the guarantor of world trade.[87] Its own balance-of-payments deficits, which had fueled the twenty-five-year postwar boom, led to a flow of dollars abroad and exposed the U.S. gold reserves to instant depletion. Thus President Nixon in 1971 renounced gold convertibility. With no external discipline for U.S. currency, world exchange rates could no longer be pegged to the dollar. Currency rates floated, producing greater economic uncertainty and distortions in international trade and investment. For instance, countries had greater freedom to maintain an overvalued currency (which meant that their exchange rate against other currencies was higher than its purchasing power indicated), which artificially stimulated imports for the country and rendered its exports relatively expensive. So, too, countries were less constrained to maintain a reasonable balance-of-payments position. The era since the demise of the Bretton Woods system has been characterized by "a lack of any form of cooperation or coordination in exchange rate or monetary policies on a global scale. The floating system itself could not have been expected to offer an automatic mechanism to correct imbalances and instabilities resulting from independent, uncoordinated policies motivated solely by national self-interest."[88] NODCs were freer to continue payments deficits and to overvalue currencies—policies that ultimately impelled them to seek huge foreign loans.

By the end of the 1960s, moreover, the official lenders were being supplanted by private banks as the source of development loans. Just as the supply of funds by official lenders did not keep pace with the inflation of the 1960s, private international banking institutions were reentering the arena of international lending. U.S. banks opened overseas branches in the 1950s so that they could serve the global financial needs of their multinational corporate clients.[89] In 1963 the U.S. government created an incentive for greater use of foreign branches when it created the interest equalization tax on foreign borrowing from U.S. banks. The tax did not apply to bonds issued abroad by branch offices of U.S. banks. This, together with the 1965 Voluntary Foreign Credit Restraint Program of voluntary ceilings on bank loans to foreign entities and the Office for Foreign Direct Investment Guidelines mandatory in 1968, preventing multinational corporations from sending too much money to their foreign subsidiaries, generated an explosion of overseas branches.[90] Thirteen U.S. banks had branches in 211 locations in 1965 (gross assets $8.9 billion); by 1974, 125 banks had 732 branches (gross assets $140.5 billion). Foreign loans as a portion of total U.S. bank loans increased from 3 percent in 1960 to 15 percent in 1972.[91]

The "Euromarket" was the result of this flow of U.S. bank assets abroad. "Eurodollars" (or U.S. currency abroad) were freely and continuously exchanged, placed in loan, and invested in London and other exchanges. The risks of a typical medium-term $10 million loan of Euromarket funds could be spread by syndication, whereby several banks would participate in the loan, and a "rollover" of the loan every six months at prevailing interest rates.[92] Most of the NODC sovereign loans were made on the Euromarket after 1970, and the Euromarket's growth enabled it to meet developing countries' demands for credit.[93] Well before the OPEC price increases of 1973, there was a global money market whose goals dovetailed almost perfectly with those of developing countries; the latter wanted to borrow a lot of money, and the former wanted to lend it. While it is true that there would have been pressure on the large international banks to recycle the petrodollars through loans to NODCs, that does not explain the banks' continued eagerness to lend, especially in 1980–81. Indeed, this enthusiasm for such risky loans seems at odds with the widely held view that bankers are risk averse. The mania of NODC, and especially Latin American, loans was uncritical and mildly irrational. The hypothesis suggested here is that bankers as a group shared a "mentality of expansion" that justified large-scale lending which appears risky only in light of subsequently understood facts. That mentality can be understood by reference to three structural themes.

Short-Term Benefits and the Lemming Phenomenon. Decisions to make loans are made by bank officers, whose career goals influence these decisions. Once American banks had established so many foreign branches, the officers in charge of them had to justify the investment by generating loans. If a banker heading up a foreign branch office in the 1970s did not make loans, that banker's career went nowhere. The successful Eurobanker was one who, like Walter Wriston, made loans one day and worried about the consequences later.[94] Very little monitoring of these loans was attempted by bank management. If foreign private demand slackened but foreign sovereign demand was strong, the sovereign loans were made.

In the short term these loans were quite profitable. Banks typically charged "up front" fees, such as a commitment fee of 1 percent, and various servicing or management fees; if a bank put together a loan package for a group of banks, it would also receive a syndication fee. Interest rates on these loans usually were one or two points above market (LIBOR). Nothing advances a banker's career like short-term profits, and the more foreign sovereign loans the greater the profits. In 1970 the profits of Chase Manhattan Bank included $108 million from domestic loans, $31 million from foreign loans; in 1976 the figures were $23 million and $108 million, respectively. Other banks showed similarly impressive earnings figures.[95] Because large-scale banking is both fiercely competitive and close-knit (everyone knows everyone else), good profits for one bank from international lending created a lemming phenomenon: if Citibank is making a lot of money lending money in Latin America, our bank will be left behind if it does not lend money there as well, bankers thought. Walter Wriston was the lemmings' leader. Much of the expansion was thus defensive in nature.

Failure to Appreciate Country Risk. The initially favorable short-term profits were not reliable indicia of the true value of these loans, for there were serious long-term risks involved. "Country risk" is "the possibility that sovereign borrowers of a particular country may be unable or unwilling, and other borrowers unable, to fulfill their foreign obligations for reasons beyond the usual risks which arise in relation to all lending."[96] Surprisingly, few banks did country risk analyses of their noncollateralized loans to developing countries and their enterprises. Three reasons, two of them suggesting systematic flaws in the way banks went about their business, contributed to the banks' failure to appreciate these risks sufficiently.

One reason for underestimating country risk is that the decision-making structures of banks caused them to have short institutional memories. Quite simply, even the managers of the largest banks had very little experience in foreign sovereign lending until the 1960s. And *their* experience had been very favorable, the leading Latin American borrowers having grown vigorously and made regular payments on bank indebtedness for twenty years. Decision makers, in banks as elsewhere, often are more sensitive to vivid current news than to historical patterns; the former makes more of an impression on the memory and hence is more likely to come forth as one considers a problem.[97] The vivid, readily available current information is then often overgeneralized, as decision makers uncritically assume that they are representative of the relevant data.[98] The future will probably resemble the present. For these reasons a bank manager defending a decision to lend a lot of money to Brazil and Mexico in 1974 was far more persuasive than one arguing that in the 1930s those countries defaulted, because the recent "hard" data supported that manager. Moreover, once loans were made to these countries, "cognitive dissonance" among the decision makers biased their analyses of later loan requests by overemphasizing good news about foreign sovereign lending and underappreciating the doubts and risks.[99] These psychological mechanisms suggest one reason why the euphoria of this mania period was almost self-regenerating.

Banks also believed that diversification would spread the risk of default, based upon the conventional view that economic performance of borrowers in different countries is subject to divergent risks.[100] Yet this view ignored the experience of the 1930s, when the worldwide Depression affected sovereign loan repayments in a wide range of countries. While some external global events would affect some countries and not others, a great many events, such as interest rate increases and a recession, would affect almost all countries. The amount of systematic, or nondiversifiable, risk in international lending was simply misunderstood by bankers. Moreover, to the extent that country risk can be managed by geographic diversification, the banks failed to follow a rational policy, for the leading banks concentrated most of their loans in similarly situated Latin American states.[101]

A third reason banks did not worry much about country risk was that they assumed political checks on default: the developing country would not default because that would exclude it from future loans essential to its growth development, and if there were a default the U.S. government would step in and rescue the banks.[102] Such an assumption may also have been optimistic, for Latin American countries had frequently defaulted on loans in the nineteenth century. Additionally, the banks may not have appreciated the potential congressional hostility to any kind of "bail-out" of the banks.[103] Finally, recent econometric studies suggest that it is in the borrowing country's self-interest to default when the debt-servicing burden becomes too high, even though default would exclude the country from international money markets.[104] Notwithstanding all these problems with the third reason, it was in most ways a valid assumption, because of the unique public importance of the large international banks. On the one hand, because of their commitment to growth development, Latin American countries would be loathe to force an outright schism with the banks, which controlled 90 percent of the funds available for such development. On the other hand, national regulators view the survival and prosperity of the large international banks as an important public policy, as any major bank failures could trigger a financial panic. For that reason the regulators in the United States and other Western countries were perceived as "lenders of last resort," which would in fact bail out the banks if trouble developed. To a certain extent, the banks' cocky political optimism may have been perceptive—since Western governments have, quietly, bailed out the banks in part.

Lack of Regulatory Constraints. The decline of the Bretton Woods system and the phenomenal growth of private international money centers resulted in an international financial system that is "a private system with only marginal official participation."[105] The Euromarket, where most of the loans were made, is unregulated—there are no central banks, no exchanges, no domestic laws to check the stampede of bankers to make sovereign loans. Of course, the private participants themselves, the banks, are subject to national regulation to assure that shareholders do not lose their investments, or depositors their accounts, because of poor lending policies on the part of banks. The government regulators, however, had no greater understanding of country risk in the 1970s than the banks did.[106] And even if they had understood the problem, there were political reasons for them to do nothing but hope that the risks would not materialize. As Federal Reserve Board Chairman Volcker candidly admitted in 1983, bank regulators were loathe to establish classifications that might be offensive to particular countries.[107] Indeed, federal regulators encouraged private bank lending to developing countries, because it removed pressure for the United States and the international financial institutions to make such loans in a period in which they did not have the resources to do so.[108]

Under the Bretton Woods system, there were stricter limits on the ability of NODCs to become heavily indebted, and when they did take on debt, it was on concessionary (bargain) terms from Western countries or multilateral lending institutions. This public order was eclipsed in the 1970s by massive, largely unconstrained, private lending. The corollaries of the demise of Bretton Woods and the mania-to-panic syndrome were that (1) the rapidity with which international lending developed charged it with an ideology of expansion parallel to that found in developing countries; (2) the risks of this sort of lending were systematically underestimated because of the competitive pressures to report increased current profits; and (3) the ideology of growth and accumulation of risks were not checked by federal regulators, because existing regulatory philosophy was blind to the possibility of overlending to sovereign debtors.

For these reasons, Western banks automatically welcomed the massive OPEC deposits and immediately, even uncritically, used them to make more massive loans to developing countries from 1973 to 1979. The power of these structural causes of the debt crisis can be seen after 1979. Although the new OPEC price increase gave an enormous new influx of funds into the Eurodollar market, the level of country debt and bank exposure was already high and cause for concern. The federal regulators in 1979 instituted a system requiring bank consideration of country risk and encouraging diversification of lending practices.[109] Yet the momentum of developing country sovereign lending continued and in fact accelerated. The 1979 federal guidelines were a substantial failure, and the level of bank exposure increased dramatically.

The nine major United States banks had 137 percent of their equity on loan to Brazil, Mexico, and Argentina in mid-1982, compared with 114 percent when the 1979 federal regulation was initiated.[110] The period of euphoria persisted far longer than any objective analysis would have justified, especially after minicrises concerning the debts of Mexico, Peru, Zaire, and Poland between 1976 and 1981.[111] The largely private system of international finance was not a system that worked very well.

The Self-perpetuating Nature of the Debt Crisis: Informal Redress for Lenders and Foreign Sovereign Borrowers

Once it became clear that the debtor countries had been borrowing far too much and the banks had been lending far too much, bank lending largely dried up.[112] But there was no crash; countries did not renounce their debt, and lenders did not stop lending altogether. Instead, the formerly euphoric bankers, their bad investments (NODCs), and the once-written-off public sector (IMF and the United States) negotiated a series of measures to avert a crash. This mode of crisis resolution is attributable to two peculiarities, the lack of reliable legal remedies available to the banks and the borrowing countries and the reemergence of public lenders of last resort to back up the system.

The first peculiarity of the debt crisis is the dearth of legal remedies. Some commentators have written or assumed that countries cannot be sued for repudiation of their public debt.[113] As a matter of law they are wrong, but in practice such lawsuits are not very effective remedies. Sovereign loans are typically not backed up by collateral that the banks can attach in the event of default, but they do have acceleration and elaborate cross-default clauses.[114] That is, if the Mexican government fails to make timely payments of principal and interest, its creditors can demand that the entire loan amount fall due (be accelerated) *and* that all other loans to the Mexican government, its political subdivisions, and its state trading companies also fall due. The right of acceleration, of course, does the banks little good if they cannot enforce it through legal process. A lawsuit in Mexico would not likely be successful, but as a formal matter a lawsuit in the United States against Mexico would in most instances be possible. Federal subject matter and personal jurisdiction in lawsuits against "foreign states" (including political departments or subdivisions and most state trading companies) is governed by the Foreign Sovereign Immunities Act of 1976 (FSIA).[115] Such jurisdiction exists "as to any claim for relief . . . with respect to which the foreign state is not entitled to [sovereign] immunity."[116] Two bases exist for denying state immunity in lawsuits to enforce the terms of sovereign loan agreements. One basis is the waiver of state immunity in most sovereign loan agreements.[117] Under the FSIA, if the foreign state debtor "has waived its immunity either explicitly or by implication" in the loan agreement, it is not immune from suit to enforce the terms of the loan agreement.[118] A second basis for denying immunity is that a sovereign default on a bank loan would fall under the FSIA's "commercial activity" exception.[119] The act of state doctrine might bar adjudication in a few, rare, instances.[120]

Thus in most cases foreign states can be sued if they breach their loan agreements with U.S. banks. The problem would be to collect the judgment, for these states may not have sufficient assets in the United States, and most of the assets found here would probably be immune from attachment to enforce the judgment. The modern theory of immunity gives foreign states greater protection against losing their assets through attachment than against being sued. Under the FSIA only the "property in the United States . . . used for a commercial activity in the United States" can be attached if the judgment is against the country itself or its departments or subdivisions.[121] Also, unless there is a specific waiver, the property attached would have to be that "used for the commercial activity upon which the claim is based," namely, the loan.[122] The funds held by the state's central bank for its own account are expressly immunized by the FSIA.[123] In short, very little of the country's property in the United States will be available to satisfy any judgment accelerating and demanding payment on the country's public debt. If there are cross-default clauses in the loan agreement, the debt of state trading companies can also be accelerated, and any judgment against trading companies can be executed against any of their properties or funds in the United States, with certain exceptions.[124] But the central government's debt judgment would still remain largely uncollected in most instances.

The peculiar dearth of formal legal sanctions against sovereign borrowers that fail to make payments contributed to the uncontrolled borrowing spree of the developing countries. Without easily enforceable legal remedies, banks were not in a position to place restrictions on their sovereign loans, such as limitations on the use of the borrowed money or a disclosure requirement or ceilings on the country's total debt.[125] As a result, the countries were allowed to borrow as much as they wanted—which was too much. More important, the banks had insufficient incentives to monitor aggregate sovereign borrowing carefully and to develop a "maximum level of sustainable debt" for each individual country.

Additionally, the weak legal sanctions left the international credit market particularly vulnerable to a contagious collapse of confidence. Without formal legal protection, a bank's immediate response to country repayment problems is to stop lending money. When one important bank stops lending to a country, the others may become nervous and try to follow the same strategy. Soon no one will lend.[126] That is only the banks' immediate response, however. There are incentives and pressures to revive lending flows if cooperative mechanisms can be created extralegally. Because the leading lenders have so much of their paid-in capital on loan to individual countries, if the countries in question were to threaten default, the banks would all but have to lend "new money" even after the crisis of confidence. This phenomenon of "involuntary lending" is also the result of the legal peculiarities of sovereign lending. To prevent a total loss of a sizable chunk of its assets, the bank will rationally commit a smaller chunk of assets to new loans that bear high risks of loss and further commit the bank to that country.[127] Because the solvency of the big money center banks is a matter of national concern, federal regulators, too, have a stake in preventing default and will commit public funds to that goal—bridge loans, export credits, guarantees. Furthermore, the government will help "persuade" the banks with smaller relative exposure (and some reason to stop lending altogether) to join the big banks' efforts, as Professor Wellons demonstrates.[128]

So long as it continues to embrace the ideology of growth, the sovereign borrower, too, is a captive of the situation. If a private company's debts exceed its assets, it may voluntarily go into bankruptcy reorganization proceedings to reorder and reduce its external debt. There is no bankruptcy proceeding for sovereign states, only payment moratoriums and default.[129] Because the banks' response to a default would be to exclude the state from international credit markets, the sovereign borrower in chronic need of growth development capital will have a strong incentive not to default. (Thus, notwithstanding talk of a "debtors' cartel," Latin American countries are committed to avoiding default or extended moratoria.) But the countries do need an authority to rehabilitate their financial viability. The institution most analogous to a bankruptcy court is the IMF—which can provide short-term relief and, more important, give its imprimatur to a "reorganization" program that will restore solvency to the country. The international debt crisis has revived the IMF by making it a critical "honest broker between debtor countries and their creditor banks, . . . ultimate judge of the appropriate mix between the magnitude of a heavily indebted developing country's adjustment effort and the commitment to it of new external finance."[130]

While lack of traditional legal remedies has thus made the international debt crisis a self-perpetuating one, it has also generated constructive extralegal mechanisms to cope with the crisis. That is, because neither the banks nor the countries have an easy legal remedy (foreclosure or bankruptcy), they are forced to cooperate with one another and with the United States and the IMF to create equivalent solutions by negotiation. Hence follow the series of debt restructuring negotiations, in which the borrowing country will agree to an IMF program to improve its current account deficit, in return for new funds from the IMF and the group of banks and an extended time in which to repay its foreign debt. These negotiated agreements have served the ordering functions in this international sovereign context typically served by formal, coercive legal rules in private party settings.[131] First, and most important, the restructure process has compelled the Latin American political systems to make the hard decisions that paralyzed them earlier. Although the IMF austerity plans have not necessarily been the best approaches, they have at least forced countries to adopt realistic policies. Second, the process has enforced collective discipline on the banks. Acting through advisory groups, the banks have accomplished what the federal regulators never required: a group determination of the country's level of sustainable debt and a rescheduling of repayment terms based on that determination. Third, the process has fostered better informed decisions. IMF country risk evaluations are made available to the banks, as is more accurate information from the debtor countries themselves.

The forced dialogue between lenders and debtor countries cannot entirely eradicate the structural barriers to a wholly satisfactory resolution of the debt crisis, though. Beneath the negotiations are deep chasms of disaster. On the one hand is the possibility that the IMF austerity measures will destabilize individual countries or entire regions because of the unrest caused by lean years after so much growth.[132] That is, like the Great Depression, the debt-induced austerity measures might destabilize existing governments and generate mass unrest, perhaps even some kind of revolution in some countries. On the other hand, if the borrowing countries do not raise enough capital, there is the possibility of default, which does severe damage to the international financial system and might lead to the failure of leading U.S. banks.[133]

The International Debt Problem in the Context of Development Theory

The structuralist explanation helps to place the current international debt crisis in the broader perspective of institutional history and dynamics. The structures of international finance and Latin American politics show the natural evolution and resolution of the debt crisis. Note, however, the limitations of the structuralist explanation. Its historical focus is the period after World War II. And by emphasizing the way institutions function, this structuralist explanation does not address historical patterns or issues of social justice and fairness. A larger historical and normative context for examining the origins of the international debt crisis is development theory. The debt crisis can be explained by several of the competing development theories. Conversely, the debt crisis sheds light on the validity of the development theories themselves.

It is impossible here to perform a comprehensive analysis of the debt crisis under every one of the many schools of development theory. All that can be done is to explore, rather provisionally, the explanatory value of three paradigms of economic development: the modernization paradigm, which is closely tied to the process by which Western Europe and the United States developed; the dependency paradigm, generated by Third World (especially

Latin American) scholars as a response to their perception that development and modernization are myths perpetuated by capitalist countries to render other countries permanently dependent upon and subservient to their capital and technology; and a world systems paradigm, which views the world economic system as an interdependent one where the leading industrial economies play the significant ordering role, but newly industrializing countries are seeking to join their ranks, sometimes with success. The modernization paradigm is not a satisfactory context for explaining and understanding the international debt crisis; the crisis underlines severe problems with that theory of development. The dependency paradigm is, normatively, a more persuasive context for examining the debt crisis, but its static analysis does little to explain the complex history (that is, how the crisis came about and affects different countries in different ways). A world systems paradigm provides a helpful description of the current situation as a crisis in the capitalist world system in which the post-1966 dysfunctions of core state economies threaten the ability of certain newly industrializing countries to advance in the world system as well as the ability of the core states to preserve their own predominant role.

The Modernization Paradigm

Development theory emerged as a systematic discipline only after World War II, in part as an ideology for Western countries to explain and defend their dominance of the postwar economy. The modernization paradigm of development evolved among Western or West-influenced economists and sociologists.[134] Development was seen from an evolutionary perspective. An "underdeveloped" country today was expected to evolve into a "developed" country tomorrow. The evolutionary process was basically imitative, the underdeveloped country being said to follow the steps taken by the United States and Western Europe in the nineteenth and early twentieth centuries, until their economies became mature ones characterized by continuous internal capital accumulation, industrialization, self-perpetuating growth. "The ruling paradigm of the economics of development rests on the classical-neoclassical view of a world in which change is gradual, marginalist, nondisruptive, equilibrating, and largely painless. . . . Once initiated, growth becomes automatic and all-pervasive, spreading among nations and trickling down classes so that everybody benefits from the process."[135]

What would stimulate Western-style self-sustaining growth in the so-called underdeveloped economies? One framework for answering that question after World War II was Keynesian economics, which had been perceived as useful in pulling the "underemployed" Western economies out of the Depression. Keynes demonstrated that an increase in aggregate consumption and investment would have a multiplier effect in the economy, increasing the level of economic activity.[136] In the 1950s two Keynesians, Evsey Domar and Roy Harrod, posited that in underdeveloped countries each increase in output provides the groundwork for further growth because part of it is reinvested; once income levels become consistently high enough to yield a certain level of reinvestment, then growth becomes self-sustaining.[137] Hence, for these scholars, capital accumulation became the main factor in the process of economic growth.

A key concern of emerging development theory was how "a community which was previously saving and investing 4 or 5 percent of its national income or less, converts itself into an economy where voluntary saving is running at about 12 to 15 percent of national income or more."[138] Much of the literature focused on social and economic "traps," such as high population growth and inefficient consumption patterns, which threatened to maintain a country in a Keynesian low-level equilibrium (indefinite stagnation). Although Domar and Harrod seemed to assume that the capital needed for development could be generated within developing countries, these traps indicated that much more capital was needed and that it would have to come from outside the developing countries. The goal of development was to provide massive inflows of capital that would stimulate a balanced growth (Keynesian general equilibrium)—thereby breaking the "vicious cycle of poverty" (the traps).[139] The sources of such seed money were foreign aid and loans, state investment, foreign direct investment.

Arthur Lewis added a second reason for infusions of external capital. He argued that underdeveloped societies are typically "dualistic," an advanced modern sector coexisting with a traditional sector. Industrialization financed by foreign capital (loans or direct investment) was a way out of this sociological conundrum. The idea was that capital-fueled growth in the industrialized sector would gradually absorb the underutilized labor force in the traditional sector, thereby drawing the whole country into modernized social and economic structures.[140] Neoclassical economists have added the idea that free international trade and investment are "engines of development." Free trade in the world economy yields benefits for underdeveloped countries by stimulating industries in which they have a comparative advantage and by reducing factor price discrepancies in the world.[141] To the extent that trade is constrained by tariffs and other barriers, the same spreading of benefits can occur through Western multinational enterprises that transfer their technological innovations through the world economy and create their own internal markets, which are efficient and wealth-enhancing for the host countries as well as the multinationals.[142]

A final group of theorists generated historical models, patterned on the experience of Western countries, for the evolution of a traditional, underdeveloped society to a modern, entrepreneurial one. The most celebrated is the five-stage model created by Walter Rostow.[143] From traditional society (stage 1), the country creates an improved infrastructure and a new entrepreneurial class as preparation for take-off (stage 2). The critical take-off stage (stage 3) is the period in which the last major obstacles to economic development are removed, and the share of net investment and saving as a part of national income doubles to 10 percent or more. At that point, growth and development become self-sustaining, and as the country travels the road to maturity (stage 4), modernization spreads from the dynamic sectors to other parts of society, which are then integrated into the country's overall growth. The inexorable result is the mass consumption society (stage 5). The idea that underdeveloped countries can go through roughly the same stages or phases of development that England and the United States experienced has had a strong and broad influence.

The central concepts of the modernization paradigm were widely accepted by policymakers in the 1950s and 1960s.

1. Asian, African, and Latin American countries can "develop" along the same historical process as Western industrial countries.
2. The key to development is capital investment.
3. Trade, investment, and loans from industrialized countries will help the linear process of development.

It was the basis for Western infusions of foreign aid and the United Nations' proclamation of the 1960s as the "Decade of Development." And, although its concepts are strongly ethnocentric, the modernization paradigm was accepted, at least in part, by the leaders and technocrats of most developing countries.

Does the modernization paradigm explain the origins of the international debt crisis? In its pure theoretical form it clearly does not. Indeed, quite the opposite. Faith in the modernization paradigm probably contributed to the current international debt crisis. The modernization paradigm teaches that once growth begins, perpetual growth will automatically follow.[144] In the 1960s and early 1970s, Brazil, Mexico, and other Latin American countries achieved impressive rates of GDP growth and domestic saving and investment. Based on the modernization paradigm, both bankers and Latin American leaders reasonably assumed that these countries had reached some kind of self-perpetuating economic growth, and the continued growth of these countries after 1973 (subsidized in large part by foreign debt) only confirmed those presuppositions. Of course, as noted previously, there were other institutional forces at work in favor of massive new lending in the 1970s, but the pervasive belief in modernization theory certainly helps explain the long-lived euphoria of so many intelligent people—from Western bankers to Third World technocrats to federal bank regulators.

Of course, only the pure or popularized form of the modernization paradigm can be so characterized, for several of the theorists explored the non-linearity of development even under the modernization model. The debt crisis suggests that "late developing" countries in Latin America and elsewhere will not proceed in the same linear way as the "early developing" countries of the United States and Western Europe. Descriptive political science scholarship suggests that late developing countries rely more heavily on a strong interventionist state for growth, face severe population pressures concomitant with GDP growth, and tend to have corporatist channels that appropriate the fruits of the economic advance to nonproductive elites.[145] Sociological and anthropological studies suggest that modernization theory grossly oversimplifies the effect of a "modern sector" on the remainder of a traditional society. The former will not automatically absorb the latter.[146] Brazil was once thought to be a classic case of modernization through the five Rostovian stages, but its economic expansion has crashed not only into high oil prices, world recession, and rising interest rates, but also poor policy planning, internal tensions, and an increasing (rather than receding) division between modern and traditional segments of society. Luiz Bresser Pereira, a leading historian of Brazil's economic development, sees that country moving toward a condition of "industrialized underdevelopment," in which part of the economy creates manufactured export goods within a Western social and physical infrastructure, while a larger part of the economy remains undeveloped, if not marginalized from the dynamic sector.[147]

The international debt crisis poses a larger challenge to the modernization paradigm. It tends to refute modernization theory's proposition that large-scale capital accumulation is necessary and sufficient for growth and development. The debt crisis reveals starkly how external capital can impede a country's development. The growth rates of most Latin American debtor countries were less than 2 percent for 1984, and they may be depressed for several years, in part because most of each country's trade surplus must be paid over to Western banks as debt servicing payments.[148] Capital accumulation will do a country no good if the capital is not appropriately used, if the terms of its acquisition are unfavorable, or if external conditions (such as interest rates) change drastically. Furthermore, plentiful capital does not automatically generate growth when there are internal structures that impede the effective utilization of that capital. Classical economist Ronald McKinnon argues that the level of savings and investment in an economy is less important than the existence of internal social, economic, and political barriers to the effective matching of capital and economic opportunities.[149] For example, when infusions of capital are controlled by the state or by Western multinational enterprises, small-scale entrepreneurs (the real engines of development) might find themselves unable to obtain funds for their own expansion. McKinnon and other thinkers suggest that big capital infusions are not at all necessary to development; developing countries would be better off to create capital through an endogenous process of firm growth rather than through outside infusions that are misdirected by structural impediments. Japan, which developed rapidly and without much outside capital, may be the appropriate model for late-developing countries.[150]

Finally, the debt crisis may be the occasion to question the modernization paradigm's emphasis on economic growth as measured by materialist indexes. The debt crisis reveals that a country can enjoy tremendous growth even while impoverishing the bulk of its people and mortgaging its future. For instance, Brazil's rapid growth development has marginalized 80 percent of the country's population, making many of them worse off in the 1970s than they were in 1960.[151] The austerity measures of the last two years, moreover, have been borne by these same people. Mexico's rapid growth development between 1950 and 1970 also went largely to the top 30 percent of the population.[152] Uncritically adopted from classical economics, the idea of growth may be an inadequate basis on which to build a development policy for Latin American countries, for it ignores distributional consequences (the unfairness of increased income going exclusively to the elite class), leaves out immeasurable things that are nonetheless critical to the country's well-being (environmental purity, health, community feelings), and overemphasizes superficial statistical measurements without considering the need for constructing economic, social, and political structures that will benefit the country in the long term.[153]

In short, the international debt crisis confirms doubts about the modernization paradigm. Empirically, the paradigm cannot deliver on its promise of linear growth for Latin American economies. Normatively, it may rest upon an excessively narrow view of development itself. Alternative objects of development need to be more seriously considered. For example, François Perroux urges more attention to nonmaterialist features of community development and a dialectic that seeks a balance between autonomy and foreign inputs, atomistic independence and social cooperation, industry and agriculture.[154] Perroux and other theorists point the way toward considering development which is responsive to human needs, endogenous and self-reliant, ecologically sound, and grounded in a transformation of social, political, and economic structures of the country.

The Dependency Paradigm

The prevailing paradigm, the modernization paradigm, came under strong intellectual challenge in the 1950s and 1960s. Marxists and other thinkers of the Left found modernization theory a mere smokescreen for continued imperialist domination in the postcolonial era following World War II.[155] They argued that underdevelopment was a continuous historical status imposed by capitalist domination, for the capitalist industrialized countries required subordinate markets and sources for investing their surplus capital once they had overgrown their national boundaries. Latin American economists and sociologists criticized modernization theory as an unrealistic portrait of the reality they saw.[156] International trade and investment failed to lead to economic expansion and success and, indeed, impeded the natural development of their countries, because the terms of trade and investment systematically favored developed countries. Raúl Prebisch divided the world into "core" states, which benefited from trade, and "peripheral" states, whose raw materials and labor were still being exploited.[157]

Although different authors formulate the dependency approach in many different ways, its central thesis is that global interests of metropolitan capitalist classes determine world development processes and power relationships to their advantage and to the detriment of the other countries of the world.[158] What this means for poorer countries is either permanent underdevelopment or, at best, "associated-dependent development," where the host country abandons its indigenous values and acquires a secondhand version of metropolitan capitalism enjoyed by a small band of the local elite. This central tenet involves three corollary ideas.[159] First, the major impediment to development is not lack of capital (internal), but rather an international division of labor (external), in which the core countries specialize in manufactured goods and the peripheral countries supply raw materials and labor. The periphery is dominated by the core, politically, culturally, and economically. Second, adverse terms of trade and domination lead to the systematic transfer of the periphery's productive surplus to the core, which invests it for its own economic growth. In this way, development in the core states implies underdevelopment in the peripheral states. Underdevelopment is the result of the same historical processes as development: the metropoles "develop," while the satellites "underdevelop." Third, because the periphery is doomed to underdevelopment through its dependency links with the core, and because the interest of the dominant states is in maintaining the periphery's underdevelopment, the only true path to development is delinkage from world trade. That is, the developing country should adopt a radical program of endogenous economic growth.

Early dependency theory focused on the subordinating effects of world trade: the surplus value created by trade tended to go to industrialized countries, and commodity-producing countries fell further behind in a regime of free trade. In the 1960s dependency theorists argued that a more potent engine of the asserted Western economic hegemony was the multinational corporation, which set up operations (branches, joint ventures, subsidiaries) in various countries.[160] Drawing from dependency theorists' critique of multinationals' investment and some of the recent literature addressing the dominating aspects of foreign external debt, it is possible to construct an explanation for the international debt crisis based upon the dependency paradigm.[161] Under this approach, outlined in figure 3–3, the connection between the underdeveloped country and the industrial West creates a vicious cycle in which more foreign investment leads to more debt, which leads in turn to a double dependency.

The beginning of the vicious cycle of debt is the desire of the underdeveloped country's elites to emulate the West, which is itself an ideological dependency.[162] Material dependency flows from the next step: the elite seek more capital and technology, which are provided by two debt-creating sources. The government has consistently played a major role in the modernization of Latin American countries by creating infrastructures, subsidizing certain segments of the economy, and establishing state trading and manufacturing companies to supply the domestic and export markets. The government's activities generate debt in two ways. Because tax revenues are insufficient to pay for the increased public sector expenditures and domestic financing of the public debt was largely unavailable, the public sector debt is typically financed by borrowing from Western lenders.[163] Because government projects are given high priority and Western firms are often more experienced suppliers of goods and services, government-led development heavily relies on imported goods and services. Capital goods imports contribute to current account deficits, which also are financed by external loans.

The second source of capital and technology has been direct foreign investment by Western multinational enterprises. Under conventional theory, an advantage of direct foreign investment is that it provides countries with new industry without creating new debts. Dependency theory argues that this has not been the case: not only does foreign investment place much of the domestic economy under foreign control, but it has contributed to current account deficits and, thereby, to the growing external debt. To begin with, the foreign investor will often not contribute any outside capital at all, but will establish operations based upon local capital (which is more readily available to the creditworthy foreign multinational).[164] Although the foreign-owned subsidiary will generate some exports, they are often sold to other subsidiaries in the multinational chain and may be underpriced to avoid tariffs and other taxes. In any event, the balance-of-trade impact of the exports will typically be offset by the subsidiary's import of raw materials and other inputs from other firms in the multinational chain; the imports will often be overpriced.[165] Within the host country market, the subsidiary will expect to make supernormal profits, either because the market for its goods in the host country has little competition or because the product is sharply differentiated from possible competitors' products.[166] Those profits will be repatriated to its parent company abroad.[167] In short, according to dependency theory, on a year-to-year basis the capital investment plus exports generated by multinational subsidiaries are less than repatriated dividends or royalties plus imports.

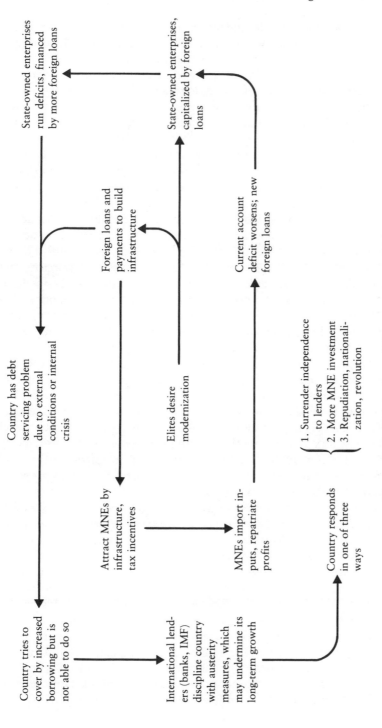

Figure 3–3. Dependency Theory's View of Debt

As a result of development dependent on multinational enterprises, Latin American countries such as Brazil and Mexico have suffered chronic trade imbalances, which have also contributed to growing indebtedness.

Under conventional theory, subsidiaries of multinational corporations make long-term contributions of technology and industrial growth, which should ultimately strengthen the host country's current account position. Dependency theory argues, however, that the long-term effects of direct foreign investment are enervating rather than strengthening. While their activity may expose the host country to technology through licensing agreements or domestic joint ventures, the technology is typically not top of the line and its use is often hedged in by restrictive contractual provisions.[168] More important, exposure to technology is of little use if the host country does not develop the capacity to improve on that technology domestically; this is not a necessary consequence of direct foreign investment, either because the technology is not completely shared with the host culture or because the host culture lacks the institutions or incentives to develop its own innovations. The research and development for the multinational—the brain work—is still done in the West; only the manufacturing—the hands-on work—is done in foreign subsidiaries.[169] Most important, foreign-owned companies come to dominate the most dynamic sectors of the economy (the main export industries or the most profitable import substitution ones), depriving local entrepreneurs of valuable business opportunities and experience and ultimately swallowing them up or driving them out of business.[170] Domestic enterprises that might compete with the multinational's subsidiary find themselves at a tremendous competitive disadvantage because they have less capital and less access to both domestic and foreign capital markets, which makes them less able to compete through mass advertisements, product development and differentiation, and research. The magnetic pull of the foreign-owned company ultimately extends to the talented entrepreneurs, who sell out or merge with the powerful competitor.

According to dependency theory, growth fueled by government spending or direct foreign investment tends to create substantial external indebtedness. As explained, the process by which the country comes to depend on external borrowing is itself harmful, because it discourages the mobilization of domestic savings (there being no need to create indigenous mechanisms when money is easily obtainable from abroad) and creates a structural dependency on foreign imports rather than domestic inputs, on foreign technology rather than local innovation, and on foreign entrepreneurial leadership in many of the leading manufacturing and mineral extraction industries. Furthermore, to the extent that the government encourages indebtedness as a means to fast growth, that process creates further distortions in the economy: exports become less competitive in world markets, domestic investment is misallocated, and income distribution may be skewed (in favor of the already-existing elites).

Finally, a large external debt is in itself undesirable, according to dependency theory. Servicing the debt consumes an increasing portion of the developing country's income and ultimately becomes a negative flow. More money is paid out in servicing payments than is sent into the country. In this way the debt "becomes a self-sustaining and continually growing phenomenon completely beyond the control of the economic policy of the local authorities," and as a result "the creditor countries, through their national credit organs and also the international bodies [IMF and World Bank] in which they usually wield a preponderant influence, do their best to control the economic management of the debtor countries."[171] In short, developing countries linked up with Western multinationals mortgage their futures twice, first by turning many of their resources over to foreign companies, and second by incurring massive external debts. In both situations the country loses its freedom without advancing even its material interests.

The dependency paradigm is a persuasive perspective for analyzing the international debt crisis. As developing countries have become increasingly integrated into the international system of trade and multinational investment in the last three decades, their external debt has indeed increased—both absolutely and as a ratio to exports (appendix B, tables B–1 and B–8). Although the source of external indebtedness varies from country to country, public sector deficits and outflows by multinational operations have been the main sources of the external debt in most of the countries. Notwithstanding their greater economic development, Latin American balance of payments shifted from net exports in 1950 to net imports in 1970 (appendix B, table B–9), a trend greatly magnified after 1973. These conclusions are difficult to dispute.

It is less clear whether these countries would have done better in material terms without the external debt. On the one hand, in most years between 1954 and 1979, Latin American economies (GDPs) grew more rapidly than their accumulations of debt, although the level of debt grew more rapidly than the level of exports (appendix B, table B–8). Some analysts of the debt crisis believe that the indebtedness was put to productive use.[172] And, they argue, to the extent that the borrowed money was "wasted" (not put to long-term productive use), it was most often wasted by the governments themselves—through graft and corruption, distorting subsidies to unprofitable domestic sectors, losses by poorly run state trading companies. On the other hand, dependency theorists might respond that there was little if any "real" growth after 1954, because population increases absorbed most of the GDP growth in the 1960s, and in the 1980s population increases are outstripping GDP growth.[173] The level of external debt and high interest rates have made the developing countries net exporters of capital to the United States, an exaggerated version of the dependency theory's critique. And what growth there has been goes to the collaborative elites, the local surrogates for the multinationals of the core countries, because the "productive" investments were in capital-intensive industries that provided very few jobs for the masses.[174] As for the allegedly wasted loans, one must remember that most of the waste in the late 1970s was through capital flight of money from Latin America to United States and European banks, which openly sought and competed for these new deposits.

The debt crisis also bears out the dependency paradigm's view that Western core countries have built-in advantages (capital, technology, social, and physical structures), which tend to perpetuate their ascendancy over countries on the periphery. The core countries can usually absorb external shocks better because they have more diversified economies, more effective political systems, and more resources on which to fall back.[175] They control the levers of finance and investment by which the world itself responds to major crises. Hence, when a crisis occurs, a disproportionate share of the sacrifices will be made by the borrowing countries' growth and development. For example, the effect of stringent IMF austerity programs and the banks' reluctance to lend money has been postponement of needed capital formation in Latin America, sharp drops in real wages, and severe curtailment of GDP growth in a period of population pressures.[176] Another consequence is that Latin American countries are at the mercy of the core states' economic decisions. The Federal Reserve System's restrictive monetary policies in 1979–80 and the enormous federal deficits of the last few years have been crippling for Latin American debtor countries, for which each percentage point increase in the real interest rate means a billion dollars more in yearly debt-servicing payments. Moreover, the debtor countries' prospects of ever digging out of the hole of debt are contingent upon the West's economic recovery *and* a relaxation of the recent trends toward protectionism, and upon following the policy constraints imposed by the restructuring agreements between the debtor countries and the IMF and the commercial banks.

The international debt crisis is the most severe economic crisis facing Latin America since the Great Depression. In one way it is worse. The Depression cut Latin America off from Western markets, thereby stimulating some indigenous entrepreneurship in import substitution. The current debt crisis threatens to tighten ties of dependency by bleeding Latin America of capital and impelling it to rely more on multinational enterprise investment. In normative terms the debt crisis seems to vindicate the dependency paradigm's indictment of the unfairness and domination inherent in Latin America's relationship with industrial countries.

In historically explanatory terms, however, the dependency paradigm is not wholly satisfactory, for two reasons. First, it seems oversimple in arguing that dependent, underdeveloped countries inevitably sink further into their pit so long as they are tied to the dominant countries. This is just not so. For example, Spanish Latin America in 1970 was significantly less dependent on single commodity export and upon the U.S. market than it was in 1950 (appendix B, tables B–10 and B–11). The reason is that the Western technology has helped these countries to diversify. Brazil is no longer just an exporter of chocolate and caffeine to satisfy the addictions of the Western middle class, for in the 1970s it became an important exporter of technologically sophisticated manufactured goods.[177] For all of their debt problems, Venezuela (a member of OPEC) and Mexico (not a member but sometimes an ally) are hardly powerless producers of raw materials; both countries are trying in the long term to transmute their oil profits into industrial development. Even more striking is the success story of South Korea, which on a per capita basis is more heavily indebted than the main Latin American countries. While it is dependent upon Western loans and technology, it is hard to say that the country's material growth has been impeded by foreign dependence or that the foreign debt has grown more rapidly than the country's ability to service it (exports grew by 11 percent in 1983, for example). Likewise, Taiwan is dependent upon Western loans and technology, yet has established industries that compete successfully with American multinational companies worldwide. Neither of these countries is stuck on the periphery, and the debt crisis does not seem to have impeded their economic development, for both countries have strong governments that responded decisively to the external shocks.[178] Generally, dependent countries were not all equally vulnerable to the debt crisis. A recent study by Bela Belassa argues that the "inward-oriented" economies were more vulnerable than "outward-oriented" ones to the external shocks of 1973–82, because the former accumulated more debt and then failed to take strong policy responses when the situation deteriorated.[179]

Second, the debt crisis indicates that core countries are also dependent. Just as the debtor countries are dependent upon the Western banks to obtain development funds, so the banks and indeed the whole Western financial structure have become dependent upon the willingness of the debtor countries not to default on their loans (as they regularly did in the nineteenth century). Although probably in a superior position to the borrowing countries, the banks are surprisingly vulnerable. If even just one of the major debtors were to default or if several debtors formed a cartel and declared a moratorium, a number of large banks might become insolvent, with a general financial panic and loss of faith likely to result in the remaining banks. One lesson of the debt crisis is that the banks and the borrowing countries are at each other's mercy; the debtor countries can default, wreaking havoc upon Western banks, which can then exclude the debtor countries from capital markets, impeding their further development.

A World Systems Paradigm

The Third World's dependency paradigm and the West's modernization paradigm are both incomplete accounts of the history of postwar economic development in the world. The international debt crisis casts doubt on the determinism of both paradigms: development is neither inevitable nor fore-closed. On the other hand the two theories provide certain insights and are in fact complementary views of the same phenomena. One might even say they establish a dialectic suggesting a third, synthetic approach to economic development. Thus the westernization suggested by the modernization paradigm is set against indigenization of the dependency paradigm, suggesting a synthesis of universalization. Not surprisingly, one important new direction for development theory has been toward models based upon the global interdependence of the states of the world community and the need for developmental cooperation.

Global viewpoints became very popular in the 1960s, in part due to ecological and population concerns of the 1960s and the notion of a "global village." Various United Nations' studies, Third World demands for a new international economic order, and worldwide reformist proposals such as those of the Brandt Commission Report presupposed a one-world approach to problem solving.[180] Business school theorists and economists stressed the increasing importance of international trade and multinational corporations as sources of economic integration in the world.[181] What unified all of these views was the realization that there is a world economy that is a structural whole and that the constituent parts are dependent (in varying degrees) on what goes on in the whole.

Immanuel Wallerstein's world systems model is one historical approach to a global interdependence paradigm. Wallerstein (employing Prebisch's core–periphery terminology) argues that the "capitalist world system" was created in the sixteenth century through the emergence of core states in Western Europe which had strong governments and money-based economies dominated by a dynamic bourgeoisie, risk-taking international merchants, and mass-producing industrialists.[182] The capital-oriented dynamism of the entrepreneurial class in those states extends far beyond the political borders of the state and serves as an organizing influence within the arena of the world system it creates. Thus peripheral areas supply cheap labor and raw materials to the industrial network of the core states. "Semiperipheral" (Wallerstein's extension of the terminology) areas have trade and industry but are not the dynamic sectors of the world economy; they are buffers between the dynamic core states and the passive periphery.[183]

Wallerstein's model is obviously heavily influenced by dependency theory but avoids some of the theory's explanatory drawbacks. For one thing, it is not a static analysis: states and areas can move from one arena to another (core to semiperiphery, and vice versa). For example, Wallerstein traces the decline of Spain from core status to the semiperiphery because of its structural socioeconomic weakness in the sixteenth century. Its own repeated debt crises (five defaults on foreign loans between 1550 and 1650) were merely symptoms of its slippage from core to semiperiphery.[184] Wallerstein does not believe it easy for a country to break through to a higher level in the world system, but he says there are, nonetheless, "limited possibilities of transformation within the capitalist world-economy."[185] More important, Wallerstein envisions the possibility of a global change to a socialist world system, which would smooth out many of the malign distributional consequences of the capitalist system.[186] Notwithstanding the problems with core state dominance, Wallerstein's response is not to withdraw from the world system, since it yields many advantages, but to transform the system into a larger cooperative mechanism. By assuming a single world state, the debt crisis could take on entirely new possibilities. The world socialist government could simply tax the banks and the global corporations and redistribute the funds to the indebted areas.

Because Wallerstein's and other global historical approaches to development theory are relatively novel, they require several imaginative leaps to apply them to explain the origins of the international debt crisis. The attempt that follows is simply one way to view the crisis along these theoretical lines, with the hope that the larger view sheds some light on the nature and possible resolution of the crisis. The focus of this global approach is not discrete economic events or structures specific to individual countries, but rather the trends and dislocations that have occurred in the world system and the way in which those large-scale trends and dislocations help explain the origins of the debt crisis.

The thirteen English colonies on the eastern shore of North America were originally part of the world system's colonial periphery in the seventeenth and eighteenth centuries. Late in the eighteenth century, they moved into the semiperiphery, for they had a dynamic middle class, indigenous merchants, and nascent industries. By 1900 the United States was on a par with other core countries, and after World War II it was the preponderant core country in the world. The capitalist world system after 1945 was largely molded by the United States.[187] The liberal norm of free trade and direct foreign investment was adopted in the Bretton Woods Agreements and in the later General Agreement on Tariffs and Trade, not to mention dozens of bilateral commercial treaties entered into by the United States and West European countries with one another and with less developed countries. The United States was the world's largest market, and the leading exporter of manufactured and agricultural goods. The dollar was the keystone of the world financial system, and the international financial institutions established by the Bretton Woods Agreements (IMF, World Bank) provided development assistance, fixed exchange rates, and monitored trade balances.

For more than twenty years, the world system enjoyed this Pax Americana. The United States was the sparkplug and organizing force of the world system, but within that world system there was substantial jockeying for historical position. The countries of Western Europe recovered from the devastations of World War II and remained at the core, albeit clearly subordinate to the United States. In 1956–57 six countries formed the European Economic Community, with the purpose of coordinating their economic and trade policies and creating a substantial internal market that would abet the further recovery and development of the member states' economies. Japan also recovered and joined the core through a very successful policy of using and improving on Western technology through indigenous development.

Just as the West European countries were adapting to a reduced importance in the core and Japan was joining the group of core societies, the periphery of the world system was expanding after World War II to include countries in Africa and the Middle East. Just as the periphery was expanding, many of the countries in the old periphery were themselves attempting to move up to the semiperiphery and ultimately (like Japan) to become core states. Latin American countries, especially Brazil, Mexico, and Argentina, were among the chief newly industrializing countries (NICs) of the period after 1945.[188] The development strategy of the Latin American and other NICs was tied to the capitalist world system led by the United States, with technology and capital coming from U.S. aid and loans, the international financial institutions growing out of the Bretton Woods Agreements, and U.S. multinational corporations. The United States was their chief exporter of capital goods and chief importer of the products of their new industrialization. The NICs were, it is true, dependent upon the United States and other core countries. But, as a historical matter, their strategy was based upon political realities. Absent a revolution and delinking from the world system such as that employed by the People's Republic of China in the 1940s or Cuba in the 1950s (both with mixed success) the NICs were going to be dependent in any event. Given the social structures of the Latin American NICs and (more important) their proximity to the intimidating political and economic power of the United States, a revolutionary delinkage may not have been a plausible strategy in the 1960s and 1970s. Instead, these NICs opted to improve their position in the world system, just as Japan had done after World War II.

More important, the United States was dependent upon the other core countries and the NICs of the semiperiphery for its own continuing position, as events after 1966 established. To the extent that the Bretton Woods system was based upon the convertibility of the dollar into gold *and* continuing U.S. trade deficits, it was bound to become unraveled at some point. That point came in the 1960s, when government deficits to finance the Vietnamese War combined with the trade deficits to trigger an almost twenty-year cycle of inflation.[189] Increasingly vulnerable to international demands that dollars be converted into gold, the United States in 1971 renounced convertibility. The oil price shocks of the 1970s revealed the extent to which the Pax Americana had been dependent upon cheap sources of energy. Growth in the U.S. economy became less impressive; recessions, sometimes combined with high inflation, seemed to characterize the economy in the 1970s, capped off by the major recession after 1979. After 1966 the world system entered into a new period of uncertainty about the economic future, because the sparkplug U.S. economy misfired repeatedly and the international financial stability formerly guaranteed by the United States unraveled.

The dysfunction of the world system after 1966 presented both challenges and opportunities to the NICs. One challenge, obviously, was whether those countries could continue their ascent in the face of higher oil prices, uncertain export markets, and (after 1978) unusually steep real interest rates. Linked to the challenge, though, was the opportunity most of the NICs had to seize the moment—that is, take advantage of the economic uncertainty to assure their rise in the world system, much as Japan had seized the moment after World War II.[190] NICs that met the challenges of the 1970s and exploited the faltering Western economies to improve their own position as exporters of manufactured and technological goods were Taiwan, Singapore, Hong Kong, and South Korea. Other NICs coped with the challenges but failed to move forward in the world system and may even have slipped somewhat because of the oil price dilemma. India, Egypt, and Eastern Europe would be examples of these NICs. A third group of NICs tried to emulate the success of Taiwan, Korea, Hong Kong, and Singapore but overextended themselves and failed. The debt crisis arose out of their historic failure. Most of the Latin American NICs—Mexico, Brazil, Argentina, Venezuela, Chile, Peru—are in this third category of countries, which tried to seize the moment but failed. Their growth has been severely curtailed, and the still-crushing interest and principal payments on their foreign debt may harm their development prospects for the next decade or more.

Historically and descriptively, the international debt crisis is a reflection of failure by many NICs to seize the moment and advance in the world system.[191] In the wake of the external shocks of 1966 to 1982, some countries have continued their ascent; others have fallen back. Why did some countries advance and some countries decline or stagnate? Part of the answer, oddly, may lie in the unique dependency of the advancing NICs. Taiwan and Korea have in some ways benefited from their special relationship with the United States as the result of the latter's resistance to world communism: they have received massive military and economic aid, favorable trade conditions for the critical U.S. market, and important flows of technology.[192] Likewise, their trade ties with Great Britain have provided Hong Kong and Singapore with numerous advantages, including early colonial encouragement and patronage of local entrepreneurs.[193] The "four tigers" are evidence that dependency ties need not stifle, at least in the short run and medium run. But a question then arises. How did the four Asian NICs escape the downside results of dependency that seem to afflict (to some degree) all of the Latin American NICs? Three endogenous reasons are a starting point for explaining why these countries have "succeeded" in the world system, for the time being.

One reason is the role of the state. Bruce Cumings has characterized their governments as "bureaucratic-authoritarian industrializing regimes," in which the state is ubiquitous in the economy and society and relatively autonomous of specific groups and interests.[194] These strong governments have contributed to the rapid industrialization of these states, and their continued success notwithstanding the debt crisis, in two ways. First, in Taiwan, South Korea, and Hong Kong, the state was a tool for indigenous capital accumulation and efficient use. The governments established state enterprises and guided development, but subjected those enterprises to market discipline or even privatized them.[195] Second, the governments of the Asian NICs have responded decisively to external shocks, such as the ones after 1966 (especially 1979–82): measures were taken to prevent currency overvaluation, to contain government spending and public sector deficits, and to turn a profit in the state enterprises.[196] Perhaps the most striking difference between the Latin American NICs and the Asian NICs lies in the degree of political coherence. The latter can make short-term sacrifices that the former typically cannot, because the stronger government structures of the Asian countries enables them to formulate and implement strong policy goals independently of the interests of special groups. In contrast to the shortsighted use of foreign debt simply to postpone hard political choices in Latin America, South Korea and Taiwan used their indebtedness as preparation for growth and made prompt and effective short-term sacrifices in response to unexpected shocks.

Another reason for the relative success of Taiwan, South Korea, Hong Kong, and Singapore is historical. Their special relationships with the United States or Great Britain are historically somewhat lucky, as is their choice of export industry. Much of the economic dynamism in the four tigers has been generated by exports of clothing or textiles.[197] The textile industry is not capital intensive. Thus small entrepreneurs have dominated production, and the role of multinational enterprises has been modest in the countries (with the exception of Singapore).[198] A further advantage is that there has been a relatively sustained demand for textile products from the 1960s onward, although the Asian NICs have already begun to diversify their exports. The point is that the Asian NICs have developed their own entrepreneurial dynamism, which helps them cope with new challenges.

A final contrast between Asian and Latin American NICs is social and cultural. While the judgment is at best an informed impressionistic one, it appears that one component of the success of Asian NICs has been a more equitable distribution of income (in Taiwan, for example, capitalism has actually narrowed income disparities, which were not large originally).[199] And the societies as a whole appear more goal-oriented, hardworking, determined to forge ahead. Herman Kahn, for example, has argued that societies based upon the Confucian ethic of hard work, responsibility and duty, and willingness to cooperate in group endeavors have some advantage in the capitalist world system.[200] These intangible factors have given incentives to groups of society to contribute to the social product (and to make sacrifices in response to crises) and has created a broader internal market. In contrast, the gross inequalities in most of the Latin American countries deprive them of internal markets and kill incentive (not to mention the sociopolitical risks all this entails).[201] In Taiwan, farmers own their land, and agrarian production has been an important support for development. In most of Latin America, landowning is still concentrated in the archaic elites, and the most recent attempt to change that (Allende's nationalization of estates in Chile) met with political upheaval and military reaction.

By focusing on a combination of exogenous and endogenous factors, the world systems model is a more sophisticated tool for explaining the historical dimensions of the international debt crisis. But this historical, descriptive analysis should not obliterate the normative analysis. Like dependency theory, world systems theory sees development in the capitalist system as an exploitive phenomenon—a zero-sum game in which Taiwan's win is Argentina's loss. The role of Wallerstein's semiperiphery is to exploit the periphery and to be exploited by the core. The fairness concerns of dependency theory are sounded anew: the Latin American debtors are participating in a financial system increasingly stacked against them. It may be hard for them to dig out of the debt problem, not only because of the imposing transfer payments they are making to Western banks, but also because they are losing export markets to other NICs, which coped with the debt problem in different ways.

Conclusion

This chapter has presented three contexts in which the international debt problem can be analyzed. The short-term economic perspective focuses on the complex interconnected events and decisions that immediately caused or generated the debt "crisis" starting in 1982. It is a mechanical perspective, and I mean "mechanical" in its benign sense: it seeks to discover what went wrong in an otherwise acceptably operating system. The long-term structuralist perspective is more historical and systematic: it examines the system itself and, in this case, finds that there were certain risks built into the system. The broadest perspective is that of development theory, which views the debt problem as a manifestation of dysfunctions in the way economic subsystems change and interrelate. This perspective is also more explicitly normative, for it wonders whether the system itself is fair and what strategy an economic subsystem might follow in response to its evaluation of its prospects within the existing system.

As is the case with so many other issues of private international law, perspective is important. Different perspectives are appropriate in different circumstances. For example, the bank creditors and their counsel, the borrowing countries and their counsel, and even the national and international financial regulators usually, if not always, think about the international debt problem from a short-term, operational perspective, because their task is simply to deal with the local manifestations of the problem. Indeed, their job should never be underestimated, for it involves not only skill, but also substantial creativity. These day-to-day participants are dealing with a classic legal problem—the debtor does not have enough money to pay all its creditors—to which there is no established legal set of remedies. Hence, the participants have had to create a legal regime of rights and remedies by negotiation. In negotiating restructuring arrangements, the shocks-and-mistakes explanation explored in this chapter is a very useful intellectual construct, for it identifies the reasons individual borrowing countries have been unable to service their external indebtedness, the ways in which the different contributing reasons have interacted, and the basic mechanical policies that will restore the borrowing country to creditworthy status. Unless a fresh disaster strikes (a revolution or new external shocks), classical economic theory underlying the shocks-and-mistakes explanation is a context that will probably prevent a major breakdown in the short term.

The short-term perspective has also been useful in galvanizing large groups of lawyers and economists into action. From 1982 through 1984 the international debt problem has indeed been perceived as a crisis. As country after country felt the external shocks and made similar policy mistakes, the prospect for a system breakdown seemed not remote, and a great quantity of intellectual talent created workable, if imperfect, short-term solutions. The problem, of course, with the short-term economic perspective is that it tends to be too ad hoc, muddling through each situation without trying to generate long-term solutions to entrenched problems. If more of the participants viewed the international debt problem from the longer term structuralist perspective, they might be able to fashion more lasting solutions—and to minimize the prospect of future crises. Thus, thoughtful planners for both the banks and the debtor countries realize that there is a "maximum level of sustainable debt" for each country and that future sovereign lending should be sensitive to such limit.

The structuralist perspective teaches that better recognition of the risks of sovereign lending on the part of the banks and the countries may not be enough to head off future breakdowns, however, because there are powerful incentives within the countries' political systems and the banks' management that will stimulate overlending under certain circumstances. One structural origin of the debt problem is the erosion of the Bretton Woods system of international finance. That system cannot be resuscitated, but new thought should be directed at increasing the role of multilateral institutions in international sovereign lending and controlling the role of the banks. The international debt problem is a policy "crisis" for international finance, because it dramatizes the insufficient direction for sovereign lending and borrowing in the post–Bretton Woods era.

The first two perspectives of the international debt problem are from within the existing system of finance and development that have been molded by Western thinkers, institutions, and ideas. The third perspective looks at the system itself and asks whether it is coherent and fair and useful. Inspired by a *New Yorker* cover, sociologist and development theorist Andre Gunder Frank asserted in his essay the *Sociology of Development* that the modernization paradigm which has been the basis of most Latin American development policy and Western capital transfers revolves around "twin gods"— Santa Claus and Sigmund Freud.[202] Underdeveloped countries in the South achieve economic development, first, by receiving gifts from the friendly Santa Claus of the North and, second, by learning the lessons taught by Sigmund Freud, such as improvement by self-examination. The international debt problem has exposed the wishful thinking involved in this modern bit of mythology. Santa Claus has only delivered thistles to Latin America lately, and Freudian self-analysis provides little solace when these countries are making outrageous sacrifices due in large part to events beyond their control (the shocks, the mildly irrational behavior of the Western system of international finance). According to the development perspective, the crisis is the questioning anew of the received wisdom about how countries develop and whether in the capitalist world system there is much prospect for improvement of the lives of most people in the world.

In early 1984 an idea occurred to several Latin American political leaders. There is an international debt problem or crisis only if we recognize the legitimacy of paying unprecedented real rates of interest on loans fueled by transfer payments from our own productive capacity. It makes no sense for our people to pay out more money to the banks than we achieve as a current accounts surplus after cutting imports to the bone and expanding exports to our breaking point. The leaders discussed forming a debtors' cartel and declaring unilateral moratoria on servicing their loans. Westerners for whom the modernization paradigm (Santa Claus and Sigmund Freud) is the only conceivable view of development were unnecessarily dismissive of this idea. And the more accommodating approach of Latin American leaders and the banks themselves suggest that this is not an idea whose time has come. But it is an idea whose time might come.

Notes

1. The IMF uses the term *nonoil developing countries* (NODCs) to include those countries whose oil exports do not constitute two-thirds of the country's total exports or whose oil exports are less than 100 million barrels per year. (Even though Mexico and Venezuela have been net oil exporters and the oil exports constitute more than two-thirds of their total exports in the 1980s, those countries, too, will be included as NODCs.)

2. Like most of the other "statistics" used in this chapter, the ones in text are approximations gathered by transnational organizations such as the IMF. Different numbers will be reported by different sources. For slightly different estimates of Latin American debt, compiled at about the same time, see "Latin America Moving away

from Brink of Debt Crisis," *Washington Post*, January 20, 1985, p. H6, cols. 3–6; "Bankers, Preparing for 1985 Debt Talks with Third World, Are Warned Not to Let 1984's Successes Go to Their Heads," *Wall Street Journal*, December 28, 1984, p. 16, cols. 1, 2.

3. See International Financial Markets and Related Problems: Hearings Before the House Committee on Banking, Finance and Urban Affairs, 98th Cong., 1st sess. (1983), pp. 73–77. Paul Volcker, chairman of the Board of Governors of the Federal Reserve System, as of June 1982 testified that claims on NODCs by the nine largest U.S. banks constituted 10.6 percent of total assets, 222 percent of total capital; claims on Argentina, Brazil, Mexico constituted 112.5 percent of total capital. [Cited hereafter as International Financial Markets Hearings.]

4. See Andrew Quale, chapter 7 of this book.

5. William Cline, *International Debt: Systemic Risk and Policy Response* (Washington, D.C.: Institute for International Economics, 1984), pp. 8–11; see Cline, *International Debt and the Stability of the World Economy* (Cambridge: MIT Press, 1983), pp. 20–22.

6. These responses and the following discussion in text are based upon World Bank, *World Development Report* (Washington, D.C.: World Bank, 1984), p. 25.

7. This distinction between upper-income, lower-income, and middle-income developing countries is based on that in Organisation for Economic Co-operation and Development, *External Debt of Developing Countries: 1983 Survey* (Paris: OECD, 1984), pp. 10–11, 49.

8. According to World Bank, *World Debt Tables* (Washington, D.C.: World Bank, 1983), p. viii, 80 percent of NODC debt in 1982 was owed or guaranteed by the state. According to "New Debt Repayment Terms Expected," *Washington Post*, August 29, 1984, p. D8, cols. 3–4, almost 70 percent of the Latin American external debt in 1984 was owed by the public sector.

9. See Staff of Subcommittee on Foreign Economic Policy of the Senate Committee on Foreign Relations, 95th Cong., 1st sess., "International Debt, the Banks, and U.S. Foreign Policy" (1977), pp. 49–51; Pierre Dhonte, *Clockwork Debt: Trade and the External Debt of Developing Countries* (Lexington, Mass.: Lexington Books, 1979), p. 45; [Secretary of Treasury] Regan, "The United States and The World's Debt Problem," *Wall Street Journal*, February 8, 1983, p. 32, col. 3.

10. Real interest rates in the United States on indebtedness between 1976 and 1980 were as follows:

Year	Long-term Debt (%)	Short-term Debt (%)
1976	2.3	− 0.2
1977	1.5	− 0.5
1978	0.9	− 0.2
1979	0.7	1.3
1980	2.1	2.1

Source: IMF, *World Economic Outlook* (1984):120–21, tables 2.6, 2.7.

11. Thomas Enders and Richard Mattione, *Latin America: The Crisis of Debt and Growth*, Studies in International Economics (Washington, D.C.: Brookings Institution, 1984), pp. 7–9, table 1; p. 65, appendix table B–6.

12. See Irving S. Friedman, *The World Debt Dilemma: Managing Country Risk* (Philadelphia: Council for International Banking Studies, 1983), pp. 27–50, 63–74.

13. For example, "Mideast Oil Money Proves Burdensome," *Wall Street Journal*, June 6, 1974, pp. 1, 29, contrasts the caution of Chase Manhattan's David Rockefeller with the optimism of Citibank's Walter Wriston.

14. That is, the current account deficits of the NODCs had been exceeded by huge surpluses for most of the OPEC states, which deposited most of their revenues in U.S. and European banks. Conventional sources of loan opportunities, such as mortgages and business expansion, were not readily available, especially during the recession of 1974–75.

15. See generally Darrell Delamaide, *Debt Shock: The Full Story of the World Credit Crisis* (New York: Doubleday, 1984), pp. 34–37; Lewis Solomon, "Developing Nations and Commercial Banks: The New Dependency," *Journal of International Law and Economics* 12 (1976):325, 326–34.

16. Delamaide, *Debt Shock*, pp. 43–45.

17. For an interesting personal account, see Louis Schirano, chapter 2 of this book.

18. See International Financial Markets Hearings, pp. 381, 386 for a statement by Richard Dale of the Brookings Institution. Exposure of eight leading U.S. banks to Argentina, Brazil, Mexico, and Venezuela on January 1, 1984, ranged from Continental Illinois' 83.9 percent of capital to Citicorp's 154.3 percent to Manufacturers Hanover's 200.3 percent. *The Latin American Times*, no. 58, April 16, 1984, p. 8.

19. In 1979 the federal regulators instituted the Interagency Country Exposure Review Committee (ICERC), which was charged with administering a new system for evaluating country risk. The system had four elements: (1) assessing and reporting the country exposures of each bank, (2) evaluating the banks' internal systems for reviewing country risk, (3) classifying the credit risk of countries whose external payments have been (or are likely to be) interrupted, (4) commenting on the risks associated with each bank's large exposures in particular countries (International Financial Markets Hearings, pp. 53–54, 84–89). The ICERC had virtually no effect, it appears, on the escalating foreign sovereign debt, in part because its guidelines were only hortatory, too timid, and too late in the cycle of lending.

20. In response to congressional dissatisfaction with previous efforts, the regulators submitted a Joint Memorandum on a Program for Improved Supervision and Regulation of International Lending, reprinted in Proposed Solutions to International Debt Problems: Hearing Before the Senate Committee on Banking, Housing and Urban Affairs, 98th Cong., 1st sess. (1983), pp. 24–52. The joint memorandum proposed a five-point plan: (1) strengthening the existing program of country risk evaluation, (2) increased disclosure of banks' country exposures, (3) a system of special reserves for questionable foreign loans, (4) new rules for fee accounting, and (5) improving international financial cooperation (pp. 25–26). Congress embodied most of the regulators' proposals in the International Lending Supervision Act of 1983, Public Law 98-181, 97 Stat. 1153, codified at 12 U.S.C. §§ 3901–3912. See Cynthia Lichtenstein, chapter 8 of this book.

21. [Former Brazilian Planning Minister] Mario Henrique Simonsen, *The Financial Crisis in Latin America* (Rio de Janeiro: Getúlio Vargas Foundation, 1983), suggests that so long as the rate of export growth is greater than the interest rate, debt servicing problems should not develop. Under this criterion, NODCs in general and Latin

American countries in particular were not in trouble in the late 1970s (see appendix B, table B–5). Although this approach has been utilized by some leading commentators (for example, Cline, *International Debt*, pp. 6–8), it is not completely satisfactory because it assumes that no new borrowing occurs in the given year. When the country is pretty much committed to borrowing more money each year, and the existing debt must be serviced at the current interest rate, an export growth rate exceeding the interest rate does not suggest that the country has no problems.

22. Roger Kubarych, chapter 1 of this book.

23. 1983 OECD Survey, pp. 37–38.

24. Fifty-six percent of LDC debt and 58 percent of debt service payments were in dollars for 1981–83 (ibid., p. 39). Although 10 percent or more of the overall international syndicated financing in 1980 was accomplished in currencies other than the dollar, only 1.4 percent of the syndicated loans to the five main NODC borrowers (Mexico, Brazil, Argentina, Korea, the Philippines) were made in such currencies, according to Andrew Mohl and Dorothy Sobol, "Currency Diversification and LDC Debt," *Federal Reserve Bank of New York Quarterly Review* (Autumn 1983), p. 19, note 1. (The Mohl and Sobol article is reprinted as appendix A of this book.)

25. Samuel Lichtensztejn and José Manuel Quijano, "The External Indebtedness of the Developing Countries to International Private Banks," in J.C. Sánchez Arnau, ed., *Debt and Development* (New York: Praeger Publishers, 1982), pp. 185, 208–09. The debt obtained on the Eurocurrency market showed a remarkable shortening of maturities; while 62.5 percent of the loans to developing countries had maturities greater than seven years in 1974, only 8.6 percent had such maturities in 1977 (only 5.0 percent and 4.7 percent had such maturities in 1975 and 1976, respectively). Ibid., p. 209, table 11.

26. See ibid., p. 214, table 13, which shows a commitment fee payable on that part of the loan which has not been made during the preloan period, 0.5 percent per annum; a participation fee to banks in the syndicate, 0.625 percent; and a management fee to the managing bank or agent, 0.375 percent per annum are typical extra fees charged NODCs by commercial banks.

27. *Latin America's External Indebtedness: Present Situation and Prospects* (Washington, D.C.: Inter-American Development Bank, 1977), p. 25.

28. IMF, *World Economic Outlook* (1982), p. 173.

29. Cline, *International Debt*, pp. 11–12.

30. IMF, *Annual Report 1983* (Washington, D.C.: International Monetary Fund, 1984), pp. 26–27, chart 10.

31. IMF, *World Economic Outlook* (1983), p. 170, table 1.

32. Cline, *International Debt*, p. 13.

33. IMF, *International Financial Statistics* (May 1983):56–57.

34. Cline, *International Debt*, p. 13. The specific line items, according to his table 1.4 (in billions of U.S. dollars), are: $260 billion for oil price increases in excess of inflation, $41 billion for interest rates higher than the 1961–80 average, $79 billion in terms of trade loss, and $21 billion due to lower export volume as a result of the world recession.

35. See appendix A.

36. Enders and Mattione, *Latin America*, p. 16, table 3, and p. 19, table 4.

37. Bela Belassa and Desmond McCarthy, *Adjustment Policies in Developing Countries 1979–82*, April 15, 1983, conclude that "[t]he benefits Mexico derived

from improvements in its terms of trade, resulting from higher petroleum prices, were offset by the adverse effects of the slowdown of world demand for its exports," while Enders and Mattione (*Latin America*, p. 19, table 4) conclude that Mexico suffered no adverse effects in its nonoil exports. Both studies found substantial adverse effects as a result of higher interest rates. The different conclusions with regard to Peru are minor; Belassa and McCarthy found no adverse shocks in 1979–80, but a 2 percent shock in 1981. In contrast, Enders and Mattione concluded that Peru came out slightly ahead in the period 1979–82.

38. Discussion of policies to be followed by NODCs may be found in Belassa and McCarthy, *Adjustment Policies*, pp. 6–9; IMF, *Annual Report 1983*, pp. 34, 42–43.

39. According to Enders and Mattione, *Latin America*, p. 20, table 5, Argentina suffered a negative shock of $13.4 billion, which was compounded by capital flight of $14.3 billion between 1979 and 1982. Mexico felt a positive shock of $11.7 billion, which was erased by capital flight amount to $18.7 billion. Venezuela's positive shock ($19.1 billion) was not offset by capital flight of $13.0 billion. Roger Kubarych (chapter 1) estimates that 40 percent of all bank lending from 1979 to the end of 1981 ($40–$50 billion) may have ended up as capital outflows from the debtor countries.

40. Enders and Mattione, *Latin America*, p. 22.

41. Commercial bank lending to developing countries fell by $23 billion in 1982, with the main Latin American borrowers (Mexico, Brazil, Argentina, Chile) being hit hardest. See World Bank, *Debt and the Developing World: Current Trends and Prospects* (Washington, D.C.: World Bank, 1984), an abridged version of *World Debt Tables*, 1983–84 edition.

42. The consequences of Mexico's development policies from 1979 to 1982 are explored in more detail in Ariel Buira, "The Exchange Crisis and the Adjustment Program in Mexico," in John Williamson, ed., *Prospects for Adjustment in Argentina, Brazil, and Mexico: Responding to the Debt Crisis* (Washington, D.C.: Institute for International Economics, 1983), p. 51.

43. Details of the 1982–83 restructuring of Mexico's external debt may be found in Joseph Kraft, *The Mexican Rescue* (New York: Group of Thirty, 1984); Enrique Tapia, "Mexico's Debt Restructuring: The Evolving Solution," *Columbia Journal of Transnational Law* 23 (1984):1.

44. Argentina's problems are explored in more detail in José Pastore, "Progress and Prospects for the Adjustment Program in Argentina," in Williamson, ed., *Prospects for Adjustment in Argentina, Brazil, and Mexico*, p. 7.

45. The 1983 restructuring is described in "Stand-By Arrangement, Compensatory Financing Approved for Argentina," *IMF Survey* (February 7, 1983):38–39.

46. See "Argentina Gets Loan from IMF of $1.66 Billion," *Wall Street Journal*, December 31, 1984, p. 12, col. 1; "Bankers Said Skeptical of Argentina Plan," *Washington Post*, December 4, 1984, p. E1, col. 2.

47. See Cline, *International Debt*, p. 18.

48. See Enders and Mattione, *Latin America*, pp. 23–24; Belassa and McCarthy, *Adjustment Policies in Developing Countries*, table and notes dealing with Brazil's adjustment to external shocks; Carlos Diaz-Alejandro, "Some Aspects of the 1982–83 Brazilian Payments Crisis," *Brookings Papers on Economic Activity* (1983):515, for excellent analysis of the economic background.

49. See Edmar Bacha, "The IMF and the Prospects for Adjustment in Brazil," in Williamson, ed., *Prospects for Adjustment in Argentina, Brazil, and Mexico*, pp. 31,

32–33; "Fund Approves Package of Assistance for Brazil Totaling SDR 5 Billion," *IMF Survey* (March 7, 1983):65, 76.

50. See "Brazil Gets $6.5 Billion in New Loans," *New York Times*, January 28, 1984.

51. For these countries, the pattern was similar to that in Argentina, Brazil, and Mexico: external shocks, failure to cope, resultant inflation and (sometimes) capital flight, drying up of new bank credits, confession of inability to service debts, a rescue package by the IMF, the banks, and (sometimes) the U.S. government. Thus Chile was a severe disadjuster, following a highly expansionistic growth policy until 1981, fueled mainly by foreign debt (since domestic saving was very low). Highly overvalued exchange rates led to capital flight and undermined the country's export position. As a result, credit dried up in 1982 (this would probably have occurred even without the Mexican and Argentine problems), and agreements for new loans and rescheduled debt were made with the IMF and the banks in 1983. See Enders and Mattione, *Latin America*, pp. 25–26.

   Although Peru had small positive results from the external shocks, they were overwhelmed by other adverse developments in 1982, including an overvalued currency, excessive public sector deficits and the resulting inflation, disappointing export growth caused in part by natural disaster (El Niño), and limited availability of new credit. In the summer of 1983, Peru obtained $830 million in commercial bank financing (new money plus rescheduled debts), together with $1 billion through the Paris Club's rescheduling of official indebtedness. See ibid., p. 29.

52. See Cline, *International Debt*, p. 18.

53. Charles P. Kindleberger, *Manias, Panics and Crashes: A History of Financial Crises* (New York: Basic Books, 1978).

54. Thus, £ 21 million was on loan to the newly independent Latin American states by 1825, and the foreign indebtedness continued to grow during the century (generally in the form of bonds, not bank loans). Despite regular defaults on the debt (especially a massive one in the 1870s), British investment in Latin America stood at £ 179.5 million in 1880 (£ 123 million invested in state bonds) and £ 995.3 million in 1913 (£ 314.3 million in state bonds). Overall, Latin America has been the largest consumer of industrial country capital in both the nineteenth and twentieth centuries. See Georges Corm, "The Indebtedness of the Developing Countries: Origins and Mechanisms," in Sánchez Arnau, ed., *Debt and Development,* pp. 15; 29–35; 45, table 5.

55. Major sources for my discussion of Latin American sociopolitical evolution and for the general information in table 3–1 are David S. Palmer, *Peru: The Authoritarian Tradition* (New York: Praeger Publishers, 1980), pp. 26–33; Thomas E. Skidmore and Peter H. Smith, *Modern Latin America* (New York: Oxford University Press, 1984), pp. 46–70, esp. table 2.1; Gary W. Wynia, *The Politics of Latin American Development*, 2d ed. (New York: Cambridge University Press, 1984); Howard Wiarda and Harvey F. Kline, "The Latin American Tradition and Process of Development," in Wiarda and Kline, eds., *Latin American Politics and Development* (Boston: Houghton Mifflin, 1979), p. 1. The basic point of Wiarda and Kline's study is that Latin American society has evolved in fundamentally different ways from North American society since the seventeenth century. Their table 2.1, on p. 23, ibid., shows the following:

Latin America	North America
Authoritarian, absolutist, centralized, corporatist	More liberal, early steps to representative rule
Catholic and orthodox	Protestant and pluralist
Feudal, mercantilist, patrimonialist	Capitalist and entre- preneurial
Hierarchical, two-class stratified, rigid	More mobil and multiclass
Scholastic, rote memory, deductive	Empirical, scientific, inductive

56. On Latin American modernization before 1930, see generally Roberto Conde, *The First Stages of Modernization in Spanish America*, translated by T. Talbot (New York: Harper & Row, 1974); see Palmer, *Peru*, pp. 18–67, with emphasis on Peru, but general analysis of Spanish America as well; J.F. Rippy, *British Investment in Latin America, 1822–1949* (Salem, N.H.: Ayer, 1977).

57. The discussion in the text is the chronology of main political events in se-lected Latin American countries after 1930, presented in appendix C. Wynia, *Politics of Latin American Development*, and Wiarda and Kline, "Latin American Tradition, pp. 30–40, provide a good analysis of the major sociopolitical changes discussed in the text paragraph.

58. In countries following this model, the society is dominated by elites that ac-cept democratic institutions unless they threaten the elites' vital interests. Elections may be held, but democratic governments are punctuated by military coups when the government challenges a vested interest or appears incapable of managing the country. After several years of authoritarian government, there may be another coup, or new elections may be held. See Samuel Huntington, "Will More Countries Become Demo-cratic?" *Political Science Quarterly* 99 (1984): 193, 210, who develops a cyclical model and argues that it can pose real obstacles to long term democratic institutions; Roett, chapter 9, applies the cyclical model to Latin America.

59. See appendix C for a chronology of transitions in Brazilian politics. On Brazil's political history after 1930, see, for example, Peter Flynn, *Brazil: A Political Analysis* (Boulder: Westview Press, 1978) [political history 1889–1977]; Ronald M. Schneider, *The Political System of Brazil: Emergence of a "Modernizing" Authori-tarian Regime, 1964–1970* (New York: Columbia University Press, 1971); Thomas E. Skidmore, *Politics in Brazil, 1930–1964: An Experiment in Democracy* (New York: Oxford University Press, 1967).

60. See appendix C for a chronology of transitions with politics of these coun-tries. For historical and political analyses of individual countries, see, for example, Robert J. Alexander, *Bolivia: Past, Present, and Future of Its Politics* (New York: Praeger Publishers, 1982); Robert Heller Dix, *Colombia: The Political Dimensions of Change* (New Haven: Yale University Press, 1967); Daniel H. Levine, *Conflict and Political Change in Venezuela* (Princeton: Princeton University Press, 1973); Leo Lott, *Venezuela and Paraguay: Political Modernity and Tradition in Conflict* (New York:

Holt, Rinehart & Winston, 1972); John D. Martz, *Ecuador: Conflicting Political Culture and the Quest for Progress* (Boston: Allyn & Bacon, 1972); Palmer, *Peru*; Peter H. Smith, *Argentina and the Failure of Democracy: Conflict among Political Elites* (Madison: University of Wisconsin Press, 1974); Peter G. Snow, *Political Forces in Argentina* (New York: Praeger Publishers, 1979); Martin Weinstein, *Uruguay: The Politics of Failure* (Westport: Greenwood Press, 1975).

61. For Mexico, see Judith Adler Hellman, *Mexico in Crisis*, 2d ed. (New York: Holmes & Meier Publishers, 1983); Roberto G. Newell and Luis F. Rubio, *Mexico's Dilemma: The Political Origins of Economic Crisis* (Boulder: Westview Press, 1984); Leon Vincent Padgett, *The Mexican Political System*, 2d ed. (Boston: Houghton Mifflin, 1976). For Chile, see Barbara Stallings, *Class Conflict and Economic Development in Chile, 1958–1973* (Stanford: Stanford University Press, 1978); see also Brian Loveman, *Chile: The Legacy of Hispanic Capitalism* (New York: Oxford University Press, 1979).

62. See Lott, *Venezuela and Paraguay*; Thomas W. Walker, *Nicaragua: The Land of Sandino* (Boulder: Westview Press, 1981).

63. See Samuel Huntington, "Will More Countries Become Democratic?", p. 210, which shows that the authoritarian–democratic cycle *is* the system; change is the norm.

64. This has been called the "living museum effect": before a new group can participate in the political process, it must show the established elites that it is powerful and is willing to respect the rights of already established groups. See Charles Anderson, *Politics and Economic Change in Latin America* (Princeton: D. Van Nostrand, 1967). Thus the power structures will either co-opt the rising group or will repress it. The third alternative is a genuine social revolution such as that in Cuba of 1958. See Wiarda and Kline, "Latin American Tradition," p. 42.

65. See Wiarda and Kline, pp. 81–82; Philippe Schmitter, "Military Intervention, Political Competitiveness, and Public Policy in Latin America: 1950–1967," in Abraham Lowenthal ed., *Armies and Politics in Latin America* (New York: Holmes & Meier Publishers, 1976), p. 120.

66. See Newell and Rubio, *Mexico's Dilemma*, pp. 121–26; Raymond Vernon, *The Dilemma of Mexico's Development: The Roles of the Private and Public Sectors* (Cambridge: Harvard University Press, 1963), pp. 188–93.

67. Some useful sources on the political and socioeconomic forces that contributed to Allende's overthrow include Jean Carrière, *Landowners and Politics in Chile: A Study of the "Sociedad Nacional de Agricultura" 1932–1970* (Amsterdam: Centrum Voor Studie en Documentatie Van Latijns Amerika, 1981); Kenneth Medhurst, ed., *Allende's Chile* (London: Hart-Davis MacGibbon, 1972); Sandro Sideri, ed., *Chile 1970–73: Economic Development and Its International Setting* (Hingham, Mass.: Kluwer Academic Publishers, 1979).

68. The typical pattern is the following: (1) The middle class became increasingly important in the early twentieth century, and the Depression gave them intellectual force by discrediting the oligarchs' policies. (2) The Depression was an economic blow to the country, but it also provided incentives for local industry to develop, potentially a source for new economic growth opportunities. (3) Between 1945 and 1955, rapid growth based on import substitution began. At some point in the 1950s, the government moved from encouragement to active financial involvement in industrial development.

For specific country patterns, see the following references: R. Loring Allen, *Venezuelan Economic Development: A Politico-Economic Analysis* (Greenwich: Jai Press, 1977), pp. 103–13, which shows that Venezuela had a high growth rate from 1950 to 1957, recession from 1958 to 1962, and uneven growth from 1962 to 1975; Markos Mamalakis, *The Growth and Structure of the Chilean Economy: From Independence to Allende* (New York: Yale University Press, 1976), pp. 89–99, which describes the struggling Chilean economy from 1930 to 1955, after which major growth gains were registered in Chile; Palmer, *Peru*, pp. 85–93; Luiz Bresser Pereira, *Development and Crisis in Brazil, 1930–1983* (Boulder, Colo.: Westview Press, 1984), pp. 9–13, 15–19; Donald Syvrud, *Foundations for Brazilian Economic Growth* (Stanford: Hoover Institution Press, 1974), pp. 12–41 for the ideology of growth-controlled government policy after 1940s, with steady growth until 1962–64 slump.

69. See generally United Nations, *The Economic Development of Latin America in the Post-War Period* (New York: The United Nations, 1964); Skidmore and Smith, *Modern Latin America*, pp. 51–64; Wynia, *The Politics of Latin American Development*, pp. 111, 128–29.

70. See Newell and Rubio, *Mexico's Dilemma*, p. 158, graph VI-1, which shows that Mexico's GDP grew in constant prices at an average annual rate of 6.8 percent between 1958 and 1970; Manuel Gollas, "External Debt and Economic Growth: Mexico," in Antonio Jorge, Jorge Salazar-Carillo, and Rene Higonnet, eds., *Foreign Debt and Latin American Economic Development* (Elmsford, N.Y.: Pergamon Press, 1983), pp. 139, 141, table 1, which shows that Mexico's GDP grew at an average annual rate of 9.2 percent in 1954–55, 6.7 percent in 1956–70, and 5.3 percent in 1971–72.

71. See Werner Baer, "The Brazilian Growth and Development Experience: 1961–1975," in Riordan Roett, ed., *Brazil in the Seventies* (Washington, D.C.: American Enterprise Institute for Public Policy Research, 1976), pp. 41, 47, table 1, which shows that Brazil's GDP grew 9.3 percent in 1968, 9.0 percent in 1969, 9.5 percent in 1970, 11.3 percent in 1971, 10.4 percent in 1972, and 11.4 percent in 1973.

72. According to Mamalakis, *Chilean Economy*, p. 92, Chile's growth was 3.7 percent from 1950 to 1954; 3.9 percent from 1955 to 1960; 5.4 percent from 1960 to 1965. See Wynia, *Politics of Latin American Development*, p. 200, on Venezuela. According to Mary Sutton, "Stucturalism: The Latin American Record & the New Critique," in Tony Killick, ed., *The IMF and Stabilization: Developing Country Experiences* (New York: St. Martin's Press, 1984), p. 19, table 2.1, and p. 27, table 2.5, Chile's GDP growth after 1964 ranged from 6.9 percent in 1966 to 11.2 percent in 1975; Peru's GDP growth ranged from 0 percent in 1968 to 6.9 percent in 1974.

73. See Douglas Graham, "Mexican and Brazilian Economic Development: Legacies, Patterns, and Performance," in Sylvia Hewlett and Richard Weinert, eds., *Brazil and Mexico: Patterns in Late Development* (Philadelphia: Institute for the Study of Human Issues, 1982), p. 13; p. 21, table 3.

74. Luiz Bresser Pereira has shown that import substitution was the basic development strategy for Brazil between 1930 and 1961 and has generated a model of development based upon this strategy: (1) The needs of the domestic market, limitations on import capacity (war, tariffs), and governmental stimuli create possibilities for import substitution. (2) The government builds an infrastructure of transportation, communication, and education. (3) Entrepreneurs take advantage of the import sub-

stitution possibilities and whatever infrastructure the country has and enter into a business that can displace existing imports. (4) The indigenous import substitution businesses are very successful (high profits). Investment was channeled into sectors offering the highest and most rapid return on investment—in which a relatively small investment yields large increases in production. (5) Industrial growth attracts more people to the urban areas and produces higher wages and increased consumption. See Pereira, *Development and Crisis in Brazil*, p. 32–44; p. 45, figure 2.1.

75. Stefan Robock, *Brazil: A Study in Development Progress* (Lexington, Mass.: Lexington Books, 1975), pp. 158–63; after 1964, "Brazil became a technocratic government under military guardianship" (p. 153). This incident was representative of a larger phenomenon: the *embourgeoisement* of the military. After World War II, an increasing number of military officers came from middle class backgrounds (or adopted middle class points of view). Hence, many of the military coups of the 1960s were inspired by essentially middle class growth aspirations. See David G. Becker, *The New Bourgeoisie and the Limits of Dependency: Mining, Class, and Power in "Revolutionary" Peru* (Princeton: Princeton University Press, 1983); José Nun, "The Middle Class Military Coup," in Claudio Veliz, ed., *The Politics of Conformity in Latin America* (London: Oxford University Press, 1967), p. 66.

76. See Baer, "Brazilian Growth and Development Experience," p. 48, table 2; William Cline, "Brazil's Emerging International Economic Role," in *Brazil in the Seventies*, p. 63, places the shift to export expansion in 1967–68.

77. See Pereira, *Development and Crisis in Brazil*, pp. 152–58.

78. See appendix C for a chronology of the shifts from authoritarian to democratic rule in Argentina, Bolivia, Brazil, Ecuador, El Salvador, Guatemala, Honduras, Panama, Peru, and Uruguay.

79. See Pereira, *Development and Crisis in Brazil*, pp. 37–40; Werner Baer, Isaac Kerstensetzky, and Annibal Villela, "The Changing Role of the State in the Brazilian Economy," *World Development* (November 1973):23; Graham, "Mexican and Brazilian Economic Development," pp. 31–33.

80. See Jean-Louis Reiffers, *Transnational Corporations and Endogenous Development: Effects on Culture, Communication, and Science and Technology* (New York: Unipub, 1982), pp. 23–24.

81. For standard authorities preaching this gospel, see, for example, Charles Kindleberger, *International Economics*, 4th ed. (Homewood, Ill.: Richard D. Irwin, 1968), pp. 483–85; Paul A. Samuelson, *Economics*, 7th ed. (New York: McGraw-Hill, 1967), pp. 636–40; Susan Strange, "Debt and Default in the International Political Economy," in Jonathan D. Aronson, ed., *Debt and the Less Developed Countries* (Boulder, Colo.: Westview Press, 1979), pp. 7, 8.

82. According to Graham, "Mexican and Brazilian Economic Development," p. 28, foreign debt was 1.04 times direct foreign investment in Mexico in 1967, 2.51 in 1975; comparable ratios for Brazil are 0.95 in 1967, 1.50 in 1975. See Albert Fishlow, "Latin America's Debt: Problem or Solution," *Columbia Journal of World Business* (Spring 1982):35, 36.

83. Pereira, *Development and Crisis in Brazil*, pp. 170–72. Note, though, that debt as a fraction of GDP actually declined in 1971–73, due to the large growth rate, which offset the increase in debt (ibid., p. 172, table 8.5). See also Philip Wellons,

"Brazil: Financing the Miracle," in Wellons, *World Economy and Credit: The Crisis and Its Causes* (Cambridge, Mass.: Harvard University Press, 1983), pp. 3, 15, where Brazil is claimed to be better off due to external borrowing.

84. Kindleberger, *Manias, Panics and Crashes*, pp. 41–54, 78–96, 107–15; see Charles Kindleberger, "Debt Situation of the Developing Countries in Historical Perspective," paper delivered at a symposium sponsored by Eximbank, April 21, 1977, reprinted in Stephen H. Goodman, ed., *Financing and Risk in Developing Countries* (New York: Praeger Publishers, 1977), p. 3; Jonathan Aronson, "The Politics of Private Bank Lending and Debt Renegotiations," in Aronson, ed., *Debt and the Less Developed Countries*, pp. 283–84.

85. A useful summary of the creation, rise, and fall of the Bretton Woods Agreements can be found in Michael Moffitt, *The World's Money: International Banking from Bretton Woods to the Brink of Insolvency* (New York: Simon & Schuster, 1983), pp. 13–40. See also Jonathan Aronson, *Money and Power: Banks and the World Monetary System* (Beverly Hills, Calif.: Sage Publications, 1978). The roles of the IMF and the World Bank are described in Robert Ayres, *Banking on the Poor: The World Bank and World Poverty* (Cambridge: MIT Press, 1983); John Williamson, *The Lending Policies of the International Monetary Fund* (Washington, D.C.: Institute for International Economics, 1982).

86. See Albert Cizauskas, "International Debt Renegotiation: Lessons from the Past," *World Development* 7 (1979):199.

87. See generally Delamaide, *Debt Shock*, pp. 38–40; Moffitt, *World's Money*, pp. 29–40, tracing the process by which the burdens on the United States imposed by the Bretton Woods Agreements became too great, from 1960 to 1971.

88. Preface, David Bigman and Teizo Taya, eds., *Floating Exchange Rates and the State of World Trade Payments* (Cambridge, Mass.: Ballinger Publishing, 1984), p. v; see Tamir Agmon, Robert Hawkins, and Richard Levich, Introduction, in Agmon, Hawkins, and Levich, eds., *The Future of the International Monetary System* (Lexington, Mass.: Lexington Books, 1983), pp. 1, 2–3.

89. Moffitt, *World's Money*, p. 44.

90. See House Committee on Banking, Finance and Urban Affairs, 96th Cong., 1st sess., The Operations of U.S. Banks in the International Capital Markets (1979), p. 8; Aronson, *Money and Power*, ch. 4.

91. See Moffitt, *World's Money*, p. 50. A distillation of table 7–2 of J. Andrew Spindler, ed., *The Politics of International Credit: Private Finance and Foreign Policy in Germany and Japan* (Washington, D.C.: Brookings Institution, 1984), p. 187, shows the progression of overseas banking from 95 foreign branches in 1950 to 211 in 1965 (assets: $8.9 billion) to 532 in 1970 (assets: $52.6 billion) to 900 in 1982 (assets: $388.5 billion).

92. See Delamaide, *Debt Shock*, pp. 41–42.

93. Created in the 1950s, the Eurodollar market grew at a compound annual rate of 37 percent between 1965 and 1971, in large part because of the tax incentives for keeping dollars abroad noted in text. According to Philip Wellons, "International Banks and Balance of Payments Finance in the Mid-1970s," in Wellons, *World Money and Credit*, p. 23, p. 59, Table A, the Eurodollar market expanded from $145 billion in 1971 to $305 billion in 1973 to $565 billion in 1976 to $1155 billion by December 1979. By June 1980, the Euromarket was $1270 billion.

94. Moffitt, *World's Money*, at 55; on p. 56. Moffitt says that Wriston epitomized the new breed of international bankers. See also Delamaide, *Debt Shock*.

95. See Moffitt, *World's Money*, p. 52, table 1, for specific profit figures for top ten multinational banks, broken down into domestic and international segments. International earnings as a percentage of total earnings increased from 17.5 percent for the top ten U.S. banks in 1970 to 50.8 percent in 1976, before falling back to 48.0 percent in 1981 (p. 53, table 2).

96. Group of Thirty, *Risks in International Bank Lending* (New York: Group of Thirty, 1982), p. 6.

97. See Richard Nisbett and Lee Ross, *Human Inferences: Strategies and Short-comings of Social Judgment* (Englewood Cliffs, N.J.: Prentice-Hall, 1980), pp. 45–60; Amos Tversky and Daniel Kahneman, "Judgment under Uncertainty: Heuristics and Biases," *Science 185* (1974):1124, reprinted in Daniel Kahneman, Paul Slovic, and Amos Tversky, eds., *Judgment under Uncertainty: Heuristics and Biases* (Cambridge: Cambridge University Press, 1982), p. 3; see also James March and Herbert Simon, *Organizations* (New York: Wiley, 1958), which points out that institutions and companies are subject to many of the same decision-making biases as individuals are.

98. See Nisbett and Ross, *Human Inferences*, pp. 17–28, 37–42; Tversky and Kahneman, "Judgment under Uncertainty," pp. 4–11. Experimental results show that decision makers do generally believe in the (erroneous) "law of small numbers"—that a small sample will yield representative results. This mistaken belief causes decision makers to have unrealistic expectations about the stability of observed patterns and replicability of prior beneficial experiences. Tversky and Kahneman, "Belief in the Law of Small Numbers," *Psychology Bulletin 2* (1972):105, reprinted in Kahneman, Slovic, and Tversky, *Judgment under Uncertainty*, p. 23.

99. According to the theory of cognitive dissonance, once a decision maker becomes even tentatively committed to a decision, she will tend to view subsequent evidence as more supportive of the decision than it really is and will tend to avoid or denigrate nonsupportive evidence. See Leon Festinger, *Conflict, Decision and Dissonance* (Stanford: Stanford University Press, 1964); Irving Janis and Leon Mann, *Decision Making: A Psychological Analysis of Conflict, Choice and Commitment* (New York: Free Press, 1977), pp. 171–72, 213–14.

100. See Richard Dale and Richard Mattione, *Managing Global Debt*, Brookings Institution Staff Paper (Washington, D.C.: Brookings Institution, 1984), pp. 23–24; Goodman, "Bank Lending to LDCs: Are Risks Diversifiable?" *Federal Reserve Bank New York Quarterly Review* (Summer 1981):10; Ingo Walter, "Country Risk, Portfolio Decisions and Regulation in International Bank Lending," *Journal of Banking and Finance* (March 1981):77.

101. Minority Staff, House Committee on Banking, Finance and Urban Affairs, Global Debt and International Financial Stablity, in International Financial Markets Hearings, pp. 137, 144–46.

102. See Elena Folkerts-Landau, "The Regulatory Origins of the International Debt Crisis," *Bankers Magazine*, September–October 1984, p. 44.

103. For example, when Federal Reserve Chairman Paul Volcker appeared before the House of Representatives in 1983 to urge regulatory cooperation in working out the problems with foreign sovereign loans, he was peppered with hostile questions

and attacks against using any tax dollars to assist the banks in their restructures. "One of the most difficult questions . . . was why the banks loaned the money. If the banks make a profit, they don't share it with the taxpayers. Why should the taxpayers share in the losses?" Remark of Representative Wylie, International Financial Markets Hearings, p. 94; see ibid., pp. 90–91, 98–99, 119–21.

104. See Jonathan Eaton and Mark Gersovitz, "Debt with Potential Repudiation: Theoretical and Empirical Analysis," *Review of Economic Studies 48* (1981):289; J. Sachs, LDC Debt in the 1980s: Risk and Reforms, National Bureau of Economic Research Working Paper 861, February 1982.

105. Moffitt, *World's Money*, p. 71.

106. Federal Reserve Chairman Paul Volcker testified that the traditional regulatory methods were not well-suited to evaluating country risk: "Individual bank examiners were not generally equipped to evaluate economic conditions and prospects of countries. . . . The traditional criteria for formally 'classifying' or 'criticizing' loans were developed for private borrowers or local governments, and were not readily adaptable to consideration of 'transfer risk' or evaluating sovereign entities." International Financial Markets Hearings, pp. 41, 52.

107. Ibid., pp. 52–53.

108. Wellons, "Brazil," p. 127, says that the State Department encouraged loans to Zaire in 1979 and generally encouraged lending to NODCs; see also Folkerts-Landau, "Regulatory Origins of the Debt Crisis," p. 49; Cynthia Lichtenstein, chapter 8, shows that federal financial regulators encouraged loans to Indonesia in 1970s and were criticized by Congress; International Financial Markets Hearings, p. 141.

109. See note 19.

110. See note 18.

111. Mexico suffered a brief foreign exchange crisis in 1975–76, but it did not lead to a formal debt renegotiation. By the end of 1981, the commercial banks had engaged in multilateral debt renegotiations with six NODCs (Peru, Zaire, Jamaica, Turkey, Nicaragua, Sudan) and had initiated negotiations with two others (Bolivia and Costa Rica). Friedman, *World Debt Dilemma*, pp. 127–33.

112. Carlos Diaz-Alejandro, "Latin American Debt: I Don't Think We Are in Kansas Anymore," *Brookings Institution Papers on Economic Activity* (1984): 335 and 350, table 4.

113. For example, see Dale and Mattione, *Managing Global Debt* pp. 20–21, where it is assumed that legal redress is not available against a defaulting government if sovereign immunity is invoked.

114. For examples of acceleration and cross-default clauses, see Model Mexican Restructure Agreement, Article IX (July 1983). See John Mendez, "Recent Trends in Commercial Bank Lending to LDCs: Part of the Problem or Part of the Solution?" *Yale Journal of World Public Order 8* (1982):173, 193–94, describing cross-default clauses and their effects.

115. Public Law 94-583, 90 Stat. 2891 (1976), codified at 28 U.S.C. §§ 1330, 1332(a), 1391(f), 1441(d), 1602–1611 (1982). I have analyzed the statute in William Eskridge, "The Iranian Nationalization Cases: Toward a General Theory of Jurisdiction over Foreign States," *Harvard International Law Journal 22* (1981):525.

116. 28 U.S.C. §§ 1330(a) (1982). An oddity (if not an idiocy) of the FSIA is that it combines sovereign immunity, subject-matter jurisdiction, and personal juris-

diction inquiries into a single statutory test: if the "foreign state" is not immune under §§ 1605 through 1607, it not on'y loses the sovereign immunity defense, but subject-matter jurisdiction is established and (if proper service is made) personal jurisdiction exists as well. Hans Smit, "The Foreign Sovereign Immunities Act of 1976: A Plea for Drastic Surgery," *1980 Proceedings of the American Society of International Law* (1981):49, 50–60.

117. A detailed waiver of immunity clause is Mexican Agreement, § 13.08.

118. 28 U.S.C. § 1605(a)(1) (1982).

119. Id. § 1605(a)(2); see Jackson v. People's Republic of China, 550 F.Supp. 869 (M.D. Ala. 1982).

While at least one U.S. court had before 1976 characterized public loans as government activities for which foreign states were immune from suit, see Victory Transp. Inc. v. Comisaria General de Abastecimientos y Transportes, 336 F.2d 354, 360 (2d Cir. 1964), cert. denied, 381 U.S. 934 (1965) ("public loans" are inherently governmental acts, for which states require immunity from suit), Congress made clear that public loans were to be considered commercial activities under the Act. See H.R. Rep. No. 94-1487, 94th Cong., 2d sess. 10 (1976).

120. See Allied Bank Int'l v. Banco Credito Agricola de Cartago, No. 83-7714 (2d Cir. Apr. 23, 1984) (an act of state doctrine bars adjudication of Costa Rican default on debt; panel granted rehearing).

121. 28 U.S.C. § 1610(a) (1982).

122. Id. § 1610(a)(2).

123. Id. § 1611(b)(1).

124. Id. § 1610(b).

125. In the case of corporate borrowing, bond covenants restrict the corporation's payment of dividends, its total indebtedness, maintenance of assets to secure the debt, and periodic disclosure of information so that the creditor may monitor the debtor's financial status. Because these covenants are practically unenforceable against sovereigns, they are typically not included in soverign loan agreements. See Dale and Mattione, *Managing Global Debt*, p. 21 and n. 34.

126. The contagious collapse works as follows. (1) Since it has no legal redress, a bank with loans to a sovereign state will react to the state's prospect of default by cutting off further loans. (2) If all the banks follow this strategy, then the country is placed in an untenable position, for even healthy Third World economies need commercial or other loans for their sovereign and private sectors. (The banks' cut-off of funds may apply to the private sector as well as the public.) (3) Once the bank has lost confidence in the ability of country X to service its debts over time, it will reevaluate its lending policy to adjacent country Y (which probably should have been done long ago) and may cut off credit to country Y as well. Again, the other banks do the same, and country Y might be forced into default, even though it is better able to service its debts than is country X.

127. "The basic dynamic of forced lending is that the lender with existing exposure will increase the exposure with new loans as long as the new funds are judged likely to enable a firming-up of the previous exposure rather than to be merely a throwing of good money after bad" (Cline, *International Debt*, p. 72). Involuntary lending will occur when "(a) the reduction in the probability of country default thereby achieved, *multiplied by* previously outstanding loans, *exceeds* (b) the terminal probability of

default (after the new loans) as *multiplied by* the amount of the new loans" (ibid., emphasis in the original). For this analysis, the probability of a moratorium (suspension of principal and interest payments) is counted as 20 percent to 40 percent of a default (ibid., p. 73).

128. Philip Wellons, chapter 6 of this book.

129. See Clifford Dammers, "A Brief History of Sovereign Defaults and Rescheduling," in David Suratgar, ed., *Default and Rescheduling: Corporate and Sovereign Borrowers* (Washington, D.C.: Euromoney Publications, 1984), p. 77.

130. E. Walter Robichek, "The International Monetary Fund: An Arbiter in the Debt Restructuring Process," *Columbia Journal of Transnational Law 23* (1984):143, 146.

131. On the ability of negotiation and other informal means to serve as the functional equivalent of a formal legal regime see William Stoever, *Renegotiations in International Business Transactions* (Lexington, Mass.: Lexington Books, 1981), esp. ch. 7; Melvin Eisenberg, "Private Ordering through Negotiation: Dispute-Settlement and Rulemaking," *Harvard Law Review 89* (1976):637.

132. See the warnings about too harsh an austerity in Riordan Roett, chapter 9; see also Roett, "Democracy and Debt in South America: A Continent's Dilemma," *Foreign Affairs 62* (1984):695.

133. See, for example, "Brazilian Debt Moratorium 'No Longer Taboo'," *Latin American Times*, no. 60, p. 22 (1984); "Dangers of the U.S. Recovery," and subsequent articles, *Latin American Times*, no. 58 (1984), p. 1 ff.

134. Compare Bjorn Hettne, *Development Theory and the Third World* (Stockholm: Swedish Agency for Research Cooperation with Developing Countries, 1982), pp. 11–38, on the origins and evolution of the modernization paradigm, with Gerald Meier and Dudley Seers, eds., *Pioneers in Development* (New York: Oxford University Press, 1984), essays by early modernization theorists reevaluating their positions.

135. Jeffrey Nugent and Pan Yotopoulos, "What Has Orthodox Development Economics Learned from Recent Experience?" *World Development 7* (1979):541, 542.

136. J.M. Keynes, "The Marginal Propensity to Consume and the Multiplier," in Keynes, *The General Theory of Employment, Interest, and Money* (1936), pp. 113–31, ch. 10.

137. Evsey Domar, *Essays in the Theory of Economic Growth* (New York: Oxford University Press, 1957); Roy Harrod, *Economic Essays* (1952), pp. 254–90.

138. Arthur Lewis, "Economic Development with Unlimited Supplies of Labour," *Manchester School of Economics and Social Studies 22* (1954):139, 155.

139. Ragnar Nurkse, *Problems of Capital Formation in Underdeveloped Countries* (New York: Oxford University Press, 1953), was a leading advocate; he did not view the cycles or traps as structural ones, but rather just as obstacles that could be surmounted by money. See also Albert Hirschman, *The Strategy of Economic Development* (New Haven: Yale University Press, 1958); Gunnar Myrdal, *Economic Theory and Underdeveloped Regions* (London: Duckworth, 1957).

140. See Arthur Lewis, *The Theory of Economic Growth* (London: Allen and Unwin, 1955); Lewis, "Economic Development with Unlimited Supplies of Labour"; see also Lewis, "Development Economics in the 1950s," in Meier and Seers, eds., *Pioneers in Development*, p. 121.

141. Jacob Viner, *International Trade and Economic Development* (Oxford: Clarendon Press, 1953). See Hettne, *Development Theory and the Third World*, pp. 24–25. As early as 1949, however, classical economists questioned whether the gains of trade would be evenly divided between underdeveloped and developed countries. The so-called Singer–Prebisch thesis was that underdeveloped countries producing primary commodities received few of the trade advantages. The strategy they should pursue, then, is not to pursue existing comparative advantages, but rather to create new advantages by industrialization. See H.W. Singer, "The Distribution of Gains Between Investing and Borrowing Countries," in American Economic Association, *Readings in International Economics* (1968):306.

142. See, for example, Richard Caves, *The Multinational Enterprise and Economic Analysis* (Cambridge: Cambridge University Press, 1982), pp. 261–78; Alan Rugman, *Inside the Multinationals: The Economics of Internal Markets* (New York: Columbia University Press, 1981), pp. 22–27, 133–55.

143. Walter W. Rostow, *The Stages of Economic Growth: A Non-Communist Manifesto* (Cambridge: Cambridge University Press, 1960); see Rostow, ed., *The Economics of Take-off into Sustained Growth* (New York: St. Martin's Press, 1963); Rostow, *Politics and the Stages of Growth* (Cambridge: Cambridge University Press, 1971); Rostow, "Development: The Political Economy of the Marshallian Long Period," in Meier and Seers, eds., *Pioneers in Development*, p. 229.

144. "Once the snowball [economic growth and development] starts to move downhill, it will move of its own momentum, and will get bigger and bigger as it goes along" (Arthur Lewis, "Industrialization in the British West Indies," *Caribbean Economic Review* 2 (1950):36).

145. Sylvia Hewlett and Richard Weinert, "Introduction: The Characteristics and Consequences of Late Development in Brazil and Mexico," in Hewlett and Weinert, eds., *Brazil and Mexico: Patterns in Late Development*, p. 1.

146. R. Stavenhagen, "Siete tesis equivocados sobre America Latina" [Seven Erroneous Theses about Latin America], *Desarrollo Indoamericano* 4 (1966), states that Latin American countries are intrinsically dualist: the modern sector will not "draw in" the traditional sector. See Andre Gunder Frank, *The Sociology of Development and the Underdevelopment of Sociology* (1969). Anthropological theory has shown how in underdeveloped societies the penetration of "modern" (Western) modes of culture and economic arrangement has been limited by indigenous structures that will not go away. See, for example, C.A. Gregory, *Gifts and Commodities* (London: Academic Press, 1982); Arthur Lowry, Legislating the Nuclear Family in Zaire: Integrating the Core and the Periphery, unpublished manuscript, November 14, 1984, University of Virginia School of Law.

147. Pereira, *Development and Crisis in Brazil*, pp. 214–16.

148. According to "Latin Debt: Postponing the Burden," *New York Times*, September 23, 1984, sec. 3, p. 1, cols. 2–4, growth for Brazil, Mexico, and Venezuela was between 1.0 percent and 1.5 percent in 1984. For these countries and for Argentina, most or all of the positive trade balance was used to pay interest on the external debt.

149. Ronald McKinnon, *Money and Capital in Economic Development* (Washington, D.C.: Brookings Institution, 1973).

150. Ibid., pp. 170–74; Hughes, "Debt and Development: The Role of Foreign Capital in Economic Growth," *World Development* 7 (1979):95.

151. It appears that most, if not almost all, of Brazil's real growth has gone to those already well-off. According to Guy Pfeffermann and Richard Webb, "The Distribution of Income in Brazil," World Bank Staff Working Paper No. 356 (1979):10, table 1, the poorest 40 percent of Brazilian households had 9.8 percent of the GDP in 1960 but only 7.8 percent in 1976; the richest 10 percent had 50.0 percent of the GDP in 1960 and 53.6 percent in 1972. For criticisms, both normative and positive or economic, of Brazil's industrialization policy in light of the unequal distribution of its benefits, see Marco Aguiar, Marcos Arruda, and Parsifal Flores, "Economic Dictatorship Versus Democracy in Brazil," translated by T. Groth, *Latin American Perspectives* (Winter 1984):13; Peter Knight, "Brazilian Socioeconomic Development: Issues for the Eighties," *World Development* 9 (1981):1063.

152. Newell and Rubio, *Mexico's Dilemma*, pp. 121 ff., 159, 161, point out that income going to poorest Mexican families declined between 1950 and 1967. Graham, "Mexican and Brazilian Economic Development," compares income inequality in Brazil and Mexico on p. 45, table 12.

153. In the 1970s, the concept of "another development" (or "alternative development") was accepted by many scholars who rejected the normative assumptions or consequences of the modernization paradigm. As popularized by the Dag Hammarskjold Foundation and *Development Dialogue*, another development is (1) needs-oriented (geared to meeting both material and nonmaterial needs of all groups in society), (2) endogenous and self-reliant, (3) ecologically sound, and (4) based upon structural transformation. See M. Nerfin, ed., *Another Development: Approaches and Strategies* (1977), p. 10; Hettne, *Development Theory*, pp. 75 ff. See also, John Friedman, Ted Wheelwright, and John Connell, eds., *Development Strategies in the Eighties* (Sydney: Development Studio Colloqulum, 1980).

154. François Perroux, *A New Concept of Development* (Paris: UNESCO, 1983).

155. See Samir Amin, *Imperialism and Unequal Development* (1977); Paul Baran, *The Political Economy of Growth* (New York: Monthly Review Press, 1957); Andre Gunder Frank, *Capitalism and Underdevelopment in Latin America*; Peter Limqueco and Bruce McFarlane, eds., *Neo-Marxist Theories of Development* (New York: St. Martin's Press, 1983).

156. Most of the scholarship in this area grew out of the United Nations Economic Commission for Latin America, known in Spanish as the Comision Economica para America Latina (CEPAL). For the CEPAL critique, see Fernando Cardoso, *The Originality of a Copy: CEPAL and the Idea of Development* (1977); Fernando Cardoso and Enzo Faletto, *Dependency and Development in Latin America*, trans. Marjory Urguidi (Berkeley: University of California Press, 1979); Theodore Moran, *Multinational Corporations and the Politics of Dependence—Copper in Chile* (Princeton: Princeton University Press, 1974), pp. 66–71, 79–83.

157. See Raúl Prebisch, *Economic Survey of Latin America* (New York: United Nations, 1950); Raúl Prebisch, *Economic Survey of Latin America and Its Principal Problems* (New York: United Nations, 1950); see Raúl Prebisch, "Five Stages in My Thinking on Development," in Meier and Seers, *Pioneers in Development*, pp. 175–77.

158. "By dependence we mean a situation in which the economy of certain countries is conditioned on the development and expansion of another economy to which the former is subjected. The relation of interdependence between two or more economies,

and between those and world trade, assumes the form of dependence when some countries (the dominant ones) can expand and can be self-sustaining, while other countries (the dependent ones) can do this only as a reflection of that expansion, which can have either a positive or a negative effect on their immediate development." Theotonio Dos Santos, "The Structure of Dependence," *American Economic Review* 60 (1970):231. For a survey of the evolution and expression of the dependency paradigm, see, for example, Corporaso and Zare, "An Interpretation and Evaluation of Dependency Theory," in H. Munoz, ed., *From Dependency to Development: Strategies to Overcome Underdevelopment and Inequality* (Boulder, Colo.: Westview, 1981), pp. 43–56; G. Palma, "Dependency: A Formal Theory of Underdevelopment or a Methodology for the Analysis of Concrete Situations of Underdevelopment?" *World Development* 6 (1978):881.

159. See generally Andre Gunder Frank, *Latin America: Underdevelopment or Revolution* (New York: Monthly Review Press, 1969), pp. 3–19; Hettne, *Development Theory*; Francis Snyder, "Law and Development in Light of Dependency Theory," *Law and Society* 14 (1980):723, 747–61.

160. Some of the main works directed specifically at multinationals' exploitation of host countries include Celso Furtado, *Obstacles to Development in Latin America*, translated by C. Ekker (Garden City, N.Y.: Anchor Books, 1970); Richard Barnet and Ronald Muller, *Global Reach: The Power of the Multinational Corporations* (New York: Simon and Schuster, 1974); C.F. Bergsten, T. Hurst, and T. Moran, *American Multinationals and American Interests* (Washington, D.C.: Brookings Institution, 1978); N. Hood and S. Young, *The Economics of Multinational Enterprise* (New York: Longman, 1979); Stephen Hymer, "The Multinational Corporation and the Law of Uneven Development," in *The Papers by Stephen Herbert Hymer, The Multinational Corporation: A Radical Approach*, edited by E. Cohen et al. (Cambridge: Cambridge University Press, 1979). For a useful digest of the competing arguments, see Thomas Biersteker, *Distortion or Development? Contending Perspectives on the Multinational Corporation* (Cambridge, Mass.: MIT Press, 1978).

161. There is surprisingly little scholarship dealing with the debt crisis from the perspective of dependency theory. One historical treatment is Corm, "Indebtedness of Developing Countries."

162. Barnet and Muller, *Global Reach*, p. 140.

163. See generally Hewlett and Weinert, "Late Development in Brazil and Mexico," pp. 2–6.

164. See Furtado, *Obstacles to Development in Latin America*, pp. 58–70; Barnet and Muller, *Global Reach*, pp. 152–53 (according to U.N. studies by Fernando Fajnzylber, U.S. multinationals financed 83 percent of their Latin American investment locally; other studies indicate that, from 1960 to 1970, 78 percent of multinational operations in Latin America were financed out of local capital).

165. "[I]n countries which impose a percentage limitation on the repatriation of profits," which includes many Latin American countries, "overpricing imports and underpricing exports are good ways to repatriate more profits than the local government allows." Barnet and Muller, *Global Reach*, p. 159; see also pp. 157–61. See M. Brooke and H.L. Remers, *The Strategy of Multinational Enterprises: Organization and Finance*, 2d ed. (Marshfield, Mass.: Pitman Publishing, 1970); Aharoni, "On the

Definition of a Multinational Corporation," in A. Kapoor and P. Grub, eds., *The Multinational Enterprise in Transition* (1972), p. 11.

166. Peter Evans and Gary Gereffi, "Foreign Investment and Dependent Development: Comparing Brazil and Mexico," in Hewlett and Weihert, eds., *Brazil and Mexico*, p. 111 and p. 164, table A–6 shows a high return on investment for multinationals in Brazil and Mexico.

167. Fifty-two percent of the profits of U.S. manufacturing subsidiaries in Latin America were repatriated, even though 78 percent of the investment funds needed to generate that dollar of profit came from local sources (Barnet and Muller, *Global Reach*, pp. 153–54).

168. See C. Michalet, *Transfer of Technology and the Multinational Firm* (Paris: OECD, 1976), summarized and evaluated (favorably) in Miguel Wionczek, "Technology Transfer Through Transnational Corporations," in Miguel Wionczek, *Some Key Issues for the World Periphery* (Oxford: Pergamon Press, 1982), pp. 265, 267, 274.

169. J. Behrman, *National Interests and the Multinational Enterprise* (Lexington, Mass.: Lexington Books, 1970), pp. 59–67. Indeed, the foreign subsidiary may attract the bright host country scientists and technicians away from more productive national projects, and even export them to the West, thereby contributing to the celebrated "brain drain" from these countries (Barnet and Muller, *Global Reach*, pp. 162–63).

170. See Evans and Gereffi, "Foreign Investment and Dependent Development," pp. 140–44; R. Newfarmer and W. Mueller, "Multinational Corporations in Brazil and Mexico: Structural Sources of Economic and Noneconomic Power," Report to the Subcommittee on Multinational Corporations of the Senate Committee on Foreign Relations, 94th Cong., 1st sess. (1975), pp. 35–38, 149–52; Richard Newfarmer, "TNC Takeovers in Brazil: The Uneven Distribution of Benefits in the Market for Firms," *World Development* 7 (1979):25.

171. See Corm, "Indebtedness of Developing Countries," p. 77.

172. Notwithstanding the borrowing binge of NODCs in the 1970s, domestic savings increased in these countries from 19 percent in 1960 to 21 percent in 1980, and gross domestic investment increased from 21 percent to 27 percent. World Bank, *World Development Report* (Washington, D.C.: World Bank, 1982), p. 118; see J. Sachs, "The Current Account and Macroeconomic Adjustment in the 1970s," *Brookings Institution Papers on Economic Activity* (1981), pp. 201–68. William Cline suggests that these figures indicate the external debt was not used to finance local consumption, for in that event local investment and savings would be expected to drop (Cline, *International Debt*, p. 16).

173. See Graham, "Mexican and Brazilian Economic Development," pp. 46–48: annual rate of population growth was 3.3 percent for Mexico in 1970–75 and 2.5 percent for Brazil in 1970–80; labor force growth 3.7 percent for Mexico in 1970–80 and 2.0 percent for Brazil in 1970–80.

174. See Barnet and Muller, *Global Reach*, pp. 166–70.

175. F. Perroux, *A New Concept of Development*, p. 139.

176. See Diaz-Alejandro, "Latin American Debt," pp. 360–67. Changes in aggregates at constant prices, 1980–81 to 1982–83, are found in these pages, as follows:

	GDP	Population	Capital Formation	Real Wages
Argentina	− 7%	3%	− 31%	− 3%
Brazil	− 1	4	− 11	1
Chile	− 12	3	− 62	− 4
Columbia	2	5	− 10	7
Mexico	1	5	− 32	− 24
Venezuela	− 1	6	− 17	− 3

177. Coffee constituted 42.0 percent of Brazil's export of goods in 1965–69, but only 32.6 percent in 1968–72, 21.7 percent in 1973, and 12.6 percent in 1974 (Baer, "Brazilian Growth and Development," p. 50, table 5).

178. See Bela Belassa, "Adjustment Policies in Developing Countries: A Reassessment," World Development 12 (1984):955.

179. Outward-oriented economies (Korea, Taiwan, and Singapore) relied on vigorous export promotion and import substitution to respond to the shocks of 1973–82 and accepted short-term growth reductions; inward-oriented economies (Brazil, Argentina, Mexico) financed the 1974–76 shocks by external debt but had to undertake deflationary measures after 1980 (ibid., pp. 966–71). Belassa's conclusion is that "[t]he policies applied led to economic growth rates substantially higher in outward-oriented than in inward-oriented economies, with the differences in growth rates offsetting the differences in the size of external shocks several times" (p. 971).

180. See Independent Commission on International Development Issues, North–South: A Program for Survival, Brandt Commission Report (1980), emphasizing crisis in the world system and the need for international cooperation; Hettne, Development Theory, pp. 55–58.

181. For example, as observed in Osvaldo Sunkel and Edmundo Fuenzalida, "Transnationalization and Its National Consequences," in J.J. Villamil, ed., Transnational Capitalism and National Development: New Perspectives on Dependence (Hassocks, Sussex: Harvester Press, 1979), growth of multinational companies has fostered an internationally integrated market of goods and services.

182. Professor Wallerstein's theory is set forth in The Capitalist World Economy (Cambridge: Cambridge University Press, 1979), a collection of his essays. See also Immanuel Wallerstein, The Modern World System I: Capitalist Agriculture and the Origins of the European World-Economy in the Sixteenth Century (New York: Academic Press, 1974); Immanuel Wallerstein, The Modern World System II: Mercantilism and the Consolidation of the European World-Economy, 1500–1750) (New York: Academic Press, 1980). Wallerstein has also written numerous articles and is the editor of a series of volumes on Political Economy of the World-System Annuals.

183. Wallerstein's "core-periphery" terminology is, obviously, taken from dependency theory and, in particular, the writings of Raúl Prebisch (see note 157). His category of "semiperipheral" countries is more original. The role of the semiperiphery is explicated in Immanuel Wallerstein, "Dependence in an Interdependent World: The Limited Possibilities of Transformation within the Capitalist World Economy," African

Studies Review (April 1974):1, reprinted in Wallerstein, *Capitalist World Economy*, p. 66; Immanuel Wallerstein, "Semiperipheral Countries and the Contemporary World Crisis," *Theory and Society* 3 (1976):461.

184. Wallerstein, *Modern World System I*, pp. 164–95. As Wallerstein notes, Spain's decline was the result of its economic and financial inability to manage a large empire. Interestingly, there is a parallel between Spain's dependence on foreign loans and a similar dependence in the 1970s on the part of its former western hemisphere colonies. "Genovese bankers monopolized the profits from the exploitation of American mines; Genoese outfitters controlled the provisioning of the fleets. . . . Far from reacting, the monarchy became more and more involved in dangerous financial disorders that tied it to the capitalist machinery on the far side of the Pyrenees; at first this tie was indispensable, then ruinous, and finally sterile." (Jaime Vicens Vives, *Approaches to the History of Spain*, 2d ed. (Berkeley: University of California Press, 1970), pp. 97–98; see J.H. Elliot, "The Decline of Spain," *Past and Present* (November 1961):52, 69.)

185. Wallerstein, "Dependence in an Interdependent World," p. 66. This essay focuses on the possibility that semiperipheral countries can become core ones. Professor Wallerstein envisions this possibility in times of crisis or economic downturn, when core producers will tend to compete with one another for investment opportunities in semiperipheral countries or for their products or raw materials (ibid., p. 99). Only some countries of the semiperiphery can move "up," though, because "a semiperipheral country rising to core status does so, not merely at the expense of some or all core powers, but also at the expense of other semiperipheral powers" (ibid., p. 101).

186. Immanuel Wallerstein, "Crises: The World-Economy, the Movements, and the Ideologies," in A. Bergesen, ed., *Crisis in the World-System* (Beverly Hills, Calif.: Sage Publications, 1983), p. 21.

187. See Philip McMichael, "Social Structure of the New International Division of Labor," in E. Friedman, ed., *Ascent and Decline in the World-System* (Beverly Hills, Calif.: Sage Publications, 1982), pp. 115, 119–24.

188. The concept of newly industrializing countries was developed in the late 1960s, when economists realized that certain "developing" countries were predominant in trade relations with the developed countries. They imported far more from the West than all other developing countries combined, and they exported manufactured goods to the West in much greater amounts. The NICs most often mentioned in the 1960s were Argentina, Brazil, Chile, Colombia, Mexico, Hong Kong, India, Singapore, South Korea, Taiwan, and Yugoslavia. See Colin Bradford, "The Rise of the NICs as Exporters on a Global Scale," in L. Turner and N. McMullen, eds., *The Newly Industrializing Countries: Trade and Adjustment* (1982), pp. 7, 9–10. To that list might be added oil-exporting countries such as Venezuela, Nigeria, Saudi Arabia (and other oil-producing Arab countries).

189. McMichael, "New International Division of Labor," argues that the political hegemony of the United States disappeared with America's humiliation in Vietnam and the rise of Europe and Japan. Contributing to the loss of economic hegemony were (1) the growing U.S. government deficit and its accompanying inflation, (2) a deteriorating trade balance, and (3) the rise of the Eurodollar market, in part due to

U.S. capital controls policy. "In short, as revealed in the rise of the Eurocurrency system, the decline of U.S. hegemony devolved a growing power to the international capital market as a force shaping global economy" (p. 125). "Given the particular features of U.S. hegemonic decline, the structuring of global economy is undertaken increasingly by transnational capital, which internalizes world exchange relations as one of its circuits" (p. 126).

190. Andrew Tylecote and Marian Lonsdale-Brown, "State Socialism and Development: Why Russian and Chinese Ascent Halted," in Friedman, ed., *Ascent and Decline in the World-System*, pp. 255, 278–81, argue that Japan ascended in the world system because it had or developed the basic sociopolitical institutions needed for progress:

> The economy is structured around independent enterprises linked primarily by market relationships and controlled by workers democratically.

> State intervention should be limited to high-technology sectors which are by nature interdependent. State management should be through monetary and fiscal policies and taxes or subsidies.

> The most important aim of state management of the market is to reduce inequality. On the other hand, incentives are preserved, because the more efficient control more resources and have more authority. Another type of motivation is also fostered: the widening of one's frame of altruism, by conceptualizing the firm as a "family" whose members one wants to help.

> Strict control of market relations was maintained (and has been only slightly relaxed even after Japan reached the core). Thus trade is restricted, and multinationals are not permitted free entry.

191. According to Henrik Marcussen and Jens Torp, *The Internationalization of Capital: The Prospects for the Third World* (Uppsala: Zed Press, 1982), pp. 158–60, crisis in the core countries gives opportunities for some countries of the periphery to advance.

192. See Shirley Kuo, *The Taiwan Economy in Transition* (Boulder: Westview Press, 1983); Paul Kuznets, *Economic Growth and Structure in the Republic of Korea* (New Haven: Yale University Press, 1977); George Crane, "The Taiwanese Ascent: System, State, and Movement in the World-Economy," in Friedman, ed., *Ascent and Decline in the World-System*, pp. 93, 99–102.

193. See generally Alvin Rabushka, *Hong Kong: A Study in Economic Freedom* (Chicago: University of Chicago Press, 1979); Kunio Yoshihara, *Foreign Investment and Domestic Response: A Study of Singapore's Industrialization* (Singapore: Eastern Universities Press, 1976).

194. Bruce Cumings, "The Origins and Development of the Northeast Asian Political Economy: Industrial Sectors, Product Cycles and Political Consequences," *International Organization* 38 (1984):1, 7, 28.

195. Crane, "Taiwanese Ascent," p. 105: "Taiwan's ascent has been a function of both the favorable climate of the world-system as a whole and the role of the state enterprises." In both South Korea and Taiwan, the government has been "a tool for capital accumulation." A. Amsden, "Taiwan's Economic History: A Case of *Etatism* and a Challenge to Dependency Theory," *Modern China* 5 (1979):341, 342.

196. "South Korea Booming: Officials Say Debt Is Manageable," *Washington Post*, October 21, 1984, pp. K1, K5, reports that notwithstanding enormous external debts, South Korea is improving its economic position because of tight government supervision, stringent fiscal policies; see Cumings, "Northeast Asian Political Economy," pp. 35–40, on the success of Taiwan.

197. See Clive Hamilton, "Capitalist Industrialization in the Four Little Tigers of East Asia," in P. Limqueco and B. McFarlane, eds., *Neo-Marxist Theories of Development* (London: St. Martin's Press, 1983), pp. 137, 152–53: textiles were 40 percent to 50 percent of total exports in Hong Kong and 50 percent in Taiwan in 1979, and 34 percent in Korea in 1971–73. Singapore's exports have been concentrated in electronics, electrical machinery, and petroleum goods (ibid., p. 164).

198. In the early 1970s, foreign-controlled firms accounted for 10 percent of Hong Kong's manufactured exports, 20 percent of Taiwan's, 15 percent of Korea's, 70 percent of Singapore's (ibid., p. 166).

199. See generally Samuel Ho, *Economic Development of Taiwan, 1860–1970* (New Haven: Yale University Press, 1978), p. 165; Crane, "The Taiwanese Ascent," p. 98.

200. Herman Kahn, *World Economic Development: 1979 and Beyond* (1979), p. 121; see also David McClelland, *The Achieving Society* (New York: Irvington Publishers, 1961); David McClelland and David Winter, *Motivating Economic Achievement* (New York: The Free Press, 1969).

201. See, for example, Marcelo Selowsky, "Income Distribution, Basic Needs and Trade-Offs with Growth: The Case of Semi-Industrialized Latin American Countries," *World Development* 9 (1981):73. In an analysis concentrating on Brazil, Mexico, Peru, Colombia, Ecuador, Selowsky shows how severe income inequalities hamper the development of Latin American states.

202. Andre Gunder Frank, "Sociology of Development and Underdevelopment of Sociology," in Frank, *Latin America: Underdevelopment or Revolution*, pp. 21, 77.

Part II
Dynamics

4

Sovereign Debt Restructure: A Perspective of Counsel to Agent Banks, Bank Advisory Groups, and Servicing Banks

Alfred Mudge

S overeign debt restructure is contractual agreement between individual debtor and individual creditor with respect to the debt in question, and nothing more. The basic questions are always the same: who pays, lends, or defers payment of how much, when, and at what price? These are currently multi-hundred-billion-dollar questions. The basic players are always the same: the universe of debtors in a country (including the sovereign and other debtors in both the public sector and the private sector) and the universe of creditors and lenders outside the country (including the International Monetary Fund (IMF) and other multilateral agencies, bilateral governmental creditors, the international banking community and more). Restructure begins to occur when some debtors sign financing agreements with some creditors to answer a few of the basic questions for a finite period of time. Given the magnitude of both the basic questions and the universe of basic players, it is fair to assume that all of the basic questions will not be answered in unison, at once and forever, and that the restructure process will continue, piece by piece. It is also fair to assume that the financing process will continue in a voluntary lending market after debtors emerge from a combination of restructuring existing debt and economic recovery as creditworthy and economically and financially viable borrowers.

Sovereign debt is restructured country by country. The current wave of simultaneous restructures of the sovereign debt of many countries increases the complexity of the process. Some countries continue a process begun in recent years. Some are now initiating the process. Both debtors and creditors increasingly compare the partial answers to the basic questions reached by other players in the process. Creditors want most favored creditor protection.

This chapter was previously published under the same title in *Columbia Journal of Transnational Law* 23 (1984):59.

Debtors want most favored debtor treatment. Each restructure is negotiated separately in its own factual context and in the context of other past, present and future restructure negotiations. Each restructure is potential precedent for the next. The process is increasingly politicized in both debtor and creditor countries and receives increasing coverage in the press around the world. Some hope for an immediate and ultimate common solution. Short of printing and distributing to debtors for effective and immediate payment to creditors several hundred billion bona fide U.S. dollars, an immediate and ultimate common solution is an unlikely prospect.

There are no general rules, and the solution to yesterday's problem is not the answer to today's question. The solution for the Kingdom of Oz simply will not work for the Republic of Zo. The problems of Oz and Zo and their respective creditors may be similar in some respects, but economic recovery and the restructure process inevitably will differ. Each situation is *unique,* and the word applies equally to the country; to its economy, financial difficulties, domestic politics and diplomatic relations; to the debt profile of its borrowers in the public and private sectors; to the constellation of its multilateral, governmental and private creditors; to the composition of its agent banks and bank advisory group; and to the basic requirements and feasible alternatives to initiate the process of economic recovery and sovereign debt restructure.

There are many participants in the process and each participant will have many perspectives on both the process and the other participants. This chapter will describe four principal actors on the banking side of the restructure process: bank creditor, agent bank, bank advisory group, and servicing bank.

Bank Creditor

A bank creditor is simply a bank that has extended credit to a debtor in the public sector or private sector of a country. Each individual bank creditor is an important principal in the restructure process. But the individual portfolios and different frames of reference of banks in the international banking community vary enormously.

Many banks have significant exposure to both the public and private sectors in any given country. Some banks may have concentrated their activity with only one sector and in some cases with only one borrower. Other banks have significant relationships with a large number of borrowers in both sectors. The existing debts represent a broad spectrum of relationships—from syndicated loans to the sovereign and its governmental agencies, to single bank loans to private sector borrowers. The existing agreements governing the existing loans also vary enormously.

Additional factors creating a different frame of reference for each bank creditor would include its exposure to other countries; its prior experience in the restructure process; the interplay of bank regulations, accounting practices and financial reporting requirements applicable to the bank; and the attitude to and role of the bank's home country to the debt restructure of a particular country. The frames of reference for banks from two different countries may differ in any particular restructure. Further, the frames of reference for any particular bank may also differ from restructure to restructure.

There is no common starting point of bank creditors in the restructure process except that no one bank wants to finance the repayment of another bank and each has a different portfolio, frame of reference, understanding of the economy and financial difficulties of the country and the debtors to such bank. Each bank creditor will participate in the restructure process only if it perceives that other bank creditors are doing their part. Each bank creditor also has its own legal counsel, and all bank creditors have the theoretical option either to participate in the restructure process or to impede the restructure process and possibly initiate litigation seeking enforcement of existing agreements governing existing debt.

Agent Bank

An agent bank is a bank appointed to act as agent for the banks party to a syndicated credit agreement under which many banks simultaneously extend credit to a borrower. The terms of the agency are contractual and generally are set forth in the credit agreement, including the specific role, function, and responsibilities of the agent bank in the administration of the syndicated credit agreement. The role of an agent bank is thus a formal role derived from the blend of agency law and the specific contractual provisions in the credit agreement creating the specific agency. An agent bank frequently is actively involved as a manager in arranging a financing prior to the signature of a syndicated credit agreement, but the formal role of agent bank begins with the execution of the syndicated credit agreement. Each agent bank normally retains its own counsel in the original preparation of a credit agreement and subsequently in the performance of the functions of the agent bank under a credit agreement.

The banks party to a syndicated credit agreement may represent a relatively homogeneous collection of banks, but frequently the syndicate will contain the full spectrum possible in the universe of bank creditors. A syndicated credit agreement typically will prohibit modification of the basic payment terms (restructure) unless all banks consent. The credit agreement will also typically provide for ratable sharing, among the entire syndicate, of payments received individually by any one bank. While each bank generally retains the individual right to sue the debtor for amounts owed to such bank, any individual recovery is diluted by the sharing provision in the absence of an (infrequent) exception for the rewards of litigation initiated by an individual bank. Acceleration of the entire debt outstanding under a syndicated credit agreement generally requires consent of a bank majority, measured by debt outstanding under the credit agreement, although in some cases the agent bank may accelerate on its own initiative. Thus, while each bank may individually sue on the debt then due and payable to it, generally no bank may accelerate and sue on all debt outstanding to it under a credit agreement unless the entire debt is accelerated by a bank majority or the agent bank. In a bank vote under a syndicated credit agreement, the vote of each bank creditor may be affected by factors that differentiate bank creditors generally but are extraneous to the specific credit. Moreover, the position of each bank may be affected by its sale of silent participations to other lenders which, while not contractual creditors under a syndicated credit agreement, may have a right under a separate participation agreement to instruct or veto the position of the actual contractual creditor in a vote by all the banks party to the syndicated credit agreement. Where a contractual creditor has sold multiple silent participations in any one credit to several participating banks, each participant may have the right to instruct or veto the position of the contractual creditor in a syndicate vote affecting acceleration, amendment, waiver, or modification of the payment terms.

In short, the agent bank is subject to the crossfire of conflicting views, instructions and votes from the spectrum of contractual creditor banks under a syndicated credit agreement. Moreover, each contractual creditor that has sold participations to other banks is subject to the same crossfire from its participants.

The potential cross pressures within one syndicated credit agreement are real, but additional frictions are possible. First, many banks are agent banks under more than one syndicated credit agreement with the same or different debtors in a country. Unless all syndicates concur on the appropriate action to be taken in a default situation, there are potential conflicts of interest where the same institution is agent bank under more than one syndicated credit agreement. If the potential conflicts become real, an agent bank may resign or be removed by a syndicate vote. Second, a bank creditor frequently is party to more than one syndicated credit agreement for the same or different debtors in a country. Thus, each bank is caught in the potential crossfire of different bank democracies under different syndicated credit agreements to which it is a party. Third, each institution acting as an agent bank may also be a bank creditor under (1) syndicated credit agreements for which it is agent bank, (2) single bank agreements under which it is the sole bank creditor, (3) syndicated credit agreements for which it is not an agent bank but only one bank in the syndicate, and (4) a credit agreement pursuant to which it has sold silent participations to other banks.

Fundamental default in the payment obligations by debtors in the public sector and private sector of a country obviously creates the potential for conflict and litigation between debtors and creditors. But equally real is the potential for conflict and litigation among bank creditors on a broad range of issues within the context of the many different existing agreements governing existing debts. Different bank creditors, agent banks, and silent participants may have different understandings and viewpoints on a number of issues:

1. What the underlying financial and economic situation is;
2. Whether a default has occurred and is material;
3. Whether to accelerate payment, waive prompt payment, or do nothing for the time being;
4. Whether, when, and how best to implement the sharing provisions in syndicated credit agreements;
5. Whether, when, and how best to obtain payment for all banks under syndicated credit agreements in order to avoid the need to implement the sharing provisions;
6. Whether to attach assets, set-off, litigate under one credit agreement between one debtor and one bank creditor irrespective of the actions taken by other bank creditors under other agreements, and whether to precipitate similar action under the universe of existing credit agreements between all debtors and all creditors in a country;
7. Whether to extend new money as an individual bank, as a small group of banks or as the universe of banks in the international banking community and, if so, on what terms and conditions; and
8. Whether to restructure existing debt and, if so, which debt between which debtors and which creditors, for how long, at what price, on what terms and conditions, and by what contractual agreement among which parties.

In some situations it is possible to address and answer these issues solely in the context of the individual existing agreements governing separate existing debts. Each agent bank then will have the fundamental responsibility and role in the context of the syndicated credit agreement for which it is agent to address these issues with debtor and bank creditors party to the syndicated credit agreement. In other situations, however, these issues simply cannot be addressed by any single bank creditor, bank syndicate, or agent bank in the limited context of one existing agreement. In order that any proposed answer be realistically considered for any individual existing agreement, a broader context and bigger answer is necessary. The more severe the situation is recognized to be, the greater will be the appreciation among bank creditors and agent banks that a common approach and consensus is needed among all bank creditors and agent banks in the international banking community. This role is provided by a bank advisory group.

Bank Advisory Group

The formation of a bank advisory group frequently coincides with the public announcement or recognition that there are fundamental payment defaults by debtors in the public and private sectors of a country and that voluntary and competitive borrowing and lending in the international capital market cannot satisfy the foreign exchange needs of the country. In contrast with an agent bank, whose existence and responsibilities are formalized under the combination of contractual agreement and agency law, the formation and role of a bank advisory group is informal and without legal recognition, either as a matter of contract or as a matter of law. The formation and role of a bank advisory group are also without legal consequences in the restructure process in the absence of basic agreement between individual debtor and individual creditor with respect to the debt in question.

General Description of a Bank Advisory Group[1]

The restructuring of the debt of a country frequently involves one or more bank advisory groups. The primary focus of the activities of such groups will vary from the debt of one private sector borrower in the country (the Steering Committee for Grupo Industrial Alfa, S.A.), to all public sector debt of the country (the Bank Advisory Group for Mexico), to the debt of the public sector and the private sector (the Bank Advisory Committee for Brazil). Different terms are used to refer to such a group; bank advisory group, bank steering committee, and bank working committee are common references. While any such group may advise or steer other actors in the debt restructuring process, it is also frequently advised and steered by other actors. The term "bank advisory group" will be used here.

As noted by the minister of finance of one Latin American country, from the debtor's viewpoint there is a thin line between "advisory" and "adversary." By composition each bank advisory group represents the creditor side of the negotiations. At the same time, there is more to the role of a well-functioning bank advisory group than simply seeking to obtain the most favorable conditions for the bank creditors. The bank advisory group can work closely with the debtor to identify the substantial areas of common interest on which a successful restructuring must be based, and can counsel the debtor on those avenues of approach that are or are not likely to be viewed sympathetically by the banking community at large. A bank advisory group, however, is quite different from advisors who may be retained and paid by the debtor. The debtor's advisors represent only the debtor, not the creditors. While out-of-pocket expenses of a bank advisory group are frequently paid by the debtor, it is rare that member banks are paid any fee. In the unusual situation where a fee is paid, this should be disclosed to nonmember banks.

There is no formal role for a bank advisory group, and the activities of each bank advisory group will vary from one situation to another. The function of a bank advisory group has been described as acting as a communications link between the debtor and the international banking community in the efforts of all to reach a consensus and mutual contractual agreement on a comprehensive financing package to answer the basic questions: who pays, lends, or defers payment of how much, when, and at what price? The answers may include both the restructuring of existing debt and new money facilities. The effort will involve significant contact back and forth among the debtor, bank creditors, and agent banks (including banks and agents not represented on the bank advisory group), the IMF, other multilateral agencies, central banks, national treasuries, bank regulators, bank accountants, and the public press. The success of the efforts by both debtor and bank advisory group to propose and implement a comprehensive financing package depends on the credibility of both debtor and bank advisory group with the other actors in the process, and on the ultimate acceptance by the international banking community of any proposal that emerges from discussions between the debtor and the bank advisory group. If the effort is to succeed, it is important that the bank advisory group maintain sufficient contact with and be sensitive to the concerns of the larger banking community throughout the process. This may be done through regional coordinators or subcommittees. It is also important that the larger banking community communicate its concerns to the bank advisory group in timely fashion.

The formation of a bank advisory group, itself an informal process involving the debtor and the banks concerned, typically is announced by coordinated but separate communications to bank creditors by both the debtor and the bank advisory group identifying both the members and the chairman or cochairmen. The formation of a bank advisory group has no legal consequences and neither creates nor changes any legal or contractual relationship among the debtor, the bank advisory group, or the banks at large. Existing contractual and legal relationships among debtors, bank creditors, and agent banks continue irrespective of the formation of a bank advisory group. The membership of a bank advisory group should credibly represent the universe of the debtor's bank creditors. The membership should be sufficiently broad to understand and be responsive to the different business concerns and regulatory and accounting environments of the debtor's creditor banks, but not so large as to compromise efficiency. The ultimate effectiveness of a bank advisory group depends upon the creativity, energy, and experience of the individuals representing each member bank, and membership by any bank on a bank advisory group should be understood to be a commitment to provide appropriate personnel and support.

Cross membership among bank advisory groups exists in several senses. A bank may be both on the bank advisory group for the public sector debt of a country and on the bank advisory group for a private sector debtor in that country. Similarly, the same bank (in some cases represented by the same individual) may be a member of the bank advisory groups for the public sector debt of several countries. The advantage of cross membership is that it enhances both the experience and ability of a bank advisory group. On the other hand, it also may be desirable to spread the work burden among different banks and individuals and to include on each committee banks that do not serve on other committees at the same time. While some members of a bank advisory group also may be agent banks under one or more syndicated credit agreements, many agent banks may not be members of an advisory group; and some members of a bank advisory group may not be agent banks.

Members of a bank advisory group are not managers for a syndicated financing, and membership on a bank advisory group does not alone imply any commitment by a bank to restructure existing debt or provide new financing (although the debtor and other group members are likely to assume that there is an implied commitment to work toward a constructive solution). Experience nevertheless demonstrates that during the process of formulating and implementing a comprehensive financing package, debtors have requested, and the members of bank advisory groups occasionally have provided, interim financing or bridge loans.

Identification of the information needs of debtor, bank advisory group, and bank creditors is frequently one of the first activities of a bank advisory group. Information on the economic and financial circumstances of the debtor and on the categories and amount of debt is critical to the development, proposal, and implementation of a comprehensive financing package. While a bank advisory group may help identify the mutual information needs of all parties, it is the debtor and the banks at large who must exchange the needed information.

The ultimate proposal and implementation of a comprehensive financing package inevitably represents a compromise among the debtor, the bank advisory group, and the international banking community. Other actors may make their own contributions and compromises in the process, such as the IMF, multilateral agencies, governments, bank regulators, and accountants. The process will involve first the proposal of the basic business terms followed by its implementation through appropriate documentation. Consensus and acceptance by all of the entire package, both the basic business terms and the implementing documentation, is frequently required for the package to work at all.

Given the need for ultimate compromise, consensus, and general acceptance, it is the inevitable role and function of a bank advisory group to examine and test alternatives with the debtor, among the members of the bank advisory group, and with the other actors in the process. If this role and function is performed effectively and an effective consensus emerges from the discussions between the debtor and the bank advisory group, it will increase the prospects that the international banking community will accept both the basic terms and the implementing documentation of any comprehensive financing package that emerges from the discussions between the debtor and the bank advisory group. All should be aware that ultimate acceptance by the banks at large will require time, response to the legitimate questions and concerns of the other banks, and possible modification to reflect these concerns. Success requires three elements—(1) effective commitment and communication by the debtor and members of a bank advisory group, (2) effective understanding of the difficulty of the effort, and (3) the need for compromise by all interested parties—and a little bit of luck.

The ultimate success of the proposal and implementation of a comprehensive financing package by debtor, bank advisory group, and bank creditors will depend on whether both the terms of the package and future economic and financial developments unrelated to the terms of the package combine to permit the restoration of a creditworthy and economically and financially viable debtor. Unfortunately, neither debtor nor bank advisory group nor bank creditors can predict future events that will ultimately determine the success of their current efforts. All must realistically recognize that the financing process will continue, in one way or another, with or without a continuing role for a bank advisory group.

Selected Problems Facing a Bank Advisory Group

While debt restructure is simply contractual agreement between individual debtor and individual creditor with respect to the debt in question, restructure occurs only in the context of the implementation of a comprehensive financing package involving many individual debtors and creditors and many different existing debts. The basic challenge to a bank advisory group is to work constructively with the debtor and to facilitate communications between debtor and the international banking community in the process of identifying a comprehensive package. Selected problems to be faced in the process include the scope, conditions, and documentation for a bank financing package.

Scope of a Bank Financing Package. The scope of a bank financing package is determined by the answers to three questions: (1) Does the package include both lending new money and restructuring existing debt or just one of those elements? (2) Which maturities and categories of existing debt to bank creditors are to be included in any restructure? (3) Does the package relate to debtors in both the public sector and the private sector, or just to one sector or just one debtor? The answer to the first two questions will vary significantly depending on the underlying factual situation in each case, but a general comment on the third question is merited.

On one level the distinction between the public sector and private sector is important because the sovereign (including most public sector debtors) is not subject to any bankruptcy court and the sovereign will generally stand behind all public sector debt in the restructure process in order to preserve access of the entire public sector to the credit markets. Local country bankruptcy laws, however, generally do apply to the private sector (and some public sector debtors in some cases), and any restructure of this debt may be subject to the actual or threatened supervision of a local bankruptcy judge.

On a second level the distinction between the public and private sectors may be irrelevant to the bank creditor with exposure to both sectors in a country. If a sufficient number of bank creditors with exposure to both public and private sectors insist on a restructure or solution for their problems in each sector, simultaneous restructure of both the public and private debtors may occur. Nationalization may instantaneously move a debtor from the private sector into the public sector. Where there is significant private sector debt denominated in foreign currencies, exchange rates and the availability of foreign exchange to the private sector will be factors in the assessment by a bank creditor of its country risk. Government policies may frequently affect the ability of private sector debtors to restructure their own debt and to recover economically and financially in the context of the economic adjustment program implemented by the government for the entire country. A private company operating profitably in local currency simply cannot pay foreign currency debt unless it can obtain foreign currency. Where exchange controls exist, the price and availability of foreign exchange depend on the sovereign. The payment of private sector foreign currency debt may become the responsibility of the sovereign as a practical matter, if not a legal matter. The extent to which the restructure of private sector debt is linked to the restructure of public sector debt is, understandably, a real variable in each case. The greater the linkage, the more complex and time consuming the entire process. The greater the linkage, the greater the risk that the package is so comprehensive that it cannot be effected on a coordinated basis. The greater the bank exposure to both public and private sectors, the greater the requirement that the linkage question be addressed.

Conditions of a Bank Financing Package. Debt restructure is conditional in two senses, factual and contractual. The restructure process simply may not in fact occur unless the necessary external conditions exist. The anticipation and identification of the necessary external conditions is a mutual challenge to both debtor and bank advisory group. Factors that may be conditions in any individual case include financing from or restructure by multilateral and bilateral official sources, the existence and implementation of a national economic adjustment program, a stand-by or extended fund facility with the IMF, and clarification by bank regulators and bank accountants of the effect of the implementation of any proposed bank financing package. In this context factors that may critically affect the reaction of bank creditors to a proposed financing package are nonfinancing issues such as the regulatory, accounting, and disclosure consequences, and requirements of implementing a proposed financing package. It is thus important to consider the proposed financing package from the viewpoint of its potential effect on legal lending limits, reserve requirements, the status of interest accrual, capital requirements, and disclosure requirements. Given the different regulatory and accounting environments affecting banks in the international banking community and given the fact that frequently no bank creditor will proceed to restructure unless substantially all other bank creditors also proceed, the importance of clarification by bank regulators and accountants as a factual condition to restructure is obvious.

Debt restructure is also conditional in a contractual sense, that is, the restructure agreement specifically will include contractual terms stipulating conditions to be satisfied in order for the restructure to be effective as a matter of contract. It is critical that the stated conditions be realistic and that the test to determine satisfaction be clear.

A common condition requires that substantially all comparable debt to all bank creditors be subject to the restructure agreement before the agreement is effective as to any debt of any one bank creditor. Other conditions may incorporate the factual conditions mentioned previously. Contractual conditions in restructure agreements must be drafted for the specific restructure context and with a view to implementing effectively the restructure agreement after signature. For example, new money credit agreements frequently contain a contractual condition that the borrower is not in default under other loan documentation. While reasonable in a voluntary lending environment, such a condition in a restructure agreement (which by definition is signed in the context of general payment default under many existing agreements) makes little sense in its normal formulation without appropriate exceptions permitting the restructure agreement to become effective.

Documentation for a Bank Financing Package. There are two basic types of agreements to implement a comprehensive bank financing package: a credit agreement providing for new incremental loans and a refinancing or restructure agreement providing for the adjustment of the payment terms of debt outstanding under existing agreements. A bank financing package may contain both types of agreements and it is critical to understand the distinction between the two types.

A new money credit agreement is comparable to credit agreements executed in a voluntary lending environment. There is a new money commitment for each bank, and the credit agreement stipulates the conditions upon which new funds are disbursed. The distinguishing elements of recent new money credit agreements implemented in a restructure context relate to the size of the new money commitments (several billion U.S. dollars is a pattern), the number of banks required to commit in order to justify the commitment by any bank (more than 500 has been frequent), and the options for different currencies and interest rate elections (multiple currencies and several interest-rate options in each currency is a pattern). Despite the increased size and complexity of new money credit agreements in a restructure context, the substance of a new money credit agreement remains the same—the new lending commitment of each bank is identified by a new numerical amount agreed to with the execution of the new money credit agreement. Once executed, the new money credit agreement operates within its own contractual context and basically without reference to the debt outstanding under the universe of existing agreements between multiple debtors and bank creditors.

In contrast, a refinancing or restructure agreement relates to existing debt outstanding under numerous existing agreements between numerous debtors and numerous bank creditors. The restructure agreement must be drafted to operate effectively and consistently with respect to all debt subject to restructure. The restructure agreement operates with respect to historical facts and not a negotiated new number as in the case of a new money credit agreement. The facts and mechanics in each individual situation will vary, but the success of the restructure effort depends on the ability of debtor and bank advisory group to prepare documentation appropriate for the individual situation. The success also will depend on whether bank creditors at large are satisfied that the restructure agreement is appropriate in the circumstances and treats all debt subject to restructure of all bank creditors on a comparable basis. In some situations the mechanical and clerical complexity of preparing a restructure agreement to deal with the universe of existing debts between multiple debtors and creditors has justified the formation of an operations subcommittee within a bank advisory group in order to consider viable alternatives to the mechanical and operational issues. The basic requirement is that the restructure agreement work effectively to implement the basic business deal from the viewpoint of bank creditor, agent bank, and servicing bank.

While quite different in their mechanical operation and effect, a new money credit agreement and a restructure agreement are executed within the same context: the debtor is facing fundamental economic and payment difficulties, and the purpose of each agreement is to assist the debtor to recover and to protect the interests of the lending banks. This context requires a realistic assessment by all of all provisions of the agreement. Covenants and events of default in particular should be reviewed to provide sufficient flexibility for the situation and to protect the interests both of bank creditors and debtor over time. Exceptions to the usual covenants and events of default frequently will be necessary to avoid the situation in which the debtor is in default on the day of signature.

Servicing Bank

A servicing bank is a bank that emerges from the restructure process to perform the mechanical and clerical functions normally allocated to an agent bank under a syndicated credit agreement, but there are several differences between an agent bank under an original syndicated credit agreement and a servicing bank under a restructure agreement.

An agent bank has voluntarily assumed, and frequently competitively won, that function in a voluntary lending environment. In contrast, a servicing bank assumes the function in the restructure context where the coordinating functions must be centralized in order to permit the restructure process to occur at all. A servicing bank may be a member of the bank advisory group. It is critical that the servicing bank have the operational ability to coordinate and administer a restructure agreement involving the large number of bank creditors involved in the restructure process.

The mechanics of restructuring many existing debts outstanding in many currencies under many existing agreements are complex, and the restructure agreement must be specific as to the functions of a servicing bank. Particularly complex is the transition from operating under multiple existing agreements to the uniform provisions of a common restructure agreement. There is a need for clarity from all viewpoints: debtor, bank creditor, agent bank, and servicing bank. An effective bank advisory group will consider all viewpoints in preparing a draft restructure agreement for review by all.

Conclusions

As said at the start, sovereign debt restructure is contractual agreement between individual debtor and individual creditor with respect to the debt in question. The basic business terms and documentation to implement restructure must be acceptable to individual debtor and creditor with respect to each item of debt subject to restructure. The responsibility to determine ultimate acceptability remains with each debtor and creditor. When existing debt is outstanding under syndicated credit agreements, pursuant to which many banks have extended credit to a debtor, the basic business terms and documentation also must be acceptable to the agent bank and all other banks party to the syndicated credit agreement. Generally, the business terms and documentation also must be acceptable to each bank holding a silent participation in debt payable to another bank. When the restructure condition of each bank creditor is that all other bank creditors also restructure all of their debt, the jury of independent judges of business terms and the restructure documentation expands exponentially. In addition to passing judgment of an infinite jury, the bank financing package must be structured so that it in fact can be implemented. The conditions to restructure must be consistent, not mutually exclusive. The restructure agreements must work from the operational viewpoint of debtor, bank creditor, agent bank, and servicing bank.

The challenge to all principals on the banking side of the restructure process (and to their respective counsel) is first to see the vague shape, then to help design, and then to construct the small eye of the needle which represents a consensus of debtors, bank creditors, agent banks, bank advisory groups, and servicing banks. In short, the fundamental requirements for sovereign debt restructure are the ability to compromise and to achieve consensus. The ultimate irony is that once a consensus is reached and implemented, the basic questions have been answered for just a finite period of time. The process of compromise and consensus building will continue as part of an ongoing financing process, hopefully in a voluntary lending environment, if the combination of the restructure package and external factors permits economic and financial recovery and the restoration of normal debt service.

Note

1. The following general description of a bank advisory group is based on a paper prepared jointly with Mark Walker, Esq. of Clearly, Gottlieb, Steen, and Hamilton for the Institute of International Finance.

5
Debt Restructure Agreements: Perspective of Counsel for Borrowing Countries

James Hurlock

The international debt crisis continues. Although short-term responses have been devised by public and private creditors of defaulting sovereign borrowers since the current round of sovereign insolvencies began in 1975, there remain today a number of debtor countries that are not servicing their external debts and have no near- or long-term expectations of doing so under present circumstances. Indeed the process of debt restructure[1] has typically been insensitive not only to the immediate situation and requirements of the sovereign borrower, but also to its long-term capital and growth needs. The banks have often taken the inflexible position that no restructuring of debt was possible unless the borrowing country first agreed to pay all interest arrearages, including penalties and interest on interest, and was willing to mortgage virtually all of its national assets. In return, the banks would agree to lend "new money," frequently needed to pay the back interest, and to reschedule loans immediately due. In 1984, however, there was some indication that lenders would under certain circumstances accept a more accommodating, longer-term approach to solving the debt problem of sovereign borrowers.

In 1984 Mexico was permitted by its commercial bank creditors to reschedule more than the current year's maturities of its external debt at what were termed "concessionary rates." It is said that this longer-term approach at slightly more reasonable rates was a reward for Mexico's willingness to accept the IMF's prescriptions for belt tightening, which in turn produced an improvement in Mexico's net foreign currency position.[2] The idea that Mexico has been rewarded for good behavior by its benevolent creditors is important, not because it will somehow "solve" the continuing financial problems in Central and South America, but because for the first time a sovereign's commercial creditors have agreed that a debtor country has a sustainable level of debt that can be supported but not exceeded.

Unfortunately, the risk accepted by the creditors in taking this approach in the case of Mexico, which is a significant oil-producing country, is quite unlike the risk that will have to be taken in applying this principle, as it eventually must be, to countries less well endowed and apparently less deserving of creditor countries' attention and support. Contrast, for example, the relative liberality of the 1984 restructuring of Mexico's debt with the one agreed to in December 1984 between Argentina and its bank advisory group. The latter would reschedule maturities of loans due only in 1985, and much of the new money would go to repay $750 million in back interest owed the banks and $750 million owed the United States under a prior bridge loan. Notwithstanding the tighter terms of this agreement, many banks (as of December 1984) are reluctant to sign on.[3] In other words, before we can take the 1984 Mexican restructure as a sign of hope, its vision must be expanded to other countries less able than Mexico to demonstrate in the short term their ability to respond to the dictates of the IMF.

From the perspective of borrowing sovereigns, other recent developments have been discouraging. One is the increase in strategic behavior among the constituents of the lending community. In the late 1970s and early 1980s, the existence of an IMF program and timely drawing under it was the sole conditional relationship between the IMF and commercial bank restructuring and new money facilities. The IMF's greatly increased role in resolving the 1982 Mexican crisis changed and complicated the relationship profoundly. Currently, borrowing sovereign states may expect to encounter in negotiation what are for them unmanageable cross currents of pressure being exerted by the IMF, the World Bank, Western governments, and the commercial banks, as each tries to force the others to accept prior and bigger commitments as a condition to its own participation. Thus, no one is willing to lend new money unless other institutions also extend new credit, and all of the lenders—including the official ones that are supposed to take a broader, "world interest" view—pressure the borrowing country to adopt draconian austerity policies to produce large positive trade balances. The pressure on developing countries to mortgage future growth, or even a survival standard of living for its people, in order to make current principal and interest payments on their debts is enormous.

Notwithstanding these events, the problem for counsel to the sovereign borrower remains very much unchanged. That problem is simply the continuing impossibility of negotiating appropriate solutions on a short-term basis for each country's debt problems; the solutions negotiated too often offer little realistic hope of long-term rehabilitation of the country's creditworthiness. Most often the short-term (or short-leash) approach proposed by lenders seems to respond not at all to the financial and political realities of the situation, but instead responds to the alleged effect on the international banking community of lower earnings and disclosure of nonperforming loans. The assumptions made by bank economists regarding estimated foreign currency inflows are optimistic at best and purely phantasmal at worst. The often heard explanation that the situation can be reviewed in six months or a year to correct errors saps the credibility, energy, goodwill, and resolve of both sides. Worse, it ignores the political facts of life, which may give the current government of the sovereign limited time and scope for maneuver in solving the debt problem.

Against this background, I propose to examine the role of counsel for borrowing countries in responding to creditor demands in the negotiations and contracts generated by sovereign debt restructuring. Additionally, I want to suggest some of the directions in which the process ought to be heading.

Role of Debtor Country's Counsel and the Dilemmas of the Restructure Process

Once a borrowing country and its creditors determine that the country can no longer make principal and interest payments on its external indebtedness, there ensues a long process of negotiations leading up to a restructure of all or part of the external indebtedness.[4] Within this context the duties of counsel to a foreign sovereign borrower are unchanging, even as the process evolves, and include the following. First, counsel develops with the help of others an information base for determining how much is owed to whom by the sovereign and its constituents and the details of the maturities, interest-rate calculations, and other legal characteristics of the various debts. Then, the debts must be classified in terms of priority, both legal and political. This is no easy task, for in developing countries there is often no one person with knowledge of all the country's outstanding debt, and no central collection of debt instruments. Even when the country does have systematic records, they may be inaccurate. Consequently, it is usually difficult, if not impossible, to draw conclusions about the current status of the outstanding debt from the sovereign itself. Hence, counsel for the borrowing country often must ask each of the lenders to provide this information, a most unsatisfactory way to represent a client.

Second, representatives of the lenders and the sovereign must research and analyze the constitutional and legislative requirements affecting payment of external indebtedness. Frequently, a government is unaware of the constitutional and legislative requirements imposed upon it in borrowing and repaying debt. When default occurs, the parties may discover that rescheduling or restructuring is not possible without an act of legislature, which, as a political matter, can be obtained only with difficulty and delay. Also, the legal status, authority, and administrative strength of the country's central bank must be studied and a determination made as to whether it does or does not own the country's foreign exchange reserves. A further judgment as to the relationship in the future between private and public sector debt must be made, with consideration given to the mechanics for changing, if necessary, the present relationship to that which is desired.

Third, counsel should analyze the sovereign's economic structure to determine an appropriate approach to rescheduling or restructuring the outstanding debt and future borrowing. Counsel must ascertain the manner in which the sovereign trades to obtain foreign currency earnings (which will be needed to service the external debt), to assure that no unnecessary or unreasonable restraints are placed on that trade. One point often overlooked in a country's default is that many developing countries have state-controlled economies: many or most of the manufacturing or commercial enterprises are owned or controlled by the state rather than by private capital.[5] Hence, restructuring of sovereign debt must at all costs avoid impairing the day-to-day business activities that are essential to the country's economic well-being and its prospects of earning hard currency through expanding exports.

Fourth, once sovereign's counsel have informed themselves, they are prepared to assist their client in initial discussions with a bank steering or "advisory" committee which undertakes to represent the entire universe of commercial bank creditors for the purpose of negotiating the restructuring of debts owed to the banks.[6] Typically, the initial meeting between a sovereign and its banks' steering committee has usually found the steering committee demanding the repayment in full of all outstanding commercial bank debt without discrimination in relation to multilateral and government-to-government debt, which is ordinarily kept current. It is somewhat hard to take such a demand seriously, because everyone recognizes that certain lenders and certain kinds of debt have priority, but nevertheless the point of departure is the same.[7]

A further demand initially made by the bank steering committee is adherence to the basic terms of solution recently negotiated with other countries, on the perfectly legitimate ground that the banks cannot be seen to favor one debtor over another. It is equally true, however, that the current solution, if it be a solution, for Poland has no necessary relation to what may be the requirements in Costa Rica. The total level of sustainable debt will be different for each country, as will the prospects for export-led trade surpluses, successful control of inflation, and reduction of public sector deficits by strong government policies, as well as the overall composition of the country's debt burden. These variables ought to influence the interest rate charged, the amount of debt rescheduled, and the treatment of interest arrearages more than they traditionally have.

The banks will also require that any arrearages of interest be brought current, usually with payment of interest on interest and penalty interest, which requirement often requires new loans. Other options are, of course, available to the banks—capitalization of overdue interest, freezing the interest so that no compound interest accrues, reducing overdue interest—which would improve the borrowing country's long-range ability to pay in many cases. But the banks usually require payment of back interest as a preliminary condition so that they can continue to accrue interest on their loans and to avoid writing off any significant part the credits now carried on their books at full value less a general undesignated reserve. These objectives are not unreasonable from the perspective of the banks, but they may not accord remotely with the financial condition and expectations of the borrower. Similarly, the banks will normally limit dicussion of restructuring to current maturities, with the resolution of problems represented by later maturities to be left for the future. The 1984 Mexican restructure is a departure from this pattern, but the 1984 Argentina restructure appears to follow it.

Finally, the banks have been requesting various fees in connection with the restructures. For example, the 1982–83 Mexican restructure required the obligors to pay each bank a "restructure fee" of 1 percent of the credits rescheduled and to pay the servicing bank (the bank coordinating the restructure for that obligor) a "servicing bank fee."[8] Additionally, the obligor agreed to reimburse the servicing bank for all documented and reasonable costs and expenses connected with the bank's preparation to act as servicing bank, its preparation and execution of the restructure agreement, and its investigation of events of default.[9] Not surprisingly, these "costs and expenses" are often rather high. In connection with the rescheduling of the debt of one very small country in 1984, the printing bill for the agreement alone came to $470,000. Some of the individual fees are mind boggling, and in the aggregate the fees for restructuring can become quite unreasonable burdens on a debtor country.

While it is generally not part of this initial discussion between sovereign and commercial bank lenders, the occasion of default has normally caused the banks to withdraw the short- and medium-term lines of credit that are generally essential to the country's trade mechanisms. The problems that led to default—which are essentially problems of liquidity—are thus further exacerbated.

Against this background, the sovereign and its advisers, including counsel, seek to negotiate a restructuring of external debt which responds realistically to the political and financial facts as they see them. Politically, there are limits on the sacrifices a government can demand of its people and the various interest groups without creating a political crisis.[10] If the size of the country or other considerations may permit the lenders to remain aloof from or to take a more cynical view of these political constraints, such liberty is not available to the governmental representatives of the sovereign, whose ability to gather domestic legislative support and perhaps to preserve their own terms in office depend on not only finding a solution to the debt problem but also creating and maintaining a viable domestic economy. Financially, the borrowing country is often unable realistically to accommodate the bank's standard demands for full repayment of principal and interest arrearages, current "market" interest rates, penalty interest, short- rather than long-term reschedules, and myriad fees. In short, the fact is that borrowing countries often have legitimate political and financial objections to the banks' standard terms. Yet their negotiating position, however well founded, is seldom more than weak. Strength is found, if at all, in the magnitude of a particular sovereign's debt and the threat that it represents to the stability of the world's banking system.[11]

At present both borrowers and lenders have stated publicly, though perhaps the self-congratulation is premature, that we have muddled through: borrowing countries have made enormous sacrifices, and the banks have made some concessions. It is a fact, however, that there exist today a number of failed restructurings where current payment of interest as well as principal is not being made. The same fate is not unthinkable for Mexico or Brazil.

Borrowing Country's Needs in the Restructure Agreement

The central dilemma of the representative of the borrowing country in the restructure negotiations is to negotiate a deal that is satisfactory to the banks but does not cripple the country's economy (hence, its ability to generate exports to earn hard currency which can be used to service the debt). In this respect principal emphasis should be given to those mechanical aspects of a restructuring agreement which are and will be essential to success. Among these are agreement on definitions affecting what debt is to be considered for restructuring, the identity of the borrower, the breadth of the negative pledge clause, the scope of the cross default clause, the extent of the waiver of sovereign immunity, as well as formulations regarding the calculation of interest rate and the relevance of the IMF and World Bank support, and the need for new money which will add to net capital inflows that will support continued imports.

Indebtedness

Generally, the definition of external indebtedness should be limited to debt for borrowed monies denominated in a foreign currency and payable outside the country. Other kinds of external debt may lend themselves readily to other forms of treatment including repayment in local currency or renegotiation on a different basis. Publicly issued debt generally should be excluded unless a ready means for a consensual restructuring exists or unless it is held by institutions otherwise participating in the restructuring. Short-term debt and trade debt should be and have been subject to different programs. Generally, the restructure just involves external debt to the state and its subdivisions, department, and agencies, although sometimes private sector debt is also included. Such a decision is largely a function of the magnitude of private sector debt and the extent to which private debtors have and will continue to be allowed to generate their own sources of foreign exchange.

Borrower and Default Clauses

The definition of the "borrower" is of great importance in various contexts. The standard World Bank definition of borrower for negative pledge clause purposes is, in effect, the government and all entities owned or controlled by the government.[12] In a country characterized by a state economy, this definition will inevitably sweep in everything—including the local hotel and the corner gas station as well as the state airline and the country's maritime fleet. Such breadth in defintion may have devastating effects in the context of the negative pledge clause as well as the cross-default clause.[13] The effect today is that the World Bank definition and the technical defaults under it and consequent cross defaults under most other external debt instruments has most Third World debt in technical default. The usual representation in new instruments and restructurings as to the nonexistence of defaults perpetuates the problem.

The borrower ought normally to be defined as the sovereign state and its agencies and departments which do not have independent juridical status, not including the central bank unless it is such an agency or department. As the central bank is usually the owner of the country's reserves, it is ordinarily in the interests of both borrower and lender to forbid the creation of a lien on such reserves (through the negative pledge clause) and, at the same time, to free such reserves from attachment by any one of many differently situated lenders by excluding the central bank and its assets from coverage under the definition of borrower.

Negative Pledge and Cross-Default Clauses

The negative pledge clause is another area of important responsibility for counsel to a sovereign in a restructuring. This clause is a covenant by the obligor or the guarantor pledging that it will not create or allow liens on the property or revenues.[14] If you do it for one, you must do if for others. When combined with a broad definition of "borrower," all or most of the public sector in a country where public enterprises perform most commercial and manufacturing activities, the negative pledge clause could theoretically tie up most forms of day-to-day trade financing and, effectively, eliminate short-term commercial credit. With a default clause to enforce this limitation, financing of the country's trade could be crippled.

For this reason, the negative pledge clause should be severely limited. The World Bank normally grants but one exception, the purchase money mortgage, to its total prohibition of the creation of liens on the assets of the borrower. Commercial lenders have been quicker to see the point than the World Bank; thus, the 1982–83 Mexican restructure agreement contained eleven separate exceptions.[15] But it is still the case that most legitimate and necessary trade and project financing will run afoul of inartistic negative pledge clauses. Only the acceptance of information concerning the working of the sovereign's economy, which most lenders do not have, will solve this problem. The irony is that the sovereign and its commercial bank lenders are almost equally affected, the former by an imposed paralysis on the financing of its normal trade and development activities, the latter by an inability to do trade, short-term, and project financing by reason of the very restrictions they have imposed.

The same kind of excesses can be found in cross-default formulations, where potential defaults by any of the entities included in the definition of borrower, whether or not called, may create a default for the borrower generally.[16] Such a default is available to any lender, including the most recalcitrant. From the sovereign's perspective, an exclusion should be sought for defaults relating to debt not exceeding a minimum amount, in order to reduce the potential mischief that can be caused by inconsequential lenders. The loss of enforcement power this position allegedly creates for the other lenders has been much discussed but little demonstrated.

Interest Rates on Restructured Indebtedness

Typically, new money and rescheduled debt bear something approaching the current market interest rate—expressed in terms of X percent above the London Interbank Offer Rate.[17] The rate will then typically float with the market, currently running 8 percent to 10 percent above the rate of inflation (virtually unprecedented in this century).[18] This abnormally high interest rate is in addition to the fees discussed previously. It has become increasingly clear that a large number of small and medium-sized borrower countries are not able to carry the interest and fee burdens imposed upon them in restructurings of external debt. The proof is found in the failure of these restructurings.[19]

The time may well have come to borrow again from the techniques of domestic bankruptcies, where in appropriate cases a limit must be imposed on the interest burden that lies within a realistic judgment of the country's ability to pay. If the estimate proves to be low and the country's performance better than anticipated, the amount of interest payable can be increased on the basis of a flexible formulation. But the increase or repeated increase in a country's stock of debt by the lending of "new money" to pay back interest or the capitalization of interest differentials to the same effect does little but exacerbate the situation. Banks may argue that the charging of less than a market rate of interest (whatever that may be in the case of a defaulted sovereign) will force the write-down of loans, as well as nonaccrual of interest under relevant national regulation. If interest at a capped rate is being paid, the latter seems improbable, and it has yet to be demonstrated from a regulatory point of view that loans operating under an interest cap would be subject to a greater percentage of write-off than is now the case. Disclosure requirements would obviously apply, but with arguably less serious results than the disclosure of loans which are classified on a nonaccrual basis.

Waiver of Sovereign Immunity

Most sovereigns do not today contest the need to accept a waiver of sovereign immunity as part of their foreign borrowing, and restructure agreements typically include a clause waiving immunity of the obligor, guarantor, and the central bank, as well as consenting to the jurisdiction of specified courts.[20] There is, however, a question as to how far that acceptance should go. Prejudgment attachment is one element of such acceptance that may well be excluded both to avoid the harassment that can result and to free negotiations with steering committees which inevitably will occur on such occasions from the diversion of attention and debilitating effects of such initiatives by individual creditors. It can be argued that creditors in fact lose nothing by forgoing such acceptance, since a well-advised sovereign will have taken reasonable steps to avoid attachment and, more important, creditors as a class do not normally benefit from the race to the court house door. They certainly did not in the case of Iran, notwithstanding imaginative and unfortunately expensive efforts in the United States, France, and Germany.

The Role of the IMF

Finally, the increasing involvement of the IMF, World Bank, and others in the structure of restructuring agreements appears to be a mixed blessing. The increased role of the IMF in sovereign restructuring has generally been beneficial, if occasionally precipitate. The efforts by other lenders in the context of loan documentation to impose upon the IMF duties that it may not wish to assume (or to assume publicly) is less helpful and puts the sovereign in a position where it is even less in control of its destiny than is otherwise the case. A recent effort by the IMF to condition its agreement for a new program on the provision of structural adjustment credit to be furnished by the World Bank and the commercial bank creditors left the sovereign dependent on institutions and their schedules of priority over which it had no control and little persuasive effect. In addition, the commercial bank creditors required that the IMF designate for the ensuing year the foreign currency shortfall that would need to be covered. This is the kind of information that no party has yet successfully generated. The implications of incorrect estimation were clear, and it was clear that the parties were creating more problems than were being solved. In many respects the less involved or more aloof posture of the IMF a few years ago was easier to accommodate in sovereign restructuring negotiations. The apparent growth in competition among the IMF, the World Bank, and the commercial banks in terms of who will contribute how much in what order does give the impression to the sovereign of being involved in somebody else's battle that is being fought in the wrong place at the wrong time.

Conclusion

The points discussed are hardly exhaustive of the problems faced by counsel representing sovereigns engaged in restructuring of external debt. They do include some of what seems to be new and some of what seems to be crucial to representing adequately the sovereign's interest. In conclusion, a good restructuring agreement should be realistic. Some specific suggestions include the following:

1. Repayment and interest obligations imposed on the sovereign should lie within its realistically estimated ability to pay. Banks and borrowing countries should work out the level of sustainable yearly payments and adjust the payments upward only if the country's exports do better than anticipated.

2. The creditors should have an expectation of receiving payment in appropriate amounts as soon as possible in the light of the sovereign's political requirements and the economy's need for essential imports.

3. The sovereign should have freedom in terms of its economic structure to trade profitably and to accumulate appropriate foreign exchange reserves.

4. A negative pledge clause should be agreed to which responds to the economic realities of the debtor. A cross-default clause should be agreed to which protects both debtor and creditors from precipitate action and unnecessary relation to immaterial events.

5. The maintenance of international monetary reserves in an unencumbered form should be assured for the benefit of all creditors.

6. Appropriately limited tax indemnities should be agreed. The world need not be covered.

7. A limitation on set-off rights should be stated which limits set-off to accounts held by the specific lender. Otherwise negative pledge clauses may be breached.

8. An appropriate percentage of holders required for a waiver or an amendment of a restructuring agreement should be designated.

Conversely, the following results are to be avoided:

1. An agreement that is in default or will be in default on the day of signature.

2. An agreement under which the recovery of the economy in the sovereign is unnecessarily impeded.

3. An agreement that violates the domestic laws of the debtor or that will be politically offensive and in the long-term detrimental to the interests of those with whom the lenders have negotiated their agreement.

Notes

1. The debt restructuring process is described by Alfred Mudge in chapter 4 of this book.

2. See "Mexico, Foreign Banks Agree to Work Out Plan to Reschedule Several Years of Debt," *Wall Street Journal,* June 6, 1984, p. 37, col. 2; "Banks Give Ground on Mexico Debt Terms in Exchange for Close Watch on Economy," *Wall Street Journal,* August 30, 1984, p. 23, col. 1.

3. See "Bankers Said Skeptical of Argentine Plan," *Washington Post,* December 4, 1984, p. E1, col. 3 and E8, col. 1. In early 1985 Brazil and its bank creditors were negotiating a restructure of much of Brazil's external debt. See "Brazil to Resume Talks on Restructuring Debt," *New York Times,* January 3, 1985, p. D8, col. 5.

4. See also my treatment of the role of counsel for borrowing countries, "The Legal Treatment of Sovereign Default: The Borrower's Perspective," in David Suratgar, ed., *Default and Rescheduling: Corporate and Sovereign Borrowers* (Washington, D.C.: Euromoney Publications, 1984), pp. 103, 106.

5. See generally United Nations Department of Economic and Social Affairs, *Organization, Management and Supervision of Public Enterprises in Developing Countries* (New York: United Nations, 1974); W.G. Friedmann and J.F. Garner, eds., *Government Enterprise: A Comparative Study* (1970).

6. The steering committee and particularly its chairman do not have an enviable task. The banks are invariably of several different nationalities and are incorporated in jurisdictions having different political relations with the sovereign. The banks themselves have a variety of dissimilar interests as regards their credits to the sovereign and, depending on their size and relative exposures as well as the trading interest of their domestic customers, are likely to have individual agendas not easily reconciled. Finally, given the proliferation of such committees, the banks may be

unable to avoid the fact that the authority and level of exposure of its participants may be disparate or less than sufficient for the task. If in turn the chairman is not a person of some ability, the chances of the committee acting in an effective and constructive manner are greatly reduced.

7. The traditional ranking puts multilateral debt, IMF, World Bank, Asian Development Bank, and similar institutional debt first. It is an article of faith that this debt is not defaulted upon or rescheduled. Even in a default situation, institutional debt is normally paid on a current basis. Second priority is assigned to bilateral government debt, and a third priority is publicly issued debt. The relationship between publicly issued debt and commercial bank debt is little understood. Trade creditor debt is ranked fourth, followed by secured debt, short-term debt and local currency debt.

8. Model Mexican Restructure Agreement, Article III, §§ 3.01–.02 (Final Draft July 27, 1983).

9. Model Mexican Restructure Agreement, Article XIII, § 13.05(a). Mexico, the guarantor, agreed to pay certain expenses of the bank's advisory group. See § 13.05(d).

10. For the political problems in Latin American borrowing countries, see generally Howard Wiarda and Harvey Kline, eds., *Latin American Politics and Development* (Boston: Houghton Mifflin, 1979).

11. William Cline, *International Debt and the Stability of the World Economy,* (Washington, D.C.: Institute of International Economics, 1983), pp. 74–82, concludes that in 1983, one-half or more of the total new bank lending to developing countries was "involuntary lending," based upon the banks' fear of default on existing loans if new money were not advanced.

12. A negative pledge clause provides that the sovereign borrower shall not create liens or charges on its assets or revenues in favor of other creditors. For an example of a standard negative pledge clause in World Bank agreements, see Georges Delaume, *Legal Aspects of International Lending and Economic Development Financing* (New York: Oceana Publications, 1967), pp. 251–55. In commercial bank syndicated loan agreement, assets of sovereign borrower include assets of the country's political subdivisions, agencies, and central bank (Michael Bradfield and Nancy Jacklin, "The Problems Posed by Negative Pledge Covenants in International Loan Agreements," *Columbia Journal of Transnational Law* 23 (1984):131, 135).

13. See text accompanying note 16.

14. See Delaume, *Legal Aspects of International Lending,* pp. 251–55, for the World Bank clause; see Bradfield and Jacklin, "Negative Pledge Covenants," 134–35, for the clause used in many syndicated sovereign loan agreements.

15. Model Mexican Restructure Agreement, Article IX, § 9.04(a), provides that the guarantor (Mexico) shall not, during the term of the restructured loans:

> (a) *Negative Pledge.* Create or suffer to exist, nor permit any Governmental Agency to create or suffer to exist, any Lien, upon or with respect to any of the present or future properties (including, without limitation, oil, gas and International Monetary Assets) or revenues of the Guarantor or any Governmental Agency, in each case to secure or provide for payment of External Indebtedness, or any interest or other amount payable in connection therewith, of any Person, other than:

(i) Liens upon any property acquired or held by any Governmental Agency incurred to secure the purchase price of such property or to secure External Indebtedness incurred for the purpose of financing the acquisition of such property; or

(ii) Liens existing on such property at the time of its acquisition, *provided* that the aggregate principal amount of the External Indebtedness secured by the Liens referred to in clause (i) above and this clause (ii) does not exceed 120% of the purchase price of such property at any time outstanding; or

(iii) Liens in favor of the Bank for International Settlements or other multilateral monetary authorities or central banks or treasuries of sovereign states other than the United Mexican States securing extensions of credit the duration of which does not exceed one year; or

(iv) Liens on cash collateral accounts or readily marketable securities securing obligations with respect to a letter of credit issued in the course of ordinary commercial banking transactions (and expiring within one year thereafter) to finance the importation of goods into the United Mexican States; or

(v) Liens on property acquired (or deemed to be acquired) by the Guarantor or any Governmental Agency under a financial lease, or claims arising from the use or loss of or damage to such property, *provided* that (A) any such Lien secures only rentals and other amounts payable under such lease and (B) such property was not owned by the Guarantor or any Governmental Agency at any time prior to becoming subject to such lease unless at the time of the acquisition of such property contractual arrangements contemplated that such lease would be executed; or

(vi) Liens which arise pursuant to any order of attachment, distraint or similar legal process arising in connection with court proceedings so long as the execution or other enforcement thereof is effectively stayed and the claims secured thereby are being contested in good faith by appropriate proceedings, *provided* that any such Lien is released or discharged in any case within one year of its imposition; or

(vii) Liens arising by operation of law (and not pursuant to any agreement) which have not been foreclosed or otherwise enforced against the properties to which they apply; or

(viii) Liens securing or providing for the payment of External Indebtedness incurred in connection with any Project Financing, *provided* that the properties to which any such Lien applies are (A) properties which are the subject of such Project Financing or (B) revenues or claims which arise from the operation, failure to meet specifications, exploitation, sale or loss of, or damage to, such properties; or

(ix) Liens in existence on the date hereof, *provided* that such Liens remain confined to the properties presently affected thereby and properties which become affected by such Liens under contracts in effect on the date of this Agreement and *provided further* that such Liens secure or provide for the payment of only those obligations so secured or provided for on the date hereof or any refinancing of such obligations; or

(x) Liens arising in connection with contracts entered into substantially simultaneously for sales and purchases at market prices of precious metals; or

(xi) any Lien on Exportable Assets securing External Indebtedness incurred to finance the business of producing and/or exporting such Exportable Assets, *provided* that (A) such Lien applies only to goods which are expected to be sold or documents evidencing title thereto and the proceeds of any insurance thereon, and the proceeds of sale of which are expected to be received, within 12 months after such goods or proceeds become subject to such Lien and (B) such External Indebtedness (i) is incurred in the normal course of business, (ii) is to be repaid primarily out of proceeds of sale of the Exportable Assets subject to such Lien and (iii) does not arise out of financing provided by the lender with a view to obtaining repayment of other External Indebtedness or on condition that other External Indebtedness be repaid and (C) such Lien is not on oil or gas or the right to receive payment for oil or gas.

A similar negative pledge is imposed on the obligor in § 9.03 of the model agreement.

16. For example, in the Model Mexican Restructure Agreement, the specified "Events of Default" included not only the public obligor's failure to make specified payments or perform specified covenants pursuant to the Restructure Agreement (Article XI, § 11.01(a)–(c)), and not only the obligor's, the guarantor's, or the central bank's failure to observe or perform any term, covenant, or agreement in the restructure agreement (§ 11.01(d)), but also the following:

(e) The Obligor, the Guarantor, Banco de Mexico or any other Governmental Agency shall fail to pay any External Indebtedness (other than in respect of the Credits) of the Obligor, the Guarantor, Banco de Mexico or such other Governmental Agency, as the case may be, in an aggregate principal amount of in excess of U.S. $10,000,000 (or equivalent) for any such obligor or U.S. $75,000,000 (or equivalent) for all such obligors collectively, or any interest or premium thereon, when due (whether at scheduled maturity or by required prepayment, acceleration, demand or otherwise), and such failure shall continue, unless waived in writing, after the applicable grace period, if any, specified in the agreement(s) or instrument(s) relating to such External Indebtedness, *provided* that

(A) any such failure to pay interest or premium on any External Indebtedness by any Governmental Agency shall not constitute an Event of Default unless either (x) such unpaid interest and premium, together with other amounts payable with respect to such External Indebtedness, satisfies one of the aggregate tests set forth above in this subsection (e) or (y) such failure to pay shall continue unremedied for 15 days after written notice thereof shall have been given to the Guarantor by any Person,

(B) any such failure to pay by any Governmental Agency whose aggregate External Indebtedness is less than U.S. $25,000,000 (or equivalent) shall not constitute an Event of Default unless such failure to pay shall continue unremedied for 10 days after written notice thereof shall have been given to the Guarantor by the Servicing Bank or any Bank,

(C) with respect to External Indebtedness of a Mexican Public Sector Borrower which constitutes Specified Debt under the Restructure Principles, any such non-payment when due shall not constitute an Event of Default under this subsection (e) until the day on which the Restructure Agreement contemplated in such Restructure Principles with respect to such Specified Debt becomes effective in accordance with its terms and such Specified Debt shall not be paid when due in accordance with the terms of such Restructure Agreement, and

(D) the foregoing proviso (C) shall not apply to any such Specified Debt with respect to which any creditor initiates legal proceedings or takes any other action or exercises any other contractual or legal remedy in order to receive payment of such Specified Debt, or interest or premium thereon, on terms more favorable than contemplated in the Restructure Principles; or

(f) As a result of any actual or purported default or event of default, any External Indebtedness (other than in respect of the Credits) of the Obligor, the Guarantor, Banco de Mexico or any other Governmental Agency is accelerated or declared to be due and payable, or required to be prepaid (other than by a regularly scheduled required prepayment) prior to the stated maturity thereof; or

(g) Any default or event of default (other than a payment default described in subsection (e) above) contained in any agreement(s) or instrument(s) relating to External Indebtedness (other than in respect of the Credits) of the Guarantor and/or Banco de Mexico in an aggregate principal amount of in excess of U.S. $10,000,000 (or equivalent) shall occur and shall continue after the applicable grace period, if any, specified in such instrument(s) or agreement(s), if the effect of such default or event of default is to permit the acceleration of the maturity of such External Indebtedness in an aggregate principal amount of in excess of U.S. $10,000,000 (or equivalent) . . .

(h) The Guarantor or Banco de Mexico shall admit in writing its inability to pay its debts as they come due or shall declare a moratorium on the payment of its debts or the debts of any Governmental Agency, it being understood that the request to restructure the Specified Debt of Mexican Public Sector Borrowers in accordance with the Restructure Principles and any action, statement or declaration relating thereto does not and will not constitute any Event of Default hereunder; . . .

(q) Any Mexican Public Sector Borrower other than the Obligor shall enter into a Restructure Agreement relating to Debt-Subject to Restructure that provides or is amended to provided for payment terms more favorable with respect to principal, interest or restructure fees than those provided in the Restructure Principles;

. . .

17. Model Mexican Restructure Agreement, Article III.

18. See Roger Kubarych, chapter 1 of this book, tables 1–1 and 1–2.

19. See Thomas Enders and Richard Mattione, *Latin America: The Crisis of Debt and Growth,* Brookings Institution Studies in International Economics (Washington, D.C.: Brookings Institution, 1984), pp. 23–29.

20. For example, Model Mexican Restructure Agreement, Article XIII, § 13.08, "Consent to Jurisdiction; Waiver of Immunities."

6
Business–Government Relations in International Bank Lending: The Debt Crisis

Philip Wellons

Much of the discussion of the international debt crisis has focused on the renegotiation of debt by bankers and borrowing countries, with the International Monetary Fund (IMF) as an important third party. Such a focus ignores an important set of players. Rescheduling is complicated. It involves many parties (many private lenders, sovereign governments and their state agencies, international financial institutions) and is an ongoing process. The restructuring of international debt affects a range of complex legal and business relationships. Many involve the government, whose influence is typically felt at various stages of the process. That is, the bargain struck in the rescheduling process does not just affect the relations and interests of banks and debtor countries. Restructuring agreements also affect the relationships between banks and governments *and* among the banks themselves.

This chapter focuses on the political and business interests and tensions that are being played out in the debt crisis. It is concerned particularly with the "politics" of rescheduling[1] as seen from the perspective of big banks in the Group of Five: France, West Germany, the United Kingdom, the United States, and Japan. These are the banks that make the major decisions about international sovereign lending—where the money is to go, what the terms will be—and then try to put the syndicates together or involve other banks in the market. These banks typically have deep historic roots in their home countries, from which they gradually expanded to meet the needs of their main corporate clients.[2] Today the big international banks in the Group of Five countries are the largest banking institutions in the world. They have enormous and diverse assets, a network of branches in both industrial and developing countries, experience in numerous financial markets, and worldwide connections (see table 6–1).[3] Most of the sovereign lending done in the 1970s was undertaken by these banks. Because of the transnational frame of their operations, the political concerns of these big international banks are complex.

Table 6–1
Major International Banks in Group of Five

| | Rank in Top 300 | | Total Assets (billions of dollars) | | Number of Foreign Branches | | | |
| | | | | | Developed Countries | | LDCs | |
	1975	1978	1975	1978	1975	1978	1975	1978
United States								
Bankamerica	1	1	66.7	94.9	64	85	133	174
Citicorp	2	3	54.3	87.1	64	67	161	167
Chase Manhattan	4	10	40.7	61.2	57	59	127	128
Manufacturers Hanover	16	26	28.3	40.6	18	27	22	28
Morgan Guaranty Trust	19	34	25.8	38.5	31	26	23	24
United Kingdom								
Barclays Bank	9	19	33.0	48.7	73	71	103	123
National Westminster Bank	11	21	32.2	45.3	7	25	3	5
Japan								
Dai-Ichi Kangyo Bank	10	8	36.4	73.3	17	17	16	16
Fuji Bank	13	11	31.7	61.2	13	17	19	19
Sumitomo Bank	15	12	31.5	63.6	16	18	13	13
Mitsubishi Bank	17	13	30.1	62.7	15	16	14	16
Sanwa Bank	18	14	29.1	61.6	15	17	17	18
Industrial Bank of Japan	25	18	23.9	53.3	20	22	16	23
Tokai Bank	33	22	22.9	45.9	10	14	6	7
Mitsui Bank	36	24	22.3	44.1	13	16	18	16
Taiyo-Kobe Bank	38	25	20.1	42.0	9	10	7	5
Bank of Tokyo	28	36	25.9	43.1	39	42	54	53

West Germany

Deutsche Bank	6	34.9	80.3	25	28	40	37
Dresdner Bank	14	28.3	61.6	28	29	33	37
Westdeutsche Landesbank	21	25.5	51.3	20	18	2	5
Commerzbank	26	21.6	48.4	28	35	28	31

France

Banque Nationale de Paris	5	39.2	78.2	34	37	54	60
Credit Lyonnais	7	35.0	74.1	25	26	36	38
Société Generale	8	33.5	66.9	18	29	20	32

Source: United Nations Centre on Transnational Corporations, *Transnational Banks: Operations, Strategies and Their Effects in Developing Countries* (New York: United Nations, 1981), pp. 124–125, table I-1.

The big international banks take political action at several different levels. Each level has different players with different stakes; different resources are available to the various players, who form different sorts of coalitions. At the *Home Level* the players are the banks from the same home country, the home government, and other interest groups at home. In most of the Group of Five, domestic banking is heavily regulated, transborder banking much less so. This phenomenon not only encourages international banking, but creates strategic possibilities for the big banks. At the *International Level,* the complexity increases. Banks from a variety of different countries are involved with a variety of different governments and multilateral financial institutions, such as the IMF, the World Bank, the Bank for International Settlements (BIS), and others. Finally, at the *Borrower Level* the borrowers, particularly the governments as borrowers, introduce another set of players to be reckoned with. The political dynamic becomes still more complex. It is useful to think about the banks' interests in terms of these three political levels.

Marx and Lenin notwithstanding, the goals of the banks relate to economic matters: cost, competitive positioning in the industry, profit opportunities. It follows that the political activities of international banks typically flow from their market interests: the big banks appeal to government authority to preserve or improve their competitive positions, for example. The international debt crisis has presented the big international banks with a potentially disastrous situation: default by debtor countries would ruin the banks' profitability or even render some of them insolvent. In working out new loan arrangements, the big banks want to minimize their losses and preserve or advance their market positions. Politics is a mechanism to achieve these goals.

In discussing these political dimensions, I distinguish between two types of politics in sovereign debt restructuring. In the short run, restructuring problems involve political relations among banks, particularly as big banks and their government allies try to keep the smaller banks from bailing out of their exposure in the debtor countries; in the longer term, restructuring involves political jockeying as governments and different groups in the banking community try to get others to put new funds into the system. In addition, banks use governments and government policies to improve their competitive position in the industry in the long run—after the restructuring is done and countries are growing again. Again, there are two levels. One has to do with the relationships among the leading international banks, as when one leader tries to improve its position against the others, whether in general or in particular markets. The other level involves leader–follower relationships, particularly efforts to keep the followers investing over the long run, while at the same time reducing their ability to disrupt markets as they did in the late 1970s.[4] The following sections explore these two arenas of politics, the restructuring process and the postrestructuring balance of competitive power.

Politics in the Restructuring Process

The restructuring of the external public and private debts of borrowers in developing countries (DCs) in the last decade have typically followed this scenario:[5] much of the debt consists of large-scale "syndicated" loans, that is, loan packages arranged by one or more big international banks but participated in by many more. After the external shocks of 1979 through 1982 (oil price increases, higher interest rates, recession), the debtor country at some point has insufficient cash flow in foreign exchange to service the debt. Hence, the debtor will ask the banks to reschedule a large part of the debt (typically that falling due in the short term) and ask them to lend new money as well. Acting through an "advisory group," the banks negotiate a restructuring along these lines, to prevent a default or an extended moratorium. In most instances the big international banks have the largest relative exposure, and thus the main incentive to accommodate the public or private DC borrowers. Their strategy is to keep the borrower solvent, but without their having to bear all of the costs. This process generates two levels of political maneuvering by the big international banks.

Interbank Politics

With regard to the politics among the banks in a restructuring, the central problem is to keep the "outliers" in. The outliers are the banks with the relatively small exposure. If the borrower which is a less developed country (LDC) were to default, such banks would not lose very much, either absolutely or relatively, whereas the big banks in many cases stand to lose a great deal in both senses. But it is important to keep the outliers in, because their contributions of new money are necessary or useful to keep the debtor solvent, for the time being. Also, if some banks drop out of the restructuring and get away with it (*their* loans are paid off), the whole process unravels, as other larger banks will be tempted to try the same gambit. How do the big banks, the ones that put together and sold the syndicated loan in the first place, keep the small banks in? While the relative levels of involvement by the various lenders are obviously important, in the typical case market forces alone are inadequate. As a result the big banks turn to political forces to accomplish what the market cannot.

At the *Home Level,* the big international banks will try to involve their governments to pressure the small outlier banks into signing onto the restructure (extending the maturities of their loans and agreeing to lend new money to the borrower). The Group of Five governments, of course, have a substantial incentive to intervene if the restructuring involves large sums of money on loan to a sovereign borrower. As a financial regulatory matter, the governments want to prevent a default or write-off on loans that might cause the failure of one or more of the big banks, thereby triggering a financial panic. As a foreign policy matter, the governments want to maintain good trade and financial relations with the debtor country. In many instances, therefore, the government would see the need to intervene in some way for its own interests.

For these reasons, when the Mexican crisis erupted in August 1982, the Board of Governors of the U.S. Federal Reserve System and the Treasury Department and (to a lesser extent) the central banks in other industrial countries played active roles in working out measures to avert a default on most of Mexico's public debt.[6] In December 1982 the Mexican bank advisory group, consisting solely of big international banks, recommended that the banks lend $5 billion in new money to Mexico, the IMF made its own assistance conditional upon that level of new lending. The big banks had reason to agree. The outliers had less incentive, and their initial inclination often was to demur. Some refused to join such a new loan agreement, willing to take their chances with a Mexican default. Paul Volcker, chairman of the Federal Reserve Board, however, urged them to join the package; officers of the Federal Reserve Board and the Treasury Department put pressure on the small banks. By March 1983, 526 banks had signed on to the $5 billion package.[7] Much the same thing may be happening with regard to the December 1984 tentative restructuring package worked out between Argentina and its advisory group (again, consisting only of the big banks): the small banks do not like the terms, but the big banks pressure them to join the package, assisted by the U.S. government, which conducts an active campaign in favor of the agreement.[8]

At the *International Level* the big banks of the dominant industrial country in a particular region take the lead, often backed up by the central bank of their country. In 1982 the U.S. Federal Reserve Board not only helped prevent immediate defaults by Latin American countries, but also coordinated central bank efforts in other Group of Five countries to back up the work of the advisory groups, which were dominated by U.S. banks. The idea is that banks in general will follow the lead of the banks and government from the dominant industrial country. U.S. banks and government regulators have generally taken the leadership positions in the restructuring of Latin American debt, while European banks have assumed the main responsibilities for problems with East European debtors.

Even though banks generally accept this rough division of labor, they do not accept other loss-sharing or risk-sharing features. In connection with the 1982–83 Mexican crisis, I interviewed Japanese bankers who were quite angry at the terms that the American banks had proposed for the rescheduling. In their view the U.S. banks should have picked up a share of new credit larger than their pro rata share of outstanding loans. One reason was that the capital flight from Mexico in the period building up to the crisis had gone disproportionately to American banks. From the Japanese point of view, because U.S. banks benefited the most from events leading up to the crisis, the Americans ought to bear more of the cost. But the Japanese chose not to push the issue very hard in the renegotiations because in their view Mexico is a country for which the United States is responsible. The Japanese banks thus agreed to follow the American lead despite the inequity. Perhaps they thought that if South Korea ever gets in trouble, the American banks should follow the Japanese lead in South Korea.

Interbank politics at the *Borrower Level* also pulls in the government, as illustrated by the experience of small U.S. banks during the 1982–83 Mexican restructuring. Those with a small exposure in Mexico threatened to cause trouble if Mexico did not allow them to fail to review or extend their loans as they fell due. In response pressure on U.S. banks came from the governor of the regional Federal Reserve Bank and from the Office of the Comptroller of the Currency. Although the government officials say they made very few phone calls to urge small banks to cooperate, the fact is that there do not have to be many such calls. Even in the relatively large American banking community, word-of-mouth multiplies the force of those calls. There certainly do not have to be many such calls in the smaller, more oligopolistic banking communities of Japan and Western Europe. The borrowing country's government also exerts pressure on the outliers. Although the borrowing country government exercises far less leverage over small banks than do their home country governments, it may in some instances have leverage. The borrowing country can, for example, threaten to default on the loans of renegade banks: either the small banks agree to the big banks' restructuring proposal (and get something) or they lose their entire loan principal and risk permanent exclusion from selected loan markets. This selective coercive default strategy seems to have been used by Costa Rica against a U.S. bank that refused to participate in the collective restructure agreement,[9] but it may not be used explicitly in many other renegotiations. More commonly the borrowing country's government plays a marketing role for the restructuring proposal. Finance Minister Herzog de Silva of Mexico became something of a bankers' hero as a result of the "success" of the 1982–83 Mexican restructuring, and the December 1984 tentative restructuring of Argentina's debt is being sold to the small banks by Argentine officials themselves, in addition to efforts of officials of the big banks, their home governments, and the IMF and other multilateral institutions.

Governmental interest and involvement in interbank politics of sovereign debt restructuring has been ubiquitous. It occurs at each level. It involves the home governments of the international banks and, sometimes, borrowing country governments as well. An important general conclusion is that in these interbank politics the governments ally themselves with their big international banks.

Bail-out Politics

Bail-out politics is the big banks' effort to get some government to pay some of the costs or bear much of the burden of a sovereign debt restructuring. The problem for the big banks with large exposure is to get others to put in new money. Whether or not the exposed banks themselves put in new money, they want new funds to come into the problem country, either to support growth or to help them reduce their exposure to the extent possible, since they can never fully get out. The politics vary with the level. At the *Home Level,* the goal of the big international banks is to persuade their home governments to be a source of funds for the ailing debtor country or to manage the economy so as to reduce the pressure on the debt-ridden LDC.

The problem for the big banks at the *Borrower's Level* is to have the borrower government as an ally. Obviously desirable in negotiating public sector debt (whether the debt is that of the government itself or that of a state-owned enterprise), this is also important in the rescheduling of private sector debt. The cooperation of the borrower's country and its central bank is essential to the export of capital to service the debt, at the very least. In 1982 Mexico instituted stringent limits on foreign currency exchange that prevented many solvent private debtors from making scheduled payments. The banks faced regulatory requirement to reclassify the loans if payments were not kept current; the result would be to require the banks to raise additional capital. To solve the problem (which was temporary), the banks enlisted the aid of the Mexican central bank and the Federal Reserve Board: the central bank set up a peso account for each lender, and the private debtors made peso payments into the account, to be paid over to the lender by the central bank as dollars became available; the Federal Reserve Board and other regulators said that this met all regulatory requirements.[10]

In other instances the banks will ask that the state become the guarantor of the private sector debt.[11] In the case of Alfa, Visa, and some of the other bankrupt conglomerates in Mexico, for example, the banks devoted a fair part of the negotiations to bringing in the Mexican government as guarantor. In that case the critical element was the political dynamic within Mexico: the relative power of the technical people in the government and the power groups outside the government. Whether the Mexican government would come in to help the banks depended on domestic politics in Mexico—on what the government technocrats could get from the private sector.

At the *International Level,* the strategy of the big banks is to encourage multilateral financial institutions such as the IMF or BIS to supply new money. Thus the advisory group dominated by big international banks will usually not recommend advancing new money to an illiquid sovereign borrower unless the IMF agrees to advance money, on condition of the country's agreement to an IMF austerity program. This strategy, of course, is one that the IMF has learned to deploy as well. In connection with the 1982 Mexican crisis, the banks assumed the IMF would advance substantial amounts of new funds, perhaps relieving them of that onus. The IMF managing director, however, took the position in November 1982 that he would not recommend an IMF loan unless the banks assured Mexico $5 billion in new money. The banks reluctantly agreed.[12] This is an example of double conditionality: the international institution forwards new money only if the banks will, and the banks will forward new money only if one or more international financial institutions will.

Very often the politics at the *Home Level* and the *International Level* are connected by the notion of regional dominance. U.S. banks are responsible for Latin America because of their country's greater geopolitical and trade relations there. For the same reason the banks are more likely to persuade their home government to advance money in Latin America than they would be in arguing for new U.S. loans to Poland, for example.

The interesting point about this phenomenon is that the United States seems to make significant distinctions as to its level of support for different Latin American countries. One need not look far to understand why the U.S. government is more involved in Latin America than in Poland. But it is also accurate to say that the U.S. government did more in Mexico than in Brazil. Table 6–2 compares the assistance the U.S. government provided Mexico,

Table 6–2
U.S. Government Assistance in Restructures (Volume and Timing)
(billions of U.S. dollars)

	Mexico	Brazil
Financial support		
Commodity credit	$1.00 (one weekend August 1982)	$0.25 (June 1983)
Swap/BIS	1.00 (one weekend August 1982)	1.23 (September 1982)
Oil reserve	1.00 (one weekend August 1982)	—
Eximbank	—	— (promised mid-1983)
Total	$3.00	$1.48
Pressure		
International	Mobilized central banks of other OECD countries	Failed to get much new money from other Group of Five governments
Domestic	Fast and thorough pressure campaign timed to reassure banks to accept Mexican restructure	Informed from start, but no active pressure on small banks until after May 1983

with U.S. assistance to Brazil. The absolute volume of funds in the first year was twice as high in Mexico as it was in Brazil. Moreover, the help came much faster. For Mexico these funds were arranged in a very short period of time (over a weekend), compared to many months for Brazil. By a more qualitative measure the pressure that the U.S. government exerted on behalf of the rescheduling process in the two countries was much greater for Mexico than for Brazil both at the international level and also at the home level. What accounts for the different United States' policy reaction?[13]

From bankers and others involved in these transactions, I have heard several different arguments to explain U.S. policy. One argument is that Brazil *wanted* the United States to go more slowly. The Brazilians did not want to be treated like the Mexicans. The Brazilians did not want to take the official route of rescheduling and, for their own political reasons, preferred a gradualist approach.[14] It is also argued that people did not recognize the Brazilian problem as fast. But while the Brazilians did not give even their own bankers as much information about their performance as they had in the past, it had been clear for several years leading up to the actual crisis that Brazil had severe problems. In any event why would the U.S. government choose to acquiesce in the Brazilians' interpretation of what was good U.S. policy? There are several different answers. Perhaps the United States was more concerned about the impact of a crisis in Mexico than in Brazil—the impact on the U.S. financial system, on the U.S. economy, and on U.S. foreign policy concerns.

As table 6–3 shows, however, the U.S. financial system was not substantially more exposed in Mexico than in Brazil at the end of 1982. The numbers are high and imposing in both Brazil and Mexico, and although slightly bigger in Mexico, the $6 billion difference between the two is not, for policy responses, significant. The market share of U.S. banks in both countries was about the same, as was the exposure of the biggest banks, according to Salomon Brothers. Lending as a share of capital in Mexico was 60 percent, and in Brazil was 54 percent. This is a lot of money in both countries. The differences for the U.S. financial system are not large enough to justify a substantially different response by the U.S. government.

Differences in equity interests are also not helpful to explain U.S. policy. In fact, direct U.S. investment in the two countries suggests the United States would move more quickly for Brazil. As a result of Mexican national control policies, foreign direct investment by the United States in Mexico was about 60 percent of that in Brazil at the end of 1982. Out of the total $221 billion U.S. investment worldwide, Mexico's share is even smaller than Brazil's 4 percent. The difference in treatment of the two countries cannot simply be a result of our foreign direct investment there.

U.S. domestic politics and national security policy emerge as most important. Enormous differences exist in U.S. trade with the two countries (see table 6–3). Recorded trade by the United States with Mexico was almost 8

Table 6–3
Economic Measures of U.S. Interests, End-1982
(billions of U.S. dollars)

	Mexico	Brazil	Total
All U.S. banks' exposure			
Amount	$25	$19	
Market share	39%	34%	
Exposure/capital			
Top 9 U.S. banks	60%	54%	
Amount	($14)	($12)	
U.S. foreign direct investment			
Stock	$5.6	$9	$221
Share	2.5%	4.1%	100%
U.S. exports			
Flow	$17.8	$3.8	$224
Share	7.9%	1.7%	100%

percent of all exports at the end of 1981. U.S. trade with Brazil is a much smaller share. The clear balance in favor of Mexico on trade translates into jobs, and so into political issues. If one adds to that the long border, the immigrants, the cultural connections, one concludes that very close social and economic ties to Mexico that shape domestic U.S. politics explain this special treatment for Mexico.

These U.S. interests—trade, culture, and security—are outside the financial system. Comparison of the Mexican and Brazilian restructurings suggests that banks wanting to ensure their home government's active support should rely on factors other than simply the state of the financial system. The details, however, were managed primarily by players within the financial system.

In reviewing many of these reschedulings, one finds the big banks adopt a strategy similar to that used in Mexico. They want their home governments to become involved, but only up to a point. While few bankers will acknowledge this publicly, two implicit goals emerge from their behavior. The first goal is to keep the management of the problem *within* the financial system. Once the debate reaches beyond the financial system, with congressmen asking pesky questions, banks and their regulators have much less control.[15] The banks' second goal is to shift the costs of rescheduling *outside* the financial system. Trade-offs must inevitably be made: somebody has to pay a price in all these reschedulings. The trade-offs are not limited to direct lending by home government, but include other, more indirect, sacrifices that the political process will force onto nonbank groups. For example, in connection with the 1983 Brazilian restructuring, that cost to the United States included reducing trade barriers for Brazilian exporters to the United States. At a broader level, in the United States the compromise over the 1983 IMF quota bill included an increase in U.S. government expenditures for domestic housing.[16] Germans negotiated similar trade-offs in the Polish rescheduling.

Banks' Competitive Positioning for the Longer Run

Less elaborately choreographed is another type of behavior, political in that it involves governments. Big banks must think about their long-run positions in world markets. Among the many ways to classify these markets, I distinguish here between markets for leaders and markets for followers. In each of these markets the international debt crisis affords opportunities for the big international banks not just to maintain, but also to improve, their competitive positions. And, not surprisingly, one of the means they may use is the manipulation of various governments.

Competition among Leading Banks

While most behavior in a restructuring is designed to cut losses, long-run concerns prompt a lead bank to try to emerge from a restructuring in a better competitive position vis-à-vis other lead banks than before. The ambitious bank may, for example, aim to displace existing leaders, often including lenders from its own country.

At the *Borrower Level,* if one assumes that the country or its state trading companies will return to a position of liquidity,[17] a big international bank can position itself for a larger share of the loan market in that country if it plays a prominent and constructive role in the restructuring. By building up a favorable network of connections within the LDC government, the leader bank can emerge from the crisis with a competitive advantage over other leader banks. One example of this phenomenon was the restructuring of the debt for Pertamina, the Indonesia state oil company, in the 1970s. Citibank, a major leader before the crisis, found that Morgan Guaranty took the main leadership role in the rescheduling, a big syndicated loan that gave Morgan a leadership position it had not held in Indonesia before. Morgan took advantage of strategic opportunities in the debt crisis.

Citibank executives have concluded that the bank will benefit if it takes a more aggressive role in the current round of restructurings. When the Mexican crisis erupted in the latter half of 1982, William Rhodes of Citibank emerged as the key figure for the big banks and not just because Citibank was the main lender to Mexico. Rhodes had personal relationships with the Mexican finance minister and at least one important IMF official, and (by all accounts) can get along with anyone, from Walter Wriston of Citibank to Paul Volcker of the Federal Reserve Board. Rhodes's success in managing the enormous problems arising out of the arduous Mexican restructure has probably redounded to the benefit of Citibank, and he subsequently was named chairman or cochairman of the bank advisory committees for Brazil, Argentina, Peru, and Uruguay.[18]

The debt restructuring affects big bank competitive positions at the *Home Level.* An interesting example of the effects of debt restructuring in the home level can be found in Japan. Japanese bankers have established a national center for international finance akin to the Institute for International Finance in Washington, D.C. The Ministry of Finance and the central bank of Japan established the center, staffed it with eighty or more people from banks all over the country and funded it with contributions from all banks. Ostensibly, the center enables Japanese banks to analyze countries better and thus avoid the debt problems that they encountered in the past. The competitive dynamic, however, was more complex. A few Japanese banks are now challenging Bank of Tokyo for positions of international leadership. The Bank of Tokyo has played a dominant role in managing the work of the reschedulings in country after country around the world. According to one of the center's officers, "the center will help take some of the pressure off the Bank of Tokyo in the reschedulings." That is a polite way to say that at issue is a reduced role of leadership for the premier foreign exchange bank in Japan, one that used to be half-owned by the emperor and that has had very close ties with the government for the last 100 years. Reversible though it may be, the strategic shift within the country occurs in the arena of debt rescheduling as well as credit extension.

Competition between Leaders and Followers

Finally, politics enters the competitive relation between followers and leaders. Banks can use government policy and the regulatory system for strategic ends at the *Home Level.* Take a bank with offices in fifty or more countries around the world, concerned about competitive lending by smaller banks that has in the past reduced margins. By characterizing this as ad hoc lending, done without proper country risk analysis, the big bank can approach its regulators and say: "We think that the legal or regulatory system ought to require participants as well as leaders of a loan to have visited the country." Consider the effect of this sort of regulation. The big international banks already have organizational structures to do country risk analysis.[19] The smaller banks would have to develop such structures, which would be expensive for them to do. The result would be to narrow the range of competitors for transborder loans. This example is not wholly hypothetical. The big international banks have made suggestions of this sort, and the U.S. regulatory trend since 1979 has been to require greater bank attention to country risk.[20]

At the *Borrower Level,* it is easy to see how the big international banks might work to improve their competitive position vis-à-vis the smaller banks. The pattern of debt restructuring has seen close cooperation between the bank advisory group, dominated by the leader banks, and the financial experts and political powers of the borrowing country. The personal relationships thereby formed ought to help the big banks, like Citibank, in the post–debt crisis loan market. Borrowing countries may unofficially close out follower banks from their markets, because the followers have shown themselves to be so obdurate in many of the restructures. In connection with the 1983 Mexican restructuring and the 1984 (tentative) Argentine restructuring, the big banks put together the deal, the small banks put up a public fuss, and the big banks twisted arms and brought the small banks into line. This type of cooperation may help the big international banks improve their competitive positions in the long run.

Conclusion

The premise of this discussion is simple. Banks' strategic goals are economic. They are concerned with positioning in the market, reducing costs, and keeping other players in the game. Economic though the goals may be, the domestic political process is very important to the bank. A big bank with an antagonistic relationship to its own government, or afraid because the legislature may step in, is in a very different position from a bank with close ties to its home government. In Japan bureaucratic politics play a very important role, and appear to lead to different outcomes. As a group Japanese banks tried to escape from Mexico, then rallied under the leadership of the finance ministry, and as a group returned.

The home government plays an extremely important role. The big banks' relationship with their home government is crucial. Notwithstanding the internationalization of banking in the last decade or so, when a crisis comes, the banks fall back on their home government for help. What kind of help they can expect and how banks mobilize political support vary depending on their home country. With respect to bank loans to LDCs on enterprises in those countries, the borrowing country government (and its political process) and various international financial institutions also assume importance to the big banks. From the banks' perspective, the political interests of the home country in borrowing countries and the political process of borrowing countries ought to play a central role in any kind of country analysis that the banks are doing. By understanding and using that process, big banks are in a position to manage their assets more effectively and even to improve their long range competitive positions.

Notes

1. I use the term "politics" or "political" to refer to matters about which the banks must deal with governments or want to involve governments in order to obtain an outcome to their liking.

2. See Philip Wellons, *World Money and Credit: The Crisis and Its Causes* (Cambridge, Mass.: Harvard University Press, 1983):24–26; Robert Aliber, "International Banking: Regulation and Growth," *Columbia Journal of World Business* (Winter 1975):12.

3. The "banking titans" in the United States are as follows (with their assets as of June 30, 1983, in billions of dollars):

Citicorp ($130.2)

Bank America ($121)

Chase Manhattan ($81.5)

Manufacturers Hanover ($63.3)

J.P. Morgan & Co. ($59.2)

Chemical New York ($48.9)

Continental Illinois ($41)

First Interstate Bankcorp ($40.8)

Bankers Trust New York ($37.7)

Security Pacific ($37.7)

William Quirk et al., "Will an Underdeveloped Countries Debtor Cartel Squeeze the Big Banks," *Business and Society Review* (Fall 1983):4.

4. In the late 1970s smaller banks offered credit to developing countries, thereby forcing spreads down and ending the club that had earlier been successful in keeping loan margins wider.

5. See generally Alfred Mudge, chapter 4 and appendix B of this book.

6. See Joseph Kraft, *The Mexican Rescue* (New York: Group of Thirty, 1984), pp. 1–40, for an excellent account of the events of August 1982.

7. Ibid., p. 54. According to a lawyer working with the advisory group, when a small bank balked "we brought appropriate pressure to bear—sometimes from state or federal regulators; sometimes from figures in the local community; sometimes from other bankers" (quoted ibid., p. 53). Bank regulators in other countries performed the same type of lobbying campaign as the U.S. government's (ibid.).

8. "Bankers Skeptical of Argentine Plan," *Washington Post,* December 4, 1984, p. E1, col. 2.

9. Allied Bank International v. Banco Credito Agricola de Cartago, No. 83-7714, slip op. at 5–6 (2d Cir. Apr. 23, 1984) (rehearing by panel granted).

10. See Kraft, *The Mexican Rescue,* p. 47.

11. For example, see William Cline, *International Debt: Systemic Risk and Policy Response* (Washington, D.C.: Institute of International Economics, 1984).

12. See Kraft, *The Mexican Rescue.*

13. The conclusions that banks draw about what accounts for the difference may well affect their lending in the future. For example, a leading New York bank decided to pull out of Brazil to the extent possible and increase its exposure in Mexico over the next years because of this distinction.

14. See, for example, Carlos Diaz-Alejandro, "Some Aspects of the 1982–83 Brazilian Payments Crisis," *Brookings Papers on Economic Activity* (1983):515.

15. See Cynthia Lichtenstein, chapter 8 of this book.

16. Interviews, November 1983.

17. This is an assumption supported by the leading econometric projections. See Cline, *International Debt,* pp. 39–69; Thomas Enders and Richard Mattione, *Latin America: The Crisis of Debt and Growth,* Brookings Institution Studies in International Economics (Washington, D.C.: Brookings Institution, 1984).

18. See Kraft, *The Mexican Rescue,* pp. 23–24.

19. See Irving Friedman, *The World Debt Dilemma: Managing Country Risk* (Philadelphia: Council for International Banking Studies, 1983), pp. 251–82, which describes country risk decision making and organizational structures at eleven big U.S. banks.

20. See Lichtenstein, chapter 8, for analysis of the 1979 Interagency Country Exposure Review Committee, the 1983 International Lending Supervision Act, and the 1984 regulations pursuant to the Act.

Part III
Directions

7

The International Debt Roller Coaster: Time for a New Approach

Andrew C. Quale, Jr.

I t is time to adopt a new, more realistic approach to the international debt crisis. Ever since August 1982, when Mexico stunned the financial world by announcing it was broke, the debtor countries, the commercial banks, the International Monetary Fund (IMF), and the creditor nations have been involuntary and hapless riders on the international debt roller coaster. The troughs have been deep and unsettling, with talk of debtors' cartels and repudiations. As recently as March 1984, when interest rates were rising again, Argentina was refusing to come to terms with the IMF, and commercial bank lenders were forced to reduce their earnings because of Argentine arrearages on interest. The Argentine minister of finance was hardly sympathetic, saying in effect: "That's their problem not ours."[1] Other debtor nations, although not necessarily supporting the hard-line approach of Argentina, met first in Quito and then later in Cartagena and Washington, D.C. in 1984 to consider their common problems and the possibility of adopting a common approach.[2]

At the end of 1984, however, the roller coaster was climbing. Interest rates fell somewhat toward the end of the year, the worldwide economic recovery seemed to be proceeding apace, Brazil and Mexico were negotiating the outlines of an agreement in principle for a long-term rescheduling, and Argentina appeared to have reached, at least temporarily, an agreement with the IMF and, tentatively, the banks.[3] A large sigh of relief was audible from many of the players affected.[4] But is the roller coaster ride over? Hardly. The ride is going to be a long one—perhaps ten to fifteen years—and, undoubtedly, there will be more troughs before it ends.

In spite of this glimmer of hope, it is essential to recognize that the debt crisis is not a temporary economic or financial problem (as originally believed) but is a political, social, and strategic problem of major proportions for all concerned, particularly the United States. It is time, therefore, to take a new

This chapter has been updated with references to developments that have occurred through January 1, 1985.

approach to this problem and for the key parties to stop trying to muddle through from one deadline to the next, but to join forces to develop a more coordinated, long-term plan for each of the countries affected. It is also time for the U.S. government, in cooperation with U.S. commercial banks, to assume a more active leadership role in this process. If it does not do so, the initiative could ultimately be taken by the debtor nations, with potentially destabilizing consequences.

Pressures have been mounting from many of the concerned parties to adopt some form of new, long-term approach to the debt problems of the debtor nations which would more realistically reflect the abilities of such countries to service their debt in a politically and socially acceptable context. The debtor nations have been insistent in expressing their anguish at the sacrifices they have been making by "adjusting" their economies such that the rate of growth for some countries has declined by as much as 5 percent per year.[5] Ministers of finance and central bank presidents are being replaced regularly, serving as scapegoats for the economic ills that have befallen their countries. Strikers and rioters have protested the deflationary economic policies throughout Latin America, threatening existing democratic regimes or the process of returning to democratically elected governments. Latin American leaders met in Quito, Ecuador in January 1984 and, although they professed *not* to be establishing a debtor's cartel, issued the "Quito Declaration and Plan of Action" urging that a new approach to the debt problem be adopted.[6] Besides agreeing on certain basic criteria, these countries agreed to exchange, on a confidential basis, information relating to the terms of refinancing and rescheduling that each has negotiated or is in the process of negotiating. The next step after shared or common knowledge may well be shared or common negotiating positions.

Even some commercial bankers have become increasingly concerned about the debt crisis and how it is being handled, and have expressed such concern publicly. The *New York Times* quoted one banker as stating: "We're living a bizarre and dangerous charade. We're trying to pretend that everything is okay with debt repayments, that we're coming out of the woods, and we're losing precious time."[7] The chairman of the Bank of America has been quoted by the *Wall Street Journal* as stating that bankers are "going through a kind of re-thinking period" and debtors need more time to repay principal and interest.[8]

The IMF, which ordinarily works diligently but quietly and without engaging in public criticism of its member nations, has recently stated through its managing director that if the United States does not reduce its budget deficit, thereby bringing about a reduction in the real rate of interest and curtailing the dramatic net inflow of capital into the United States, the debt crisis will continue.[9] Paul Volcker, chairman of the Board of Governors of the U.S. Federal Reserve System, has repeatedly urged similar policies, noting recently that "successful management of the debt problem can continue [only] so long as certain fundamentals are respected," including "continuing growth among the industrial countries as a whole, maintenance of open markets for the products of developing countries to compete fairly in world markets, and reasonable stability in financial markets (or better yet, declining interest rates) which in turn rests on keeping inflation and budgetary deficits under control."[10]

More important, the IMF's managing director and the Federal Reserve's chairman also called for a longer range approach. Chairman Volcker was described early in 1984 as having urged the Mexican government to seek to reopen refinancing agreements with commercial banks covering some $20 billion in order to get the banks to reduce the interest rate charged on their loans and to extend the maturity.[11] Volcker raised the possibility that caps be placed on interest rates so that they would not exceed a specified amount even if the general level or rates rose.[12] This was an especially telling suggestion, since at that time the Federal Reserve's own monetary policies seemed to be pushing interest rates up. Martin Feldstein, former chairman of President Reagan's Council of Economic Advisors, urged in May 1984 that "the time has come" to develop a long-term approach to the world debt crisis, including the adoption of some form of interest caps.[13]

Thus, pressures have been mounting from all quarters—the debtors, the IMF, the U.S. government, and some bankers—that a new approach to the debt crisis must be taken. What should be the parameters or elements of such an approach? What should be the contributions of the various parties involved? How should the costs be shared? How can an approach be structured so as to minimize the suffering and costs to the debtor nations and the risks and costs to the lenders, while at the same time ensuring stability and acceptable growth for the debtor nations and the integrity of the lenders' outstanding loans?

The purpose of this chapter is to answer these questions, or at least to suggest answers. A basic shift in approach to managing the debt crisis is needed. The first phase of the crisis can be characterized as an ad hoc, muddling through approach. That approach is no longer suitable. A new, second, phase is called for, in which long-term, more realistic solutions are adopted.

Phase I: The Current Approach, or "Muddling through"

The commercial banks and public policymakers were surprised by the crisis which started in August 1982 and snowballed since then. As country after country declared its inability to make scheduled payments of principal and interest, the objective of the bank lenders, the IMF, the Bank for International Settlements, and the U.S. government and other Western governments during this phase I has been, first and foremost, to keep money flowing into the debtor nations so as to avoid default.[14] This at times has required nearly superhuman efforts by the IMF, the U.S. Treasury, and the commercial banks, working both separately and together. Although they have gradually been lowered, interest-rate spreads and fees were initially very high, as much as two points and more over the London Interbank Offered Rate (LIBOR) in the case of interest. Maturing principal payments have been rescheduled for relatively short periods of time, one to two years. "New" loans have been made to enable the borrowers to pay interest.

The underlying assumption (or perhaps hope) of these restructuring arrangements was that the debt crisis was a short-term, liquidity problem, not a long-term, structural problem.[15] The banks hoped, therefore, that with interim financing the debtor nations would gradually be able to work themselves out of their debt burdens through a combination of increased export earnings (resulting from rapid growth and recovery in the United States and other OECD nations), growth of the debtors' domestic economies (so that their debt burdens would decline relative to the magnitude of the economy), and a decline in interest rates.[16] The debtor nations were strongly encouraged to assist this process by adopting IMF adjustment programs designed to cause such nations to live within their means by reducing inflation, budgetary deficits, and imports and, in so doing, to create a substantial net trade surplus.

This first part of the rescheduling effort, characterized here as phase I, has been a considerable success for several of the principal debtor countries if viewed in terms of its short-term, stabilizing objectives. Indeed, the adjustment programs adopted by Brazil and Mexico have been extraordinarily successful in producing a substantial trade surplus to service foreign debt. For example, it was estimated in 1984 that Brazil and Mexico would both have trade surpluses in excess of $10 billion apiece, but that most of their surpluses would be paid to foreign creditors.[17] Thus, the patient appears to have been temporarily stabilized. But the illness has not been cured. Indeed, in light of the extensive net outflow of capital, the patient is still bleeding. What is the problem?

There are, of course, many problems, both serious and persistent. In general, the debt crisis is merely an element of an international and global disequilibrium that is unprecedented in some respects. The most salient features of this disequilibrium are the following:[18]

1. Real, as distinguished from nominal, interest rates are at nearly historical highs.
2. Net capital flows among nations have become dramatically altered. The United States is now a substantial net *importer* of capital from the developing countries, as well as Europe and the Middle East, whereas the less developed countries, particularly the Latin American nations, have become net *exporters* of capital.

3. Trade among certain nations has become grossly unbalanced. The United States, for example, is experiencing a massive trade deficit.
4. The U.S. dollar has become considerably overvalued in comparison to many other currencies.
5. The external debt burdens of many countries are greater than they are capable of servicing.

In attempting to respond to this global disequilibrium, including the debt crisis in particular, debtor countries have had to adopt policies that generate enough surplus hard currency to service their debt. The policies adopted by the debtor nations have had a range of consequences including the following. First, as a result of the adoption of adjustment policies, some debtor nations have drastically reduced imports in an effort to produce a trade surplus for use in servicing their debt. For example, Mexico's imports declined by 66 percent between 1981 and 1983, and Venezuela's fell 50 percent in just one year, from 1982 to 1983 (figure 7–1). Second, because of these adjustment policies and the curtailment of imports, the growth rate of some of the debtor nations fell by as much as 16 percent per capita from 1981 to 1983 (figure 7–1). Third, the massive cutbacks in imports have decimated intraregional trade among the debtor nations, thereby reducing export earnings of their neighbors. Fourth, in spite of the high level of imports by the United States, the most troubled debtor nations of Latin America have benefited little, with the more developed nations of Asia (Taiwan, South Korea, Singapore, Hong Kong) being the principal beneficiaries. Fifth, the debt burden of the debtor nations, as reflected by the ratio of the *real* interest rate being paid on their debt to their export earnings, has remained high.[19]

Thus, the overall effect of these policies on the debtor nations has been to produce for some of the larger debtor nations substantial surpluses in their trade balance, but with the result of domestic economic stagnation and contraction, bordering on depression. More significantly, such trade surpluses, although unprecedented in amount for some of the debtor nations, are still not sufficient even to cover the interest due on their debt, much less to repay any principal. Moreover, with the economies of most of the debtor nations stagnating, it is unreasonable to expect that their productive capacity and, particularly, their ability to produce more exports, will increase significantly, if at all.[20] Thus, it was not surprising that, although phase I was "successful" in that there were no repudiations, maturing debt was rescheduled, new loans were made to help the debtors meet their interest obligations, and adjustment programs yielded substantial trade surpluses, nevertheless, most of the debtor nations still do not have a realistic chance of paying even the interest on their debt, while also maintaining socially and politically acceptable levels of domestic economic programs and per capita income.[21] That is the bad news.

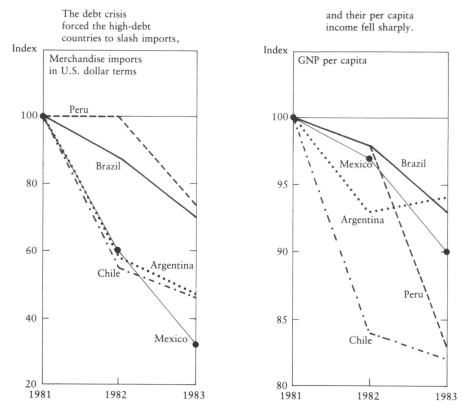

Source: Federal Reserve Bank of New York, *Sixty-ninth Annual Report* (1984), p. 20. Reprinted with permission.

Figure 7–1. Impact of the Debt Crisis on Latin American Imports and Per Capita Income

The good news is that dramatic progress has been made with the two largest debtors, Mexico and Brazil. Mexico has completed phase I of the rescheduling effort, in the sense that it has rescheduled its current principal maturities and met or exceeded the economic goals entailed in its IMF program. In 1983 Mexico had a current account surplus of $5.5 billion, well above the IMF target of a $3 billion deficit, and its projected performance in 1984 was substantially better.[22] This improved economic performance has made it easier for Mexico and its bank advisory committee to reach a preliminary agreement on a multiyear rescheduling of debt at lower rates.[23] In essence Mexico is the first of the debtor nations to begin to enter phase II, in which the debt burden is approached on a long-term basis.

At the beginning of January 1985 Brazil commenced negotiations for a multiyear restructuring, which could lead to the rescheduling, over fourteen to sixteen years, of its debt obligations maturing in the next six years or so.[24] Perhaps more significant is the dramatic progress made by the Brazilian economy. Brazil's current account deficit in 1983 was $6 billion despite a dramatic cut in imports; for 1984 the deficit was estimated to be only $1.8 billion, which reflects (in part) higher than forecasted export earnings.[25] Similarly, the Brazilian economy was estimated to have grown by 4.1 percent in 1984,[26] which means per capita income rose slightly, compared to a decline in per capita income of about 7 percent between 1981 and 1983.[27]

Thus, for the two biggest debtor nations the muddling-through phase (phase I), seems to have worked. Both Mexico and Brazil are embarked on the beginning of phase II. This is hardly to say that Mexico and Brazil are out of the woods. Their debt burdens could again become overwhelming. That will depend upon the confluence of internal domestic factors, such as excessive inflation or governmental deficits and political or social unrest, or external factors, such as an increase in international interest rates, slower growth in the developed countries of North America and Western Europe, or disequilibrium in flows of trade and capital.[28]

Moreover, many of the other debtor nations have faired less well. Of the remaining major debtor nations, Argentina, Chile, Peru, the Philippines, and Yugoslavia are still experiencing severe problems in making payments on their external debt or renegotiating unmanageable debt. Some of the smaller debtor nations, such as Bolivia, Ecuador, and several Central American nations, are also encountering great difficulty in making scheduled payments or in rescheduling their external debt.[29] For all of these countries, including even Brazil and Mexico, it is time to consider a new, more realistic approach.

Phase II: A New Approach

In outlining a new, phase II approach to the debt crisis, I will focus first on the fundamental problem to be solved and then will propose actions the debtor nations, the banking community, Western governments, and multilateral institutions such as the IMF might take to respond to such problems.

The Fundamental Problem: Net Capital Outflows and Acceptable Growth of Per Capita Income

The overriding problem that must be confronted by the debtor nations, the IMF, the United States and other OECD governments, and the commercial banks in phase II of the debt crisis boils down to one question: How can the borrowing nations' debt be serviced sufficiently so that the quality of this debt on the books of the lenders will be maintained, while at the same time the net outflow of capital from such nations is held to a level that enables their real income per capita to grow at politically acceptable rates?

The nature of this dilemma can be illustrated by two sets of data, one for a group of large debtor nations and the other for a single debtor nation. Fourteen major debtor countries experienced an estimated net outflow of capital in 1983 of $20 billion in order to pay a portion (not all) of the interest due on their debt.[30] The total interest due on their debt for 1983 was approximately $50 billion, and the total amount of principal due was approximately $25 billion. The difference between such principal and interest payments and such net outflow is accounted for by new loans, reductions in reserves, capital investment, postponement of principal payments, and so forth. For 1985 it is estimated that the principal payments becoming due will jump to $50 billion unless new reschedulings such as those proposed for Mexico and Brazil extend principal repayment obligations further into the future. The net capital outflows for these nations will increase to an estimated $30 billion by 1986 unless, again, reschedulings slow the pace somewhat. Traditionally and for many years, these same countries had been net *importers* of capital and such net capital inflows had been used to fuel their economic development. Although these countries may be able to support capital outflows of this magnitude for a few years, they cannot do so over the next ten to fifteen years without severe political and social consequences.

At the end of 1984 Argentina's debt was approximately $45 billion, and it accrued interest at the rate of approximately $6 billion to $6.5 billion per year.[31] Its estimated balance of trade and nonfinancial services for 1984 was a very substantial (for Argentina) $3.7 billion, reflecting a high level of exports and reduced imports. Argentina's net balance of financial services was a negative $5.9 billion. As a result Argentina's current account was a negative $2.2 billion. Thus, if Argentina used all of its trade balance of $3.7 billion to pay the interest on its debt, it would suffer a net capital outflow of this amount, yet would still fall $2.2 billion short in paying the interest due. Even if it were successful in borrowing this shortfall, it would nevertheless experience a net capital outflow of $3.7 billion per year. Although Argentina is a country wealthy in resources and productive capacity, it is unclear whether it can socially and politically absorb such an outflow of resources.

The statistics indicate a problem for a group of borrowing countries, and a severe problem for one of the largest borrowers. The figures also suggest a number of possible remedies: reduce interest rates, extend maturities, adopt adjustment programs, increase exports, and so on. Before analyzing some of these, it may be helpful to ascertain to what extent such remedies might be expected to alleviate the debt burdens in the near term.

A recent paper published by four members of the staff of the Board of Governors of the Federal Reserve System provides useful insight into this question.[32] The authors reached the following conclusions based upon past trends and their projections for the external positions of eight developing nations through 1990. The authors' first conclusion was that the debt burden could be reduced rapidly by reductions of *real* interest rates or equivalent changes in the present value of outstanding external debts. Such reductions in real interest rates were found to be clearly more important for the short-run prospects of the debtor nations than the other factors to be described.

Second, the study concluded that faster economic growth in the industrial (OECD) countries and the associated increases in export earnings for the debtor nations would provide little relief for the debtor nations for the next two years. (The study assumed that OECD growth would be 3.4 percent in 1984 and remain at 3 percent from 1985 through 1990.) Such a rate of growth, however, if sustained, would have a powerful effect on debtor countries' export earnings by 1990. Thus, according to the Federal Reserve Board's paper, higher OECD growth rates will not have a significant impact on the debt burden of these countries relative to their flow of exports for a number of years. Moreover, the rise in export earnings associated with higher growth rates could well be offset by a concomitant increase in imports.[33]

Third, adjustment policies in the debtor nations which give rise to substantial trade surpluses will not materially reduce the debt burden over the next two years, although they could have a significant impact by 1990. Fourth, continued capital flight from the debtor nations which does not generate an inflow of foreign exchange earnings could offset much of the improvement in the debt position of the debtor nations which otherwise would flow from growth in the OECD countries and appropriate adjustment policies.

Some Recommended Actions

In light of the foregoing data and analysis, the following actions are worthy of consideration.

1. The level of real interest rates should be reduced substantially.
2. Principal maturities should be rescheduled over a long period.
3. Sound adjustment programs should be adopted by the debtor nations.
4. An adequate flow of new financing should be maintained.
5. Effective domestic policies should be adopted by the debtor nations to discourage capital flight and encourage investment by both foreigners and residents, including the repatriation of capital by residents.
6. Trade policies should be adopted that will encourage exports not only with the developed nations, but also with the debtors' neighbors.

7. The United States and other OECD nations should adopt monetary, fiscal, and trade policies that take into account their effect on the debtor nations.

Implementation of these proposals will require a coordinated effort by the United States and other OECD governments, the debtor countries themselves, the commercial banks, and the IMF and other multilateral financial institutions.

Reduction in Real Interest Rate. Clearly the most effective and immediate relief that can be provided to the debtor nations is a meaningful reduction in the level of real interest rates, which have been at extraordinarily high levels for the last four years.[34] In order for certain of the debtor nations to be able to meet their current obligations (forgetting for the moment any attempt to repay principal) without devoting an unreasonably large percentage of their export earnings or incurring excessive additional debt, real interest rates must drop. The emphasis must be on a reduction in *real* interest rates (nominal interest rates minus the rate of inflation) rather than on *nominal* rates. Thus, most debtor nations would be able to support high nominal interest rates of, say, 20 percent, if the rate of inflation were also 20 percent.

A reduction in real interest rates can be brought about in essentially two ways: a reduction in the market rates, which have recently been at high *real* levels, due in significant part to the unprecedented U.S. budget deficit and to the efforts of the Board of Governors of the Federal Reserve System to respond to such deficit, or a reduction in the actual rates being charged by the lenders. Although interest rates dropped appreciably in late 1984, it may be unrealistic to expect that the Federal Reserve Board will be able to effect a significant further reduction in U.S. interest rates in order to assist the developing countries since, in so doing, domestic inflationary pressures might be renewed.[35] Moreover, in spite of Chairman Volcker's frequent criticism, the high U.S. budget deficit is likely to continue, the financing of which will result in a constant upward pressure on rates. Therefore, attention must be focused on reducing the rates of interest charged by the bank lenders.[36] It is perhaps unfair to focus only on the commercial bank lenders, but unfortunately for them they have become the most flexible and significant holder of claims on the larger debtor nations and, at least at the present time, the official lenders, particularly the United States, are politically unable or unwilling to provide significant financial assistance.

How much of a reduction in real interest rates will have a meaningful impact on the debtor nations? An examination of a somewhat oversimplified hypothetical involving Argentina may help establish some parameters. As noted previously, Argentina's foreign debt as of year end 1984 was approximately $45 billion, and interest accrued at the rate of approximately $6–$6.5

billion per year.[37] Argentina's imports of goods and services have been reduced to $4.7 billion, while exports are approximately $8.7 billion, resulting in a very substantial trade surplus of approximately $4 billion. Assuming all of the trade surplus is available to pay the interest on the debt, an additional $2–$2.5 billion is needed to pay interest. One way to close this gap is, of course, to borrow more money, but this simply accelerates the treadmill. Another way would be to reduce interest rates. A reduction of interest rates on the $45 billion debt would reduce interest payments, and hence close the gap, as follows:

Reduction in Interest Rate	Reduction in Interest Payments (millions of U.S. dollars)
1%	$ 450
2	900
3	1,350
4	1,800
5	2,250

In order for Argentina's net trade surplus to be sufficient to cover the interest payments on its debt, the current rate of interest would have to be reduced by 5 percentage points. Thus, if Argentina is currently paying 12 percent to 12.5 percent interest on its external debt, the interest charge would need to be lowered to approximately 7 percent to 7.5 percent. The problem is that it is not reasonable to expect the commercial banks to make such a concession.[38] What reduction in interest rates could the commercial banks afford without undue hardship? Can the U.S. government help the U.S. banks in some way?

To put these figures in perspective, it is helpful to view them in the context of the net earnings and capital of one of the major money center banks, Manufacturers Hanover Trust Company. Manufacturers Hanover had loans outstanding to its major debtor countries in the following amounts in billions of U.S. dollars as of September 30, 1984:[39]

	Total Amount on Loan	Loan Amount on Nonaccrual Status
Argentina	$1.4	$ .700
Brazil	2.4	1.800
Chile	.8	.015
Mexico	2.0	.025
Venezuela	1.1	.026
Total	$7.7	

If Manufacturers Hanover were to reduce the interest rates on its loans to just these five countries, its earnings could fall as follows:

Reduction in Rate	Reduction in Earnings (millions of U.S. dollars)
1%	$ 77
2	154
3	231
4	308
5	385

How do these figures compare with the capital and income of Manufacturers Hanover's holding company, the Manufacturers Hanover Corporation? The holding company's total shareholders' equity as of December 31, 1984, was $2.67 billion and its net income for all of 1983 was $337 million.

For Manufacturers Hanover, a 5 percent reduction in interest rates for these five countries would have eliminated its 1983 income. Other large banks would also be significantly affected by such reductions. Obviously, a straight reduction of interest rates in the range of 3 percent to 5 percent would be difficult for Manufacturers Hanover and the other banks to bear. Assuming that some reduction may be necessary, how can it be structured so as to minimize accounting and regulatory burdens on the banks?

One approach to consider would be to reduce interest rates to a level below the applicable market level, but then capitalize the difference and issue new notes evidencing such capitalized interest. A number of techniques are available for effecting a reduction in current interest rates through interest capitalization. One technique is the variable maturity loan pursuant to which the debt service payments remain constant but, if the applicable market rate of interest (which, presumably, is a floating rate) rises above a specified level, the rate of amortization of principal will decrease or, indeed, become negative (that is, foregone interest will be added to principal in order to keep the periodic service payments constant). This technique has been used in recent years in the United States in home mortgage financing.

A slight variation on this would be to establish a fixed rate of interest which the debtor can afford to pay out of export earnings and then capitalize the excess interest which otherwise would have been applicable by adding such excess as principal at the end of the loan. A somewhat more complicated technique would be to fix a rate of interest for the loan and provide that, to the extent that market rates exceed such level, the excess will be capitalized and, to the extent that market rates fall below such rate, the debtor will continue to pay the higher rate, but the excess of such higher rate over the market rate will be credited to reduce principal.

One might argue that these interest capitalization techniques are, in effect, no different than what is occurring now when the banks lend "new money" which is immediately repaid to the banks as interest, a device sometimes referred to in the trade as *rolling up* interest. However, there may be some advantages to reducing rates and capitalizing the difference in comparison to rolling up interest. A reduction in the level of interest rates being charged currently could be viewed by the debtor nations, as well as by the IMF and certain political interests (such as the United States Congress), as a meaningful concession or contribution by the banks to match the sacrifices made by certain debtor countries in adopting, at times, harsh domestic adjustment programs. The capitalization of interest, in contrast to rolling up interest, does not involve the making of a "new" loan, which may not be received warmly by the boards of directors, shareholders, and even regulators of certain banks. Moreover, if the rate of interest is reduced to a more manageable level, the debtor will be in a stronger position to fulfill its existing loan obligation, with the result that the quality of the loan in question will be enhanced. This remains true even if a bank creditor treats, for accounting purposes, the capitalized interest notes differently from the principal indebtedness owed by the same debtor.

The principal disadvantage of capitalizing interest would appear to be that some banks are concerned how this would be treated for accounting purposes, specifically whether:

1. The existing principal indebtedness must be reserved against or otherwise carried at a reduced value;
2. The capitalized interest would be accruable for purposes of income determination; and
3. The capitalized interest notes would be carried on the books at face value or at a reduced value.

According to the Financial Accounting Standards Board, even if the rate of interest on a restructured loan were to be significantly reduced, the bank creditor would not thereby have to write down such loan.[40] Indeed, so long as the rate of interest does not go below zero, the loan need not be written down. The amount of the capitalized interest notes could be carried as assets in their face amount on the books of the bank creditors, provided that the accountants were satisfied that the notes were ultimately collectible. If the restructuring arrangement were coupled with the adoption of an appropriate domestic adjustment program and other measures designed to improve the debtor's ability to pay its indebtedness, the accountants would probably be able to allow such interest income to be accrued and also to book such notes as assets at their face value without requiring the establishment of a reserve or the writing down of such assets. Depending on its ability to add to reserves, however, a bank might be inclined to establish a partial or full reserve against such capitalized interest notes. In so doing, however, it would not necessarily be required to reserve against the principal indebtedness owed by such debtor.

If, however, accountants are not willing to permit the accrual of capitalized interest, the magnitude of the reduction in income to the banks resulting from such interest capitalization proposal will most likely be more than they could realistically be expected to absorb.

The adoption of such interest capitalization techniques should not, in and of themselves, require the banks to maintain special "allocated transfer risk reserves" pursuant to the International Lending Supervision Act of 1983,[41] since the quality of the banks' assets would not have been "impaired by a protracted inability of public or private borrowers in a foreign country to make payments on their external indebtedness," and the situation does not exist that there are "no definite prospects for an orderly restoration of debt service."[42]

It would be hoped that the bank regulatory authorities and the accountants could contribute to solving any problems raised by the foregoing interest capitalization proposals by assisting in the structuring of arrangements along the foregoing lines, which would not impose an excessive burden on the profit and loss and balance sheet statements of the banks, yet would also avoid overstating the income or assets of the banks.

The foregoing approach accomplishes no miracles. Indeed, the total debt of a borrower would rise by the amount of the capitalized interest notes. However, this arrangement would help preserve the quality of the banks' outstanding loans to the debtor nations, since the debtors' ability to service such loans would be enhanced. The banks would appear to have considerable flexibility in how they account for the capitalized interest notes. Establishing such level of reserves, if any, as they believe appropriate and as their current profit situation would accommodate under the circumstances, would be workable.

An additional way in which the U.S. bank regulatory authorities might be able to assist the banks in reducing the real rate of interest to the debtor nations, without the necessity of obtaining funding from or the approval of Congress, might be to permit banks to discount with their Federal Reserve Bank some of their debtor nation paper. Assuming the discount rate to be 8½ percent, the banks could reduce the interest rates on their loans to, say, 9 percent or 9½ percent on their loans and still make a modest profit. Since the average yield that banks have been earning over their cost of funds increased appreciably by the end of 1984, the banks should be in a better position to absorb a reduction in their profits on such loans.

The recent negotiations relating to the long-term rescheduling of the debt of Mexico and Brazil have contemplated a reduction in the interest rate spread over the base rate to as low as 1¼ percent. In addition, the parties are proposing to use a base rate, such as LIBOR or the U.S. certificate of deposit rate, which more closely reflects the banks' cost of funds than does the prime rate. These concessions by the banks are meaningful and well deserved by Mexico and Brazil. It is questionable, however, whether such reductions will be sufficient to enable even these countries to service the interest and make significant principal payments on the debt over the long run; so further reductions should probably be considered.

Assuming that it is possible to make some meaningful concessions on interest rates, should all the debtor nations be entitled to the same reductions? If the precedent is established for one, will all expect to receive it? Because each country's situation is different, each country should probably be treated separately and on an ad hoc basis. Indeed, because of the effectiveness of their adjustment programs and the sacrifices they have made, some debtors may be more deserving of interest concessions than others. Other countries, by contrast, may be needier. However, should a Colombia, which has exercised greater care and discipline in its borrowing practices and in its foreign exchange management policies than most of the other debtor nations, be entitled to no concession or a smaller concession merely because its situation is less desperate? If so, would it not be unfair to Colombia, indeed punishing it, to deny it lower rates because it has behaved more responsibly? These questions illustrate some of the problems that may be encountered in connection with making meaningful concessions on interest rates.

Extend Maturity Dates of the Debt. Since the debtor nations cannot generate enough surplus foreign exchange to meet their interest obligations, it is inevitable that principal repayments must be extended far into the future. This should be done as promptly as possible in order to avoid the inconvenience and insecurity of brinksmanship rescheduling negotiations. In consideration of doing this, however, the creditor banks are entitled to insist that the debtor nations take appropriate (but not excessive) domestic adjustment measures, which under certain circumstances may involve IMF standby programs. If a debtor nation is unwilling to adopt such measures or to stick to them, then it should not have the benefit of long-term rescheduling or of concessionary interest-rate reductions of the type described. This is the part of phase II already in progress in the cases of Mexico and Brazil.

Adoption by the Debtor Nations of Sound Adjustment Programs. Mexico and Brazil have shown how much foreign exchange resources can be generated by an effective adjustment program. Unfortunately, such programs, as well as those adopted by other countries, have had a substantial cost. Trade surpluses have been produced primarily by driving down imports and, generally, by causing negative growth. The resultant suffering and social and political unrest have been substantial. It is believed that such severe adjustment programs cannot be maintained for more than several years, and certainly not for the ten to fifteen years expected duration of the debt program.[43]

It is also recognized that the governments of some of the debtor nations are lacking in either the will or the power to implement adjustment programs strong enough to accomplish the needed results. These include Argentina and Venezuela, which may be strong enough economically to survive without a strong adjustment program, and countries such as Chile, Peru, and the Philippines, which perhaps are not, and whose political situation may not be able to bear the strains of a strong program.[44]

In spite of the political difficulties, effective adjustment programs, whether structured by the IMF pursuant to a standby agreement, or adopted by a debtor government on its own initiative, are clearly needed. Debtor nations should be encouraged by the banks and the IMF to adopt the necessary programs and should be rewarded if they carry them out. At the same time the banks should be sensitive to the differences among debtor nations in the types of adjustment programs that are appropriate. Whereas a tough IMF standby program may be appropriate for one country, another country's government may have evidenced sufficient discipline and will to adopt an adjustment program on its own initiative so that an IMF program may not be necessary. The Colombian government, for example, rejected recommendations to adopt an IMF standby arrangement, yet has, on its own initiative, implemented effective adjustment programs. If a debtor, without apparently adequate justification, is unwilling to implement or carry through an adequate program, however, consideration should be given to withdrawing interest-rate concessions and other benefits that may have been granted.

Maintenance of the Flow of New Financing. Additional financing is obviously needed to close the gap between the debtor's interest obligations and the amount of net trade surplus the debtors can reasonably be expected to generate without politically unacceptable consequences. Nor is it reasonable to expect that a significant reduction by the lenders in interest rates can fully close the gap. The burden of providing this new financing is currently being shared by official lenders and the commerical banks. Thus, of approximately $7.3 billion in new funds needed by Argentina, it is expected that the IMF and members of the Paris Club will provide $3 billion and the commercial banks over $4 billion.[45] Is it reasonable to expect the banks to continue to make such a large contribution? To the extent possible, this burden should fall more on the official lending agencies, especially the IMF and the OECD nations. These agencies should perhaps carry the primary burden for long-term balance of payments gap financing, while the commercial banks focus more on short-term trade financing and lines of credit. Ideally, the IMF should either be provided with sufficient additional capital resources or the authority to raise such resources in the international capital markets. Unfortunately, the political prospects in the United States for providing such additional support to the IMF are bleak, if the attitude evidenced by Congress toward the 1983 IMF legislation is any indication.[46] The U.S. government should take the initiative, nevertheless, in finding ways to obtain this additional financing. Until such financing is available, the commercial banks, by being the only flexible actor on the stage and by needing to preserve the quality of their already outstanding loans, will continue to be pressed into service.

Policies to Discourage Capital Flight and Encourage Domestic and Foreign Investment. One of the most disturbing causes of the debt crisis has been the flight of capital from the debtor nations. The estimates as to the magnitude of such capital flight are startling. One estimate found more than $40 billion in capital flight from Mexico, Venezuela, and Argentina alone between 1979 and 1982.[47] Staff members of the Board of Governors of the Federal Reserve System estimated that between 1974 and 1982 substantially more than 50 percent of the increase in external debt of Argentina and Venezuela was due to capital flight.[48] In addition, Roger Kubarych of the Federal Reserve Bank, New York, estimates that 40 percent of all bank lending from 1979 to the end of 1981 may have ended up as capital flight from the debtor countries.[49] Such flight has, at times, been coupled with corruption and extortion by officials of the debtor nations. More commonly, it is the consequence of governmental policies of debtor nations which discourage domestic investment and encourage the holding of hard currency assets. Such data make it particularly galling to the commercial bankers who are being called upon to provide new money to service debt that may never have benefited the borrower in the first place. The debtors themselves are also justifiably angry in having to make sacrifices to service such debt.

What can be done to reduce capital flight? First and most fundamental, a debtor nation must create a political, social, and economic environment in which domestic savings and investment can be preserved and enhanced. If the real rate of interest paid on domestically invested savings is negative, inevitably people will be encouraged to invest in nonproductive commodities or similar assets or to invest abroad. Thus, the debtor countries must lower their inflation rates, so that they do not exceed local interest rates. Second, carefully structured foreign exchange restrictions may, on balance, discourage or prevent capital flight. The difficulty, of course, is that the mere implementation of such restrictions (if there previously were none) may incite capital flight.[50] Moreover, the ease with which such measures may be evaded and the schemes that are developed to evade or avoid them are legendary. However, if a genuine effort is made to enforce such measures and the penalties are sufficiently stiff, the too common attitude that "everybody does it" and that evasion is a national pastime may be put to rest. If such measures fail, consideration should be given to more draconian devices, such as obtaining the cooperation of the tax and other authorities of the countries receiving such capital. The problems of developing an effective capital flight discouragement program are, indeed, enormous, but so are the benefits. Therefore, the careful attention of both the debtor and developed nations to this problem is warranted.

During the late 1960s and all through the 1970s, foreign investment was barely tolerated by some of the developing countries in Latin America, or, at least, not warmly welcomed.[51] Such nations, apparently for reasons of nationalistic pride, preferred to follow a path of development relying on foreign debt financing rather than equity financing. That this policy was misguided is evident to many of the debtor nations now, and they are gradually loosening the restrictions on foreign investment. This trend should be encouraged and accelerated, because it does not increase the burden of external debt and, as a result of the oversight by the foreign investors, such investment is likely to be more efficiently employed and therefore more productive than public debt financing.[52] But a mere change in policy or law may not be sufficient to convince a reluctant foreign investor, who sees nothing but problems, particularly debt problems, hanging over the debtor nations, to invest in such countries. This is unfortunate because, although problems do exist, this may be a highly opportune time for foreign investment in the debtor nations, the U.S. dollar being high, the debtor nations in desperate need of foreign exchange and therefore likely to be quite flexible in accommodating new investment, and many domestic businesses being available at bargain prices. The debtor nations need to embark on a campaign to convince foreign investors that they are indeed welcome and that attractive investment opportunities exist.

Encourage Exports to Both Developed and Debtor Nations. The need to encourage exports is apparent. Attention should be focused, however, on increasing regional trade, especially within the Latin American nations, which fell off dramatically due to the efforts of the debtor nations to drive down imports, thereby resulting in beggar-thy-neighbor trade policies.[53]

The commercial banks can assist in increasing the trade of the debtor nations by restoring the trade financing lines that in some instances have been severely cut. In so doing, it is reasonable for the bank lenders to insist that such trade financing be carefully documented and monitored in order to ensure that the funds provided are financing actual trade transactions. The official lending agencies can also assist in expanding their trade financing facilities. Additionally, the United States and other OECD nations should take greater steps to reduce the barriers imposed by their own countries to imports from the debtor nations.

Adoption by the Creditor Nations of Economic Policies That Are Conducive to Alleviating the Debt Burden. In pursuing their own domestic economic policies, the United States and other OECD nations should be sensitive to the effect that such policies may have on the debtor nations and their debt burdens. At the present time, of course, the debtor nations are adversely affected by the unusually high real interest rates prevailing in the United States. The debtor nations are probably benefited, on the other hand, by the high value of the U.S. dollar, which encourages exports from the debtor nations to the United States. It is doubtful, though, whether such benefits compensate for the costs of the high interest rates.

Moreover, the uncertain outlook for the U.S. economy, with its substantial budget and trade deficits, portends even further problems for the debtor nations. A significant part of the U.S. budgetary and trade deficits is being financed by an inflow of capital from the rest of the world. As a result, interest rates are perhaps appreciably lower and the dollar exchange rate appreciably higher than they would be absent such capital inflow. If such inflow slows or stops, and the U.S. budgetary and trade deficits are not cut correspondingly, interest rates may rise and the exchange rate may fall, both of which events will weigh heavily on the debtor nations.

Conclusion

The key players in the debt crisis, the debtor nations, the commercial banks, the IMF, and the U.S. government, have accomplished yeomen feats under great pressure in the past two years in rounding up new financing, often at the eleventh hour, to avoid defaults and to reschedule hundreds of billions of dollars of debt. During this first phase of the debt crisis, the goal was to meet the immediate problem by getting a quick fix loan to pay interest and to reschedule near-term principal payments, thereby avoiding the next payment default, on the assumption (or, perhaps more realistically, the hope) that for most debtor nations the problem was one of temporary illiquidity, not of long-term structural adjustment. Although great progress has been made with Brazil and Mexico, the two largest debtors, it is now evident that the massive debt burdening the debtor nations constitutes a long-term structural problem that perhaps can only be cured over the next ten to fifteen years and only then with major contributions and sacrifices from the key players. The debt crisis has entered phase II; and it is time, therefore, for a new approach.

The solution to the debt crisis lies in concerted, coordinated action by all the key players. Although many steps can be taken that would help alleviate the debt burdens, the following are of particular importance.

1. The level of real interest rates borne by the debt must be substantially reduced, perhaps by as much as several points, and perhaps close to the lenders' actual cost of funds.
2. Principal payments should be rescheduled as far as fifteen or more years into the future.
3. The debtor nations must adopt and follow sound adjustment programs consistent with the maintenance of politically, socially, and economically acceptable levels of growth.

4. New financing must be provided, particularly by the official lenders, to fill the gap between the debtor nations' debt-servicing needs and their trade surpluses, if any.

5. The debtor nations must adopt effective policies to encourage domestic and foreign investment within their own countries and to discourage the flight of capital.

6. Both debtor and developed nations should adopt trade policies that will reduce the barriers to trade and encourage exports of the debtor nations.

7. The OECD countries, particularly the United States, should pursue domestic economic policies that are sensitive to, and supportive of, the needs of the debtor nations.

Good progress has been made to date in coping with the debt crisis, particularly with respect to Brazil and Mexico. The key players have in general made major contributions and sacrifices, although some debtor nations have contributed less than perhaps may be called for. The U.S. Congress has also not distinguished itself in seeking a solution. Despite the progress, however, further major contributions and sacrifices will be needed from all the players in order to avoid repudiation, default, or forgiveness, which, historically, has been the usual way out for sovereign nations that have become so heavily burdened with debt. Because of the potential threat posed by the debt crisis to political stability and democratic institutions in some of the debtor nations, it is in the strategic interest of the United States to assume more initiative and leadership in finding a long-term solution. If it does not, the initiative will be taken by others.

Notes

1. See generally "No Magic Wand for Argentina's Debt Dilemma," *Wall Street Journal*, March 29, 1984, p. 33, col. 1; "Argentina Nears Showdown with Bankers," *Wall Street Journal*, March 1984, p. 32, col. 1.

2. See "After Cartagena: Latin Debtors Hope for New Remedies," *Wall Street Journal*, June 25, 1984, p. 31, col. 2.

3. See "Bankers Said Skeptical of Argentina Plan," *Washington Post*, December 4, 1984, p. E1, col. 2, describing tentative agreement between Argentina and its bank advisory group; "Argentina Says Progress Made in IMF Talks," *Wall Street Journal*, August 13, 1984, p. 21, col. 1, on the agreement between Argentina and IMF on austerity measures.

4. See "International Conference on Debt Considers Alternative Approaches," *Washington Financial Report 43* (Bureau of National Affairs, November 19, 1984): 786. Testimony by Federal Reserve Chairman Paul Volcker, other regulators, and economists or scholars in August 1984 hearings before the House Foreign Affairs Committee was similarly optimistic. See Problems of the International Debt: Hearings Before the House Committee on Foreign Affairs, 98th Cong., 2d sess. (1984) [cited hereafter as 1984 International Debt Hearings].

5. See "What Harm Is Global Debt Crisis Doing? It's Slowly Reducing Trade World-Wide," *Wall Street Journal*, August 1, 1983, p. 18, cols. 1–2.

6. For warnings of the potentially dire political, socioeconomic, and diplomatic consequences in Latin America, see Riordan Roett, chapter 9 of this book. The Quito Declaration is reproduced as appendix C.

7. "The New Crisis for Latin Debt," *New York Times*, March 11, 1984, sec. 3, p. 1, col. 2; see Louis Schirano, chapter 2 of this book, expressing the frustrations of a leading international banker with a pure ad hoc, muddling through approach.

8. "Developing Trend: Banks Are Pressured to Give Sizable Breaks on Third World Loans," *Wall Street Journal*, March 12, 1984, p. 25, col. 1.

9. See "Fund Managing Director Outlines Considerable Progress Achieved in Managing Country Debt Problems," *IMF Survey*, June 18, 1984, pp. 178, 181 [cited hereafter as IMF Managing Director's Address].

10. Statement of Paul A. Volcker, chairman, Board of Governors of the Federal Reserve System, 1984 International Debt Hearings, pp. 99, 115–16.

11. See "Mexico, Volcker Allied on Debt Strategy," *Wall Street Journal*, May 29, 1984, p. 35, col. 2.

12. See "Volcker Terms Economy Strong Despite Rates: Fed Chief Speaks Favorably of Loan Charge Ceiling for Debtor Nations," *Wall Street Journal*, May 14, 1984, p. 13, col. 1.

13. See "Feldstein Offers Assistance Plan for Debtor States," *Wall Street Journal*, May 9, 1984, p. 45, col. 3.

14. For specific accounts of such efforts in the case of Mexico, which triggered the crisis in August 1982, see Joseph Kraft, *The Mexican Rescue* (New York: Group of Thirty, 1984); Nancy Gibbs, "A Regional Bank's Perspective: An Analysis of the Differences and Similarities in the U.S. Banking Community's Approach to and Participation with Mexican Restructuring," *Columbia Journal of Transnational Law 23* (1984):11; Enrique Tapia, "Mexico's Debt Restructuring: The Evolving Solution," *Columbia Journal of Transnational Law 23* (1984):1.

15. See John Calverley, "Is the Debt Crisis Nearly Over?" *Euromoney* (October 1984):279; Jésus Silva Herzog, "Beware Extreme Solutions," *Euromoney* (October 1984):279.

16. See generally William Cline, *International Debt: Systemic Risk and Policy Response* (Washington, D.C.: Institute for International Economics, 1984).

17. "Latin Debt: Postponing the Burden," *New York Times*, September 23, 1984, sec. 3, p. 1, cols. 2–4.

18. Sources for these facts include Federal Reserve Bank of New York, *Sixty-ninth Annual Report* (1984); Richard Feinberg, "The World Debt Crisis" (August 1984), reprinted in 1984 International Debt Hearings, pp. 42–55; Roger Kubarych, chapter 1 of this book.

19. See William Eskridge, chapter 3 of this book, especially figure 3–2.

20. Carlos Diaz-Alejandro, in "Latin American Debt: I Don't Think We're in Kansas Anymore," *Brookings Papers on Economic Activity* (1984):335, 363–65, notes that debtor countries' curtailment of imports have all but cut off the flow of capital assets needed to maintain and improve the productive capacity of these countries. See also "What Harm Is Global Debt Crisis Doing?"

21. William Cline of the Institute for International Economics projects that exports of debtor countries will probably rise sufficiently to reestablish their debt-servicing

capacity by 1986, assuming about a 3 percent growth rate for industrial countries, no sharp interest rate increases, and stable oil prices. See Cline, *International Debt*. The assumption of continual growth in the next two years is a controversial one. See text accompanying notes 32 and 33 as well as the notes.

22. William Cline, "The Outlook for International Debt" (July 30, 1984), reprinted in 1984 International Debt Hearings, pp. 9, 11.

23. For details, see "Mexico, Foreign Banks Agree to Work Out Plan to Reschedule Several Years of Debt," *Wall Street Journal*, June 6, 1984, p. 37, col. 2; "Banks Give Ground on Mexico Debt Terms in Exchange for Close Watch on Economy," *Wall Street Journal*, August 30, 1984, p. 23, col. 1.

24. See "Brazil Close to Agreement on IMF Curbs," *Wall Street Journal*, December 14, 1984, p. 30, col. 4; "Brazil to Resume Talks on Restructuring Debt," *New York Times*, January 3, 1985, p. D8, col. 5.

25. Bank of Boston, *Newsletter Brazil*, December 17, 1984.

26. Ibid.

27. Federal Reserve Bank of New York, *Sixty-Ninth Annual Report*, p. 20.

28. See note 21.

29. See generally "Bankers Worry That Smaller Latin Debtors Could Be the Next to Face a Payments Crisis," *Wall Street Journal*, October 17, 1984, p. 34, col. 1; "A Wall Street Watch List," *Wall Street Journal*, June 22, 1984, p. 36, col. 1.

30. The data and estimates described in the paragraph in text are drawn from a paper by Charles F. Meissner, "Commentary on the International Debt Crisis" (August 13, 1984), portions of which appeared as Meissner, "Debt: Reform without Governments," *Foreign Policy* (Fall 1984):81–93. The fourteen debtor nations included in this data are Argentina, Brazil, Chile, Colombia, Indonesia, South Korea, Malaysia, Mexico, Peru, the Philippines, Taiwan, Thailand, Venezuela, and Yugoslavia.

31. The data and estimates described in the paragraph in text are drawn from Bank of Boston, *Newsletter Argentina*, October 9, 1984, which cites data drawn from Argentina's Memorandum of Understanding with the IMF.

32. Michael Dooley, William Helkie, Ralph Tryon, and John Underwood, "Analysis of External Debt Positions of Eight Developing Countries Through 1990," International Financial Discussion Paper no. 227, Federal Reserve Board, August 1983, pp. 21–23.

33. It should be noted that these conclusions may conflict with the assumptions used by other analysts to reach a more optimistic conclusion as to the ability of debtor countries to deal with their large indebtedness. Thus Cline, "Outlook for International Debt," 1984 International Debt Hearings, pp. 11–13, argues that OECD country growth is the most important variable in determining debtor countries' ability to solve their debt problems.

34. See Kubarych, chapter 1, especially table 1–2, showing that real long-term U.S. interest rates increased from 1 percent to 2 percent in 1976–78 to 6.6 percent to 6.7 percent in 1982–83.

35. See "Volcker Sees Eased Debt Terms," *New York Times*, August 9, 1984, p. D1, col. 6, reporting that Federal Reserve Chairman Volcker favors bank reductions of interest charged to debtor countries, (implicitly) instead of use of U.S. monetary policy to achieve that result.

36. It should be noted that along with high real interest rates, U.S. economic policy has resulted in an overvalued dollar, which in turn has produced an enormous trade deficit, which gradually can be expected to result in greater exports from the debtor nations to the United States.

37. See text accompanying note 31.

38. See Troland Link, "The Value of Bank Assets Subject to Transfer Risk," *Columbia Journal of Transnational Law* 23 (1984):75, 82.

39. Manufactures Hanover Corporation, Third Quarter Report, September 30, 1984.

40. Financial Accounting Standards Board, *Statement of Financial Accounting Standards No. 15, Accounting by Debtors and Creditors for Troubled Debt Restructurings,* ¶¶ 30 and 31.

41. Public Law 98-181, Tit. IX, 97 Stat. 1153, codified at 12 U.S.C. §§ 3901–3912.

42. 12 U.S.C.A. § 3904(a)(1)(A) & (B) (1984 Supp.).

43. See William Eskridge, chapter 3 and Riordan Roett, chapter 9 for analyses of the political systems of the Latin American borrowing countries and the unlikelihood that those countries can impose economic sacrifices on the major corporatist interests indefinitely. See also "Brazil's Hard Life With Austerity," *New York Times*, sec. 3, p. 4, col. 2, on Brazil's effort to comply with IMF rules in 1984 disrupted business and economy; "Ending Latin Debt Crisis," *New York Times*, May 2, 1984, p. D2, col. 1.

44. See generally Meissner, "Commentary," p. 18; "Bankers, Preparing for 1985 Debt Talks With Third World, Are Warned Not to Let 1984's Successes Go to Their Heads," *Wall Street Journal*, December 28, 1984, p. 16, col. 1.

45. See "IMF Approves 20 Billion Aid for Argentina," *New York Times*, December 29, 1984, p. A1, col. 2.

46. For example, when Federal Reserve Chairman Volcker appeared before the House Banking Committee in 1983 to urge government cooperation with the banks and the IMF to work out solutions to the international debt crisis, he was peppered with questions hostile to much, if any, commitment of taxpayer dollars. See International Financial Markets and Related Problems: Hearings Before the House Comm. on Banking, Finance and Urban Affairs, 98th Cong., 1st sess., pp. 90–91, 94, 98–99, 119–21 (1983).

47. See Thomas Enders and Richard Mattione, *Latin America and the Crisis of Debt and Growth*, Brookings Institution Studies in International Economics (Washington, D.C.: Brookings Institution, 1984), p. 20, table 5.

48. See Dooley et al., "External Debt Positions of Eight Developing Countries," pp. 3–4.

49. See Kubarych, chapter 1.

50. This occurred in Mexico in 1982, when foreign exchange restrictions were imposed. See Kraft, *The Mexican Rescue.*

51. Such an attitude was exemplified by Decision 24 of the Andean Pact, which narrowly circumscribed the terms on which foreign investment could be made in the Andean Pact countries. For a recent comment on the effects of this policy, see "Hindering Help: Debt-Ridden Nations Impose Many Barriers on Foreign Investors," *Wall Street Journal*, January 21, 1985, p. 1, col. 6 (Latin American states, especially Brazil,

Mexico, Venezuela, have rules that block the flow of capital that could help replace international borrowing).

52. According to IMF Managing Director de Larosiere, an expanded flow of direct foreign investment is necessary because it "represents a more secure form of external finance, and one that does not involve the accumulation of external debt. Also, it carries the advantage of being tied to productive capital formation as well as forming part of a package that includes the transfer of technology and skills" (IMF Managing Director's Address, p. 180).

53. See "The Big Debtors Try to Dig Themselves Out," *Wall Street Journal,* August 1, 1983, p. 14, cols. 1, 2.

8

U.S. Response to the International Debt Crisis: The International Lending Supervision Act of 1983 and the Regulations Issued under the Act

Cynthia C. Lichtenstein

A s Third World countries struggle to maintain interest payments on their debt obligations to Western banks, they have fallen short repeatedly since 1982, triggering a series of reschedulings of their foreign debt and considerable uncertainty as to the general health of the global financial situation. Other scholars have outlined the causes and dimensions of what most are now calling an international "crisis."[1] This chapter will address the response of the United States to the crisis. It should be emphasized initially that the U.S. response is hardly unitary. Different groups and scholarly disciplines have very different concepts of the implications of the debt crisis. Some scholars, such as Riordan Roett, argue that the precarious economic situation of the Latin American borrowing countries is a national security issue for the United States.[2] Those who espouse this view of the implications of the crisis tend to stress the interest of the United States in ensuring an adequate flow of hard-currency funds to our Latin American neighbors in order to avert a contraction in the standard of living, which might produce political instability.

Other commentators on the debt crisis stress that the current situation not only involves the economic effect of the debt on the debtors, but also implicates the health of the Latin countries' private creditors, the major multinational banks.[3] Balance-of-payments financing of certain of the developing countries has been furnished over the past ten years, not by public institutional lending, but by the recycling of funds gathered in the Eurocurrency markets by private intermediaries, the multinational banks. The present exposure of the major multinational banks on developing country debt is such that at least nine large U.S. banks would be insolvent if all of the foreign sovereign lending loan repayments were to dry up at once.[4] In short, a major international banking crisis could be triggered by sovereign debt default resulting from insufficient new funds to continue payments on prior borrowings.

This chapter was previously published in *Virginia Journal of International Law* 25 (1985):401.

It is this possibility of breakdown of the financial system that raises the political process dilemma. The U.S. bank regulators[5] are directed by their authorizing statutes to be primarily concerned, not with the foreign policy and national security aspects of the flow of funds to the developing countries, but rather with the financial prudence of bank loans and lending policies. Banking regulation exists, in theory, to safeguard depositors and investors. The United States may prefer, because of the political difficulties of foreign aid, to have the flow of funds to developing countries carried out by private intermediaries rather than by official lending. There are indications that it has been U.S. policy to encourage bank lending to less developed countries since the 1950s.[6] The dilemma for the banking regulators in the light of such a national economic policy is how to induce the private actors to lend—and restructure developing country debt—in accordance with the needs of such a policy rather than the best interests of bank owners, the investors in bank stock. This is an old dilemma: regulation may indeed be inefficient, but the private system left to itself does not always perfectly fulfill public functions. A second, and related, quandary for the regulators arises when such lending has gone sour: how to persuade the legislature that the public sector should support the private banks in fulfilling the public function of continuing lending, notwithstanding objections that government help just serves to "bail out" the banks from deserved consequences of imprudence.

The congressional and regulatory experience with the enactment on November 30, 1983 of the so-called IMF Funding Bill (of which the International Lending Supervision Act of 1983 constitutes a part)[7] illustrates these dilemmas very well. In the course of the economic summit of 1983, the Reagan administration became convinced that the general health of the international economic system required larger resources in the International Monetary Fund (IMF) to deal with the crisis situation in developing nations. The administration therefore proposed to Congress an increase in the U.S. "quota" in the IMF.[8] Many members of Congress, however, took the view that the financial crisis in the developing nations, if not caused by excessive lending by the major multinational banks, at the least had been exacerbated by such lending.[9] Moreover, Congress was concerned with the perception of some legislators that the regulators had not prevented and may even have encouraged the excessive lending. Finally, the addition to the U.S. IMF quota was labeled in some constituencies as a bail-out of the banks' own imprudence, it being assumed (with certain justification) that any new public funds would only be used to keep the interest payments owed to the private banks flowing.

This chapter will explore the political and regulatory tensions underlying the IMF Funding Bill in three steps. I will first give the background of the 1970s, when the debt to the commercial banks was incurred, and present the reasons why both the regulators and the banks failed to anticipate the risks to bank financial soundness in sovereign lending. Essentially, the tools for regulation available to regulators in the 1970s were not suitable to regulation of the new phenomenon of private bank balance-of-payment financing. Thus the congressional tussles in 1983 can be viewed as trying to give the regulators better bridles to ride their unruly horse. But the regulators themselves argued persuasively that they needed flexible and not mandatory tools from Congress to avert a major crisis in the banking system. In the second part of this chapter I will examine the legislative compromise generated by the tension between regulatory inability to control the new phenomenon and congressional outrage at what was viewed in some quarters as regulatory weakness. The compromise set some standards to discourage imprudent international lending but generally left the regulators free to react to the ongoing debt crisis. The final part of this chapter will analyze the regulations implementing the legislation and will assess their impact or lack of impact on the effective governance of international sovereign lending.

U.S. Regulation of International Lending in the 1970s

When the Mexican foreign exchange crisis erupted in August 1982,[10] the nine major U.S. commercial bank lenders had outstanding to Mexico, Brazil, and Argentina loans totaling 137 percent of their capital.[11] Were these loans to be written off, nine major U.S. banks would be insolvent. How, in a system with a supposedly intensive network of banking regulation, had this state of bank affairs come to pass? It would seem that few bankers or regulators in the 1970s fully appreciated the risks involved in sovereign lending, since losses on foreign loans had traditionally been quite low.[12] Moreover, neither the banks nor the regulators had expertise in techniques of "country risk analysis." Sovereign lending is not subject to the market test of potential insolvency used to evaluate private lending. But it is subject to "transfer risk"— the possibility that a country or its central bank that holds its hard-currency reserves may not be able to come up with the dollars needed to service its debt.

Even more important is the difficulty in determining what is a country's debt. Private banks have not had the mechanisms to force their sovereign debtors to provide good accurate financial reports of their borrowing activities, and often a borrowing country did not itself have a full account of the borrowings of its agencies.[13] Aid in the generation of adequate governmental statistics is an IMF service to member countries, but the IMF cannot, without the sovereign's permission, share with private lenders any information gathered in reports from or consultations with member countries. The private banks responded to this problem, not by limiting lending, but by setting up first the Ditchley Group and then the Institute for International Finance to gather and exchange debtor country information. Unfortunately, this inter-bank cooperation in trying to find out the financial situation of their sovereign borrowers came only after the banks had already collectively committed so much to a small group of "middle income" developing countries (including Mexico, Brazil, and Argentina) that withdrawal might have brought down the international financial system.

Even if the risks of foreign sovereign lending were not fully appreciated in the early 1970s, why did not the banks follow a prime rule of prudence and put their eggs in a greater number of baskets—that is, diversify their sovereign loans? A key theme of portfolio management is *diversification,* the avoidance of placement of assets in a class of investments that will all react badly to any given change in external economic conditions. One might have hoped that this concept would have prevented the banks from making too many loans to developing country debtors whose servicing ability would be imperiled by similar factors, such as the worldwide recession after 1979. The banks would probably have replied that there were few creditworthy sovereign borrowers and that they were under pressure to recycle into the most likely outlets the enormous volume of petrodollar deposits from members of the Organization of Petroleum Exporting Countries.

The bank regulators were hardly blind to the problem.[14] However, under the federal structure of banking regulation, the regulators have not been given the power by the legislature to force the banks to diversify; indeed, they have no power to dictate asset allocation at all.[15] For national banks (almost all the major money center banks are national banks), diversification is governed by the "single borrower" rule, which in 1982 limited the extension of credit to a single borrower to 10 percent of the bank's capital and surplus.[16] Thus the Office of the Comptroller and its bank examiners could only take action against the gross amount of extensions of credit to a limited number of similarly situated Latin American nations if the loans were in violation of the statutory single borrower rule.

The Comptroller as early as 1977 was aware of the situation and, presumably, also aware of the "transfer risk" problem. But the single borrower statute, an ancient one dating back to the original enactment in 1863 of the National Banks Act, was not drafted in terms of sovereign lending. The statute itself refers to any one "person," and in the early 1970s the regulations under the statute did not specifically address how this term should be applied to extensions of credit to foreign governments, their agencies and instrumentalities.[17] In 1977 John Heimann, then Comptroller, instructed the bank examiners to question whether or not governmental instrumentalities had separate means to repay an extension of credit (a source of revenue apart from the sovereign's budget) and whether or not the special purpose of the loan to the governmental instrumentality had been documented by the bank extending the credit. As a result of these instructions, Mexico voiced public concern that "its ability to borrow in the United States is being restricted by growing pressure on U.S. banks to limit their lending to developing nations carrying heavy debt burdens." The Mexican Ministry of Finance suggested that the new rules would force Mexico to turn increasingly "to Western Europe and Japan to meet its enormous borrowing needs."[18]

Nevertheless, the Comptroller persisted in his attempt to interpret his statutory authority to force the banks to consider seriously the total loans outstanding to governments and their instrumentalities. After meetings with counsel for the major banks and even consultation in Mexico, the Comptroller in January 1978 proposed a rule incorporating a functional test to determine what state entities should be lumped together as one "person" for purposes of the single borrower rule.[19] While it is not possible here to explore the detailed comments and proposed final rule, the point is that the Comptroller was attempting to deal, within the bounds of his statutory authority and within the confines of U.S. foreign policy needs to support the continued growth of our southern continental neighbor, with regulatory concern over the *prudence* of the banks' sovereign lending. The regulators, of course, could have stopped the lending to Peru or to Mexico or to Brazil by defining all government agencies and instrumentalities as the same "person" as the central government itself, thus limiting all covered extensions of credit to a country's public sector to 10 percent of a bank's capital and surplus, but such a regulation would have generated immediate protests from the banks (as effectively ending their capacity to compete in the international lending markets) as well as raising serious foreign relations problems.[20] In short, the single borrower statute was not and is not a useful tool for control of foreign public sector lending by U.S. multinational banks. Thus the banks continued to lend to the Latin American countries even under the new loan limitation ruling, and in the period from early 1979 to the Mexican crisis, the nine major U.S. commercial bank lenders increased the total of their extensions of credit to borrowers (both public and private) in Mexico, Argentina, and Brazil from 114 percent to the 137 percent of equity noted previously.[21]

Whatever the banks' justifications for their high level of Latin American lending prior to 1979, one wonders about the increase after the second OPEC price shock in 1979. The congressional hearings on the crisis detailed some possible reasons for continued lending, such as the advantages of being able to allocate loan fees to present earnings, which made continued loans and reschedulings attractive to bank managers under pressure to generate increased earnings each year. The main reason, though, was that the banks were in a very real sense "hostages" of their earlier optimism. Once the large banks had lent substantial sums to sovereign borrowers (or private borrowers backed up by sovereign guarantees), they had little choice but to keep on lending to those borrowers. "A key feature of the market in international lending," says Richard Dale, is that, because of sovereign immunity, "lenders and borrowers are bound together not by enforceable contractual obligations but by crude sanctions [such as repudiation by the debtor and exclusion from financial markets by the creditors], which, because they are mutually damaging, are seldom invoked. One consequence of this situation is that lenders have no control (as they do in domestic context) over the total indebtedness that country borrowers may incur."[22]

Before 1977 and the Comptroller's experiments with the legal loan limitation, federal regulatory policy more or less ignored the issue of diversification in international lending. Although federal bank examiners are supposed to monitor imprudent loan practices, as noted, they did not have statutory grounds for criticism of large loans (if not in violation of the single borrower rule as interpreted) made to developing countries and the concentration of loans to several similarly situated countries. Apart from the statutory problem, the failure to criticize loans to specific countries is understandable, since adverse classifications of certain countries by the government might have had diplomatic and political ramifications for the United States abroad. After the second OPEC price shock in 1979, the federal regulators took another tack and instituted a new system of guidelines for evaluating country risk under the direction of an Interagency Country Exposure Review Committee (ICERC). The ICERC was charged with monitoring bank exposures, evaluating banks' internal systems for managing country risk, assessing the creditworthiness of particular countries, identifying problems that could arise because of transfer risk, and bringing these problems to the attention of bank management.[23] Possibly because there were no sanctions behind ignoring ICERC classifications (and since the classifications were not made public, the market sanction could not work either), the ICERC apparently failed to prevent the escalation of risky sovereign debt. The failure of the ICERC approach has led some commentators, Richard Dale and others, to argue that jawboning for diversification is not enough—stronger, binding legal constraints are needed. But as much as the regulators might want better tools for obtaining bank prudence, they are in a classic political bind. They want to improve bank practices, but without damaging foreign friendly states or imperiling the increasingly precarious debt situation.

This political bind of the regulators in the 1970s sometimes even meant that the banks were encouraged to take or withhold action for political reasons, rather than economic ones. A classic instance of the political bind came to light in 1977 Senate hearings. The story is related here at length both to illustrate the dilemma of U.S. banking regulators and the systematic problem of using private actors for developing country financing. The story concerns commercial bank lending to the Indonesian government-owned oil company, Pertamina.[24] The government of President Suharto, which replaced the Sukarno government in 1967, had undertaken to restructure and develop the Indonesian economy. At that time, Suharto turned to an advisor and personal friend, General Ibnu Sutowo, to be in charge of the oil sector of the economy and appointed as the managers of the remainder of the economy in Indonesia a number of technocrats with economic credentials and no personal power base. Sutowo, unfortunately, never checked with the technocrats and, indeed, managed the affairs of the oil sector in the way he thought the president would want him to. He believed that in order to develop Pertamina adequately, he should borrow money. At that time there were a number of bankers anxious to utilize the deposits that they had obtained in the very liquid Eurocurrency markets of the early 1970s. Although private commercial banks were more than willing to provide financing for General Sutowo's undertakings, ultimately the technocrats in the Indonesian government, the IMF experts, and even the U.S. embassy became very worried about the extent of Pertamina's borrowings and the fact that no one, not even the general, seemed to know the total extent of the indebtedness.

In the meantime Indonesia experienced general economic difficulties, and a standby agreement with the IMF was concluded in 1972.[25] The standby agreement set a ceiling on external borrowing by Indonesia. The standby arrangement stated the total permitted amount of medium-term external debt (loan maturities of one to fifteen years) which Indonesia would be permitted to incur and still be in compliance with the economic program for its recovery worked out with IMF officials. According to the U.S. economic counselor in Indonesia at that time, the private commercial banks, which were anxious to continue lending to Pertamina, did not observe the ceiling and instead colluded with General Sutowo in drafting loan agreements that appeared to conform to the debt ceiling but in fact evaded it. The embassy directly encouraged the U.S. banks to cooperate fully with the Indonesian government (the technocrats who wanted to carry out the IMF program) in attempting to maintain the ceiling. The U.S. State Department appealed both to U.S. bank representatives in Jakarta and to the bank head offices in the United States to restrain private bank lending to Indonesia.

However, by the end of 1974, Pertamina's affairs began to deteriorate radically; and Pertamina ceased to be able to repay its obligations. In the meantime, as the result of a tightening of the Eurocurrency market following the failure of Herstatt bank, the commercial banks' excess liquidity was disappearing. At this point the U.S. embassy's role shifted significantly. Instead of pressuring the banks to slow down their lending to Pertamina, the embassy embarked on a campaign to convince the banks not to declare their unpaid loans in default and, moreover, to elicit assurances from the Indonesian government that the Indonesian central bank would support Pertamina so that it could repay the private foreign banks. In other words, after having told the banks not to lend (which advice the banks ignored), the U.S. embassy then found itself asking the banks not to call in the loans because the United States could be hurt politically.

In the end the situation was resolved. The banks did not call the loans and worked with Indonesia to muddle through the crisis. When Congress heard ι 1is story in 1977, however, it asked why the regulators had permitted the banks to make the loans to Pertamina in such an unrestrained and, indeed, uncooperative fashion. The Senate Banking Committee was particularly concerned that the banks had made loans that violated the IMF conditions on external borrowing by Indonesia and its instrumentalities. The senators seemed to assume, with certain reason, that if the IMF thought borrowing in excess of a certain level imprudent for Indonesia, the lenders could be considered imprudent for violating the IMF agreement and that this was the sort of imprudence that the regulators were supposed to control. Although Congress did not write any specific directions to the bank lending regulators concerning oversight of the international lending process by U.S. banks into the Bretton Woods Agreements Act Amendments of 1977,[26] neither did Congress forget that it had admonished the regulators in 1977 that they were supposed to be more diligent in heading off imprudent foreign loans.

The International Lending Supervision Act of 1983

When the question of additional funding for the IMF came up again in 1983, the Senate focused on the extent to which imprudent lending by the private commercial banks had contributed to the developing country economic crisis. After the Pertamina disaster and the Senate's rebuke in 1977, why had the banking regulators not been vigilant in guarding against excessively risky sovereign lending? The senators also wanted to know exactly what the regulators proposed doing to deal with the situation. The regulators' answer was a Joint Memorandum on the Program for Improved Supervision and Regulation of International Lending, submitted to the Senate Banking Committee by the Board of Governors at the Federal Reserve System, the Office of the Comptroller of the Currency, and the Federal Deposit Insurance Corporation.[27] They explained that after the 1977 concern over the role that private lending had played in Indonesia's economic crisis, and pursuant to Congress's directive in the creation of the Federal Financial Institutions Examination Council,[28] they had jointly instituted a system for uniform examination procedures for evaluating "country risk" factors in international lending by U.S. banks, the ICERC system. The Joint Memorandum reflected a sophisticated understanding of the special transfer risks associated with sovereign lending and the concerns of the regulators that the prior procedures had apparently been inadequate.

The regulators explained in the Joint Memorandum that they were indeed very concerned about the risk to the banks themselves that the enormous amount of developing country external debt represented. They intended, therefore, to integrate the country exposure reports with their reviews of capital adequacy. Banks that had overconcentrated their loans to one particular country would be required to add to their capital base.[29] In addition, the regulators proposed a five-point program they thought would "help assure earlier recognition of potential international payments problems, encourage orderly responses to these problems, and provide for stronger reserves to meet adverse conditions when they infrequently, but inevitably, arise."[30] The program contained proposals to

1. Strengthen the existing program of country risk examination and evaluation;
2. Increase disclosure of banks' country exposures;
3. Establish a system of special reserves (called *Allocated Transfer Risk Reserves)*;
4. Create supervisory rules for accounting for fees; and
5. Strengthen international cooperation with foreign banking regulators and through the IMF.

The first proposal, country risk evaluation, was an extension of the ICERC policies to avoid risk concentration and increase diversification. The third and fourth proposals, special reserves and accounting rules, were new approaches to encourage lenders to be more cautious when making new foreign loans.

The regulators appeared before the Senate committee with their suggestions. One interesting point about their proposals is that they evinced the same duality as the response of the United States to the Indonesian situation six years before. That is, the regulators were concerned with encouraging the banks to be much more prudent in their international lending and in their exposure to country risk and, at the same time, were well aware of the risk to the entire international financial system were the banks to call their loans or fail to agree to a restructuring and the input of new money to permit some continuing payment on old loans. Although the Joint Memorandum is phrased in typically cautious regulators' language, the concern of the regulators over the need for continued flow of capital to the developing nations is perfectly clear. Thus, they say that their five-point program

> has been designed to create incentives for prudent lending but without establishing arbitrary obstacles to international capital movements or preventing the continuation of credit flows to credit-worthy borrowers. Depending upon particular circumstances, continued capital flows to basically credit-worthy countries in current strained economic conditions remains appropriate—especially in the context of IMF-approved economic stabilization programs—in order to encourage appropriate adjustments by borrowers to their

problems, to maintain their capacity to service their outstanding debt, and therefore to preserve the integrity of existing bank assets.[31]

Translated, this means that congressionally imposed harsh measures against the banks will only cause them to stop any new lending, and this the system cannot afford.

The dual concerns of the regulators mirror the dual goals of national monetary control. Thus the Board of Governors of the Federal Reserve System is not only a bank regulator, but is also the central bank of the United States, an entity that together with the Treasury is responsible for participation in international monetary cooperation. It should therefore be no surprise that the Joint Memorandum stresses that "broader considerations of the stability of the international financial and economic system are at stake as well."[32] Both of the novel suggestions in the regulators' five-point program—the Allocated Transfer Risk Reserves and the rules on bank accounting for fees collected in connection with international syndicated loans—must be understood as means of utilizing private bank lending to encourage compliance by debtor countries with IMF remedial programs and of discouraging special incentives for international lending except where they are needed.

With respect to the first of the two novel proposals, the regulators proposed that they institute a system of "provisioning against certain country exposures. When a borrower has been unable to service its debts over a protracted period of time, whether or not that borrower is a sovereign, it is appropriate to recognize the risks and the diminished quality of the assets represented by these loans."[33] Generally banks, or at least banks that are subsidiaries of holding companies that raise capital in the public securities markets, are required to review their credits to determine whether all or part of specific loans should be declared losses and charged off or whether additional provisions should be made to the allowance for possible loan losses in light of such credits. The requirements for so doing arise from the necessity of the parent company to prepare certified financial statements according to generally accepted accounting principles. For better or worse, the accountants had never developed such principles to deal with sovereign loans, since "credit risk" in the case of a sovereign had not been well conceptualized. Thus, the regulators reported that countries' transfer risks were not routinely or uniformly used to adjust the net carrying value of the affected assets, although certain banks were provisioning against country exposure. To remedy that problem, the regulators proposed that they require banks to make special provisions against certain assets found to be severely affected by transfer risk problems—that is, where the countries had not been able to service debt. These reserves were to be called *Allocated Transfer Risk Reserves*.[34]

As so described, one might think that these special reserves would be a prudential provision analogous to the loan loss reserves kept by banks against credit risk on lending. However, the regulators were relatively honest in their admission that the special reserves were a goad to push banks toward desirable social behavior (supporting the regulators' view of policy necessity) and were not so much a protection for depositors and investors.

> Such provisions would be deducted from current earnings and, to the extent required by regulation, would not be included in capital for regulatory and accounting purposes. The prospective requirement for reserving, with its attendant bottom-line earnings impact, should act as a cautionary element when the initial decision to lend is being made.[35]

Because of the requirement that any such reserves imposed be deducted from current income, the proposed transfer risk reserve, so far as the banks are concerned, would operate somewhat like a tax, reducing the reported earnings of the banks. Since banks report publicly how much they earn, any reduction in reported earnings affects the value of their stock. Thus no bank would want to be required to keep a special reserve of this sort, particularly since the regulators were suggesting that this kind of reserve not be counted as part of capital. The suggestion was that the banks would have to take money out of income, put it into a special fund, and then still be subject to the regulatory objection that the bank capital is inadequate to support its lending. As a result, the proposed requirement of a special reserve constitutes a very powerful threat against banks. Regulators could use the implied threat of special reserve requirements to influence bank conduct. Therefore, when the regulators went on to say in the Joint Memorandum that "such reserve provisions would not apply to lending to a country where the terms of any restructuring of debt were being met, where interest payments were being made and where the borrowing country is complying with the terms of an IMF-approved stabilization program,"[36] it is perfectly clear that the regulators were suggesting a system of motivating private lenders to ensure country compliance with an IMF stabilization program. This is in contrast to the Pertamina situation in the 1970s, when the banks, anxious to lend, were in effect abetting Indonesian evasion of the IMF restrictions.

The other novel proposal in the Joint Memorandum was the new accounting rule for loan fees. The regulators had noticed that the multinational bank lending syndicates on sovereign loans were behaving very much like syndicates of investment bankers and were assessing a number of special fees. In addition to commitment fees generally charged in connection with loans, one or more of the banks in these syndicates were also charging "front-end" fees, agency fees, advisory fees, and expense reimbursements.[37] The special fees would be of considerable importance to banks to the extent that, as an accounting matter, the banks take them into income at the moment the lending arrangements are put together rather than treating the fees as additional interest, which under accounting rules must be accrued over the term of the loan. The regulators were concerned that some of these fees "provide an added incentive to seek out international loans in order to boost earnings immediately and, once this has occurred, to sustain past earnings levels." The regulators proposed that the fees "be treated as interest except when they are identifiable as reimbursement of direct costs."[38] Like the reserve proposal, the accounting proposal was formed so that the regulators could remove any artificial incentive for the banks to prefer sovereign balance of payment lending over ordinary commercial lending.

In recommending the transfer risk reserves, the accounting rules, and the proposals on country risk and disclosure, however, the regulators also recommended to the Senate Banking Committee that they be allowed adequate flexibility in issuing their regulations so as to ensure that the banks continue to roll over the loans, and not withdraw from the business of international lending. They thus recommended that the IMF Funding Act not include any specific legislative provisions concerning international banking supervision.[39] The Senate Banking Committee agreed that "great care should be taken not to complicate upcoming debt restructurings or to impede future prudent growth in foreign lending" but "also concluded that specific legislative action is needed to mandate permanent improvements in the supervision and regulation of international lending, to improve the timeliness and comprehensiveness of public information on foreign borrowing and lending, and to assure that appropriate accounting procedures are used to report the true results of international lending."[40] The Senate was essentially telling the regulators: We agree with your program, but we remember Pertamina and your failure to heed our admonitions in 1977. Therefore, the legislation will tell you what you have to do and will cut back on your discretion.

The Banking Committee of the House of Representatives was prepared to go even further. As far as it was concerned, the lending banks had been wicked and imprudent, and the regulators had been almost criminally lax and complacent. The House Banking Committee criticized the regulators' recommendation that they be left alone to formulate new rules. "In 1977, such a recommendation would have been meaningful. In 1983, after six years of agency assurances, a reform proposal consisting of general comments and guidelines yet to be specified . . . was insufficient. The long history of banker excess and regulatory neglect in the area of international lending made the agencies' proposal and legislative recommendation unacceptable."[41] As a result the House bill contained detailed mandatory rules, to be implemented by the Federal Financial Institutions Examination Council, which had been established in 1978 to coordinate the examination procedures of the various federal agencies and which had produced the ICERC. The House Banking Committee expressed utter lack of faith in the traditional regulators to devise or enforce adequate rules.[42]

Bashing banks and bank regulators has been a popular House sport, dating back at least to the years when populist Congressman Wright Patman headed the Banking Committee, but this initial reaction was overblown. The regulators' recommendation was a sound one, notwithstanding Pertamina and the other lapses of the prior decade. Given the precarious balance between protection against unwise foreign lending and the preservation of the international financial system through the continued flow of new money, it is necessary to allow the regulators flexibility in making the rules, so that the regulators can adjust them as the conditions change, and calibrate their enforcement to encourage the banks to be more prudent in their future lending, even as they roll over the imprudent loans made in the past. Hard-and-fast legal restrictions written into a statute ill serve the requirements of an intrinsically fluid situation.[43]

The wiser heads prevailed in the Conference Committee, and the International Lending Supervision Act is very much a compromise. Thus, the only mandatory provision in the Act is section 906(a)(1) which provides: "[N]o banking institution shall charge, in connection with the restructuring of an international loan, any fee exceeding the administrative cost of the restructuring unless it amortizes such fee over the effective life of each such loan."[44] This provision originated in the concern of some members of the House of Representatives over the addition to developing countries' debt burden of the additional charges being made in some cases as a "rescheduling fee." That provision takes away from the regulators any discretion in providing for the accounting treatment of whatever is determined to be a "fee in connection with the restructuring of an international loan." Presumably, the regulators continue to have a certain amount of discretion in determining what are "administrative costs of the restructuring" as well as what sorts of refinancings qualify as "restructurings."

The other provisions of the Act are not mandatory. Each simply directs the "appropriate Federal banking agency" (our friends the regulators[45]) to promulgate regulations to carry out the proposals of the Joint Memorandum.[46] Congress wisely permitted the regulators the flexibility they needed to manage the developing problems. Indeed, the congressional statement of purpose, "to assure that the economic health and stability of the United States and the other nations of the world shall not be adversely affected or threatened in the future by imprudent lending practices or inadequate supervision,"[47] reflects the multifaceted goals of the regulators.

Regulatory Implementation of the International Lending Supervision Act of 1983

In 1983 and early 1984 the regulators issued a series of proposed and final regulations to implement the five-point program set forth in the joint memorandum and ratified by the International Lending Supervision Act. The U.S. response to the debt crisis, or at least the response of the banking regulators, is to attempt simultaneously to respond to the congressional desire to restrain the banks in their foreign lending and to accommodate the need of the international system for continued inflow of funds to developing countries. The intention of this response is to avoid a worldwide domino effect in the system should one or more major countries be unable to pay their external bills.

Allocated Transfer Risk Reserve Rules

Section 905 of the Act incorporates the regulators' suggestions as to the possible imposition of special reserves against loans to certain debtor countries. Specifically, section 905(a)(1) provides that the regulators "shall" require banking institutions to establish and maintain a special reserve, and the section goes on to provide the necessary flexibility by saying, "whenever, in the judgment of such appropriate Federal banking agency"

> (A) the quality of such banking institution's assets has been impaired by a protracted inability of public or private borrowers in a foreign country to make payments on their external indebtedness as indicated by such factors, among others, as
>> (i) a failure by such public or private borrowers to make full interest payments on external indebtedness;
>> (ii) a failure to comply with the terms of any restructured indebtedness; or
>> (iii) a failure by the foreign country to comply with any International Monetary Fund program or any other suitable adjustment program; or
> (B) no definite prospects exist for the orderly restoration of the debt service.[48]

Presumably under this provision, if a country were continuing to make the scheduled payments on its bank loans (if not all external funding) but was also continuing to borrow new money from the private banks in violation of an IMF program, the regulators would be authorized to "encourage" the banks to stop such new lending in violation of the IMF program by the imposition of the expensive special reserves against those loans. Obviously Congress had not forgotten the Pertamina episode.

Section 905(a)(2) provides that the special reserves "shall be charged against current income and shall not be considered as part of capital and surplus or allowances for possible loan losses for regulatory, supervisory, or disclosure purposes."[49] It could be that in this provision, the regulators got more than they wished, for the Joint Memorandum merely asked for power to *choose* such treatment. Section 905(a) suggests that Congress accepted the idea that the special reserves are much more of a goad to the banks than they are true prudential reserves against lending risks.

On the other hand, Congress was aware of the necessity of not discouraging the flow of new money to a developing country in the process of rescheduling its debt. Thus, the House Committee Report notes,

> Some Members of the Committee were concerned that [the similar provision of the House bill] could cause smaller banks to stop lending to countries which are in the process of organizing their finances and desperately need credit to prevent having to default. It cannot be emphasized strongly enough that the language of the bill regarding reserves i[s] intended to be used by the Examination Council and the banking agencies to stabilize international financial conditions and assure orderly credit markets.[50]

The context of this House Committee Report makes clear that the term "orderly credit markets" means not discouraging banks from making new loans as part of restructuring agreements. This flexibility is all the more striking insofar as it came from the House of Representatives, whose general attitude toward the lending by the banks, and the oversight thereof by the banking regulators, is indicated by the House Committee Report's vehement rejection of the regulators' suggestion that legislation was not required.[51]

The regulators' response to section 905 of the Act indicates how clearly they understand the necessary role of the private banks in the continued functioning of the network of international sovereign lending. The proposed regulations concerning the special reserves were published by the three agencies in late December 1983.[52] Apart from choosing a very special name, Allocated Transfer Risk Reserve, or ATRR, for the special reserves, the proposed regulations did not expand much on the congressional language. The proposed regulations simply repeated the congressional language and asked for comments. The proposals noted that the federal banking agencies would jointly determine which "international assets" would be subject to the reserve and the amount and timing of the reserve for specified assets.[53] In other words the regulators were ensuring that there would be no "competition of laxness" among the agencies. The ATRR thus established would be 10 percent of the principal amount of those specified international assets (or a greater or lesser percentage as determined by the banking agencies).[54] Finally, the proposed regulations contained a replenishment provision. Rather than having to establish an ATRR against assets found to be impaired by the transfer risk problems as described in the statute, banking institutions would have the option to write down (against the reserve for loan losses ordinarily kept by banks) all or part of the assets subject to the special reserves and, consequently, reduce the amount of ATRR balances that would otherwise be required. In the event of the exercise of that option, however, the regulators proposed to require the allowance for possible loan losses to be replenished out of current earnings by the amount written down.[55] In other words, as proposed, the provisions for special reserves would in no case allow a bank to avoid a "hit" to its current earnings if a particular country's borrowings were found to fall into the special reserve category.

The proposals called for comments not only as to the percentage norms for the reserve and the factors to be used in determining the amount of reserves, but also "the appropriate treatment of new loans when comparable outstanding loans are subject to reserves required by this regulation."[56] The Board of Governors of the Federal Reserve System received thirty-nine responses.[57] A number of the comments from the banks are quite interesting. Virtually all the banks recognized the inevitability of special reserve rules, and their comments focused on a rational implementation that would not be so burdensome on the banks. The main criticisms related to the replenishment provision. Commenters argued that if a bank chose to write down an asset instead of establishing an ATRR, the loss reserves should be replenished only to the extent necessary to restore it to a level adequate to reflect the remaining risks in the loan portfolio. For example, Bank of America noted that the proposed rule could put banks which earlier had charged weak loans against earnings—the responsible banks—at a competitive disadvantage vis-à-vis banks that made no provisions for weak loans—the less responsible banks. This would, in turn, discourage conservative practices. The commenters suggested something to this effect: "Why don't you leave that to us? The amount of our general reserve for loan losses has traditionally been up to our discretion, and if our accountants and we determine that our general reserves are enough to cover everything—and, indeed, if we have been so prudent as to write off bad loans promptly—why should we have to replenish the general loan amount when we think it is sufficient to cover our regular loans?"

The other major point made by the comments concerned what should be done about additional loans to borrowers in a country already on the special reserves list. The banks stressed that any treatment requiring the application of the ATRR to new loans would be counterproductive. The banks noted that this would mean that the cost of new money going to countries in severe difficulty and attempting to reschedule would be even greater because of the requirement of reserves against the additional loans. The banks stressed: "You *want* us to put in new money, don't you? How are you ever going to encourage us to put in any new money to a country if we also have to reserve against it?"

The regulators' response to the comments was accommodating. The final regulation follows the good sense of the comments.[58] The major alternation of the proposed regulation accepted the banks' criticism of the replenishment provision. The final regulation does not require replenishment of the allowance for possible loan losses by the amount written down unless, in light of the banks' and the accountants' appreciation, the allowance for possible loan losses should be replenished "in such amount necessary to restore it to a level which adequately provides for the estimated losses inherent in the banking institution's loan portfolio."[59] The same provision counts write-downs in prior periods as well as reductions in principal against the allowance for possible loan losses as acceptable alternatives for an ATRR. Moreover, the agencies' preamble to the final regulations makes clear that "an ATRR normally would not be required initially for net new lending when the additional loans are made in countries implementing economic adjustment programs, such as programs approved by the International Monetary Fund, designed to correct the countries' economic difficulties in an orderly manner." The reasoning, in accord with that of the comments, was that new loans would improve the quality of outstanding credit and thus be consistent with the Act's objective of improved supervision of international lending.[60] In short, the final regulations suggest that the regulators were willing to accede to virtually all of the banks' suggestions, especially those indicating the need for continued bank involvement in the restructuring process.

Finally, and most interestingly, the regulations turned out to be completely *in terrorem*. The reserve provisions only come into effect to the extent that the ICERC determines that assets in those countries should be subject to an ATRR. (The ICERC reviews country risk exposure and the economic situation of countries in which the regulated banks have a significant amount of assets.) By the spring of 1984 the regulators had announced only five countries against which the special reserves are to be charged against income (if not already written off) and carried: Zaire (75 percent reserves), Sudan (50 percent reserves), Poland (15 percent reserves), Nicaragua (15 percent reserves), and Bolivia (10 percent reserves).[61] These are precisely the countries against whose borrowings the banks in general have already made provision in their allowance for possible loan losses. Since write-off against such coverage can under the final regulation substitute for the creation of an ATRR, it should not be expensive for the banks to comply with the Allocated Transfer Risk Reserves for those five countries.

It would not be surprising, in light of the concern of the regulators that lending to developing countries on the brink be continued in the interest of an orderly restructuring of developing country debt, if the regulators choose not to add any other countries to the list. The ironic result is that the regulators have simultaneously been able to appease Congress with the suggestion of special reserves and then, by not adding countries to the list, protected the public interest in banks' continued lending to developing countries by not punishing them, so far, with ATRRs. Thus, in this area of the special reserves, the regulators would seem to be trying both to follow the domestic political process as best they can so as to appear as dutiful regulators and still relieve the banks of what might prove, if exercised in fact, a very burdensome provision. The risk they run, of course, is yet another round of congressional blame if the accommodation does not work, the reschedulings are not muddled through, and the loans must be called in default (with no reserves).

Fee Accounting Rules

The various fees charged by banks restructuring foreign debts raised two issues that are treated in the International Lending Supervision Act. The debtor countries complained incessantly about the imposition of additional fees payable to the banks in the process of coming to agreement on a stretching out of maturities. Some members of the House of Representatives in considering the House version of the IMF Funding Bill were very much concerned with the level of up-front fees that the banks were charging in connection with the restructuring of foreign sovereign loans. If additional fees paid to a bank or banks upon an extension of an international loan represent an additional interest charge to compensate for the additional credit risks incurred with the "rescheduled" principal, then presumably such fees *should* be amortized over the effective life of the loan as extended. However, at least some banks had been taking into income the restructuring fee as of the time of signature of the restructuring agreement.[62] Congress apparently believed that this accounting treatment sometimes gave an incentive to the banks negotiating in a restructuring to provide for excessive up-front fees and thereby to add to the debt service burden on the countries in trouble. Thus section 906(a)(1) of the Act, the only wholly mandatory provision, seeks to "avoid excessive debt service burdens on debtor countries" by forbidding banks from charging "any fee exceeding the administrative cost of the restructuring" unless the fee is amortized over the life of the restructured loan.[63]

In contrast, section 906(b)(1) instructs the federal banking agencies (the regulators) to "promulgate regulations for accounting for agency, commitment, management and other fees charged by a banking institution in connection with an international loan," but in subsection (b)(2) explains that the purpose of the regulation is "to assure that the appropriate portion of such fees is accrued in income over the effective life of each such loan."[64] This provision appears to cover a broad variety of fees, including those generated by the large-scale debt restructuring committees of banks. It is clear from the legislative history of the Act that section 906(b) was enacted in response to the regulators' suggestions that the "front-end loading" (that is, placing at the initiation of the loan rather than over time) of various fees charged to the borrowing countries in connection with international syndicated loans had been creating an artificial incentive to make international loans.[65]

The concern of Congress and the regulators was well founded. Under generally accepted accounting principles, if payments by a borrower are labeled "fee for services," the full payment can be taken into income at the time the loan agreement is signed; if the fee is considered simply a way of increasing yield on the loan, then it is "interest" and should be accounted for at intervals over the life of the loan. To the extent that banks can claim fees as service-related rather than yield-related, they can gain short-term boosts in earnings. Up-front fees were not the only ones that were sometimes reported as current earnings; other opportunities abound in international syndicated lending. For reasons as to which legal anthropologists can only speculate, foreign sovereign lending syndicates of multinational commercial banks are put together in a fashion that resembles investment banking syndicates.[66] Thus, for example, the lead bank in such sovereign lending syndicates refers to its undertaking to round up the group of lenders as "underwriting."[67] Nevertheless, function followed form, the banking syndicates charged the borrowers "fees," and some banks thereby accounted for those fees as fees for services includable immediately in income.

Since large domestic borrowers are not in the habit of paying such a wondrous variety of fees to their commerical bankers, the practice of receiving and counting as immediate income these fees on international syndicated loans tends to make such activity unusually attractive to bankers concerned with maintaining or increasing current earnings. It is this practice that the regulators and Congress thought might be giving an "artificial incentive" to international lending. Thus at the time of promulgation of the final ATRR rule in February 1984, the banking regulators also issued proposed regulations on accounting for international loan fees, in accordance with Congress's mandate in section 906(b).[68]

The proposed regulations sought to cut through the various semantic distinctions among the myriad fees and to create a unified functional accounting approach that would not create artificial incentives for commercial banks to make foreign loans. Thus the proposed regulations made no distinction between fees received in connection with a restructuring (section 906(a) fees) and various other fees received in connection with international lending (section 906(b) fees). The proposed regulations simply provided that all fees received in connection with international loans other than loan commitment fees (a traditional commercial banking fee) should be, to the extent they exceed the administrative costs of the international loan, recognized over the loan period; loan commitment fees were to be deferred and amortized over the term of the combined commitment and loan period.[69] In short, the practice of front-end loading was made much less attractive. The preamble of the proposed regulation indicated that the reasoning behind the regulators' sweeping proposal was that "accounting practices should not result in artificial incentives for banking institutions to make international loans premised on the immediate recognition of all fee income."[70]

The regulators had proposed strict accounting rules in the Joint Memorandum, Congress had concurred, and the proposed regulations seem unusually firm. Nevertheless, perhaps indicating regulatory doubts about the impact on the multinational banks of their proposed rules, the proposal asked specifically for industry comment on whether the rules should differentiate between fees related to restructured loans and other international loans, whether the proposals on commitment fees made sense, how banking institutions should account for the cost of and fee income attributable to their merchant banking activities, and whether or not any aspect of the proposed rules were inconsistent with the accounting treatment for domestic loans.[71]

The reaction from the international banks was an immediate howl. The regulators received sixty-seven comments.[72] The general argument of the commenters was that whereas Congress had in section 906(a) mandatorily put a stop to the front-end loading of fees received in connection with a restructuring, Congress in section 906(b) had not mandated any particular accounting treatment for fees received in connection with international loans not involved in a restructuring. The banks commenting, therefore, asked for as narrow as possible definition of "restructuring" so as to ensure that Congress's mandate would only have to be applied in connection with loans to debtor countries that were rescheduling because of lack of foreign exchange to pay their external debt and not to loans that were refinanced for other reasons.

Moreover, and above all, the commenters wanted to ensure that they could continue to take into income as "service income" the management fees on the syndicated international loans. A reading of the London-based magazine *Euromoney* over the years gives a picture of how fierce is the competition in the Eurocurrency markets among the banks to be "lead" bank on the sovereign loans because it is the lead bank that manages to earn for itself the lion's share of the management fee for arrangement of the loan. In effect, the banks saw the utility of these fees being reduced by the new proposed regulations. The comment letters raised elaborate arguments as to why the management fees were fees for services and the extent to which the new regulation would make competition with the multinational banks' competitors, the merchant banks, much more difficult. The argument does not strike me as entirely convincing, but the regulators apparently were willing to appear convinced. The preamble to the final regulation states: "There can be little dispute that banking institutions that are 'lead' or 'managing' banks provide services, as described by the commentators, in connection with the international loan syndications. These banking institutions also frequently participate in the loan and often their share in the loan is among the largest of all participants. In such circumstances the activities of the institution in syndicating the loan are, at least to some extent, integral to the lending of funds." However, the preamble continues: "What additional portion of the syndication fees is intended to compensate a managing bank for making the loan, as compared with arranging loans for others, is not easily determined using any generalized standard and may vary from case to case."[73]

Apparently, the regulators realized that in this area they had gotten themselves into a hornet's nest. In theory, the banking agencies are regulating commercial banks that are forbidden by the Glass–Steagall Act to act like merchant banks.[74] On the other hand, the Glass–Steagall Act does not apply to participation in foreign merchant banks that do no underwriting within the United States. In short, abroad there are major U.S. multinational banks that do compete with merchant banks and have mixed commercial and merchant banking functions, just like foreign institutions. There really is no reason why such institutions should not be allowed to receive fees for arranging loans for others. The problem is, of course, that in the case of the foreign sovereign loans, the lead bank also acts generally as a lending bank, and could be viewed as merely doing what it would do in a very large domestic loan, parcelling out the portion of the loan that is too large for it to manage alone, in light of its own capital base. In this case, its functions look much more like "banking" than "underwriting."

The regulators, however, in the actual final regulation were quite subtle. They appeared to accept the banks' arguments concerning the provision of services and how, therefore, the lead or managing bank fees should be accounted for. But, as the preamble to the final regulation makes clear, there is some limitation on the ability of the lead bank to take the fee into income:

> In order to assure that, in practice, the appropriate portion of the fee is amortized, the final regulations allow the banking institution to take the fee into income when the loan is closed only to the extent that the institution can identify and document the services for which the specified fee was received. Documentation for this purpose shall include the loan agreement signed by all of the parties to the loan, which identifies the services provided and the total fee received by the institution for the provision of such syndication or management services. . . . If the portion of fees received representing compensation for such services cannot be so identified and documented, then the fee will be presumed to be an adjustment to yield [additional interest] and must be amortized over the life of the loan.[75]

Very often in loan syndications the exact amount of the management fee is negotiated between the debtor country or its instrumentality and the managing or lead banks; the other bank participants in the syndicated loan are not necessarily aware of the full amount of the fee. If the other banks in the syndicate become aware of the full amount of the management fee, they might ask questions as to why, if the sovereign could afford such a fee, it could not afford instead to pay a higher interest rate. Indeed, it has become a custom in syndicated loans to share some of the management fee with other participating banks to induce them to participate. This portion of the fee, the regulators have insisted both in the proposed regulation and in the final regulation, represents an adjustment to yield and must be amortized. It would seem clear that if, in order to take the portion of the management fee not shared with the other banks into income immediately, the lead bank must insert the amount of the management fee into the loan agreement, the result will be to enable the participating banks to demand as the price of their participation a greater portion of the management fee. To the extent that they do so, then that changes for all participating banks, including the lead bank, the accounting treatment of that portion of the fee. It will be very interesting to see how the final regulations for accounting change the drafting work of the British and American lawyers that specialize in the documentation of the syndicated loan agreements. In this instance the regulators, while appearing to accommodate the multinational banks, may have in fact found a way of tracking Congress's purpose and reducing the amount of fees for sovereign lending that can be charged "up front," thus reducing the attractiveness of foreign sovereign loans vis-à-vis domestic lending.

Conclusion

It can only be concluded, after all the dust has settled, that the U.S. Congress's response to the international debt "crisis" in the form of the International Lending Supervision Act has not changed the regulatory structure over U.S. commercial banks' international lending to any significant degree. The regulators have been given statutory authority to impose some greater discipline on lending to countries that are failing to adhere to their IMF austerity programs and to discourage any artificial preference for international lending based upon its effect on financial statements. Neither of these regulatory powers will have any significant effect on the volume of international lending by U.S. banks. The decision-making power as to prudence of international loans ends up where it started, in the hands of the management and boards of directors of the multinational banks.[76]

This tepid response is hardly surprising, for two reasons. The first reason is a theme that runs through the legislative history of the International Lending Supervision Act of 1983. Even the House recognized the necessity, for the moment, of rolling over the loans and of allowing the rescheduling process to continue with the addition of new money to keep the interest payments on the old loans current, or at least current enough to prevent a mandatory recognition of default, and a conceivable international financial breakdown.[77] The second reason was not articulated in any of the public debate in connection with the Act, but that reason may be a more important cause of the ambivalent form of the U.S. legislative and regulatory "response." That reason is the international competition for banking services. So long as states themselves are unwilling to undertake (individually, or collectively through international agencies) the necessary job of balance of payments financing, the need will be filled at a price by private banking institutions.[78] As this chapter and this volume of essays have stressed, this has been the international monetary history of the 1970s and 1980s.

These privately owned international intermediaries are hardly all American owned and regulated. The multinational banks involved in syndicated sovereign lending are British, German, Swiss, and Japanese, with considerable participation by other European Common Market or Canadian based banks as well. This is critically important. It would be very difficult for the United States unilaterally to tighten its rules of sovereign lending, considering the regulatory structure of the international lending market. The United States cannot go it alone. U.S. banks at present are more regulated in their international activities than the banks of any other nation;[79] to restrict their discretionary lending any further (or to raise the costs of their funding for such lending by imposing additional reserve requirements)[80] would only inhibit, at considerable cost to the U.S. balance-of-payments deficit, their capacity to compete with (or participate with) the other multinational banks in global lending.

Significant regulation of international lending by private institutions will have to be achieved on an international basis, either through international coordination of regulation or through a supranational regulator (impossible dream though that may seem).[81] Congress in the International Lending Supervision Act was well aware of this reality; the Act directs the chairman of the Board of Governors of the Federal Reserve System to "review the laws, regulations, and examination and supervisory procedures and practices, governing international banking in each of the Group of Ten Nations and Switzerland, with particular attention to such matters bearing on capital requirements, lending limits, reserves, disclosure, examiner access, and lender of last resort resources. . . ."[82] It is this call to international action, with respect to the international debt crisis and the role of banking supervision therein, that is the effective and appropriate U.S. response.

Notes

1. See, for example, Roger Kubarych, chapter 1 of this book.
2. Riordan Roett, chapter 6 of this book; Riordan Roett, "Democracy and Debt in South America: A Continent's Dilemma," *Foreign Affairs* 62 (1984):695.
3. This perception of the relationship between balance of payments financing by private banks and the health of the global financial system is not a new one. See James Srodes, "Governor Wallich Wants the IMF to Advise LDC Lenders," *Euromoney*, April 1977, p. 24; "Sounding Alarms on Foreign Debt," *New York Times*, September 18, 1977, sec. 3, p. I, col. 1.
4. By "insolvent" I mean that for a number of U.S. banks, the total principal amount of loans to Latin American countries exceed their capital: if these assets were to be written down to actual worth (or the Latin debtors were to repudiate the loans so as to cause their value to be recognized as zero), the capital of these banks would be impaired.

5. The chief U.S. financial institutions that participate in the short-term Eurocurrency markets are commercial banks or their affiliates. Federal regulation of U.S. commercial banks is carried out chiefly by three separate regulators: the Federal Deposit Insurance Corporation, the Comptroller of the Currency, and the Board of Governors of the Federal Reserve System. See Banking Act of 1933, 12 U.S.C. §§ 1, 221, 264 (1982). All three agencies work together to regulate U.S. commercial bank international lending, and thus the three agencies will hereafter be referred to collectively as the "regulators."

6. Hearings Before the Senate Committee on Banking and Currency, 89th Cong., 1st sess. (1955), the statement of George M. Humphrey, Treasury secretary. In the last decade the U.S. government, along with other Western governments, encouraged bank overseas lending on the theory that the private flow of funds would aid U.S. export and job markets. International Bank Lending: Hearings Before the Subcommittee on Financial Institutions Supervision, Regulation and Insurance of the House Committee on Banking, Finance and Urban Affairs, 98th Cong., 1st sess. 274 (1983), the statement of C.T. Conover, Comptroller of the Currency. Most important, however, the banks played the role of broker by recycling OPEC oil earnings back to countries with massive balance of payments deficits because of the oil shock of 1973–74. For example, International Financial Markets and Related Matters: Hearing Before the House Committee on Banking, Finance and Urban Matters, 97th Cong., 2d sess. 13 (1982), the statement of Representative Wylie. Of course, unlike a broker, the banks borrowed (by taking petrodollars in the form of deposits) in order to relend.

7. The IMF Funding Bill was enacted as Title IX of the Domestic Housing and International Recovery and Financial Stability Act, Public Law 98-181, 97 Stat. 1153, November 30, 1983, and was codified at 12 U.S.C. §§ 3901–3912. For a short but heartfelt recounting of the political difficulties of the bill, see Andreas Lowenfeld, *The International Monetary System*, 2d ed. (New York: Matthew Bender, 1984), pp. 259–61.

The legislative history of Public Law 98-181 is extremely complicated because of the extraordinary political maneuvering that seems to have been connected with it, including an amendment of the House and Senate Conference Report on the Senate floor, at which point the IMF and international lending legislation with which we are concerned in this chapter was added to the Domestic Housing Act and passed by the Senate in that form. Thus the hearings that are listed following the House and Senate reports do not apply to the bill number of Public Law 98-181, H.R. 3959, the Domestic Housing Act. The hearings that pertain to the U.S. response to the debt crisis are International Financial Markets and Related Problems: Hearings Before the House Committee on Banking, Finance and Urban Affairs, 98th Cong., 1st sess., February 2, 8, and 9, 1983 [cited hereafter as International Financial Markets]; International Bank Lending: Hearings Before the Subcommittee on Financial Institutions Supervision, Regulation and Insurance of the House Committee on Banking, Finance and Urban Affairs, 98th Cong., 1st sess., April 20 and 21, 1983 [cited hereafter as International Bank Lending]; and Proposed Solutions to International Debt Problems: Hearing Before the Senate Committee on Banking, Housing, and Urban Affairs, 98th Cong., 1st sess., April 11, 1983 [cited hereafter as International Debt Problems]. The House and Senate reports on the bills that became the portions of Public Law 98-181 that interest us here are H.R. Rep. No. 177, International Economic Recovery and Financial Stability Act, 98th Cong., 1st sess. (May 16, 1983) [cited hereafter as House Report], and Senate Report No. 122, Bretton Woods Agreements Act Amendments and International Lending Supervision, Report of the Committee on Banking, Housing, and Urban Affairs, U.S. Senate to accompany S.695, 98th Cong., 1st sess. (May 16, 1983) [cited hereafter as Senate Report].

8. One of the purposes of the IMF set forth in Article I of its Articles of Agreement is the temporary provision of financial resources to members "to correct maladjustments in their balance of payments" thereby obviating resort by members to "measures destructive of national or international prosperity." The financial resources available for IMF loans are drawn (among other sources) from contributions by member nations to the pool of currencies in the fund; each member's contribution is called its "quota." The United States is the largest contributor to the fund, and any substantial increase in IMF resources all but requires an increase in the U.S. quota.

9. Representative James Coyne, for example, criticized the "young bankers" for urging Third World countries "to borrow, and borrow, and borrow, because after all they had valuable mineral resources or commodities" and for "rushing one [after] another to every economic backwater trying to lend money at a time when they didn't really understand the credits they were dealing with." International Financial Markets and Related Matters: Hearings Before the House Committee on Banking, Finance and Urban Affairs, 97th Cong., 2d sess. 96 (1982).

10. A good account of the story of the Mexican crisis of August 1982 may be found in Joseph Kraft, *The Mexican Rescue* (New York: Group of Thirty, 1984).

11. International Financial Markets, pp. 381, 386, statement of Richard Dale of the Brookings Institution.

12. Thus in 1978, the then Comptroller of the Currency (the regulator of national banks) wrote to the chairman of the American Bankers Association's (ABA) International Banking Division requesting comment on the legal lending limit concept as it applies to international lending. The ABA replied that it saw a strong need for an increase in the established 10 percent legal lending limit as applied to foreign governments and their related entities. Specifically, the ABA noted that "[t]he inherent ability to raise revenue through the capacity to borrow, to tax, and to command the allocation of natural resources distinguishes governmental borrowers from private sector borrowers. . . . Additionally the repayment and debt servicing record of foreign governments has been stronger than that of private borrowers." Letter from Gerald M. Lowrie, executive director of government relations, American Bankers Association to John Shockey, chief counsel, Office of the Comptroller of the Currency (March 13, 1978) (available in the Office of the Comptroller). The letter was received as a comment in response to publication in the *Federal Register* of proposed rules for determining lending limits for foreign borrowers. See Proposed Rulemaking, Loans to Foreign Governments, their Agencies, and Instrumentalities, 43 Fed. Reg. 1800 (January 12, 1978) [cited hereafter as Proposed Rulemaking].

13. See James Hurlock, chapter 5 of this book, recounting these and other problems confronted by counsel for debtor countries.

14. See Srodes, "Governor Wallich Wants the IMF to Advise LDC Lenders," an interview with a governor of the Federal Reserve System.

15. See Cynthia Lichtenstein, "U.S. Banks and the Eurocurrency Markets: The Regulatory Structure," *Banking Law Journal* 99 (1982):484, 510–11.

16. 12 U.S.C. § 84 (1982). The statute and its regulations define what is meant by "single borrower" and "capital and surplus." See generally Lichtenstein, "U.S. Banks and the Eurocurrency Markets." The statute was amended in 1982, raising the limit from 10 percent to 15 percent.

17. The implementing regulations, 12 C.F.R. §§ 2.1-32.2 (1977), concerned the combining of loans to partnerships, corporations, and their subsidiaries and certain other enterprises, and so applied to parastatal organizations organized as corporations. See Proposed Rulemaking, p. 1800. The regulations did not specify, however, which governmentally-owned corporations should be combined with the sovereign itself for the purpose of the legal lending limit. Ibid., pp. 1800-01.

18. "Mexico Is Worried That New U.S. Rules Are Curbing Loans, *New York Times,* October 19, 1977, p. D1, col. 1.

19. See Proposed Rulemaking, p. 1801.

20. With regard to the foreign affairs ramifications of such a rule, consider the comment of the Central Bank of Mexico on the much milder 1978 rule proposed by the U.S Comptroller of the Currency. It begins by iterating the Central Bank's understanding of "the need to have a banking system based on a reasonable diversification of risks as well as on open practices contributing to its soundness." It goes on, however, to complain that the proposed regulation had already led some bank examiners "to adopt procedures that have been even more restrictive than those proposed," and to protest that such restrictiveness if generalized "could result in a harmful restriciton on the access of foreign borrowers to U.S. financial markets." The letter then details (as do many of the bank comment letters) *why* foreign governments should not be a single "person" for purposes of the statute: "From our point of view, the proposed regulation fails to grasp fully the particular characteristics of a 'mixed economy' such as ours. It is for us difficult to understand why the nature of such a system should affect its creditworthiness or bring about the combination of a particular borrower with the government." Letter from Gustavo Romeso Kolbeck, director general of Banco de Mexico, S.A. to John G. Heimann, Comptroller of the Currency (March 3, 1978) (available in the Office of the Comptroller). The letter was received as a comment in response to Proposed Rulemaking.

21. See International Financial Markets, pp. 381, 386, the statement of Richard Dale of the Brookings Institution.

22. Ibid., pp. 390–91.

23. The ICERC is described in ibid., pp. 52–58, 84–89 in the statement of Paul Volcker, chairman of the Board of Governors of the Federal Reserve System. ICERC is a classification system in assessing country risk. When a country has interrupted its payments, the loan is classified as "loss." If the borrower country has such problems that an interruption in payments seems likely, then the classification would be either substandard or doubtful. The majority of countries, however, came under the classifications strong, moderately strong, or weak. In determining a country's classification, ICERC will examine objective criteria of current account balance, debt service payments, and net interest payment as well as subjective criteria such as economic, political and social factors. When a bank's exposure exceeds 10 percent of its capital funds for a weak country, and 10 percent for a moderately strong country, ICERC is required to make a "special comment" on the condition in its report. The

purpose was simply to alert the banks; the regulators could not require any action by the banks.

24. The story concerning Pertamina related in the text may be found in the Senate Foreign Relations Committee's Report on the Bretton Woods Agreements Amendments Act of 1977. Senate Report No. 603, 95th Cong., 1st sess. 20 (November 15, 1977).

25. When a country seeks balance of payments assistance from the IMF, it typically enters into an arrangement in which the IMF agrees to lend it money in return for the country's commitment to an economic stabilization program. For a good explanation of the process of IMF aid to developing countries and the negotiation of standby arrangements, see Lowenfeld, *International Monetary System,* esp. ch. 2.

26. See Public Law 95-118, Title II, § 201, 91 Stat. 1967 (codified at 22 U.S.C. § 286e-1f); Public Law 95-147, § 4(a), 91 Stat. 1228 (codified at 22 U.S.C. §§ 286c, 286k).

27. Joint Memorandum (Subject: Program for Improved Supervision and Regulation of International Lending), April 7, 1983, reprinted in International Debt Problems, pp. 24–52 [cited hereafter as Joint Memorandum, with page citations to the Senate hearing].

28. Financial Institutions Regulatory and Interest Rate Control Act of 1978, Public Law 95-630, Title IX, 92 Stat. 3641, 3693 (November 10, 1978).

29. See Lichtenstein, "U.S. Banks and the Eurocurrency Markets," pp. 509–10; "Profit Rises 38.9% at Big Coast Bank [Bank America Corporation]," *New York Times,* January 22, 1985, p. D1, col. 6.

30. Joint Memorandum, p. 25.

31. Ibid., p. 26.

32. Ibid.

33. Ibid., p. 29.

34. Ibid., pp. 40–41, appendix C: "Proposed Reserve Provisioning for Credits to Countries with Severe and Protracted Debt Servicing Problems."

35. Ibid., p. 29.

36. Ibid., pp. 29–30.

37. "Front-end fees" are flat fees paid by the borrower to the lending banks, generally on the signing or disbursement dates of the credit facility; somewhat like an origination fee (for it is expressed as a percentage of the credit facility and paid to cover the administrative expenses of originating a loan), the front-end fee includes "management fees" paid to some of the lending banks in return for additional service provided or "underwriting" risk assumed (ibid., p. 51).

An "agency fee" is paid by the borrower to the agent bank to reimburse it for out-of-pocket expenses incurred in the performance of its administrative duties (telex, printing, travel, etc.) (ibid., p. 52).

"Commitment fees" compensate the lending banks for legally committing to lend to the borrower at certain terms and rate at some future time (ibid.).

"Advisory fees" are paid by the borrower to compensate a bank(s) for specific advisory services provided in connection with a transaction, such as coordinating a multibank loan (ibid.).

"Expense reimbursements"—including legal and travel expenses—are paid to banks active in arranging multi- or on-site credit facilities (ibid.).

38. Ibid., p. 30.

39. The regulators argued that their enabling statutes and the Financial Institutions Supervisory Act of 1966 gave them the authority to implement the five-point program. "In view of the existence of this authority it would not be desirable to establish rigid or inconsistent legislative rules that could limit the ability of the banking regulators to adapt the program as they gain experience with its implementation and could have the unwarranted and unintended effect of discouraging the international lending necessary to support world trade and economic recovery" (ibid., p. 33).

40. Senate Report, p. 13.

41. House Report, pp. 26–27.

42. "In the Committee's view, the testimony of the witnesses, the reports of the GAO, and other information available to the Committee, indicate that the supervisory failings which permitted the build-up of U.S. bank foreign debt is attributable to failures in supervisory follow-up by the Federal Reserve, the Comptroller of the Currency, and the FDIC, and not to the Council itself. The prominence of the Council in implementing the Act, is seen by the Committee as conducive to greater international regulatory cooperation and coordination" (ibid., p. 28).

43. No less a personage than IMF Managing Director de Larosière recently stressed to the Council on Foreign Relations that "there is also a crucial role for the commercial banks in the future, as in the past, in any constructive and meaningful resolution of the debt problems. The banks will have to continue to provide restructuring and new money on realistic terms to debtor countries implementing adjustment policies." *IMF Survey,* December 10, 1984, p. 380.

44. International Lending Supervision Act (ILSA) § 906(a)(1), 12 U.S.C.A. § 3905(a)(1) (Supp. 1984).

45. The Act uses the term "Federal banking agencies" to refer to the FDIC, the Office of the Comptroller of the Currency, and the Board of Governors of the Federal Reserve System (id. § 903(1), 12 U.S.C.A. § 3902(1) (Supp. 1984)), which are the agencies referred to as the "regulators" in this piece. See note 5.

46. See ILSA §§ 904–905, 907–909, 12 U.S.C.A. §§ 3903–3904, 3906–3908 (Supp. 1984); see also id. § 910(a), 12 U.S.C.A. § 3909(a) (Supp. 1984), providing general authority for rulemaking by the federal agencies.

47. Id. § 902(a)(1), 12 U.S.C.A. § 3901(a)(1) (Supp. 1984).

48. Id. § 905(a)(1), 12 U.S.C.A. § 3904(a)(1) (Supp. 1984); see Joint Memorandum, pp. 29–30: "such reserve provisions would not apply to lending to a country where the terms of any restructuring debt were being met, where interest payments were being made and where the borrowing country is complying with the terms of an IMF-approved stabilization program."

49. ILSA § 905(a)(2), 12 U.S.C.A. § 3904(a)(2) (Supp. 1984).

50. House Report, p. 29.

51. Ibid., pp. 26–27.

52. The Comptroller of the Currency's proposed version is at 48 Fed. Reg. 56,597 (December 22, 1983) (to be codified at 12 C.F.R. pt. 20); that of the FDIC is reported at 48 Fed. Reg. 56,764 (December 23, 1983) (to be codified at 12 C.F.R. pt. 351); and that of the Board of Governors of the Federal Reserve System appears at 48 Fed. Reg. 57,140 (December 28, 1983) (to be codified at 12 C.F.R. pt. 211). The proposed regulations and the introductions thereto are identical, and therefore the reference hereafter will be only to the Federal Reserve's proposed regulation.

53. 48 Fed. Reg. at 57,142 (proposed § 211.44). Generally, the assets would be those subject to transfer risk: the quality of the assets was impaired by a protracted inability to pay or by the absence of definite prospects for restoration of debt service.

54. Ibid. (Fed's proposed § 211.43). The ATRR is to increase to 15 percent in subsequent years.

55. Ibid. (Fed's proposed § 211.46(d)).

56. Ibid., at 57,141.

57. There were seventeen comments from U.S. banks and bank holding companies, five from trade associations, eight from foreign banks, five from Federal Reserve banks, and one from New York's Banking Department. 49 Fed. Reg. 5587, 5588 (February 13, 1984).

58. The final regulation for all three agencies was issued February 9, 1984 and appears at 49 Fed. Reg. 5587 (February 13, 1984) (to be codified at 12 C.F.R. pts. 20, 211, 351).

59. This final rule on replenishment is codified at 12 C.F.R. §§ 20.8[c][4] (Comptroller), 211.43[c][4] (Fed) and 351.1[c][4] (FDIC).

60. 49 Fed. Reg. at 5588.

61. See *Washington Financial Report* 42 (Jan. 2, 1984):3. A meeting in April of the interagency committee decided at that time not to add any other countries to the list. On the other hand, during the summer of 1984, the ICERC has put pressure on banks to be more cautious about making more loans in countries like Venezuela (not yet on the ATRR list). "Possibly Bad News for U.S. Banks," *Wall Street Journal,* August 7, 1984, p. 36, col. 2.

62. Joint Memorandum, p. 30.

63. ILSA § 906(a)(1), 12 U.S.C.A. § 3905(a)(1) (Supp. 1984).

64. Id. § 906(b)(1)–(2), 12 U.S.C. § 3905(b)(1)–(2) (Supp. 1984).

65. "The current practice of taking front-end fees into income in the quarter or year in which they are charged, rather than spread over the life of the loan is an incentive to promote international loans in order to boost earnings. Banks should be making loans based on the creditworthiness of the borrower not on short-term profitability considerations. The establishment of an accepted accounting treatment for front-end fees will contribute to the future stability of the international financial system by eliminating artificial incentives to make international loans." (House Report, 31.)

66. In the United States since 1933, investment banking, the process by which funds are raised for economic enterprises by investment banks that publicly distribute securities of the enterprise, has been separated from the business of commercial banking, the raising of funds by deposit taking and the reselling of the funds by lending. Investment bankers traditionally consider their "underwriting" a "service" for the client corporation.

67. This, of course, is a misuse of the word: a real "underwriter" is stuck with securities purchased that it cannot resell; it has a real risk. No court would ever force a single or group of lead banks to *lend* the full amount of a promised loan if the promised participants could not be found.

68. 49 Fed. Reg. 5594 (February 13, 1984).

69. Id. at 5597–98 (to be codified at 12 C.F.R. §§ 20.9(a), (b)(1) (Comptroller), 211.45(a), (b)(1) (Fed) and 351.2(b), (c)(1) (FDIC)).

70. 49. Fed. Reg. 5594, 5595 (February 13, 1984).

71. Id. at 5596.

72. The Federal Reserve Board and the Comptroller of the Currency received thirty letters from banks and bank holding companies, ten from trade associations or firms, seven from accounting firms or groups, and six from Federal Reserve banks. FDIC received fourteen letters, all duplicating comments received by the other two agencies. 49 Fed. Reg. 12,192, 12,193–94 (March 29, 1984).

73. Id. at 12,195.

74. Banking Act of 1933, 48 Stat. 162 (codified in scattered portions of 12 U.S.C.).

75. 49 Fed. Reg. 12,193, 12,195 (March 29, 1984).

76. The English scholar Richard S. Dale, who testified in the February 1983 House hearings on International Financial Markets, p. 388, strongly criticized the ICERC supervising mechanism and the reluctance of the regulators to allocate credit. He stressed his belief that "at the very least banks should be prevented from getting into a situation where they can be brought down by a single country's default." He thus recommended the imposition of a ceiling on banks' lending to country borrowers such as 25 percent of capital. This kind of radical change in the U.S. approach to control of private commercial banks foreign sovereign lending is exactly what was *not* adopted.

77. In this chapter I have been unable, given space limitations, to delve into the accounting and disclosure questions involved in international lending. The rules are set by a combination of generally accepted accounting principles, the banking regulators' call report requirements, and the Securities Exchange Commission's financial disclosure requirements for bank holding companies. The total effect, however, is to force banks to take out of reported income (and thus reduce reported earnings) any interest income they have accrued once that interest is more than ninety days in default. Until the banks in the Argentine rescheduling negotiations stopped the game by publicly announcing the actual effect on income, fear of such announced reductions in income was a card in the hands of the debtors. At some point, however, if debts due are *never* rescheduled, they must be written off as "bad" and *then* the banks could be, from the accounting point of view, insolvent. To Mr. Dale's credit, his proposal for an absolute ceiling in lending insisted that "there would, of course, have to be extended transitional arrangements, although the most heavily exposed banks might reasonably be required to increase their capital in order to expedite adjustment to the new regime." International Financial Markets, p. 388.

78. See text accompanying note 43.

79. See International Financial Markets, pp. 391–92, testimony of Richard Dale, Brookings Institution.

80. See generally, Lichtenstein, "U.S. Banks and the Eurocurrency Markets."

81. What makes the allocated transfer risk reserves provisions so interesting is their deference to the *supervising* function of the IMF in its conditionality (in the IMF restrictions on sovereign external borrowing in IMF adjustment programs).

82. ILSA § 913(1), 12 U.S.C.A. § 3912(1) (Supp. 1984).

9

The Foreign Debt Crisis and the Process of Redemocratization in Latin America

Riordan Roett

W hile the attention of the U.S. government appears to be focused almost exclusively on the drama of Central America, there is no doubt that another crisis has erupted which affects the entire hemisphere. That crisis is the international debt crisis. It has continued to expand and deepen since August-September 1982, when Mexico provided the first "signal" that Latin American states were not in a position to service their outstanding debt. Patchwork policymaking by the private commercial banks and the international lending institutions in 1983 resulted in a series of temporary palliatives. The next year brought the Argentine scare of March 31, which drew a reluctant U.S. government and four other governments in the hemisphere into the process of rescheduling payments of principal falling due. April and May 1984 brought news that the Dominican Republic and Bolivia either stopped payments or broke off negotiations with the International Monetary Fund (IMF). On May 19 the democratic presidents of Argentina, Brazil, Colombia, and Mexico issued a dramatic statement about the social costs of the debt burden and called for a meeting of finance and foreign ministers in June 1984 to establish mutual policy responses for the hemisphere. While improved balances of payments enabled the two largest debtor countries, Mexico and Brazil, to reschedule part of their debt after the middle of 1984, by January 1985, Argentina was still struggling (notwithstanding new agreements with the IMF and the banks), and Peru and Chile had fallen into arrears on interest.[1]

Those who call for a limited role for the United States in seeking a resolution of the debt crisis suffer from a dangerous myopia. The debt crisis is no longer a business-as-usual issue between the debtor governments and the private commercial banks. The world has changed dramatically since the Mexican collapse of 1982. Today the foreign debt of Latin America is a political question of the highest priority to the United States and to the national security interests of the United States in the western hemisphere. To consider the debt question as anything less undermines our future in the hemisphere and threatens to destabilize the process of redemocratization in Latin America, which is important to our security and strategic interests in the region.

This position is not held universally, of course. Walter Wriston, the recently retired chairman of the board of Citicorp, published an "op-ed" essay in the *Wall Street Journal* titled "LDCs Just Need a Little Help from Their Friends." The article compares the international debt crisis with the 1970s debt crisis in New York City. Wriston's message is that sound management and resourceful people will resolve the international crisis just as the banks and the city government salvaged New York City. He uses Mexico to illustrate his point that austerity and adjustment are effective in returning Latin American economies to good health. He states that the "Cassandras will be proved wrong." Those who argue that the social and political costs of adjustment are excessive clearly fall into Wriston's "Cassandra" category. He concludes his argument by stating that "as history has shown again and again, good people working together with an intelligent plan will still move cities, states, and the world forward."[2]

One problem with Wriston's argument is that he does not know his Greek mythology. Cassandra was proven to be right—not wrong. The tragedy was that no one believed Cassandra's prophecies. Those of us who argue that the debt has political and social aspects may well be termed latter-day Cassandras, but that does not mean, necessarily, that we are wrong in our judgment about the gravity of the debt crisis in Latin America. A more accurate interpretation of the current debt crisis is found in a *New York Times* editorial titled "The Debt Bomb Ticks."

> Britain in Dickens' time had a simple remedy for debtors: prison. Though morally gratifying, this was economic madness. Debtors denied a chance to produce can hardly repay their creditors. The lesson applies today to the otherwise different issue of third-world debt. Punishing poor or overextended peoples by burdening them with interest rates and repayments that exceed their income may be rough justice, but it damages creditors just as much.[3]

The precariousness of the debt issue in Latin America has been reinforced by the recent report of the Americas Society Western Hemisphere Commission on Public Policy Implications of Foreign Debt.[4] The report of the blue ribbon panel states that Latin America will need $60 billion in new loans between 1984 and 1986. The report argues that the private commercial banks ought to provide $40 billion of the total, with the remainder coming from governments or international financial institutions. The report goes on to point out the striking political and social implications of austerity measures in Latin America. The panel suggests that at some point regional political leaders may well recoil against 20 percent and higher rates of unemployment in the urban work force, refuse to further curb crucial imports that are essential to generate jobs, and balk at further price increases in basic foodstuffs and services for the majority of the population.

From the perspective of Latin America, the possibility of not meeting outstanding debt obligations is still palpable. Any increase of the prime interest rate raises the amount of annual payments of principal and interest by hundreds of millions of dollars. Protectionism in the industrial countries makes it more difficult for Latin American countries to export and earn the foreign exchange required to service the debt. The social pressures at home are mounting, and the fear of civil disturbance has been confirmed with the 1984 workers' demonstrations and hunger strikes in Bolivia and with riots in the Dominican Republic, which left more than fifty people dead and hundreds injured.

Increasingly, the debt issue is not only political, but it has come to focus on the key question of whether or not the new democratic governments of the hemisphere will be able to withstand the social deprivation which has accompanied their efforts to adjust their economies in response to negotiations with the IMF.[5] The future of democracy in Latin America and its response to the debt crisis are inexorably linked. And they are linked in a way that makes a satisfactory resolution of the debt situation important to the national security of this country. Between January 1979 and January 1985, nine Latin American countries (Argentina, Bolivia, Brazil, Ecuador, El Salvador, Honduras, Panama, Peru, Uruguay) have held elections to replace military governments with democratic ones. The first problem most of these new democracies have had to deal with has been the debt crisis. The austerity imposed by harsh renegotiation terms threatens that redemocratization. The crisis is immediate; the results of ignoring it may be dire. It is in the urgent interests of both Latin America and the United States that public efforts be made to ameliorate the impact of renegotiation.

Preconditions for Latin American Democracy

The classic movement of a society toward democracy is the progression in England from the near-absolute monarchy of the Norman kings to the modern parliamentary supremacy and cabinet government, accompanied by a gradual expansion of the right to vote. Such a linear model is a historical blessing made possible by a general trend of economic growth, the development of a differentiated social structure (one with a variety of classes and social, regional, occupational, ethnic, and religious groups), and a culture that emphasizes individualism and activism. The United States and Canada in the western hemisphere have had these characteristics, together with the advantage of England's institutional example, and their "progress" toward democratic governance has been even more rapid. The states of Latin America, which gained their independence from Spain and Portugal in the nineteenth century, on the other hand, have not had these characteristics. Their cultural traditions are corporatist and hierarchical rather than individualist. Economically, those societies have traditionally been less capitalist and less wealthy. The social structure has been less varied, typically dominated by entrenched elites. Traditions of orthodoxy and intellectual scholasticism have stifled broad and energetic participation in the political process. The preconditions for the linear evolution of a stable democracy have not necessarily existed in Latin America.[6]

An alternative way that democracy has developed in many Third World states is a cyclical model of alternating despotism and democracy.[7] In countries following this model, the society is dominated by elites, who nominally accept democratic institutions—until the democracy threatens real change or their vital interests. As a result, elections are held, but there is generally not a sustained succession of democratically elected governments. Governments are as often the result of military coups as of elections. Such coups would occur when a party or candidate appealing to the middle and lower classes for reform wins or is about to win an election, when the elected government challenges a vested interest of the elites, or when the government appears incapable of managing the economy and maintaining social order. After several years of authoritarian leadership, new elections are held, and the cycle starts all over again. As Professor Samuel Huntington has argued, the cyclical pattern can prove a real obstacle to the evolution of a stable democracy, more of an obstacle than a long period of authoritarian rule, for example. "In the [former], neither democratic nor authoritarian norms have deep roots among the political elites, while in the [latter] a broad consensus accepting of authoritarian norms is displaced by a broad consensus on or acceptance of democratic norms. In the one case, the alternation of democracy and despotism *is* the political system; in the other, the shift from the stable despotism to a stable democracy *is a change* in the political system."[8]

The cyclical model better describes the experience with democracy in most Latin American states during the first half of this century. Although most of the states abandoned pure government by oligarchy or single authority as the middle class and trade unions became more powerful forces, social and political conflict only engendered the cycle from despotism to democracy and back again. Brazil, for example, followed this pattern, as demonstrated in some detail by appendix C, a chronology of major political events in Latin America, by country. The Brazilian Republic was unable to cope with the economic disaster of the 1929 worldwide Depression, and a military coup in 1930 established Getúlio Vargas as president. His policies favored national unity over regional interests, industrialization, and certain labor reforms (such as the eight-hour workday and collective bargaining rights). These reforms stimulated rightist opposition, and the military took over in 1945. In the elections of 1950, however, Vargas was elected president on a vaguely populist platform. His prolabor policies contributed to high inflation and economic concern among the elites, leading to another military coup in 1954. Civilians returned to power in the 1955 elections, but the increasing social and economic problems proved no less tractable. When the economy became sluggish in the early 1960s, the military once again assumed the reins of government in 1964 and suspended elections. A series of military governments ruled Brazil for twenty-one years. In January 1985 former prime minister Tancredo de Almeida Neves was elected president.

The unstable cyclical model illustrated by Brazil has also been characteristic of Argentina, Peru, Bolivia, Ecuador, Guatemala, Honduras, Panama, and El Salvador. Several countries have followed the cyclical pattern for part of the century. Thus Colombia and Venezuela alternated between dictators and elections until the late 1950s and have had fairly democratic transitions since then. In contrast, Chile and Uruguay boasted long-standing democratic traditions until the 1970s, when each fell under authoritarian right-wing rule. (See appendix C for highlights of the major regimes in each of these countries from 1930 to the present.) Other countries have enjoyed a more constant system. Mexico, for example, has been a relatively stable one-party "democracy" since 1917. Paraguay has been governed by the same authoritarian leader since 1954.

In the last twenty years there has been a shift away from the cyclical model. At first, it appeared as a shift toward authoritarian rule, but in the long run the changes might have created some of the preconditions for more stable, evolutionary democracy in the region. In the 1940s the classic *caudillo*, or general, could seize power, overthrow a weak civilian regime, govern greedily for a few years, and drift into exile or retirement. In the 1950s and 1960s Latin America, especially the continent of South America, underwent a set of important socioeconomic changes: urbanization, industrialization, falling birthrates, technological breakthroughs, increasing direct private investment from abroad, and so forth. The role of the state in the economy expanded rapidly. As traditional urban middle class governments attempted to cope with increasing social strains and inadequate financial resources, increasingly professional military institutions developed doctrines of national development and national security. These doctrines differed from country to country. But they led to one conclusion: civilian government was inadequate to the task of socioeconomic development. Furthermore, the armed forces determined that weak civilian governments endangered their vision of national security. Military governments provided a shield against subversion.

As a result of the perceived inadequacies of the populist or middle class elected governments and the military's positive vision of a stronger, economically developed state, authoritarian regimes replaced democratic ones in the 1960s and early 1970s—Brazil in 1964, Argentina in 1966 and 1976, Peru and Panama in 1968, Ecuador and Honduras in 1972, Chile and Uruguay in 1973 (see appendix C). All of the new regimes, with the exceptions of those in Ecuador and Peru, were right-wing authoritarian; those in Ecuador and Peru were military populist experiments. Regardless of ideology, all were disdainful of democratic processes. Almost all of the authoritarian regimes closed legislatures, banned political parties and interest group activity, and censored the media and the press. In response to the national security dimension of the new regimes, the intelligence and security forces occupied prominent roles in setting the goals of the state. High among the priorities was that of eliminating dissent. Latin America plunged into a decade of human rights violations that were unprecedented in the continent's history. In light of this, the authoritarian regimes rested their right to rule—their political legitimacy—on their efficiency, their capacity to induce economic growth, and their proclaimed ability to govern decisively, without the political stalemate and social tensions that populist democratic regimes allegedly generated.

From the perspective of many, these promises appeared to bear fruit, as world economic conditions and domestic policies led to unprecedented levels of economic growth. Again, Brazil is a useful example.[9] The economic managers adopted decisive policies to combat inflation (which exceeded 100 percent per annum by the middle of the decade), such as curtailing government expenditures, strengthening tax collection efforts, and tightening credit and wages. Also, the policymakers adopted measures to reduce price distortions caused in part by the import-substitution policies of the 1950s. All of these policies brought the government deficit and inflation rate down to acceptable levels by the end of the decade. Moreover, the government vigorously encouraged business development by ambitious improvements in the country's capital, transportation, and power supply systems and by a system of tax incentives favoring certain industries or regions. Other reforms in the tax and foreign exchange policies were adopted in order to foster export diversification. These policies contributed to the "Brazilian Miracle" of 1968–74, a period of remarkable growth. Annual real growth in the gross domestic product averaged 3.7 percent from 1962 to 1967 but surged to an average of 10.1 percent per year from 1968 to 1974. The economy also opened up to significantly increased foreign trade. In the early 1970s Brazil was able to incur substantial trade deficits and to increase its foreign exchange reserves (from $400 million to $6.8 billion in 1973) by attracting foreign direct investment and loans from official and private foreign sources. Though less impressive in their results, similar growth occurred under authoritarian regimes in Chile and Argentina.

Amid the superficial glitter of growth statistics, however, lurked systematic problems with the authoritarian policies. Many argued that the growth took place at the cost of development. Workers' salaries, in real terms, fell; social security programs suffered; labor organizations were either prohibited or severely limited in their autonomy. One result was increased concentration of income. In Brazil, for example, the share of national income for the bottom

40 percent fell from 11.2 percent in 1960 to 9 percent in 1970, while the share of the top 5 percent increased from 27.4 percent to 36.3 percent.[10] Building economic miracles on such a slender segment of the population is a risky program for economic growth. And after the 1973–74 oil price shock, even the talismanic growth statistics soured. The authoritarian market managers turned out not to have been such miracle workers after all.

Additionally, the unchecked security mentality of the regimes led them to overextend their countries' resources. It led to arms build-ups at home and adventurism abroad, as the authoritarian regimes showed a tendency to revive historical rivalries and interfere in the affairs of their neighbors. Chile and Argentina spent hundreds of millions of dollars to prepare themselves for possible war in 1978 over possession of the Beagle Channel Islands. Even after democratic elections in 1980, the quasi-autonomous military establishment in Peru skirmished with Ecuador in 1981. And, of course, there was the Argentine debacle in 1982, when the military regime quickly seized, and just as quickly lost, the Falkland, or Malvinas, islands. To finance military build-ups and miniwars, as well as the ambitious public works projects and other programs adopted to secure the physical integration of these countries, the regimes were led to massive borrowing from foreign sources. Even Brazil, which was less prone to adventurism than Peru, Chile, and Argentina, borrowed heavily after 1974 in an effort to perpetuate its economic development projects. In all of these cases, the normal checks and balances of public opinion, congressional oversight, or press coverage were absent. Decisions were taken without regard for overall strategies of social integration and development.

By the end of the 1970s the experiments with authoritarian growth and government had failed. The economies were close to bankruptcy. Looming foreign debt could not be repaid. Massive infrastructure projects stood partially completed. Unemployment and social deprivation had increased. Traditional modes of life had been disrupted and little had been fashioned to take their place. By the early 1980s the signals were clear: the military was in retreat. Civilian pressures increased and reluctant military and civilian autocrats were forced to concede that they had failed. The alternative was a return to electoral politics and democracy.[11]

The Dilemmas of Redemocratization in the 1980s

Ironically, both the successes and the failures of the authoritarian regimes may have paved the way for the ultimate establishment of democracy in many of the countries of Latin America. By moving the Latin American economies into the international arena, the regimes have generated a small but important class of technocrats and businesspeople who are impressed with the

North American experience with democracy as a stabilizing influence. And by failing at their essential tasks of governance, the authoritarian regimes have stimulated a consensus in several countries that a broader based and more accountable government is necessary. The recent trend toward democracy has been encouraging. Free elections restored democratic regimes in nine countries between 1979 and 1985: Ecuador in 1979; Peru in 1980; Honduras in 1981; Bolivia in 1982; Argentina in 1983; Uruguay, Panama, and El Salvador in 1984; and Brazil in 1985 (see appendix C). A transition is planned for Guatemala in 1985. Public opposition has surfaced in Chile against the Pinochet regime, and pressure for elections has increased. Caribbean countries such as Jamaica and the Dominican Republic have consolidated their democratic governments in recent national voting.

A further irony, however, is that the very forces that undermined the authoritarian regimes may also undermine the democratic ones. The stark reality that confronts the newly elected governments is financial insolvency. There are a number of reasons for this macabre convergence of financial bankruptcy and political liberalization. As a natural consequence of the failures of military regimes in the 1970s, democratic governments have been able to reclaim long lost political space in the hemisphere. But as they return to power they discover that part of the phenomenon of the 1970s was massive foreign borrowing by military regimes. That borrowing was poorly planned, much of the money was badly spent, some was lost in corruption and venality, and little appears to have been utilized for social development purposes. The massive debt that has been accumulated by Latin American military regimes must now be repaid by their civilian successors.

While one can argue that governments inherit, and must honor, the debts of their predecessors (which is not a principle widely acknowledged in Latin America), a second element complicates the current economic scene in Latin America. At a time when democratic governments must demonstrate their efficacy—their capacity to perform, to respond to pent-up social demand—they are encountering a very bleak international economic situation. Even if the will to repay exists, the foreign exchange needed to do so is scarce and, in some cases, nonexistent. The world recession of the early 1980s sharply cut the export markets of Latin America. Protectionism continues to plague Latin American exporters. Real interest rates on loans (the nominal rate minus the rate of inflation) are still very high, and it is not clear when they will come down. This means, very simply, that a larger and larger share of what Latin America earns must be recycled to the private banks to repay interest. Little is left for needed imports or for social investment projects at home.

As Latin American governments confront mounting pressure "to honor their debts," they are urged to sign a "letter of intent" with the International Monetary Fund which will stipulate adjustment measures to be applied to the internal economy. Only when there is a letter of intent signed between the country and the IMF will the private banks agree to reschedule existing debt or approve new loans (much of which will go to pay interest and keep the accounts current). The adjustments deal with esoteric issues such as the growth of the money supply and related matters, but they also emphasize issues that are very much of concern to the majority of Latin American citizens: the real cost of food, housing, medicine, and clothing; the reduction in real wages; the elimination of government subsidies for basic commodities; and other belt-tightening measures.

There is no doubt that adjustments must be made in all the economies of Latin America (as is the case in the United States). The issue is *how* to adjust and *when*. The democratic governments are being pressured to undertake draconian cuts at the moment when their accumulated debt is massive, the export possibilities remain limited, and they need some growth to demonstrate a minimal level of concern for basic social needs in their societies. That is the issue at hand: how to provide sufficient economic "space" in Latin America to allow democratic regimes to perform adequately. Their performance, in the eyes of their citizens, will determine whether or not the democratic system will continue. Meaningful programs of adjustment, acceptable in both economic and social terms, need to be introduced with a high degree of political awareness. The very delicate political balance between the demands of the IMF and international bankers and the requisites for democratic development is different for each country. Four variations on this theme can be found by examining the interconnection of debt and politics in several Latin American countries.

Debt and Politics in Brazil

The process of democratization in Brazil has been one of transformation rather than replacement—*abertura*, the political liberalization instituted by the military government itself. Thus the government in the late 1970s partially lifted press censorship, granted political amnesty, and allowed new political parties to be formed. In November 1982 elections were held for a new congress, new state governors (not directly elected since 1965), and new municipal officials; indirect election (through an electoral college) for president was held in January 1985. One problem with this hopeful transition to democracy is the specter of Brazil's estimated $100 billion foreign debt, because the payment burden is generating social and economic ferment that may yet stimulate a rightist reaction.

In December 1982 Brazil and the IMF reached agreement on an austerity program that included the deindexing of wages from inflation, a decrease in government spending across the board, and the elimination of agricultural subsidies. The impact of such changes in a country already afflicted with high unemployment and inflation was all too predictable: days of rioting in São

Paulo in April 1983, labor demonstrations in June and July, autumn super-market invasions in Rio de Janeiro, and political opposition in the Congress. Although 1984 was a year of fewer such outbreaks, and although Brazil has made impressive progress in meeting the IMF targets, the cost has been great—substantial slashes in the level of imports, hardship for those least able to bear it, political instability and a less optimistic scenario for a return to democracy. For example, former President Figueiredo opposed a proposal for the direct election of the president and favored an electoral college plan that would favor his party, the Social Democratic party. The president feared that if direct elections were held, the winner would be a candidate unwilling to take the extreme measures needed to deal with the debt crisis. Congress in 1984 defeated a constitutional amendment calling for direct election of the president.

The intangible toll on the renewed interest in democracy is, of course, not quantifiable. At the very best, the debt crisis has stalled Brazil's attempt to develop a stable democracy. At worst, it may yet kill it. President Tancredo Neves, elected in 1985, is apparently committed to the military government's policy of austerity and accommodation to the banks. But it is still an open question whether his government will be able to satisfy *both* Brazil's foreign creditors *and* its people. Many in Brazil fear that the economic hardship and concomitant social unrest will produce *either* a series of unstable temporary governments *or* a rightist reaction which might repudiate the foreign debt or severely restrict the role of foreign banks and investment in the Brazilian economy. In either case there would be no winners. The banks stand to lose much or even all of their investments, the United States loses export and investment opportunities, and the Brazilian people lose the most, their chance for freedom.

A similar dilemma confronts two other recently elected Latin American leaders. Soon after being sworn in as Panama's first elected president in sixteen years, Nicolas Barletta in November 1984 introduced an austerity plan that provoked a ferocious reaction—marches in the streets, strikes, business protests—and left the country socially and politically divided over how to accommodate IMF demands. Julio Sanguinetti, the newly elected president in Uruguay, is also faced with the need for an austerity program that is bound to be unpopular in a country in which real wages have fallen 50 percent since 1969 and more than 15 percent of the work force is jobless.

Argentina

Argentina in 1983 repudiated its authoritarian regime for its feckless and mendacious conduct of the Malvinas/Falklands War, for "*el proceso*," the ugly covert campaign to remove citizens suspected of subversion against the government, and for economic chaos and inflation. The public consensus and the victory of a pragmatic moderate, Raúl Alfonsín, in the October 1983 election bring hope that the cycle of democracy and despotism may be broken. The foreign debt is one of the most pressing problems faced by the Alfonsín government, in large part because the military government had, in less than eight years (1976–83), increased the country's debt from $8 billion to $43 billion to pay for its adventuristic foreign policy and other schemes. In 1983 the IMF had arranged a $1.5 billion loan, but when Argentina failed to meet the goals of the accompanying austerity program the IMF withheld $1 billion. To Alfonsín has fallen the task of arranging a satisfactory austerity program, but that proved difficult in 1984, a year in which real wages had declined to 1974 levels and inflation ran at a rate of several hundred percent a year.

Negotiating an acceptable IMF program and forestalling popular unrest is becoming increasingly difficult. For example, Argentina was able to meet $500 million in interest payments on March 31, 1984, only through a complex arrangement by which $300 million came from Mexico, Colombia, Venezuela, and Brazil, to be paid back through an equal loan from the United States once an IMF program was worked out. In a bold move Alfonsín sent a letter of intent to the IMF proposing real wage increases in addition to economy measures. The premise of the letter was not unreasonable: Argentina could not reduce the importance of the armed forces, reinstate human rights, and make fundamental changes in the economy while at the same time imposing further hardship on the people. But the IMF rejected the terms of the proposal, and the United States refused to lend the $300 million. In October the government introduced a stabilization (austerity) program (including devaluation of the currency, slowdowns in wage increases, and severe reductions in public spending). As a reward, but with somewhat less than full confidence in the success of this program, the IMF and the commercial banks in December 1984 and January 1985 agreed to extend new loans and to reschedule part of the existing debt. Although he remains personally quite popular, Alfonsín barely remains in the same position in which he started—sandwiched between IMF austerity demands and the cries of his people for better living conditions. The unions are unhappy over wage freezes. Political violence is on the rise. What is at stake is not only Argentine democracy, for if Brazil retreats from its tentative movement toward democracy and if the Argentine experiment fails, there will be less pressure on the two remaining authoritarian regimes of Latin America's "Southern Cone"—Chile and Paraguay—to institute democratic reforms.

Peru

In Peru, democracy is five years old, restored in 1980 with the election of Fernando Belaúnde Terry as president, after twelve years of military rule. After taking office, Belaúnde moved forward with social programs, but his government has been frustrated by a string of natural disasters (floods in the north, drought in the south, and problems for the fishing industry) and the debt crisis. Peru obtained a $600 million IMF loan in 1982 but was unable to meet the IMF's goals in 1983. The IMF demanded a 20–30 percent devaluation and drastic spending cuts to lower the deficit. Belaúnde refused, perhaps mindful that devaluation by his government in 1967 led to a military coup. Ultimately, a compromise austerity program of budget cuts, tax increases, and a currency devaluation was agreed upon. Paying the debt consumes around half of Peru's export earnings, and the austerity measures have contributed to the worsened plight of workers (20 percent of whom have lost their jobs; wages are 60 percent of their 1973 levels). Notwithstanding these sacrifices, on January 1, 1985, Peru owed the foreign banks $250 million in overdue interest.

Debt-generated austerity has stimulated protests that threaten the government. Lima in November 1983 rebuffed Belaúnde's party by electing a Marxist mayor. After the new austerity program led to higher commodity prices, a general strike was called in March 1984. The Marxist guerrillas of the Sendero Luminoso (the "Shining Path") have spread their terrorist campaign from mountain villages to the cities, including Lima. Beset by such turmoil, the government declared a state of emergency in June 1984 and suspended constitutional guarantees. Many fear that the next "emergency" might replace the Belaúnde government with a military one or suspend the presidential elections scheduled for 1985. Although Peru's neighbor Ecuador seems to be coping with its foreign debt more successfully, its neighbor Bolivia has encountered similar problems. The democratic government of President Hernán Siles Zuazo faces the distinct possibility of a military coup if he cannot come to terms with the dual crisis of debt restructuring and depressed export prices.

Mexico

Even Mexico's more stable and long-lived democracy is being tested by the international debt payments. José López Portillo, president from 1976 to 1982, used Mexico's petroleum deposits to fuel an ambitious development program. When oil prices fell in 1981, he continued the programs and temporarily staved off currency devaluation by heavy foreign borrowing. The debt today is more than $96 billion. When Miguel de la Madrid Hurtado became president in December 1982, he inherited a country that had been forced to devalue its currency twice in one year and that had an inflation rate of more than 100 percent, a declining national output (falling by 4.7 percent in 1983), and rising unemployment. De la Madrid has complied with the accord reached with the IMF in November 1982, reducing government spending and imports. The banks responded in 1984 with a longer term rescheduling of much of Mexico's external debt.

Although Mexico has been able to renegotiate short-term loans with private banks on less unfavorable terms than previously and has a trade surplus for 1984, it faces severe problems with high unemployment and inflation. It is not clear that a moderate government, such as that of de la Madrid, can withstand the mounting political pressures generated by austerity. That is, a country so recently accustomed to substantial growth and relatively low unemployment will find low growth and high unemployment statistics frustrating, especially if they continue through the decade as they have every indication of doing. Thus in Mexico, and perhaps in the democracies of Venezuela and Colombia as well, the debt crisis does not seem to pose an immediate threat to established democracy, but it could pose a threat if debt-induced austerity continues through the decade.

The Hemisphere Debt Crisis: Implications for Latin America and for the United States

Implications for Latin America

Although the impact of the debt crisis is different in each country, certain general trends are clearly discernible. These trends have provoked increasingly alarmed responses from the countries of Latin America.

1. *Austerity has already exacted a high price in Latin America.* The combination of interest payments, IMF austerity programs, and uneven export prospects has generated a very bleak present for Latin America. Between 1981 and 1983 Latin America cut back its imports by 43 percent, thus starving its industries of needed materials and capital improvements. Latin American countries face depressed prices for commodity exports such as copper, iron ore, and sugar. And protectionism continues to grow, making export targets more difficult to achieve (in the United States, Western Europe, and Japan). The Latin American economy shrank nearly 3 percent in 1982 and 1 percent in 1983, although growth resumed in some countries in 1984. In the same period, per capita income fell by 13 percent, and unemployment and inflation rates continued to climb.

2. *Latin America's future is mortgaged, making a return to growth less likely.* Notwithstanding the recent austerity, the total debt is increasing and threatens to consume Latin American export earnings for much of the decade. The IMF, in a study released in May 1984, warned that even under optimistic economic assumptions, debt payments will take nearly one-quarter of the export earnings of Third World countries by 1987, compared with slightly more than one-fifth in 1983. The situation for Latin America is even more dramatic. Argentina's payments have consumed virtually all of its foreign exchange earnings, as is the case for Bolivia; Brazil's ratio has exceeded 50 percent; Peru's ratio has been close to 50 percent. With half or more of their

export earnings going to debt payments, some Latin American countries will not be able to import capital goods needed to serve as a foundation for future growth.

3. *The situation in Latin America could deteriorate.* The situation is dire under "optimistic" economic assumptions. It could become much worse if those assumptions do not hold up. For example, interest rates could go up. The prime bank lending rate was 11 percent in 1983, but went up in lockstep to 13 percent by mid-1984. (Later in the year, it declined once again.) The boost in the prime lending rate from 12 percent to 12.5 percent alone increased Argentina's interest payments by $200 million a year, Brazil's by $350 million, Venezuela's by $150 million, and Mexico's by $300 million. Each percentage point increase in interest rates adds about $2.7 billion to the annual external interest bill of the Latin American countries. The rising prime rate in early 1984 negated the few concessions debtor countries obtained from the banks. For example, the jump in the prime rate from 11 percent to 12 percent in April 1984 cancelled out the concessions Mexico had received from its success in meeting IMF goals. On the other hand, the decline in interest rates later in 1984 contributed to brighter prospects for countries such as Brazil and Mexico.

Moreover, the impact of rising interest rates—or rates stabilized at a high level—undermines the possibility of real growth in Latin America. An increasing prime rate obliges countries to use export earnings, earnings that are urgently needed to improve productive capacity, to pay increased interest charges. At 12.5 percent, the interest due in 1984 would equal about $45 billion, which is nearly one-half the $95 billion these countries will earn from exports (under the best of conditions). The increased debt servicing payments translate into a decline in gross national product (GNP) for these countries. Each percentage point increase in interest rates reduces the GNP of Brazil by 0.3 percent and of Mexico by 0.5 percent.[12] With an economic recession in most of the Latin American debtor states, the decline in GNP could be the difference between growth and no growth in the economy.

The issue is clear. Latin America, because of the U.S. federal deficit and a high prime interest rate, will need to export more to pay more to service its debt. Efforts to export more meet increasing protection everywhere and a weak recovery in the West European economies. Earnings from exports must go to service an increasing debt, much of which is viewed as little more than the result of financial machinations by the U.S. government and the private commercial banks. Unable to increase imports, there is little chance to rekindle the industrial growth and investment that would yield jobs and internal demand for goods and services. The vicious circle spirals upward.[13]

These factors have created potential national security dangers of great importance. To begin with, the process imperils fragile democracy in Latin America. Democratic governments in Brazil, Argentina, Peru, Panama,

Uruguay, and Bolivia may fall under the weight of debt-induced austerity. Authoritarian government in Chile may further delay any transition to democracy, either because it distrusts the capacity of an elected government to make the hard decisions needed to handle the crisis or because it believes that a return to repression will be needed to manage popular or leftist discontent with austerity. Most alarming is the possibility that the longer lived democracies of countries such as Mexico or Venezuela or Colombia might be threatened over the course of the decade, perhaps throwing those countries into the cycle of despotism and democracy which has proved so dispiriting in Latin America.

Moreover, there is some evidence that the debt crisis may radicalize existing Latin American governments or will encourage the substitution of radical governments for reasonable ones. For the first time Latin American states are deliberately walking away from the IMF and the private commercial banks—*unable* to pay, *unwilling* to pay. There are some factors making a default or unilateral moratorium attractive to debtor nations today. One benefit accruing to a nation paying interest on its debt is the ability to borrow new money. But Latin America is not currently receiving this benefit. Inter-American Development Bank figures show that in 1981 loans made to Latin America were $18 million more than payments made to banks. In 1982 the debtors paid out $5 billion more than they received in loans. The 1983 excess of payments over new loans is $17 billion, and the 1984 figure is expected to be even higher. A recent Brookings Institution study suggests that, given certain optimistic assumptons, Brazil, Argentina, and Venezuela would be better off if they repudiated their debt. The implications for the international financial system and for the private banking system in the United States must be the cause of highest concern to the government of the United States.

One can argue, of course, that it is the weak countries that are "overreacting" and that the magic of the marketplace will indeed reach out to them in the short term. Few realistic observers believe this to be true. Moreover, the democratic leaders of Latin America appear very dubious about the possibilities of recovery in the near future. In a dramatic statement on May 19, 1984, the presidents of Argentina, Brazil, Colombia, and Mexico issued a joint declaration. Since adopted by a number of other democratic leaders in the hemisphere, that declaration states the problem graphically:

> We have confirmed that the successive increases of interest rates, the perspective that there will be new increases and the proliferation and intensity of protectionist measures have created a sombre scenario for our nations and for the region as a whole.
>
> Our countries cannot accept these risks indefinitely. We have asserted our firm determination of overcoming imbalances and to restore the conditions that will renew or strengthen economic growth and the process of improving the living standards of our peoples.

. . . We do not accept being pushed into a situation of forced insolvency and continuous economic stagnation.[14]

Is this an idle threat? Or is it an expression of desperation and exasperation? The presidents' statement follows the January 1984 "Declaration of Quito" signed by the states of Latin America (reproduced as appendix D). In that statement the governments argued that the current economic crisis in the hemisphere

> originated in internal and external factors . . . which are beyond the control of our countries and place serious constraints upon the options open to us for overcoming it. The economic policies of some industrialized countries have severely affected the developing countries and, in particular, those of the region, owing to the vulnerability and dependence of our economies and their increasing participation in international economic relations. These policies have brought about the constant deterioration of the terms of trade, diminishing trade, an inordinate increase in interest rates and the sharp contraction of capital flows. The overwhelming burden of our external indebtedness forms part of this picture.[15]

Elsewhere, the document states that

> the most harmful social effects of this situation take the form of an increase in unemployment figures unprecedented in our history, of a substantial reduction of real personal incomes and of living standards, with serious and growing consequences for the political and social stability of our peoples, the persistence of which will, in time, result in further deterioration of our economies.[16]

In the latter half of 1984, these same governments have adopted a more cooperative approach. But their words of May and January should not be quickly discounted. The statements suggest that the democratic leaders of Latin America may not be willing to sacrifice growth and government services indefinitely, just to please their Western creditors.

The general thrust of the arguments for Latin America is clear. Will the United States take the leadership in responding in time and with appropriate policy measures?

Implications for the United States

The debt burden abroad has increasing relevance for the United States. The recent crisis of confidence in the banking system due to the difficulties of Continental Illinois Bank do not need to be repeated. The constant pressure of the federal deficit on interest rates is well known. One need only state a few other implications.

1. *The crisis could have serious repercussions for the U.S. economy.* As a result of IMF and other austerity programs, debtor countries have drastically slashed imports, 43 percent between 1981 and 1983. According to Department of Commerce figures, U.S. exports to Latin America dropped 42 percent to $22.6 billion in 1983, from $39.0 billion in 1981. By comparison, U.S. exports worldwide fell only 14 percent, to $200.5 billion, in the same period. The drop in U.S. exports to Latin America accounted for almost half of the $33.2 billion decline in total U.S. exports between 1981 and 1983 (see table 9–1). The Commerce Department believes that the most important factor in this precipitous decline has been the debt crisis. It is estimated that each billion dollars of trade means 25,000 U.S. jobs, which could mean that 400,000 American workers either lost their jobs or were not hired as U.S. exports shrank by $16.4 billion between 1981 and 1983.[17] Government experts expect trade with Latin America to increase substantially in 1985, but that projection rests upon the assumption that the debt crisis will not deepen. It is important to U.S. trade that this assumption be borne out.

2. *The crisis undermines the U.S. diplomatic leverage in Latin America and Western Europe.* The U.S. position in Latin America stands to deteriorate badly if it does not respond to the debt crisis. Already weakened in some countries due to our position during the Malvinas/Falklands War, and in many by current U.S. policy in Central America and the Caribbean, the United States needs to move quickly and effectively to seize leadership in the debt crisis to demonstrate our concern for democracy and for social and economic development in the hemisphere.

Moreover, if the United States does not seize the initiative, there is every possibility that Latin Americans acting collectively will do so. The increasing willingness of Latin America's states to seek multilateral positions poses a new and poorly understood assertion of Latin American leadership. Collaboration between the United States and Latin America is required. Confrontation will only strengthen the will of democratic leaders in the hemisphere to strike out on their own to seek solutions for real problems they must confront day by day.

Finally, the United States' deficit and continuing high rates of interest are generating tension within the Western alliance. The West European economic recovery is sluggish; many of our allies believe that only U.S. government action to reduce the deficit will guarantee an orderly and sustained economic recovery.

3. *The crisis threatens the long-term U.S. interest in Latin American democracy and stability.* The debt crisis is a political threat to democracy and redemocratization in Latin America. Although economic growth does not ensure that the democratic trend will continue, an easing of the indebtedness is needed to give these governments the breathing room they need to cope with the economic problems bequeathed them from prior military regimes. The

Table 9–1
U.S. Exports to Latin America Compared with All U.S. Exports
(*billions of dollars*)

	All U.S. Exports			U.S. Exports to Latin America			Latin American Share of Decline in U.S. World Exports, 1981–1983
	1981	1983	Decline 1981–1983	1981	1983	Decline 1981–1983	
Total	$233.7	$200.5	−14%	$39.0	$22.6	−42%	49%
Selected Areas Manufactured goods	154.3	132.5	−14	$29.7	15.2	−49	67
Machinery and transportation equipment	95.7	$82.6	−14	17.8	8.2	−54	73
Automobiles	7.9	4.6	−42	3.6	1.5	−54	65
Civilian aircraft	13.5	10.7	−21	1.8	0.8	−57	37
Construction equipment	6.3	2.4	−62	1.5	0.3	−79	31
Agricultural machinery	3.5	1.6	−54	0.7	0.1	−86	29

Source: U.S. Department of Commerce, Bureau of Census.

Latin American people would be better off under democratic regimes than under authoritarian ones of either the left or the right, for democratic regimes promise less repression and violation of civil liberties and more concern for fairness in addition to growth. But the United States also has perfectly selfish reasons for wanting democracy to flourish in Latin America. Because they are more "accountable," democratic governments in Latin America tend to be more "rational" in their priorities. They are on the whole less bellicose toward one another, less extreme in their diplomatic postures, more concerned with regional stability, and more amenable to long-range good relations with the United States.[18] After all, the United States is the world's leading democracy, and a basic postulate of our foreign policy has long been that the more democracies in the world, the more congenial the world is for U.S. interests. The examples of Nicaragua and El Salvador reveal that the instability of authoritarian governments in the western hemisphere can lead to particularly vexing national security problems for the United States.

U.S. Policy Responses

The debt crisis in Latin America is real. It is also political. The U.S. government must abandon its present posture of leaving the resolution of the crisis to the private commercial banks and the international financial institutions.[19] That posture threatens to further overexpose and to seriously politicize both the international institutions and the banks. To argue for a political response is not to seek a means of justifying the IMF and its adjustment programs. It is clear they need to be carefully reviewed and far better adapted to the needs of the 1980s and the need for growth and recovery in Latin America. Nor is it an effort to overlook or justify the role of the private commercial banks and their past and current lending policies in the hemisphere, which also must be modified. But if the banks are part of the problem, they are surely a part of the solution. The private banks are not responsible for the federal deficit, nor do they set the prime rate. They will also be needed in the future as Latin American recovery begins.

What is needed is a comprehensive initiative by the U.S. government to take immediate steps to review and implement programs of relief for the indebted countries of Latin America. Some will require congressional participation and action. Others will necessitate decisions by the regulatory agencies and the Federal Reserve System. Others will demand adjustments in current lending policies by the private commercial banks. But all need the leadership of the U.S. government and its industrial allies in order to design, coordinate, and implement a plan of action. Some of the elements of such a plan are described in this section.

Constructive Monetary and Fiscal Policies

The international debt crisis has been made much worse, for the banks as well as for the debtor countries, by unusually high interest rates in the United States. Real interest rates are at unprecedentedly high levels, and they have exacted a very high price from Latin American countries. The Federal Reserve Board has proved itself to be sensitive to the situation in the last year or so and has relaxed monetary pressure on interest rates. This should continue, but it is not sufficient. One continuing cause of high rates is the enormous federal deficit, and the failure of either the Congress or the administration to show much resolve in reducing it significantly. Without committing itself in any way to "debtor relief" measures for the banks and Latin America, the United States could improve the situation by taking decisive action against the deficit and reducing interest rates.

Better Loan Terms

A second area for official action would be to encourage, or perhaps even require, the commercial banks to offer loan terms that would mitigate the crisis. Loan terms could be improved by:

1. Lowering the fees that banks charge for negotiating loans;

2. Lowering the "spreads" between the prime rate and the amount above it that countries are charged;

3. Lengthening the grace periods during which a country pays little or no principal;

4. Lengthening the maturities or lifetime of the loans;

5. Writing loans for three and four years to avoid today's frantic cycles of year-to-year rescheduling;

6. Examining the possibility of capping interest rates at, say, 10 percent;

7. Changing the currency composition of loans from dollar denomination to Japanese and European denominations;

8. Altering the accounting rules for U.S. banks so they do not have to take losses on delinquent loans so quickly; and

9. Reopening previously negotiated loans, with agreement to repay them over a much longer period of time.

There has been some movement by the banks in this direction. The 1984 restructuring of Mexican indebtedness offered extended maturities and interest rates slightly above market; a similar restructuring will probably be formalized for Brazil in 1985. While this is movement in the right direction, it may not be enough relief for Brazil and Mexico, and much less relief is being offered to countries such as Argentina.

These suggestions are not panaceas; they will not solve the debt crisis. They would, however, give Latin American states needed time to consolidate democratic institutions and to foster investment in export industries, which could yield foreign exchange to pay future interest charges. *And* they would be concrete official recognition of Latin America's plight and a signal of the United States' concern for that plight.

More Official Lending

Loans from official international sources typically carry easier ("concessionary") terms, and the United States should favor greater use of these sources. Congress and the administration took one step in this direction with the 1983 IMF Funding Act. The Act not only increased the U.S. quota to the IMF, but also directed the U.S. executive director of the IMF to support changes in IMF policy to convert short-term bank debt that was made at high interest rates into long-term debt at lower rates of interest and to assure that the annual external debt service, which shall include principal, interest, points, fees and other charges required of the country involved, is a manageable and prudent percentage of the projected annual export earnings of such country.[20] Further initiatives like this one are needed. For example, the United States should call for greater lending facilities for the World Bank, the Inter-American Development Bank, and other multilateral agencies that can offer relatively easier terms than commercial banks and in which the Latin American states generally have great confidence. Specifically, the United States should support a 50 percent increase in lending capacity by the World Bank.[21]

Free Trade Policy and Development Grants

Even with an abatement of interest rates, easier terms, and a more varied source of loans, Latin American debtor states will not be able to dig out of their debt crisis without a strong export-led recovery, which may have started in 1984. The United States can provide critical assistance of two sorts. First, it should reject current pressures toward greater protectionism, both in the United States and abroad, and encourage free trade. What is needed is a joint U.S.–European effort to encourage Latin American exports as the best means of earning foreign exchange required to meet interest payments on the debt. Second, the United States should encourage the development of productive capacity in Latin America. A recent precedent is readily available. It is the Caribbean Basin Initiative, which was designed to strengthen democratic institutions in the Caribbean states by providing development grants, encouraging direct foreign investment (through official encouragement, investment tax credits, and Overseas Private Investment Corporation or Eximbank investment guarantees or loans), and removing trade barriers. The reason for the Initiative, to encourage stable democracy by fostering economic development, would apply equally well to Latin American states, where the threat to democracy may pose an even greater long-term problem for the United States. And the mechanisms (not all of which have been approved by Congress) would be a promising encouragement to an export-led recovery in Latin America.

These and other suggestions are not new. But they are increasingly urgent and require our immediate attention. Individual private commercial banks are unable to take the initiative to implement many of these; those recommendations that they can implement require a web of policy supports that protects the basic integrity of the private banking system while recognizing the need for orderly lending adjustments. The international organizations can play a crucial role, but new facilities and new funds require government action. The United States plays the crucial lead role in determining how much, and when, these institutions will receive new resources.

Conclusion

There are many reasons for the United States to revise its current position with regard to the debt crisis in Latin America. American jobs and exports suffer as a result of the crisis. Our industrial allies' recovery is linked to demand in the Third World generally and in Latin America specifically. The leadership of the United States in the global system has been found wanting on this issue, and it is essential to reassert our will to lead. But the overwhelming argument is one of self-interest and national security for our future in the hemisphere. Governments are becoming desperate. Democratic systems are besieged by rising social demands. To survive, governments must respond to internal pressures. To do so requires resources that are extremely scarce, if not nonexistent, today in Latin America. Breathing space must be found to allow Latin American economies to grow now. Growth will permit an increase in both productivity and in employment and an increased capacity to import as well as export. Unless the United States takes the leadership role in helping Latin America, we must expect even more dramatic responses than those of Bolivia and the Dominican Republic.

Responding to a reporter's inquiries about the debt crisis recently, President Raúl Alfonsín of Argentina said that "Latin America cannot take any more. It is like a reverse neutron bomb in which men and women remain alive, but all that generates wealth is destroyed. It is as though madness has taken over the financial centers."[22] Arriving in the United States for a state visit recently, President Miguel de la Madrid of Mexico stated:

Latin America is suffering the most severe economic crisis of modern times. Its peoples and governments have been obliged to implement harsh economic programs to cope with the situation. The broadest and most far-reaching solution is to recover our payment capacity so that we can meet our debt obligations to regain our purchasing power abroad, to renew the process of economic growth, and to generate employment, thereby strengthening the basis of stability.[23]

From Tierra del Fuego to the U.S.–Mexican border, the message of democratic leaders is similar: the debt crisis has posed severe limitations to growth. A continuation of such policies will inevitably challenge the democratic stability of the countries in the region.[24] Social pressures require action, as do the needs of adjustment. But the two must be understood together, not separately. The ultimate reason to do so, of course, is that both are needed to help democratic regimes survive, which is in the national security interests of the United States. The United States needs to move quickly to respond to this clear plea for help. The issue cannot be left to the initiative of private commercial banking or to the limited efforts of the international banks. It calls for political leadership at the highest levels of the Western alliance, now.

Notes

1. The status in January 1985 of the main Latin American debtors is reviewed in "Latin America Moving away from Brink of Debt Crisis," *Washington Post*, January 21, 1985, p. H1, col. 1; "Bankers, Preparing for 1985 Debt Talks with Third World, Are Warned Not to Let 1984's Successes Go to Their Heads," *Wall Street Journal*, December 28, 1984, p. 16, col. 1. Although the *Post*'s article is quite optimistic about the prospects of Mexico and Brazil, it notes continuing problems for other Latin American debtors.

2. Walter Wriston, "LDC's Just Need a Little Help From Their Friends," *Wall Street Journal*, March 13, 1984, p. 30, col. 3.

3. "The Debt Bomb Ticks," *New York Times*, March 21, 1984, sec. I, p. 22, col. 1.

4. The Americas Society, Western Hemisphere Commission on Public Policy Implications of Foreign Debt, Guidelines for U.S. Policy (February 1984).

5. This argument is well made in a recent monograph by Thomas Enders and Richard Mattione, *Latin America: The Crisis of Debt and Growth* (Washington, D.C.: Brookings Institution, 1984), p. 55.

6. "Preconditions" for a successful "transition" to democracy are analyzed in D. Rustow, "Transitions to Democracy: Toward a Dynamic Model," *Comparative Policy* 2 (1970):337.

7. See Samuel Huntington, "Will More Countries Become Democratic?" *Political Science Quarterly* 99 (1984):193.

8. Ibid., p. 210.

9. See generally Werner Baer, "The Brazilian Growth and Development Experience: 1964–1975," in Riordan Roett, ed., *Brazil in the Seventies* (Washington, D.C.: American Enterprise Institute for Public Policy Research, 1976), pp. 41–62.

10. Ibid., pp. 51–52.

11. These themes are also developed in my article, "Democracy and Debt in South America: A Continent's Dilemma," *Foreign Affairs* 62 (1984):695.

12. Pedro-Pablo Kuczynski has discussed these issues recently in "Periling Debtor Countries," *New York Times*, May 24, 1984, sec. I, p. 27, col. 3.

13. See "To Avoid Wasting the Economic Talks," *New York Times*, May 29, 1984, sec. I, p. 1, col. 5.

14. Joint Presidential Statement Calling to Meeting of Latin American Foreign Ministers and Financial Authorities to Discuss the International Debt Crisis, May 19, 1984.

15. Latin American Economic Conference, Quito, Ecuador, Declaration of Quito and Plan of Action 3, Permanent Secretariat of SELA, Print 1984.

16. Ibid.

17. For elaboration on this data, see "Latin Debt Crunch Hurting U.S. Firms," *Wall Street Journal*, May 8, 1984, p. 38, col. 1.

18. As an analogy, Michael Doyle's article, "Kant, Liberal Legacies and Foreign Affairs," *Philosophy and Public Affairs* 12 (1983):205, argues that "liberal" societies do not fight one another. Huntington, "Will More Countries Become Democratic," p. 194, argues: "Other things being equal, non-democratic regimes are likely to pose more serious challenges to American interests than despotic regimes."

19. For a recent statement of the U.S. position, see "Regan, in Paris, Spurns Allied Bid for New Approach to Debt Crisis," *New York Times*, May 18, 1984, sec. I, p. 5, col. 1.

20. Public Law 98-181, 97 Stat. 1153, November 30, 1983.

21. These policy suggestions are explored in the articles contained in Richard Feinberg and Valeriana Kallab, eds., *Adjustment Crisis in the Third World* (New Brunswick, N.J.: Transaction Books, 1984), a publication of the Overseas Development Council and volume 1 in its series U.S.–Third World Policy Perspectives.

22. "Alfonsín Says Rate Raise in U.S. Imperils Argentina's 'Social Peace,' " *New York Times*, May 11, 1984, sec. I, p. 1, col. 5.

23. "Excerpts from Remarks by the Two Presidents," *New York Times*, May 16, 1984, sec. I, p. 4, col. 1.

24. See "Hemisphere's Debt Woes Approach Breaking Point," *Wall Street Journal*, May 21, 1984, p. 34, col. 1.

Appendix A:
Currency Diversification and
LDC Debt

etween 1979 and 1982 the nonoil developing countries (LDCs) borrowed about $137 billion from commercial banks worldwide, virtually all in terms of dollars. Had these countries diversified the currency composition of their borrowings to correspond broadly with the currency composition of their trade, they would have incurred substantial savings in interest payments as well as in the conversion value of their principal.[1]

To estimate these savings, weights were assigned to various major currencies. The weights were based on the composition of nonoil LDC trade in 1980.[2]

The relative cost of borrowing was determined by comparing three-month average Eurodollar interest rates from 1979 to 1982 with three-month average Eurorates for the trade-weighted mix of currencies. The interest rate for the mix of currencies was lower in each year (table A–1).

Relative exchange rate changes are reflected in changes in the level of the trade-weighted index of the mix of currencies vis-à-vis the U.S. dollar (1978 = 100). With dollar depreciation during 1979 and 1980, the index rose slightly (appreciated) against the dollar in these two years. By contrast, the strengthening of the dollar during 1981 and 1982 caused the index to fall (depreciate) by roughly 5½ percent and 4½ percent, respectively, in each of these years.

Between 1979 and 1982, nonoil LDC cumulative net borrowings from banks amounted to $137 billion. Had this borrowing been denominated in the trade-weighted mix of currencies, its conversion value at end 1982 would have been about $125.5 billion (table A–2). This would have represented a savings of about $11.5 billion or 8½ percent over borrowing solely in U.S. dollars.

The interest rate on the trade-weighted mix of currencies was 1.48 percentage points lower than the comparable dollar rate in 1981 and 0.65 percentage points lower than that in 1982. Exchange rate changes reduced

By Andrew Mohl and Dorothy Sobol. Reprinted with permission from *Federal Reserve Bank New York Quarterly Review* (Autumn 1983):19–20.

Table A–1
Average Annual Rates of Interest

	Three-Month Eurodollar Interest Rates	Three-Month Eurorates for a Trade-Weighted Mix of Currencies
1979	11.93%	11.03%
1980	13.96	13.36
1981	16.80	15.32
1982	13.10	12.45

Table A–2
Effects on Principal of Borrowing in a Trade-Weighted Mix of Currencies
(billions of U.S. dollars)

	Trade-Weighted Index (1978 = 100)	Net Borrowings from Banks	Cumulative Borrowings	Conversion Value of Cumulative Borrowings
1979	101.2	$35.0	$ 35.0	$ 35.4
1980	101.3	38.0	73.0	73.9
1981	96.0	41.0	114.0	109.4
1982	91.6	23.0	137.0	125.5

Table A–3
Effects on Interest Payments of Borrowing in a Trade-Weighted Mix of Currencies
(billions of U.S. dollars)

	Average Cumulative Borrowings	Pure Interest Savings	Exchange Rate Savings (Loss)	Total Savings[a]
1979	$ 17.5	$0.16	$(0.02)	$0.13
1980	54.0	0.33	(0.09)	0.23
1981	93.5	1.39	0.58	1.96
1982	125.5	0.82	1.31	2.13

Note: *Average cumulative borrowings* were calculated on the assumption that the borrowings were distributed evenly throughout the year. *Pure interest savings* measures the gain from borrowing at a lower interest rate by using the trade-weighted mix of currencies. *Exchange rate savings (loss)* adjusts the interest payments for movements in the trade-weighted index against the U.S. dollar since 1978.

[a]Because of rounding, figures may not add to totals.

the value of the trade-weighted index against the U.S. dollar by 4 percent between 1978 and 1981 and by 8.4 percent between 1978 and 1982. As a result interest payments on cumulative bank borrowings by the nonoil LDC would have been lower by about $2 billion in 1981 and in 1982 (table A–3).

If maturing debt had also been rolled over into the trade-weighted mix of currencies, the savings effects would have been even greater. Additional savings would have amounted to $13 billion on the principal at end 1982 and roughly $2 billion on the interest payments in 1981 and in 1982.

In total these estimates suggest that the combined savings to the nonoil LDCs in terms of lower interest costs and exchange rate gains of diversifying their new and maturing bank debt between 1979 and 1982 could have amounted to over $30 billion.

Notes

1. To the extent that borrowing and rolled-over maturing debt took place in currencies other than dollars, our estimates may overstate the benefits. Nevertheless, data for five major nonoil LDC borrowers indicate that only 1.4 percent of syndicated loans to these countries in 1980 took place in currencies other than dollars. Although this percentage has tended to increase in recent years, totaling 11.9 in 1982, it still lags well behind the world average. For example, the percentage of all syndicated loans in nondollar currencies was 10.6 in 1980 and 20.8 in 1982. Excluding the five major nonoil LDC borrowers, these percentages were 12.8 in 1980 and 30.1 in 1982. The five nonoil borrowers include Mexico, Brazil, Argentina, Korea, and the Philippines.

2. Weights were based on aggregate nonoil LDC imports. Weight based on aggregate exports in the same year would have been almost identical. Over the past five years, the trade patterns have been reasonably stable. In our calculations, imports from Belgium and Denmark were attributed to the German mark. Imports from OPEC countries, from each other, and from those countries not accounted for in the currencies specified below were attributed to the dollar. The trade weights in percentage terms were: U.S. dollar 67.0, Japanese yen 10.5, German mark 8.5, French franc 4.8, pound sterling 4.6, Italian lira 3.0, Dutch guilder 1.6

Appendix B:
Statistics on Latin American Development and Debt

Table B–1
Nonoil Developing Countries: Current Account Financing, 1973–1982
(billions of U.S. dollars)

	1973	1974	1975	1976	1977	1978	1979	1980	1981	1982	1983
Current account deficit[a]	$11.3	$37.0	$46.3	$32.6	$28.9	$41.3	$61.0	$89.0	$107.7	$86.8	$68.0
By area											
Africa	1.9	3.2	6.6	6.1	6.6	9.4	9.9	12.9	14.0	13.2	13.5
Asia	2.6	9.9	8.9	2.7	0.8	7.2	14.8	24.3	22.2	15.6	17.5
Europe	(0.6)	4.4	4.9	4.7	8.4	6.7	9.9	12.5	10.5	7.1	4.0
Middle East	2.6	4.5	6.9	5.4	5.1	6.2	8.5	9.4	11.1	12.9	12.0
Western hemisphere	4.7	13.5	16.3	11.8	8.5	13.3	21.4	33.4	45.4	34.9	21.5
Use of reserves	−10.4	−2.7	1.6	−13.0	−12.5	−17.4	−12.6	−4.5	−2.1	7.1	n.a.
Non–debt-creating flows, net	10.3	14.6	11.8	12.6	14.4	17.9	23.9	24.1	28.0	25.1	n.a.
Direct investment flows, net	4.2	5.3	5.3	5.0	5.4	7.3	8.9	10.1	13.9	11.4	n.a.
Net external borrowing[b]	11.4	25.1	32.9	33.0	27.0	40.8	49.7	69.3	81.8	54.6	n.a.
Long-term borrowing, net[c]	11.9	18.1	27.1	28.0	24.6	37.2	36.5	47.2	62.7	41.0	n.a.
From official sources	4.9	6.8	11.7	10.5	11.4	13.8	13.3	17.6	23.0	19.5	n.a.
From private sources	6.8	11.3	15.4	17.5	13.2	23.4	23.2	29.6	39.7	21.5	n.a.

Source: IMF, *Annual Report* (1983), pp. 18, 33.

[a]Net total of balances on goods, services, and private transfers, as defined in the IMF, *Balance of Payments Statistics* (with sign reversed).

[b]Includes any net use of nonreserve claims on nonresidents, errors and omissions in reported balance of payments statements for individual countries, and minor deficiencies in coverage.

[c]On a balance-of-payments basis.

Table B-2
Nonoil Developing Countries: External Debt, 1973–1982
(billions of U.S. dollars)

	1973	1974	1975	1976	1977	1978	1979	1980	1981	1982	Average Annual Compound Rate of Change, 1973–1982
Total debt outstanding[a]	$130.1	$160.8	$190.8	$228.0	$278.5	$336.3	$391.1	$467.6	$550.8	$614.2	18.8%
By maturity											
Short-term[b]	18.4	22.7	27.3	33.2	42.5	49.7	56.8	83.1	99.2	111.9	22.2
Medium-term and long-term	111.8	138.1	163.5	194.9	235.9	286.6	334.4	384.4	451.6	502.3	18.2
By creditor											
Government	37.3	43.4	50.3	57.9	67.6	79.1	89.1	101.7	113.4	125.7	14.5
International institutions	13.7	16.6	20.3	24.8	31.0	38.4	45.6	53.2	62.7	71.0	20.1
Private	60.8	77.9	95.1	114.8	137.3	169.1	199.7	229.5	275.5	300.8	19.4
1975 Prices	169.0	175.7	190.8	218.0	250.9	281.0	294.7	308.6	331.3	357.8	8.7
Debt service payments	17.9	22.1	25.1	27.8	34.7	50.3	65.0	76.2	93.1	105.0	21.7
Interest	6.9	9.3	10.5	10.9	13.6	19.4	28.0	40.4	54.0	57.4	26.5
Principal	11.1	12.8	14.6	16.8	21.1	30.9	36.9	35.8	39.1	47.6	17.6
Ratio of debt to exports of goods and services	115.4%	104.6%	122.4%	125.5%	126.4%	130.2%	117.2%	111.0%	123.8%	143.6%	
Ratio of debt to gross domestic product	22.4	21.8	23.8	25.7	27.4	27.9	26.8	26.9	30.4	35.8	
Ratio of debt service payments[c] to exports of goods and services	15.9	14.4	16.1	15.3	15.4	19.0	19.0	17.6	20.1	23.4	

Source: IMF, *World Economic Outlook* (1982, 1983); E. Brau and R.C. Williams, *Recent Multilateral Debt Restructurings with Official and Bank Creditors*, IMF Occasional Paper no. 25 (Washington, D.C., 1983), p. 4.

[a]Covers public and publicly guaranteed debt and, where available, private nonguaranteed debt.

[b]Debt with an original maturity of one year or less; series excludes data for a number of nonreporting debtor countries.

[c]Principal and interest on medium-term and long-term debt and interest on short-term debt.

Table B–3
Debt Indicators for the Eight Largest Sovereign Debtors and for Three Other Latin American Debtors, 1973–1982

	1973	1974	1975	1976	1977	1978	1979	1980	1981	1982
Total debt (billions of U.S. dollars)										
Brazil	$13.8	$18.9	$23.3	$28.6	$35.2	$48.4	$57.4	$66.1	$75.7	$88.2
Mexico	8.6	12.8	16.9	21.8	27.1	33.6	40.8	53.8	67.0	82.0
Argentina	6.4	8.0	7.9	8.3	9.7	12.5	19.0	27.2	35.7	38.0
Spain	5.7	8.6	10.7	13.5	16.3	18.4	22.2	27.4	33.2	n.a.
Korea	4.6	6.0	7.3	8.9	11.2	14.8	20.5	26.4	31.2	35.8
Venezuela	4.6	5.3	5.7	8.7	12.3	16.3	23.7	27.5	29.3	31.3
India	10.5	11.6	12.4	13.4	14.7	15.6	15.9	17.7	18.5	n.a.
Yugoslavia	4.6	5.4	6.3	7.7	9.6	11.8	14.9	17.6	18.5	17.9
Chile	3.6	4.4	4.7	4.5	4.9	6.4	8.2	10.7	15.0	17.9
Peru	2.4	3.8	4.9	5.3	6.4	6.7	7.4	9.0	9.8	11.1
Colombia	2.8	3.1	3.4	3.6	4.0	4.3	5.7	6.8	8.3	n.a.
Debt service/exports (percentage)										
Brazil	36.7%	36.0%	40.8%	45.3%	48.7%	59.3%	65.6%	60.8%	66.9%	87.1%
Mexico	28.7	21.9	30.3	40.7	53.6	64.9	67.7	36.4	48.5	58.5
Argentina	19.9	21.3	31.9	26.2	19.1	41.6	21.3	32.2	37.5	102.9
Spain	5.2	4.2	9.3	10.7	13.3	19.5	15.7	15.5	19.0	n.a.
Korea	11.5	11.8	12.5	9.8	10.2	12.0	13.9	17.3	18.8	21.1
Venezuela	3.8	3.3	3.5	8.4	10.0	15.6	16.4	15.6	19.0	20.7
India	23.6	63.7	14.0	11.5	12.3	11.4	11.2	n.a.	n.a.	n.a.
Yugoslavia	21.7	21.7	21.1	18.3	19.4	21.0	20.8	20.0	n.a.	30.3
Chile	35.1	37.4	42.7	41.7	45.9	49.7	44.4	41.3	61.0	60.4
Peru	35.8	30.1	45.7	47.2	45.1	64.4	44.6	50.9	n.a.	53.4
Colombia	21.1	23.6	21.4	16.7	13.7	14.9	19.0	16.3	23.9	n.a.

Net debt/exports
(percentage)

	106.2%	145.9%	194.3%	195.8%	207.6%	252.5%	269.3%	259.1%	256.6%	365.3%
Brazil										
Mexico	154.6	182.0	243.8	286.5	309.7	278.2	241.7	205.7	242.4	272.7
Argentina	140.8	145.2	211.5	145.7	96.8	96.1	97.3	182.5	275.3	353.5
Spain	-4.1	21.0	37.7	60.3	60.3	37.4	30.0	46.0	66.2	n.a.
Korea	88.9	106.5	110.2	73.4	63.0	70.2	89.8	103.8	103.9	104.5
Venezuela	51.2	-5.9	-37.3	-32.9	-8.7	35.6	41.5	33.2	29.3	104.2
India	290.7	248.0	200.8	159.9	125.7	107.9	81.1	n.a.	n.a.	n.a.
Yugoslavia	76.0	75.6	88.8	81.8	100.1	110.4	133.6	118.8	99.8	113.7
Chile	239.9	183.9	250.4	170.1	169.9	178.8	131.1	121.5	192.9	274.0
Peru	138.5	151.7	258.2	286.3	280.6	260.7	141.6	143.8	204.6	259.9
Colombia	141.7	136.8	131.8	88.2	63.3	46.1	38.6	35.5	72.9	n.a.

Source: William Cline, *International Debt: Systemic Risk and Policy Response* (Washington, D.C.: Institute for International Economics, 1984), tables E–1 to E–3. Reprinted with permission.

Table B–4
Nonoil Developing Countries: Distribution of Outstanding Debt among Selected Groups of Countries, End-1982

	Major Borrowers[a]	Low-Income Countries (except China and India)	Other Countries[b]
Total debt (*billions of U.S. dollars*)	$447.0	$56.6	$108.8
Short-term debt	99.7	3.0	10.0
Long-term debt	347.3	53.6	98.8
Guaranteed, to official creditors	93.7	44.8	54.7
Other	253.6	8.8	44.1
Total debt (*percentage*)	73.0%	9.2%	17.8%
Short-term debt	88.4	2.7	8.9
Long-term debt	69.5	10.7	19.8
Guaranteed, to official creditors	48.5	23.2	28.3
Other	82.7	2.9	14.4

Source: IMF, *Annual Report* (1983), p. 30.

[a]The twenty countries (in the nonoil developing group) with the largest estimated external debts to private creditors: Mexico, Brazil, Argentina, Chile, Peru, Ecuador, Colombia, Korea, Philippines, Thailand, Malaysia, Greece, Morocco, Egypt, Yugoslavia, Israel, Turkey, Portugal, Romania, and Hungary.

[b]Residual group (including China and India).

Table B–5
Export Growth Compared with Interest Rates, 1973–1982
(Percentage)

	1973	1974	1975	1976	1977	1978	1979	1980	1981	1982
LIBOR + 1 percent	10.2%	12.0%	8.0%	6.6%	7.0%	9.7%	13.0%	15.4%	17.5%	14.1%
Export growth, nominal										
Nonoil LDCs	n.a.	36.4	1.4	16.5	21.2	17.2	28.9	26.1	5.8	-3.8
Net oil importers	n.a.	33.1	1.6	16.3	21.9	16.9	26.8	24.2	5.4	-3.8
Net oil exporters	n.a.	57.3	-0.1	18.9	18.8	18.0	40.4	35.4	7.8	-3.6
Brazil	56.1	33.2	6.1	13.5	19.7	7.2	24.2	29.3	15.7	-13.4
Mexico	26.8	31.6	-0.2	13.3	14.0	39.1	40.2	54.3	21.9	7.3
Argentina	61.6	25.8	-23.9	30.8	43.6	16.3	26.6	13.0	5.1	-15.7
Korea	85.6	29.4	9.7	60.8	38.2	31.3	13.8	15.6	21.7	2.3
Venezuela	54.4	126.8	-15.7	2.8	5.5	-0.8	50.2	36.4	10.1	-22.0
Chile	49.0	60.1	-21.7	31.7	8.1	13.8	59.0	32.2	-2.6	-3.8

Source: William Cline, *International Debt: Systemic Risk and Policy Response* (Washington, D.C.: Institute for International Economics, 1984), pp. 6–7. Reprinted with permission.

Table B-6
Economic Indicators for Selected Latin American Countries, 1979–1982

	Argentina	Brazil	Chile	Mexico	Peru	Venezuela
Real exchange rates (per constant dollar)						
1979	69.3	103.2	88.0	92.5	112.7	96.4
1980	60.2	106.9	72.0	81.7	99.4	85.7
1981	75.4	99.3	71.5	76.8	90.9	81.5
1982	132.0	105.6	93.0	116.9	96.7	79.6
Government deficits as percentage of gross domestic product						
1979	7.2	8.1	-4.8	6.8	1.7	-1.1
1980	8.6	7.1	-5.6	7.7	6.4	-1.2
1981	14.3	12.1	-1.1	14.8	8.6	3.4
1982	14.2	13.8	4.0	18.6	8.8	11.0
State enterprise deficits as percentage of gross domestic product (average 1979–1982)	3.8	4.2	0.95	6.2	3.3	3.4
Inflation, percentage per year						
1979	159.6	52.7	33.4	18.2	66.7	12.4
1980	100.8	82.8	35.1	26.4	59.2	21.5
1981	104.5	105.6	19.7	27.9	75.4	16.2
1982	164.8	98.0	9.9	58.9	64.4	9.9
Real domestic interest rate (nominal rate minus inflation)						
1979	-86.86	-20.45	n.a.	-3.25	n.a.	n.a.
1980	-28.80	-32.30	n.a.	-3.65	n.a.	n.a.
1981	-17.74	+9.45	n.a.	+3.12	n.a.	n.a.
1982	-61.38	-80.80	n.a.	-46.36	n.a.	n.a.
1983	-257.29	-154.90	n.a.	-26.10	n.a.	n.a.

Source: Thomas Enders and Richard Mattione, Latin America: The Crisis of Debt and Growth 65-66 (Washington, D.C.: Brookings Institution, 1984), table B–5 to B–8, reprinted with permission; Roger Kubarych, chapter 1 of this book, table 1–7.

Table B–7
U.S. Investment in Spanish America, 1928–1970 (Investment/National Government Revenue Ratios)
(millions of U.S. dollars)

	1936		1943		1950		1960		1970	
	Investment	Ratio	Investment	Ratio	Investment	Ratio	Investment	Ratio	Investment	Ratio
Argentina	$348	.92	$380	1.37	$356	.26	$472	.38	$1,281	.73
Bolivia	18	2.25	13	.89	11	.17	31	1.03	50[a]	.48
Chile	484	11.11	328	5.70	540	1.62	738	1.10	748	.46
Colombia	108	2.81	117	2.14	193	.89	424	1.33	698	1.01
Costa Rica	13	2.17	30	3.90	60	3.87	62	.99	101	.76
Cuba	636	9.74	526	6.31	642	2.79	956	2.36	0	.00
Dominican Republic	41	3.76	71	5.77	106	1.37	105	.69	168	.69
Ecuador	5	.67	11	1.09	14	.54	50	.63	182	1.07
El Salvador	17	2.39	15	1.88	17	.48	31	.41	71	.63
Guatemala	50	4.76	87	7.01	106	2.47	131	1.53	187	1.25
Honduras	36	5.71	37	6.49	62	4.19	100	2.54	198	2.30
Mexico	480	4.48	286	2.87	415	1.04	795	.76	1,786	.68
Nicaragua	5	1.72	4	1.90	9	.70	18	.55	65	.79
Panama	27	3.41	110	8.66	58	1.85	405	6.98	1,251	7.82
Paraguay	5	.82	9	—	6	—	13	.61	26	.38
Peru	96	2.47	71	1.84	145	1.45	496	1.51	688	.69
Uruguay	14	.16	6	.06	55	—	47	.93	73	.22
Venezuela	186	3.01	373	3.67	993	1.75	2,569	1.67	2,704	1.26
Total/Average	2,599	3.46	2,494	3.62	3,788	1.59	7,443	1.44	10,244	1.18

Source: David Palmer, *Peru: The Authoritarian Tradition* (New York: Praeger Publishers, 1980), p. 80, table 5.7. Reprinted with permission.

Table B–8

Indicators of Dependency in Spanish America: Foreign Debt and Debt/Export Ratios, 1929–1970

(millions of U.S. dollars)

	1929		1950		1970	
	Debt	Ratio	Debt	Ratio	Debt	Ratio
Argentina	$1,202.40	1.30	$ 400.00	.29	$ 1,788	1.02
Bolivia	90.96	1.78	50.00	.67	334	3.67
Chile	499.20	.71	355.40	1.26	1,734	1.07
Colombia	88.20	.71	157.50	.40	1,079	1.57
Costa Rica	18.00	.99	12.00	.21	120	.90
Cuba	70.20	.25	95.80[a]	.14	6,000[b]	2.22
Dominican Republic	18.80	.81	10.00	.11	184	.76
Ecuador	20.10	1.18	31.90	.43	179	1.05
El Salvador	19.20	1.04	22.40	.33	75	.66
Guatemala	13.80	.57	.40	.01	91	.61
Honduras	27.30	1.11	1.30	.02	65	.76
Mexico	826.20	2.49	509.10	.98	2,963	1.12
Nicaragua	2.90	.27	4.60	.17	119	1.45
Panama	16.30	2.91	13.00	.54	122	.76
Paraguay	3.90	.29	15.30	.46	82	1.17
Peru	113.00	.69	107.20	.57	858	.86
Uruguay	138.20	1.44	105.40	.42	265	.80
Venezuela	3.90	.03	249.80[c]	.22	514	.24
Total	3,172.56	1.03	2,141.20	.41	16,572	1.15

Source: David Palmer, *Peru: The Authoritarian Tradition* (New York: Praeger Publishers, 1980), p. 81, table 5.8. Reprinted with permission.

[a]1945.

[b]1973.

[c]1955.

Table B–9
Indicators of Dependency in Spanish America: Balance-of-Payments Ratios (Imports/Exports), 1930–1970

	1930	1950	1970
Argentina	1.20	.87	.85
Bolivia	.59	.85	.86
Chile	1.06	.87	.75
Colombia	.68	.92	1.03
Costa Rica	.67	.82	1.24
Cuba	.97	.84	1.25
Dominican Republic	.82	.51	1.30
Ecuador	.88	.55	1.05
El Salvador	.90	.71	.82
Guatemala	.71	.90	.90
Honduras	.42	.61	1.14
Mexico	.76	1.07	1.57
Nicaragua	1.03	1.08	1.02
Panama	5.18	2.54	2.53
Paraguay	1.07	.58	1.18
Peru	.62	.93	.68
Uruguay	.92	.78	.91
Venezuela	.37	.51	.65
Average	1.05	.89	1.10

Source: David Palmer, *Peru: The Authoritarian Tradition* (New York: Praeger Publishers, 1980), p. 83, table 5.10. Reprinted with permission.

Table B–10
Indicators of Dependency in Spanish America: Principal Export/Total Exports, 1928–1971

	1928	1947	1971
Argentina	23.8	31.0	23.7
Bolivia	77.3	71.0	48.6
Chile	47.6	63.0	73.0
Colombia	66.0	77.0	63.8
Costa Rica	63.1	47.0	28.4
Cuba	71.6	86.0	76.9
Dominican Republic	61.6	62.0	57.2
Ecuador	30.1	34.0	51.0
El Salvador	93.0	85.0	40.6
Guatemala	79.2	61.0	33.8
Honduras	80.7	47.0	51.0
Mexico	14.7	24.0	7.8
Nicaragua	58.1	40.0	22.5
Panama	70.8	50.0	56.4
Paraguay	24.0	17.0	31.9
Peru	20.9	30.0	30.9
Uruguay	30.5	43.0	33.8
Venezuela	73.7	95.0	92.2
Average	54.0	53.5	45.8

Source: David Palmer, *Peru: The Authoritarian Tradition* (New York: Praeger Publishers, 1980), p. 82, table 5.9. Reprinted with permission.

Table B–11
Indicators of Dependency in Spanish America: Principal Foreign Market/Total Exports, 1928–1971

	1928	1947	1971
Argentina	28.7	30.0	15.0
Bolivia	83.2	59.8	37.8
Chile	34.3	44.5	19.7
Colombia	77.7	88.2	38.4
Costa Rica	53.7	77.2	40.1
Cuba	72.8	66.7	50.0
Dominican Republic	44.5	41.4	74.4
Ecuador	37.4	42.4	35.9
El Salvador	29.1	77.5	23.4
Guatemala	54.2	86.4	32.7
Honduras	76.3	72.9	52.0
Mexico	68.1	76.6	62.5
Nicaragua	51.5	77.4	35.2
Panama	91.6	85.4	48.1
Paraguay	88.2	75.0	27.4
Peru	28.5	29.3	28.8
Uruguay	22.6	28.6	11.8
Venezuela	35.4	50.0	37.9
Average	54.4	61.6	37.3

Source: David Palmer, *Peru: The Authoritarian Tradition* (New York: Praeger Publishers, 1980), p. 84, table 5.11. Reprinted with permission.

Appendix C:
A Political Chronology of Selected Latin American Countries, 1930–Present

BRAZIL

1930 Brazil's First Republic (a limited democracy) ends with a military coup led by Getúlio Vargas. Vargas rules as a strong-arm dictator but modernizes Brazil.

1945 Military overthrows Vargas when it appears that Vargas will try to retain power instead of holding elections.

1946 The Second Republic begins with the inauguration of Eurico Dutra as president.

1950 Vargas wins the presidential elections. Prolabor policies and economic problems generate pressure for Vargas's ouster.

1954 Vargas commits suicide rather than resign.

1955 Juscelino Kubitschek, from the primarily middle class Partido Social Democrático (PSD), wins the presidency. He runs up a large deficit and foreign debt in an ambitious development program.

1960 Jânio Quadros elected president; he is inaugurated in 1961. He moves to bring the economy under control but resigns because of unpopular economic measures and accusations of procommunism.

1961 João Goulart, the vice president, becomes president over conservative opposition. Goulart's rule is marked by economic deterioration and the increasing influence of radical philosophies.

1964 Military ousts Goulart, ending the Second Republic. General Humberto Castelo Branco becomes president and in the next several years restricts political freedoms and strengthens the power of the president.

This chronology was compiled by Riordan Roett, Stephanie Humbert, and William N. Eskridge, Jr.

1967   General Artur da Costa e Silva becomes president. A new constitution is approved by Congress.

1969   Under General Emílio Garrastazú Médici, Brazil begins to experience its "economic miracle."

1974   Military moderate Ernesto Geisel begins Brazil on a slow path to redemocratization.

1979   Geisel outmaneuvers military hardliners to see General João Baptista de Oliveira Figueiredo, his choice as successor, become president. Figueiredo continues the slow move to redemocratization.

1985   Electoral College selects as president popular opposition leader and former prime minister Tancredo de Almeida Neves.

FIVE LARGE SOUTH AMERICAN COUNTRIES

Argentina

1930   Military coup overthrows reform president Hipólito Irigoyen, ending a seventy-year period of political stability.

1932–   Period dominated by Conservatives through controlled elections.
1943

1943   Military deposes Conservative President Ramón S. Castillo. Juan Domingo Perón, a participant in the coup, becomes minister of labor.

1946–   Perón wins presidency on Labor party ticket with support of
1955   working class. Reelected in 1951, he steadily increases right-wing authoritarian measures.

1955   Military deposes Perón, who flees the country.

1958   Arturo Frondizi wins the presidency with the support of peronistas.

1962   Military removes Frondizi when peronistas win too much power in legislative and gubernatorial elections.

1963   Arturio Illía elected president. He is unable to cope with mounting economic problems.

1966   Military coup. General Juan Carlos Onganía, a staunch conservative, installed as president.

1970	Military replaces Onganía with General Roberto Levingston in an effort to stem increasing violence and dissatisfaction.
1971	General Alejandro A. Lanusse, the junta's leader, becomes president.
1973	Héctor J. Cámpora, with the endorsement of Perón, elected president. Cámpora resigns less than two months later and Perón returns from exile and is elected president.
1974	Perón dies. Perón's wife, María Estela Martínez de Perón (Isabel), his vice-president, becomes president.
1976	Military coup in face of increasing violence and economic deterioration. Jorge Rafael Videla becomes president. He is succeeded by General Viola, who is in turn ousted by General Leopoldo Galtieri.
1982	Malvinas/Falklands War. Galtieri resigns, and General Reynaldo Benito Antonio Bignone assumes the presidency.
1983	Raúl Alfonsín wins free elections.

Chile

1920	Populist Arturo Alessandri elected president. A conservative Congress frustrates his attempts at reform.
1924	Alessandri, unhappy with military pressure, resigns. Military junta dissolves Congress and decrees new reformist laws. This is the first time a strictly military junta has governed Chile.
1925	Military overthrown with the assistance of General Carlos Ibáñez del Campo. Alessandri returns to the presidency, with Ibáñez as defense minister. The 1925 Constitution is adopted. It creates a strong executive, sets forth individual rights guarantees (extended suffrage, separation of church and state) and assures each citizen a "minimum of well-being" to satisfy personal and family needs.
1927–1931	General Ibáñez gains power and rules as a quasi-dictator. Political and social unrest force Ibáñez to resign.
1932	Forty years of constitutional democracy begins with the election of Alessandri as president. The Radical party, a middle class party, becomes the major party in government coalitions during the next twenty years.

1938   Popular Front candidate Pedro Aquirre Cerda elected president, as the left and center join forces. The government increases its role in the economy by means of the Development Corporation.

1942   Juan Antonio Ríos of the Radical party elected president after the death of Aquirre. He continues the industrialization process and institutes some social reform.

1946   Gabriel González Videla, a Radical party member, elected president after the death of Ríos.

1952   General Ibáñez is elected to the presidency with broad support. He legalizes the Communist party again. Ibáñez attempts to implement an austerity program.

1958   Jorge Alessandri Rodríquez, son of Arturo Alessandri, wins presidency with conservative and liberal support. Salvador Allende Gossens of the Popular Action Front, composed of left-wing groups, narrowly loses the election. Alessandri institutes land reform and attempts to bring the economy under control.

1964   Eduardo Frei Montalva of the Christian Democratic party wins the election. Under a "Revolution in Liberty" program, the government institutes major social and economic reforms.

1970–1973   Marxist Salvador Allende narrowly wins the presidency. Banks and the copper industry are nationalized, and the government takes over many other industries. Agrarian reform is accelerated and wages and salaries increase sharply. Allende's economic policies work for a short while, but in 1972 the economy begins to disintegrate and approaches near chaos with a 600 percent inflation rate in 1973.

1973–1984   Military attacks the presidential palace and assumes power. Allende dies in the coup. The military government, under President Augusto Pinochet Ugarte, drastically changes Chilean political traditions of liberal democracy. Congress is dissolved for the first time in Chile's independent history, political parties are banned, elections are suspended, and the press is censored. The Pinochet government is characterized by repression, and the number of Chileans killed is estimated between 3,000 and 10,000.

1981   A new Constitution becomes effective. It calls for an eight-year transition period from military rule to presidential and congressional elections in 1990. There are calls for earlier elections.

1983– 1984	Deepening economic recession and increasing demands for a return to democracy result in widespread demonstration against the government. Pinochet announces that he will not permit an acceleration of the transition period as he had previously announced.

Colombia

1930– 1945	Liberals come into power after fifty years of Conservative rule. This period is dominated by Alfonso Lopéz who brought about social and economic reforms.
1946	Conservative Mariano Ospina Pérez elected president.
1947	Violence between the two parties escalated into the period known as "la violencia," which lasts for roughly twenty years. Over 200,000 Colombians are killed.
1950	Conservative Laureano Gómez elected president without any opposition. His repressive regime amounts to a civilian dictatorship.
1953	Armed forces under Gustavo Rojas Pinilla take power. This is Colombia's only military dictatorship in the twentieth century.
1957	Rojas Pinilla is forced to resign because he does not restore a democratic government.
1958	Liberal Alberto Lleras Camargo becomes president under a bipartisan pact, the National Front. The National Front, ratified by the voters, requires a sharing of power between the Liberals and Conservatives for a twenty-six-year period, with the presidency alternating between the two parties.
1974	National Front ends and Alfonson López Michelsen, a Liberal, is elected president.
1978	Liberal Julio César Turbay Ayala elected president.
1982	Conservative Belisario Betancur wins presidential election.

Peru

1919– 1930	Authoritarian Augusto B. Leguía becomes president, ending a twenty-four-year period of civilian rule.

1931 Military overthrow of Leguía. Colonel Luis M. Sánchez Cerro wins presidential elections and rules as a dictator, suppressing a rebellion in 1932.

1933 Sánchez Cerro assassinated. Congress selects General Oscar Raimundo Benavides, a moderate, as president.

1936 Elections held. Benavides remains president even though not a candidate when an APRA (American Popular Revolutionary Alliance) candidate wins the election. Benavides brings political stability.

1939 Manuel Prado elected president. He eases up on repressive measures.

1945 President José Luis Bustamante y Rivero, a moderate, continues political liberalization.

1948 Military ousts Bustamante. General Manuel Odría assumes control.

1956 Free elections held. Manuel Prado (supported by APRA) wins presidency.

1962 Military takeover after candidates in election fail to achieve required majority.

1963 Fernando Belaúnde Terry, a moderate reformer who founded the Accion Popular (AP), elected president. Legislative opposition makes him an ineffective leader.

1968 Military coup. General Juan Velasco Alvarado chosen as president.

1968–1975 Phase I of the Revolutionary Government, an ambitious plan to transform the social, economic, and cultural structure of Peru.

1975–1977 Phase II of the Revolutionary Government. Velasco is replaced by General Francisco Morales Bermúdez Cerrutti, as the economy worsens.

1980 Belaúnde wins in presidential elections which are held in accordance with the 1977 Constitution.

1985 Presidential elections scheduled.

Venezuela

1908 Repressive regime under dictator Juan Vincente Gómez.

1936 After the death of Gómez, General Eleázar López Contreras becomes president. He allows some political liberalization.

1941	General Isaías Medina Angarita continues political and economic liberalization in his presidency.
1945	Military overthrow of Medina with the support of Acción Democrática Party (AD). AD leader Rómulo Betancourt heads a seven-man junta that brings further liberalization.
1947	First free elections held. Rómulo Gallegos of the AD becomes president.
1948	Military, worried about the extent of reforms, overthrows Gallegos. Ten-year military rule dominated by Marcos Pérez Jiménez and political repression.
1958	Pérez Jiménez flees Venezuela after general revolt against his regime. Elections held and Betancourt, the AD candidate, is elected president. Political and economic reforms instituted.
1963–1983	Democratic elections held every five years, with the following results: Raúl Leoni (AD), 1963; Rafael Caldera (Social Christian), 1968; Carlos Andrés Peréz (AD), 1973; Luis Herrera Campíns (Social Christian), 1978; and Jaime Lusinchi (AD), 1983.

SIX SMALL CENTRAL AND SOUTH AMERICAN COUNTRIES

Bolivia

1941	Formation of populist party Movimiento Nacionalista Revolucionario (MNR). Its goal is to achieve social justice and economic development free from dependence on the North.
1943	The MNR overthrows the government of General Enrique Peñaranda, and Colonel Gualberto Villarroel becomes president.
1946	Villarroel is killed as conservatives overthrow the government. The MNR is outlawed.
1947	Enrique Hertzog elected president. In 1949 Hertzog resigns in favor of Mamerto Urriolagoitia, his vice president.
1951	Victor Paz Estenssoro, secretary of the MNR, is elected president in absentia. Paz is denied the presidency as Urriolagoitia turns the government over to a military junta.
1952	MNR ousts the army, and Paz becomes president. Bolivia's social revolution begins: the army is disbanded and the peasants are armed, mining interests are nationalized and sweeping land reform

is carried out. A split in the MNR develops between the radical wing of the party and the more moderate wing. Government is obliged to borrow money.

1956–
1960
Hernán Siles Zuazo, acceptable to both wings of the MNR, becomes president. Siles, with U.S. aid, begins rebuilding army, partly to counter armed workers' militias.

1960
Paz elected president. Split between the moderate and radical wings of the MNR intensifies.

1964
Shortly after his reelection, Paz is ousted by the military. General René Barrientos Ortuño, Paz's vice president, and General Alfredo Ovando Candia head the military junta. The military assumes its role of the dominant force in Bolivian politics. The unions and militia are brought under control.

1966
Barrientos, a moderate, elected president.

1969
Accidental death of Barrientos. Luis Adolfo Siles Salinas, the vice president, assumes power. He is deposed by General Ovando Candia, former copresident.

1970
General Ovando loses his military support and is deposed by a leftist, General Juan José Torres. Political parties are outlawed and foreign companies are nationalized.

1971
Bloody coup installs Colonel Hugo Banzer Suárez. Banzer rules with a civilian-military coalition.

1973
Military officers replace civilians in government coalition. All unions and political parties suppressed. Banzer calls for elections.

1978–
1980
Turmoil in the government results when annual elections are held, but no candidate obtains a majority. Finally in 1980 Hernán Siles Zuazo of the MNR wins presidency.

Military intervenes to keep Siles from assuming office. General Luis García Meza Tejada suspends Congress and forbids all political activities. Flagrant abuses of human rights characterize his regime.

1981–
1982
Military ousts García Meza. Three military governments attempt to address the country's problems.

1982
Hernán Siles Zuazo is chosen to be president by a newly reconvened Congress. Siles governs with a coalition.

1985
Presidential and congressional elections scheduled.

Ecuador

1925   Military junta takes power from liberal government when inflation and increasing cost-of-living expenses cause civil unrest. This takeover ends an unusual eleven-year period of calm in the normally turbulent political scene. In the first ninety-five years of independence, Ecuador had forty chiefs of state.

1928   Military junta returns the country to civilian rule. Isidro Ayoro, head of the junta, wins and attempts to institute reforms. He is blocked by elite factions.

1931   Economic problems force Ayoro to resign and a new period of turbulence begins. From 1928 to 1945, none of the twenty-two presidents or chiefs of state is able to complete his term of office.

1933   José María Velasco Ibarra, who becomes a dominant figure, is elected president.

1935   Velasco forced to resign. A succession of three presidents follows.

1940   Carlos Arroyo del Rió is elected president. Velasco unsuccessfully attempts to overthrow the government, and he is exiled. Arroyo del Rió achieves some control over the economy.

1944   Only days before the election, uprisings force Arroyo del Rió to resign. The violence is caused in large part by resentment over the loss of land to Peru in a 1941 war. Velasco, returned from exile, is decreed president. He embraces the left and promises political and social changes.

1947   Velasco is overthrown and exiled by Colonel Carlos Mancheno, the minister of defense. Mancheno is then replaced by the vice president.

1948   Galo Plaza Lasso is elected president. This is a period of relative stability as Plaza, strongly committed to constitutional rule, achieves economic progress.

1952   Velasco, returned from exile, wins election as president. He is committed to constitutional rule, achieves economic progress.

1956   Camilo Ponce Enríquez, from the Conservative Party, elected president. His term is characterized by moderation, but he does not implement the reforms he promised.

1960   Velasco elected to the presidency for the fourth time. He promises sweeping reforms.

1961	Velasco forced to resign. A tax on consumer items, necessary for a deteriorating economy had caused strikes and riots. Julio Arosemena becomes president. He fails to carry out reforms and is accused of allowing communist infiltrations.
1963	Arosemena is ousted by the military, which attempts reforms, but achieves only minor progress.
1966–1968	The military, suffering from internal disagreement and eroding public support, withdraws. Two interim presidents serve.
1968	Velasco narrowly wins a fifth term as president. In 1970 he suspends the Constitution and dissolves Congress.
1972	Military, under the leadership of General Guillermo Rodriguez Lara, deposes Velasco for the fourth time and cancels elections.
1976	Rodriguez forced to resign by other military officers.
1979	Jaime Roldós elected president. He attempts to revive oil production and to continue reforms. Roldós's uncle by marriage, Assad Bucaram, leader of the country's largest political party and president of the legislature, believes Roldós should act as his surrogate. When Roldós refuses, Bucaram blocks the government's programs in the legislature.
1981	Roldós is killed in an airplane crash. Osvaldo Hurtado becomes president and continues the moderate policies of Roldós. Austerity measures are introduced.
1982	Hurtado declares state of emergency when a nationwide strike is planned over high prices. General strike occurs in major cities.
1983	Further austerity measures introduced and general strikes occur. Petroleum production increases and the economy shows some improvement.
1984	Leon Febres Cordero wins presidential election. He plans to organize the private sector to provide help for the troubled economy.

El Salvador

1913–1931	Period of relative stability. The presidency alternates between two families.
1931	Arturo Araújo, who organized the Labor party, wins presidency with the support of middle and lower classes.

Araújo is unable to control supporters who demand immediate solutions to their problems. He is deposed, and his vice president, General Maximiliano Hernández Martínez takes power. Hernández Martínez, known as "El Brujo" (the witch) because of his interest in the occult, rules with a harsh hand for thirteen years. He does, however, implement programs in education, public works and services, and land reform.

1944   Workers' nonviolent strike finally forces the increasingly ineffective Hernández Martínez to resign.

1945   General Salvador Castaneda Castro wins elections.

1948   Castaneda tries to extend his term of office, and he is deposed. Junta headed by Colonel Oscar Osorio takes power. The military founds the Revolutionary Party of Democratic Unity (PRUD). This is the beginning of the military as an institution, and its policies are reformist.

1950   Osorio elected president. He legalizes labor unions, expands industry, and introduces social security. He avoids confrontation with elite groups and does not pursue land reform.

1956   Osorio's hand-picked successor, Colonel José María Lemus, wins elections.

1960   Lemus loses much of his support as his reactions to social and economic problems become increasingly severe. Military coup of leftist officers overthrows Lemus.

1961   Counter coup brings in more conservative officers headed by Lieutenant Colonel Julio Adalberto Rivera. The Party of National Conciliation (PCN), to replace PRUD, is created by the military.

1962   Rivera elected president. Considered an honest officer, Rivera continues reforms in election laws, health, education, and begins some agrarian reform.

1967   Colonel Fidel Sánchez Hernández of the PCN wins elections.

1972   In fraudulent elections, the PCN candidate, Colonel Arturo A. Molina, becomes president. His opponent, José Napoleon Duarte, attempts an unsuccessful coup.

1977   General Carlos Humberto Romero elected on the PCN ticket. There are charges of election fraud, and disturbances are suppressed by the government. Violence from both the Right and Left begins to escalate.

1979   Military deposes General Romero. A junta composed of military officers and civilians is established, violence between right-wing and left-wing groups escalates into a civil war.

1980   Civilian junta members resign three months later, citing human rights violations and lack of reforms. New junta established. Duarte becomes a member and later heads the junta. Duarte nationalizes the banks and begins land reform.

1981   United States, under Reagan, begins an intense military and economic aid program to help El Salvador combat communists and left-wing guerrillas.

1982   Constituent Assembly election is held. Duarte receives most of the votes, but a right-wing coalition headed by Major Roberto D'Aubuisson, of the National Republic Alliance (ARENA), controls the Constituent Assembly. An agreement allows a moderate, Alvaro Magaña, to head the government. D'Aubuisson becomes president of the Constituent Assembly.

1984   Duarte wins presidential election. A moderate, Duarte hopes to achieve reforms, a dialogue with the leftists, and a reduction in human rights abuses.

Guatemala

1931   Jorge Ubico y Castañeda is elected president. While ruling as a dictator, Ubico does bring economic progress to the country.

1944   Ubico is overthrown by dissatisfied army officers, students, and professionals. Juan Frederico Ponce heads a military junta, ousted when it refuses to hold elections.

1945   Juan José Arévalo, who received 85 percent of the vote, assumes the presidency. A new constitution guaranteeing individual rights becomes effective. Social reforms are enacted but Arévalo is accused by different factions of being both too moderate and too reformist.

1950   Jacobo Arbenz Guzmán, choice of the strong Communist party, is elected president. Arbenz continues social reform, including agrarian reform. Rising Communist party influence leads to increased Anti-Americanism and take-overs of American businesses.

1954   Exiled Colonel Carlos Castillo Armas invades from Honduras with U.S. aid. Confirmed president by plebiscite, Castillo restores foreign holdings and disbands leftist parties but still continues limited reforms.

1957 Castillo is assassinated. A period of turmoil follows.

1958 Miguel Ydígoras Fuentes is elected president. Economic troubles beset the country and political turmoil grows throughout Ydígoras' presidency.

1963 Military coup overthrows Ydígoras. Colonel Enrique Peralta Azurdia, Ydígoras' minister of defense, heads the government. Terrorism is a growing problem.

1966 Julio César Méndez Montenegro, from the moderate left Revolutionary party, wins presidential elections. The army begins major attacks against guerrilla strongholds.

1968 Méndez Montenegro suspends constitutional guarantees as terrorist violence continues to escalate. The American ambassador is assassinated.

1970 Carlos Arana Osorio, the new president, declares a state of seige and launches a vigorous campaign against terrorists.

1974 General Kjell Lauqerud Garcia, the choice of Arana, is elected president amid charges of election fraud.

1978 With no one candidate obtaining a majority, Congress elects the government's candidate, General Romeo Lucas García. Violence between leftist guerrillas and the military, aided by right-wing groups, increases. Amnesty International estimates that 20,000 people have been killed by death squads since 1966.

1982 Military junta seizes power, charging that presidential elections are fraudulent. Brigadier General José Efrain Ríos Montt names himself president and suspends civil liberties.

1983 Military overthrow of General Ríos Montt. Brigadier General Oscar Humberto Mejia Victores becomes president.

1985 Elections are tentatively set for this year.

Honduras

1933 General Tiburcio Carías Andino is elected president, ending a prolonged period of instability and strife. Carías rules with dictatorial powers for sixteen years.

1949 President Juan Manuel Gálvez institutes moderate social and economic reform. Foreign investment increases.

1954   Liberal Ramón Villeda Morales wins 48 percent of the presidential vote. With no one candidate receiving the majority, Julio Lozano Diaz, the vice president, arbitrarily assumes power.

1956   Military junta removes the repressive Lozano from office.

1957   Villeda Morales is elected president. He institutes pragmatic reforms in education, social security, and land distribution.

1963   Villeda Morales deposed. Colonel Osvaldo López Arellano, a staunch conservative, assumes power.

1965   A newly elected Congress elects López Arellano as president for a six-year term.

1971   Ramón Ernesto Cruz elected by a coalition party. He attempts to deal with the economic crisis facing the nation.

1972   Military coup. López Arellano takes power once again. He makes an effort to placate the "campesinos" by limited agrarian reforms.

1974   López Arellano implicated in political scandal known as "Bananagate." United Brands Company paid $1.25 million dollars to high government officials in return for a reduction in a banana export tax. López Arellano ousted and Colonel Juan Melgar Castro assumes power. Impressive economic gains are made. Plans are drawn up for a return to a civilian, constitutional rule.

1978   Melgar is replaced with a three-man military junta, with General Policarpo Paz García at the head. Elections for an assembly to draft a new constitution are scheduled for 1980.

1980   Constitutional Assembly elected. Assembly names Paz García as interim president.

1981   Dr. Roberto Suazo Córdova is elected president. He is the first civilian president in a decade.

1984   General Gustavo Alvarez Martinez, commander of the armed forces and a staunch U.S. supporter, is ousted. He is replaced by General Walter Lopez Reyes, who calls for limits on military spending and a commitment to a peaceful solution in Central America.

1985   Presidential and congressional elections scheduled.

Panama

1940   Arnulfo Arias elected to presidency with the support of the Panamenismo, a mass nationalistic movement.

1941   Arias deposed by National Police. Ricardo Adolfo de la Guardia succeeds him.

1945   Constituent Assembly, convened because of tension between the president and the National Assembly, elects Enrique A. Jiménez president.

1948   Arias wins presidency, but takes office one year later. The leader of the National Police, Commander José Antonio Remón, manipulates the accession to the presidency. Remón, a very powerful figure, turns the National Police into the National Guard, a paramilitary organization.

1950   Arias removed from office. Ramón becomes president. While enriching himself in office, Remón also institutes social and economic reforms.

1955   Ramón assassinated. The second vice president serves out the term. Reforms discontinued.

1956   Ernesto de la Guardia, Jr. elected president. Heightened United States–Panama tension.

1960   Roberto Chiari is the first opposition leader to become president. He tries to implement moderate reforms.

1964   Violent riots are touched off over disagreements about raising the Panamian flag in the Canal Zone. Marco Auerlio Robles becomes president.

1968   Arias elected president. He is deposed after ten days in office when he attempts to remove a senior National Guard official. The National Guard sets up a provisional junta.

1969   Brigadier General Omar Torrijos becomes dominant figure in the junta, although he does not become president.

1972   National Assembly gives Torrijos military and civilian powers for a six-year term.

1977   Torrijos and President Carter sign a new treaty. The United States agrees to relinquish control over the Canal to Panama in the year 2000.

1978	Powers granted to Torrijos in 1972 expire. Dr. Arístides Royo elected president by the National Assembly. Torrijos remains an important figure in the government.
1981	General Torrijos is killed in accident. Arístides Royo takes over as president. National Guard retains its powerful position.
1982	Royo resigns. The vice president, Ricardo de la Espriella, is sworn in as president.
1984	Espriella resigns. In a close election, Nicolas Ardito Barletta wins over Arias, the three-time former president.

Uruguay

1930–1938	Conservative Gabriel Terra is president. He abolishes Congress and governs by decree.
1938	General Alfredo Baldomir, Terra's brother-in-law, becomes president. He restores free elections.
1951	President Martinez Trueba obtains electorate approval for a nine-member National Council of Government to replace the president and vice president.
1952	National Council of Government takes office. It is beset by factionalism between the Blanco and Colorado parties. Falling wool prices cause economic hardship.
1958	Voters elect to keep the Council and vote the Blanco (now called Nationalist) party to a majority on the Council. Economic problems continue to escalate, as floods the following year devastate agriculture.
1962	The Nationalist party retains its majority in the Council, but loses the majority in the General Assembly.
1966	Electorate votes for a new constitution, which returns to a presidential system of government, with broad powers to the president. Oscar Gestido, of the Colorado party, elected president.
1967	Upon the death of Gestido, Jorge Pacheco Areco, the vice-president, assumes the presidency. A financial crisis is precipitated by high public spending. The Tupamaros, a left-wing group, spearhead civil unrest.

1971   Colorado candidate Juan M. Bordaberry wins close election for president. Tupamaros continue to escalate political violence. Military begins to assume a large role in government.

1973   Bordaberry dissolves the General Assembly. He is advised by the military through a National Security Council and in effect becomes a puppet of the military.

1976   Military takeover. Aparicio Méndez is named president. The military regime is characterized by human rights violations and its harsh authoritarian rule.

1984   Government of General Gregorio Alvarez faces increasing unrest over the continuation of the military regime. General strikes paralyze the capital. As a result of public unrest, elections held in November. Civilian Julio Sanguinetti elected president.

Appendix D:
Declaration of Quito and
Plan of Action

he Heads of State or Government and the Personal Representatives of the Heads of State or Government of Latin America and the Caribbean, meeting in the city of Quito, on 12 and 13 January 1984 at the Latin American Economic Conference convened at the initiative of the Constitutional President of Ecuador, Dr. Osvaldo Hurtado—an initiative which all the Governments of the region welcomed enthusiastically—in accordance with the provisions of the Undertaking of Santo Domingo to prepare a Latin American and Caribbean response to the economic crisis affecting the region, hereby agree to the following:

DECLARATION OF QUITO

1. We reaffirm the brotherhood and solidarity of our peoples and their aspiration to live within the framework of democratic principles, and we reaffirm our unity in diversity and respect for the sovereign right of all the nations of Latin America and the Caribbean to follow in peace and freedom and relieved of all forms of foreign intervention, their own economic, social, and political paths, rejecting discriminatory or coercive economic measures for political reasons and ensuring the full exercise of human rights and the benefits of progress for all their inhabitants in an environment free of external pressures, threats and aggression.

2. We reiterate our commitment to eliminate once and for all any recourse to the threat or the use of force in the solution of international conflicts. We once again call for disarmament that will make it possible to reallocate the resources squandered on the arms race and armaments towards objectives which contribute to strengthening the development of all the peoples of the world. There is an essential link between the problems of peace and of

Issued by the *Permanent Secretariat of the Latin American Economic Conference,* January 9–13, 1984.

development, since without peace, development will be unattainable, and without development, peace will always be precarious.

3. We express our concern over the worsening of the tensions overshadowing international relations and already engulfing many areas of the planet, thereby constituting a serious threat to world peace. Latin America and the Caribbean do not resign themselves to being the arena of alien confrontation and firmly believe that the region's problems should and can be resolved in our own sphere, thereby ensuring that the Latin America area will be a zone of peace.

4. We reject the interventionism which has recently manifested itself dramatically in the region, and we stress the need to find a negotiated solution to the problems of Central America which arise from the economic, social, and political conditions prevailing in that area, to which end we lend full political support to the Contadora Group.

We are aware that at the present time Central American countries are suffering more acutely the economic problems which are affecting Latin America and the Caribbean. Consequently, we wish to offer our support to the Action Committee for the Support of Economic and Social Development in Central America (CADESCA), a Latin American regional mechanism recently established in SELA to assist, *inter alia,* in mobilizing resources for economic and social development aimed at solving the major problems of the Central American people.

5. Latin America and the Caribbean are facing the most serious and intense economic and social crisis of this century, one which is characterized by unique and unprecedented features.

6. Concerned by the economic and social setbacks of recent years which this crisis has brought about, we expound before international public opinion our profound anxiety over the conditions prevailing in the world economy which are seriously affecting the region's development and stability.

7. The crisis demands urgent solutions by means of joint actions founded on regional co-operation and on the forging of a common position aimed at strengthening the region's capacity for response. This response should be directed most immediately towards the most critical situations and at the same time form part of a medium- and long-term perspective in order also to deal with the structural causes of the crisis, thereby increasing international co-operation and making it more effective for development under conditions in keeping with the scope and seriousness of the present-day economic crisis.

8. The crisis originated in internal and external factors, and our success in surmounting it is largely dependent on the latter, which are beyond the control of our countries and place serious constraints upon the options open to

us for overcoming it. The economic policies of some industrialized countries have severely affected the developing countries and, in particular, those of the region, owing to the vulnerability and dependence of our economies and their increasing participation in international economic relations. These policies have brought about the constant deterioration of the terms of trade, diminishing trade, an inordinate increase in interest rates and the sharp contraction of capital flows. The overwhelming burden of our external indebtedness forms part of this picture.

9. The most harmful social effects of this situation take the form of an increase in unemployment figures unprecedented in our history, of a substantial reduction of real personal incomes and of living standards, with serious and growing consequences for the political and social stability of our peoples, the persistence of which will, in time, result in further deterioration of our economies.

10. In order to make the region more autonomous, we are ready to mobilize the human and material resources potential of Latin America and the Caribbean to formulate a joint response to the crisis affecting us, giving impetus to and co-ordinating the endeavours of regional institutions, for which purpose we pledge all our political will.

11. Adjustments which cause prolonged declines in production, employment and living standards are not compatible with the objectives which we pursue. Consequently, the international community must take concerted action that will enable the countries of the region to continue their development without further delay.

12. The Latin American and Caribbean response to the crisis is based on the need to complement the efforts of each country and those made at the sub-regional level by strengthening regional co-operation and integration.

13. This response calls for the firm and resolute participation of all the national sectors of our countries, and it will achieve its goals only if the benefits deriving therefrom are fully and effectively extended to the rural and urban underprivileged, who must remain completely integrated in the development process in order to enjoy a dignified life. In this context, the resolve to support, *inter alia,* actions aimed at achieving and maintaining regional food security assumes particular importance.

14. However, the region's efforts alone are not sufficient for surmounting the crisis. It is essential that they be complemented and reinforced by significant external support, principally in the area of trade and financing.

15. There is a close and inseparable link between foreign trade and international finance. Only the joint handling of the two elements which, among other effects, will enhance our countries' ability to pay—and to which ability

the debt service must be adjusted—will contribute to a positive solution of the external debt problem.

16. The attitude of the Latin American and Caribbean governments in recognizing and assuming their obligations calls for an attitude of shared responsibility by the governments of the creditor countries, the international financing organizations and the international private banks in the solution of the external debt problem, bearing in mind, furthermore, its political and social implications. Therefore, flexible and realistic criteria are required in the renegotiation of the debt, including repayment periods, grace periods, and interest rates compatible with the recovery of economic growth. Only in this way can continuity be assured in the fulfilment of the debt service.

17. We caution that it is neither fair nor rational that the countries of the region have become net capital exporters, thereby compounding their precarious economic situation which will finally prove to be contrary to the interests of the industrialized countries themselves and those of the world community.

18. Furthermore, we point out that the maladjustment between the fiscal and monetary policies of certain industrialized countries is the cause of the rise in real interest rates which has persisted despite the fact that inflation has been diminished, thereby very seriously exacerbating the present situation. We therefore ask that the international community make the adjustments necessary to eliminate the causes of this distortion.

19. We reaffirm the urgent need to take measures designed to reform the international monetary and financial system.

20. In addition to the worsening of financial problems, we are witnessing the stagnation and even the decline of world trade levels. World trade has recently ceased to play its role in stimulating the economy and has drastically reduced its contribution towards the availability of foreign exchange for the developing countries. The reduction of imports from the developing countries, imposed by the crisis, lowered trade levels to an even greater extent and has brought about a contraction of their economies.

21. We view with great alarm the increase in the protectionist measures of the industrialized countries, which to a great extent closed their markets to exports from our countries, despite the fact that the volumes exported in no way caused internal problems in the markets of those countries. We once more urge the industrialized countries to abstain from imposing new protectionist barriers and to proceed to dismantle the existing ones.

22. We maintain that actions which restrict access to markets and limit the scope of the General System of Preferences through the application of limiting

and discriminatory criteria, such as graduation, quotas, and reciprocity requirements, should be abolished.

23. The prices of export commodities dropped to extremely low levels, bringing about continuous deterioration in the terms of trade in the region. In this light, we propose to adopt and strengthen multilateral actions necessary in order to stabilize prices dynamically, thereby increasing levels of income from our exports.

24. We formally call the attention of the leaders of the industrialized countries to the seriousness of the region's economic situation, its high social cost and the need to participate urgently in measures to confront the crisis, directly through their governments and through the international organizations.

25. The energy sector is of special importance to the social and economic development of our peoples. The region will step up its efforts to achieve and maintain a high level of self-sufficiency in energy, with technological autonomy. It is consequently important to support the Latin American Energy Organization (OLADE) in attaining its objectives and in implementing the Latin American Energy Co-operation Programme (PLACE).

26. We bring to the attention of the international community our conviction that should Latin America and the Caribbean again resume their economic development, they would once again become a dynamic element in the necessary and sound recovery of the world economy.

27. Finally, in the spirit of the Buenos Aires Platform, we express our will to strengthen the unity of the developing countries and to promote a joint strategy for the revitalization and development of the world economy.

We believe that this solemn occasion is proof of the permanent resolve of our countries, despite all obstacles, to maintain the regional unity which is an essential requisite for our development.

We have agreed upon a response that includes challenges and promises. Its implementation is obviously dependent upon the efficiency of our negotiating capacity and on the diligence with which the regional and subregional institutions and organizations carry out the tasks we have entrusted them here.

Consequently, we respectfully request His Excellency, the President of Ecuador, Dr. Osvaldo Hurtado Larrea, that the Declaration and Plan of Action adopted here be formally transmitted to the Heads of State or Government of developing countries which are members of the Group of 77 and the Heads of State or Government of the industrialized countries as well as to the appropriate regional and international institutions and organizations.

We request the appropriate regional and subregional organizations to prepare reports on the progress achieved in implementing the actions and tasks which have been entrusted to them and to forward them to the Regular Meeting of the Latin American Council of SELA in order that a study and evaluation of the progress of the Plan of Action be made.

We wish to thank the people and Government of Ecuador for their magnificent hospitality and the city of Quito for having been the historical setting for this Conference.

Index

About the Contributors

James Hurlock is a partner in the law firm of White and Case in New York. He has served as an advisor to many developing countries, including Indonesia, Turkey, Sri Lanka, Costa Rica, Peru, Honduras, and Zaire. In some of these cases, he has represented debtor countries in their negotiations to restructure debt owed to commercial banks.

Roger M. Kubarych is a senior vice-president and deputy director of research of the Federal Reserve Bank of New York. He is a well-recognized economist and expert on foreign exchange markets and international finance.

Cynthia C. Lichtenstein is a professor at the Boston College Law School. Her research and teaching specialties are international and corporate finance, international economic law, and banking regulation. She is currently serving on the Board of Editors of the *American Journal of International Law*.

Alfred Mudge is a partner in the law firm of Shearman and Sterling in New York. He has represented agent banks, bank advisory groups, and servicing banks in the restructure of the debt to commercial banks in Turkey, Zaire, and Mexico.

Andrew C. Quale, Jr., is a partner in the law firm of Sidley and Austin. He represents commercial banks in creditor and debtor countries and has served as an advisor to the ministries of finance of two debtor countries. He is also adjunct professor of law at the University of Virginia School of Law.

Riordan Roett is an eminent professor of political science and is the director of the Latin American Studies Program at the School of Advanced International Studies at the Johns Hopkins University. He has published widely on Latin American political systems, especially that of Brazil.

Louis G. Schirano is a vice-president of Bankers Trust and senior credit officer for Latin America. He has been actively involved in debt restructuring for several Latin American countries.

Philip Wellons is associate professor of business administration at the Harvard Business School. Before joining the Harvard faculty, he completed a study of borrowing by developing countries on the Eurocurrency market.

About the Editor

William N. Eskridge, Jr., is an assistant professor of law at the University of Virginia, where he teaches courses in international business transactions, export sales, conflict of laws, legislation, and civil procedure. He is also the director of the Sokol Fund for Colloquia in Private International Law.

Professor Eskridge received an M.A. in history from Harvard University and a J.D. from the Yale Law School. From 1979 through 1982 Professor Eskridge practiced law with the firm of Shea and Gardner in Washington, D.C., working on the Iranian assets litigation and various matters of domestic finance. He has published articles on home mortgage finance and the international debt problem.